HOW MACHINES CAME TO SPEAK

Sign, Storage, Transmission
Edited by Jonathan Sterne
and Lisa Gitelman

Jennifer Petersen

HOW MACHINES CAME TO SPEAK

MEDIA TECHNOLOGIES AND FREEDOM OF SPEECH

Duke University Press   Durham and London   2022

Library of Congress Cataloging-in-Publication Data
Names: Petersen, Jennifer, [date] author.
Title: How machines came to speak : media technologies and
freedom of speech / Jennifer Petersen.
Other titles: Sign, storage, transmission.
Description: Durham : Duke University Press, 2022. |
Series: Sign, storage, transmission | Includes bibliographical
references and index.
Identifiers: LCCN 2021034623 (print)
LCCN 2021034624 (ebook)
ISBN 9781478013600 (hardcover)
ISBN 9781478014522 (paperback)
ISBN 9781478021827 (ebook)
Subjects: LCSH: Communication—Effect of technological
innovations on—United States. | Freedom of speech—
United States. | Freedom of expression—United States. | Mass
media and technology—Political aspects—United States. |
Technological innovations—Political aspects—United
States. | BISAC: SOCIAL SCIENCE / Media Studies | LAW /
Media & the Law
Classification: LCC P96.T42 P48 2022 (print) |
LCC P96.T42 (ebook) | DDC 302.23—dc23/eng/20211118
LC record available at https://lccn.loc.gov/2021034623
LC ebook record available at https://lccn.loc.gov/2021034624

CONTENTS

ACKNOWLEDGMENTS

This book began in many places and conversations. Its writing and research have taken place across three temporary relocations, one permanent cross-country move, and the beginnings of a global pandemic. It required a number of deep dives into different literatures and primary materials. I would not have been able to do this without the support of the institutions that gave me the time and space for research. The National Endowment for the Humanities provided support early in the project. The Lenore Annenberg and Wallis Annenberg Fellowship in Communication and the Center for Advanced Studies in the Behavioral Sciences (CASBS) at Stanford University enabled me to dive deep into the scholarship and primary materials that are the core of chapters 3 and 4. It was a joy to do this research in a place that some of the people and conversations I was researching had inhabited decades ago. Some of the "ghosts" of CASBS found a home in this book. The Institute for Advanced Technology in the Humanities at the University of Virginia — and in particular Daniel Pitti, Worthy Martin, and Cindy Girard — helped me out with computational approaches at a critical juncture in the book, shifting my approach to the middle chapters and pointing to connections I might not otherwise have found. The Institute for Advanced Study in Princeton, New Jersey, provided me physical space, the company of an amazing cohort of people, and a beautiful library in which to research and write the final chapter. Throughout all of this, my colleagues and the administration at the University of Virginia provided material and other support in innumerable ways. I will always be grateful to them for this. I owe a particular debt of gratitude to Dean Ian Baucom for flexibility and commitment to support for research. At the University of Southern California, my new colleagues have provided a wonderful, welcoming community, even when it has had to be on Zoom.

So many friends, colleagues, teachers, and students helped me along the way. Laura Stein inspired my interest in law as a site of analysis back in graduate school. My wonderful writing group, Allison Pugh, Jennifer Rubenstein, and Denise Walsh, read way too many drafts of almost all of these chapters. In addition to always pushing me to clarify my thinking and my writing, they provided mentorship and camaraderie. Thanks as well to Kyle Barnette, Hollis Griffin, Allison Perlman, and Avi Santo for comments and encouragement on chapter 2. It was a delight to reconvene our grad school writing group across time zones. And I consider myself lucky to have landed so close to Avi and Allison, in turn. Tom Streeter provided a kindred set of interests and inspiration at many conference conversations about law, policy, and technology.

I want to thank all my colleagues at CASBS for wonderful lunch conversations in our year together, but especially Brooke Blower, Chaihark Hahm, Miyako Inoue, Terry Mahoney, and Kate Zaloom, for their support and suggestions. Many thanks to Morgan Weiland for bringing the work of Laura Weinrib and Genevieve Lakier to my attention. Thanks as well to the participants in the "Sounds of Language, Languages of Sound: Themes and Tools in the Humanities" workshop at the Max Planck Institute for the History of Science and to the anonymous reviewers for the *History of Humanities*, whose comments helped improve my understanding of the history of information theory and sharpen my analysis in chapter 4.

I have had the amazing fortune of working with a number of excellent students on this book. Without their help, I would not have been able to employ the computational methodologies used in the book. I owe particular thanks to Timothy Schott for research into various methods and, along with Amanda Glass, for tireless work cataloging the terms used to define speech in a large corpus of cases. Jack Tuftie did a terrific job researching midcentury advertising as background for chapter 2. And many thanks to Soledad Altrudi for helping me find the images used in the book and to Edward Kang for editorial work on the endnotes and final stages of manuscript preparation.

The law librarians at the University of Virginia and Stanford University not only helped me find specific materials but also helped me find my way in researching legal history. I also want to thank the Law and Humanities Junior Scholar workshop participants, in particular Sanford Levison, Hilary Schor, and Naomi Mezy, for providing a friendly venue, suggestions, and encouragement to me when I was first embarking on this project and venturing into a new field.

Finally, thank you to Courtney Berger for early and continued interest in the book and to Sandra Korn and the rest of the Duke Press team for shepherding the book through the publication process. And thank you to Hector Amaya, for ongoing conversations about the book but especially for those early ones when I was figuring out its scope and shape. Throughout all the twists and turns of the past years, you and Javi have been my home.

Introduction

The "Speech" in Freedom of Speech

> *Congress shall make no law* respecting an establishment of
> religion, or prohibiting the free exercise thereof; *or abridg-*
> *ing the freedom of speech, or of the press*; or the right of the
> people peaceably to assemble, and to petition the Govern-
> ment for a redress of grievances.
>
> **—First Amendment, US Bill of Rights**

The First Amendment that most Americans hold dear is an invention of
the twentieth century. But what was behind this invention? The conventional explanation is that the set of expressive freedoms we know as free
speech—the right to speak one's mind in a public space, to engage in offen-
sive and dissenting speech or gesture, to craft aesthetic expressions of our
inner states or selves—was forged through social movements and changes
in political culture and legal thought. These histories are concerned primarily with the boundaries and purpose of democratic communication (e.g.,
the various normative bases or "theories" of free speech in legal theory) or
shifts in social and moral parameters of the law (e.g., what is obscene)—in
other words, they focus on the "free" in free speech. But the very conception of what constitutes expression—or the "speech" in free speech—has
also changed during this period. At the dawn of the twentieth century, the
"speech" of free speech referred to oratory and printed material. It was a
narrow category populated by public speakers, pamphleteers, authors, and
publishers. A plethora of activities that we would consider expressive, eli-
gible for First Amendment protection today, would not have made sense
as speech to early twentieth-century legal practitioners. Activities such as

burning flags, naked dancing, wearing symbols (such as black armbands), producing and displaying abstract art, or sitting in silent protest would not have been considered relevant to the First Amendment.

In the twenty-first century, questions about how to understand algorithmically generated speech, the role of algorithms in curating and amplifying the speech of users online, and more are provoking deep questions about the applicability and direction of First Amendment law. Whether a body of law developed under conditions of information scarcity can prove adequate to conditions of information abundance and whether utterances produced significantly by computational processes (and not only the decisions and judgments of their human designers) count as speech are pressing questions. Such questions are not only about freedoms but also about the nature and meaning of speech and expression. In order to answer these questions, we need to look at how "speech" has been constituted as an object of legal knowledge and action.

This book does just that, constructing a genealogy of the "speech" in free speech. In doing so, it rematerializes speech, showing how communication technologies and their surrounding concerns animate First Amendment law. By shifting the locus of inquiry and analysis from rights and freedoms to the legal conception of speech undergirding legal decisions in free speech cases, I show that changing media technologies and discourse on communication were important drivers in the twentieth-century transformation of how we understand and adjudicate free speech in the United States. Current legal doctrine and political rights have technocultural roots, as do some of the entrenched contemporary contradictions and impasses of free speech law and discourse.

It is, I argue, no accident that the First Amendment went through its reinvention, from granting a narrow right to speak and print (linguistic) messages to a broad right of political and aesthetic expression, at the same time as the means of communication were undergoing a radical transformation. New media technologies changed the way ideas circulated in the public sphere and even more basically the activities involved in public communication. The phonograph and photograph captured sound and images, preserving for the record what was formerly a fleeting event. Silent film conveyed stories and ideas not through words but through images and physical gestures, reanimating events and performances that had transpired in the past. And the radio uncannily extended the aura of the human voice beyond the bounds of physical copresence, in an odd mixture of intimacy and publicity.[1]

The adoption of new communication technologies not only extended communication but also in many ways transformed it. These new technologies quite literally placed people in different relation to one another as communicants. The printing press had allowed the lone writer to address an anonymous public of readers; it also provided the idea that anyone could be a pamphleteer or propagandist.[2] Film and radio, on the other hand, made most people into audiences more than proto-publishers. Today, in using the internet and mobile media, users produce information that is read by machines; we all are in a sense broadcasters, unwittingly signaling our location and interests to databases and data brokers. In these ways, communication technologies structure and restructure our very ability to speak, as well as the actions that constitute speech and its social meanings.

In the face of these changes in the material means and social possibilities of communication, philosophers, sociologists, religious leaders, politicians, and journalists all weighed in on the nature and function of communication as well as the ways in which it might go awry and imperil society. This proliferation of the means of and discourse on communication, which began in the late nineteenth century and became institutionalized in universities by the midcentury, presented new tools and questions about the nature and limits of "speech" in the law. Sites such as early twentieth-century sociological studies of influence, midcentury mass-communications research (in social psychology, sociology, political science, and finally its own discipline), and cybernetics provide many of the metaphors and models of communication that animate legal definitions and categorizations of expression. In this way, when we look into the legal constitution of freedom of speech, we find a discourse full of machines.

Take, for example, the history of the public forum. It is well known as an example in a progressive history of the First Amendment, in which more and more freedoms are granted to expression. In this case, it was the freedom to organize and discuss economic issues like work conditions. In the late 1930s, the mayor of Jersey City, New Jersey, Frank ("Boss") Hague, was notoriously anti-union, working hard to quash union organizing in the city. In 1937, Hague prevented the Committee for Industrial Organization (CIO) from distributing pamphlets and holding a mass meeting, going so far as deploying police to beat those assembled. The CIO took to the courts, bringing the case all the way to the Supreme Court. The Court handed down a landmark decision in the case, *Hague v. Committee for Industrial*

Organization (1939), stating that the public had a First Amendment right to gather and speak in public streets and parks. Such places were "public forums" dedicated to people's use and discourse, and no local official could determine who would and would not be allowed to speak in such places. Cities could no longer refuse to let labor organizers—and, in the years that followed, picketers and other peaceful protestors—use public venues to address a broad audience.[3]

This much is well known. Less well known are the terms and reasoning in the case, or the activities that were rendered as expressive. The decision and the rationales for it were deeply entwined with radio broadcasting. As Samantha Barbas has shown, the judges and justices who crafted the public forum were redressing the problems of radio: that a few broadcasters controlled access to the main platform for public discussion. The public forum was to be a platform for the working man.[4] But even more, the ways in which speech was defined, or the activities considered expressive in the case, reflected this media environment. In many prior cases, the Court had defined "speech" as the expression of personally held ideas, opinions, or beliefs. In *Hague v. CIO*, in contrast, the communication at issue was not expressing an idea but rather passing along or repeating ideas that originated elsewhere. The CIO emphasized that what they sought to do was to distribute copies of the National Labor Relations Act.[5] The literature they were distributing, then, was not technically expressing or publicizing the group's beliefs or convictions. It was not publicizing or making known something new, or expressing any original individual thought or view, as in many earlier First Amendment cases. In earlier cases, as is elaborated in chapter 1, the Court had defined speech and publication as an act of bringing something new to light. Speaking and publishing were uses of words, which represented ideas. And ideas resided in the minds of men. To speak or publish was thus to externalize such personal mental states or activity. In distinction, in *Hague v. CIO* and a set of related cases, the Court clarified that freedom of speech not only covered the freedom to speak or publish one's own sentiments (to express one's thoughts or ideas) but also contained a right to distribute information that might originate elsewhere. In this broadening of the scope of free speech, the expressive rights of individuals were re-articulated in a form that resembled the current media environment. Rather than authors publishing their ideas or interlocutors in an argument, the speakers protected by First Amendment law might act more like the transmitters or relays that enabled radio broadcasts to reach broad, unseen audiences. This decision, which momentously granted rights to the members of the public to access and use public places for advocacy and dissent, did so through conceptualizing the speech of the petitioners, and the broader public, in the shape of radio transmissions.

Moments like this, in which the justices rearticulate the meaning or scope of speech or the press, are an incredibly important, but overlooked, part of the history of free speech. Like many instances in this history, *Hague v. CIO* is usually understood as a case in which the Court recognized and expanded civil liberties through freedom of speech. In this understanding, the focus is on the articulation of rights to a formerly disenfranchised group of speakers. It is usually a plot point in a progress narrative, of the ongoing expansion of political rights to more different types of citizens and their expression. Such histories are common in both legal and media history, and they focus on the history of the rights and liberties accorded to expression. Freedom is the variable; the character and form of speech or expression, in contrast, is a constant. *How Machines Came to Speak* adds to and complicates such understandings by demonstrating the speech in free speech to be historically contingent, and its historical trajectory to be multidirectional and textured rather than linear and progress-oriented. It constructs a genealogy of "speech" as a legal category, showing how the substance and nature of expression have been articulated differently within legal documents and arguments in different historical moments, and the often surprising sources of knowledge and experience that have given form to the category.[6] In doing so, it draws on insights and methods of media studies and science and technology studies to analyze the constitution of legal knowledge about expression and the instantiation of this knowledge in the legal code.

Speech and the Politics of Classification

Today, the prevailing legal knowledge is that the "speech" of free speech law is not coextensive with commonsense understandings of speech—or communication more broadly. It does not cover every utterance we would colloquially call "speech." And it includes much we would not (such as instrumental music or burning a flag). It is often used as a shorthand to encompass both the speech and press referenced in the First Amendment and is interchangeable with the more general term "expression" (as in "freedom of expression"). It is, in other words, a term of art.[7] I argue, however, that the need for a term of art—the abstraction of the legal terminology from common parlance—is an artifact of the growing complexity of communication wrought by the development of media technologies in the twentieth century. Even as the speech in free speech has become a term of art, there has been no coherent and broad agreement about what exactly this technical term encompasses.[8] In the absence of clear conceptual definitions, justices evaluate questions of whether a particular artifact, medium, or action is an example of "speech" or "the press" by referring to earlier technologies, common sense (and experience), and contemporaneous discourse. In other words, technology and culture have shaped the legal term of art.[9]

These evaluations are important. Normative debates about how and why speech should be protected and the outcomes of precedent-setting legal decisions get most of the attention in discussions of free speech law, but modest classifications do much of the work. In First Amendment decisions, the simple determination of whether an action or artifact counts as speech or a form of expression is an important site where the scope of the law is determined. Before determining the outcome of a First Amendment case, the judges or justices must agree that the law even applies. Such decisions about coverage (does the law apply?) are places where the boundaries and limits of freedom of speech are determined, though often without a great deal of scrutiny or justification. Discussions of coverage are sites of classification, or category construction.

Science and technology studies scholarship has shown how classification and category construction enact political and moral judgments under the aegis of semantics or purely technical decisions.[10] This is true as well in the law, in which the classification of an issue or event—and the analogies employed—determines how a particular dispute is framed and discussed, which legal principles are involved, and what existing law (precedents) bind or direct legal decisions.[11] As the legal scholar James Boyle observes on this phenomenon: "The moment of typing, classifying and defining becomes the moment of moral decision. It is a fundamental way of *avoiding* moral decision for the same reason. The thing-like or reified nature of categories can operate to obscure a moral issue, to resolve by pre-theoretical definition an issue that would be troubling and painful if faced directly."[12] I take this to heart in considering speech law. In particular, this book suggests that many pivotal moments of free speech law have revolved around questions of what can be classified as speech (versus, for example, commerce or action) rather than around the more obvious questions of censorship, the extent of rights, or when the state can regulate speech in the name of public safety or national security. The moral and political stakes of the latter discussions are explicit and on display. The moral and political stakes embedded in the former classification schemes are harder to read.

This focus on classifications takes me away from the typical trajectory or historiography of free speech, which focuses on precedent-setting cases that carved out new speech rights or qualified the ability of the state to regulate speech (i.e., established standards like "clear and present danger" or "incitement"). Such precedent-setting cases do show up in this book, but they show up more often as endpoints, places where a new conception of speech, crafted in earlier, less remarked-on legal decisions, is put into play. At center stage are, instead, cases that test the boundary of speech—often cases involving communication via a new medium that did not conform to prior definitions of speech. For example, silent films presented the Court with the question of whether the projection of images of pantomime, or telling a story through physical gesture, was a form of speech or publication—or something else entirely. Radio presented the Court with an act of communication that required multiple operators in order to be completed, raising the question of which of these operators was the speaker. And computer code presented the lower courts with questions of whether a set of instructions to a machine could be considered speech.[13] The novel claims in such cases test the boundaries of the category of speech; they ask that implicit, assumed boundaries are explicitly stated, contested, and, at times, adjusted. Such cases highlight questions distinct from the more commonly analyzed cases outlining the parameters under which the state can limit expression (e.g., obscenity and incitement). Yet, as I show here, these less-famous cases and the less-obvious questions they posed have often been among the factors that determine the outcomes of more famous, precedent-setting cases.

One of the upshots of the legal trajectory assembled here is that rulings about what counts as speech not only have different, more diverse, and mundane underpinnings than what is captured in histories that focus on law and social movements, but also involve moral and normative assessments—moral and political stakes that are obscured by the seemingly neutral language of classification—beyond those discussed by most scholars interested in the First Amendment. In legal scholarship, determinations of what counts as speech are usually construed as functions of underlying normative goals, such as the protection of individual autonomy (and/or self-fulfillment), the ability to self-govern, a safety valve for dissent, and the search for truth.[14] Instead, as I will show, legal decisions concerning the parameters of speech itself are bound up in the development, use, and implications of media technologies—and the concerns about influence, access, and agency that go along with them.

The politics of how the legal category of speech is constituted goes far beyond normative concerns with truth, self-governance, stability, or autonomy. The moral stakes that are obscured in acts of the categorization of communication have to do with definitions of personhood, agency, and citizenship. Speech has long been entangled with such definitions in Western thought. In this tradition, speech suggests more than just communication. We are happy to say that trees, animals, machines, or institutions communicate. To say they speak is a more tendentious claim. Speech has been a mark of what distinguishes humans from these others. This was perhaps most famously articulated by René Descartes, for whom speech was uniquely human, a symptom of the soul; the ability to speak is what set "man" apart from both animals and machines.[15] Both machines and animals (e.g., parrots) might utter words, Descartes argued, but these words were not speech, because they were mere imitation (not their creation) and did not imply understanding.

At the beginning of the twentieth century, the term "speech" retained many of these Cartesian connotations. It signaled individual agency and creation, the externalization of mind and will. It was used to refer to transfers of meaning in which ideas were exchanged, objects represented, turns taken, and minds persuaded. Speech was self-evidently different from physical acts, from brute force to mere mechanical parroting. This distinction is sedimented in the separation of speech and conduct in First Amendment law. At the turn of the twentieth century, the distinction between the two seemed relatively straightforward. Speech was the ephemeral expression of interior mental states and ideas; the freedom to express or publicize these ideas was at the core of the First Amendment and liberal notions of freedom. It was based in a set of ideas about expression and publicity that drew both on the role of printing in the nineteenth century and on conceptions of the individual in liberal political thought. In contrast, action was physical conduct, with material consequences to person or property; as such, it was subject to legal regulation and constraint. At the center of this distinction was a seemingly clear line between regulating bodies and regulating minds. The former was necessary, while the latter was illegitimate and illegal. Not coincidentally, this meant that when workers, feminists, anarchists, and others assembled (say, in strikes, marches, or other forms we call protest today), these gatherings could be understood as displays of brute force or coercion, rather than expressions of dissent or advocacy. The mind-body distinction rendered mute idioms associated with the body—and with the poor, workers, women, African Americans, and immigrants. For example, forms of agitation from efforts to unionize workers or protest labor conditions and the hunger strikes of imprisoned suffragettes were treated as forms of disruptive conduct.[16] The way in which speech was defined and opposed to bodily action was bound up in broader discriminations. Bodies and physicality were key to the boundary drawing in each.

While this distinction is still an important one in culture and in law, changes in communication have made it harder to draw the line between speech and conduct, bodies and minds. In the late 1930s and early 1940s, justices began to consider some physical actions, like saluting the flag and picketing, as expressive and thus protected by the First Amendment. These cases gave rise to a new legal category of speech—alternately labeled symbolic speech, expressive conduct, or speech plus—in which actions doubled as utterances.[17] For most of the twentieth century, the problem of expressive conduct centered on when human bodies and their actions were immune from regulation and when they were subject to restraint (e.g., can they be restrained from burning draft cards, sitting in silent protest, dancing without clothes?).

Just as embodied forms of communication were being included in the legal conception of speech, a strain of legal discourse and argumentation turned away from bodies and individuals entirely. Rather than discussing speakers and their rights, jurists began to discuss speech without speakers, and the flow of ideas and information. Information flows on its own much better than ideas, which tend to get stuck in the minds and bodies of individuals. In legal decisions from the latter half of the twentieth century, speech was increasingly equated with information, which might be either the product of individual acts of expression or the output of institutions or machines. In this shift, it was not so much that speech was disembodied (it was already disembodied in a different way in the early twentieth century) but that the terms of this disembodiment changed. In the early twentieth century, speech and opinion were differentiated and abstracted from corporeality, understood as sites of primitive urges and action. In the latter part of the twentieth century, in contrast, speech was disarticulated from particular human speakers. Judges and justices began to debate and regulate speech without reference to the particular speakers involved—or to their rights or interests.

This way of reasoning about and ruling on speech was, I argue, associated with systems, in which the sources of speech were interchangeable and might even be unclear. Rather than being structured around acts of advocacy, persuasion, publication, and dialogue, this understanding of speech is structured around the flow of information disarticulated from particular speakers, sometimes from human speakers entirely. In reasoning about speech without speakers, the judges and justices advance what I call a "posthuman conception of speech." I use the label of posthumanism somewhat differently, and with different conclusions, than do scholars like N. Katherine Hayles or Rosi Braidotti.[18] More than dematerialization, what is posthuman about some strains of recent legal reasoning is the way speech is disarticulated from persons and the ways in which agency and subjectivity have been redescribed in the process. In calling this conception of speech posthuman, I want to draw attention both to the way that this line of reasoning disarticulates messages from speakers and to the way that minds, thoughts, and beliefs have become less central to free speech law. I mean to highlight as well the drift in sources of knowledge or expertise that inform legal reasoning about the nature and boundaries of expression, from sociology, psychology, and philosophy (which I characterize as broadly humanist) toward economics and engineering.

The posthuman conception of speech is a way of defining expression that fits, or benefits, communication systems as much as or more than it does individual subjects. Within this posthuman conception, it becomes possible to argue that freedom of speech protects not persons but messages (artifacts). In this, the locus of legal protection and equality shifts from human actors to artifacts, and it is messages themselves that deserve equal protection, whether produced by machines, commercial entities, or individuals.[19] What is posthuman here is the ability to adjudicate rights without reference either to the particular agents who might claim them or to the different social interests involved.

This genealogy, then, shows how the liberal conception of speech as an index of a human mind was joined, and in some instances replaced, by a conception of speech in which individual agents are no longer central to create a complex and contradictory set of legal approaches and political outcomes. The posthuman conception of speech has not replaced the liberal humanist one; rather it exists alongside and in tension with it today. It is arguably the contradictions between the two that animate controversies over recent Supreme Court decisions regarding corporate speech. Saying that an op-ed, monetary exchanges, and patients' medical records all convey information and thus are equal as utterances obscures important differences among them. The conception of speech employed by the

Court in *Citizens United v. Federal Election Commission* (2010), in which the Supreme Court argued that corporations had speech rights, focused solely on the flow of information. The intent of individuals—and notions of individual reason, soul, or responsibility that go with these—has little place in such classificatory logics. Yet granting free speech rights to such entities seems to provide them with liberties associated with human agents (rights-bearing individuals) and, more broadly, with traditional liberal notions of agency. I would suggest that much of what is unsettling about decisions like *Citizens United* and similar cases (e.g., granting corporations immunity from regulation based on religious convictions) is just this mixture of liberal humanist conceptions of speech and posthuman ones.

New technologies and ways of talking about communication made these changes possible and, in some cases, gave them shape. In this process of influence, I suggest, the law and the rights people enjoy (or not) are not only sociocultural but also *technocultural artifacts*. In the genealogy traced in the following chapters, technologies of communication have offered new mechanisms and models for human communication and, in so doing, shifted legal conceptions of what it means to speak.

Historicizing Freedom of Speech

In order to introduce this genealogy, it may be helpful to have first an outline of the history of free speech jurisprudence. In what follows, I offer a condensed retelling of the dominant historiography of free speech law in the United States. In doing so, I aim to provide a framework for the chapters that follow, to introduce readers to the major themes and fault lines in the development of free speech law in the United States, and to highlight my intervention.

Histories of the "Free" in Free Speech

Per the dominant historiography, modern legal interpretations of the First Amendment emerged in the 1920s and 1930s in reaction to the governmental censorship of dissent in World War I (largely the result of the Espionage Act of 1917 and anti-immigrant sentiment and politics).[20] In the nineteenth century, freedom of speech had primarily been understood as an absence of prior restraint (laws explicitly restricting speech or publication on a particular topic or requirements of governmental approval before publication) and was primarily adjudicated at the state level.[21] Generally, speech was considered a right and a responsibility, in which speakers might be held responsible after the fact for any negative effects of their speech, and the right to speak was thought by many to hinge on property rights (as in the saying that freedom of the press belongs to those who own them).[22] In the twentieth century, this nineteenth-century tradition evolved into a more robust free speech doctrine that greatly reduced the ability of the state, or the social majority, to restrict unpopular speech—what is often termed "the civil libertarian turn." This civil libertarian interpretation of the First Amendment prioritized robust debate and a plurality of views and voices as essential to democratic political processes. Protecting minority speech—often, unpopular speech—was essential to such debate and to democracy. Zechariah Chafee Jr. was the chief architect of this tradition, and Justices Oliver Wendell Holmes Jr. and Louis Brandeis were among its first converts.

This history is often painted as a more or less linear progress narrative, in which the ability of the state to regulate citizen speech in the name of security is steadily diminished and the rights of unpopular speakers (e.g., socialists, Jehovah's Witnesses, striking workers, civil rights activists) are protected. The restriction of regulation is understood as a liberal triumph that has produced a uniquely tolerant cultural and legal framework in contemporary US speech law.[23] Such histories, which dovetail with narratives of American exceptionalism, construct a simple heroes-and-villains template to deal with a set of highly complex issues that would better be painted in shades of gray.[24]

As others have pointed out, the civil libertarian turn was complicated and not uniformly progressive. Legal historians like David Rabban and Laura Weinrib point out that this civil libertarian turn, with its emphasis on political speech, overshadowed a host of other, more radical turn-of-the-century visions of freedom of speech. Feminists, utopian movements, and labor reform movements defined freedom of speech in broader and more cultural, radical, and often embodied terms, to include discussion of sex and birth control, a right to public nudity and other sexual and aesthetic forms of expression, as well as boycotts and agitation for workers' rights.[25] For many of these radicals, freedom of speech was not an end in and of itself but a means toward social justice and equality. Such expansive understandings of freedom of speech were eclipsed by the civil libertarian tradition that focused on political discourse and public opinion as the core terrain of the First Amendment. This civil libertarian tradition has given us broad protections against governmental interference in citizen speech, protecting primarily against the creation of laws that restrict speech (though not many protections against the various ways that private entities like media outlets, or even the actions of other citizens, may restrict the ability of some to speak).[26] It provided the grounds for the "two-tier" system we have today, in which political speech is at the core of what the First Amendment protects ("pure speech") and other forms of speech (e.g., artistic, sexual, commercial) are more peripheral—a system that reifies a historically contingent and gendered public-private divide, often devaluing forms of speech associated with sexuality and reproduction or the home.[27]

The civil libertarian turn, in which justices became more solicitous toward freedom of speech and more attentive to the rights of dissenting speakers, from Jehovah's Witnesses to socialists, became the dominant approach of both free speech advocates (e.g., the American Civil Liberties Union) and Supreme Court justices by the late 1930s. The justices abandoned practices like the bad tendency test, in which lawmakers could restrict speech if they could convince judges that the expression in question had a vaguely defined "tendency" to harm public safety or morals, in favor of policies that protected dissenting or unpopular speech. (In its place, the justices in the 1930s required that lawmakers demonstrate that speech posed a "clear and present danger" to justify regulation, which would be replaced by the narrower exception for "incitement" to imminent lawless action in the 1960s.) They recognized pamphlet distribution (by unpopular religious minorities), strikes, and flag salutes as protected speech. In the 1940s, the Court sought to redress the imbalance in access to the venues of public speech wrought by mass media, designating the city streets and sound trucks as vehicles for working-class speech, making it harder for local authorities to regulate speech in such venues.

While the Court in the 1930s and early 1940s had sought to redress power imbalances and the way economics structured the ability to speak, by the late 1940s the Court was becoming more agnostic on the economics of speech.[28] That the Court should be concerned only with speech, abstracted from the economic conditions that might structure it (which were, on this theory, better addressed by the legislature), became orthodoxy in the 1950s and 1960s, so that even the progressivism of the 1960s did not reach to economic issues of access, or the way that economic inequalities structured the ability to speak. The 1960s saw the formalization and expansion of some activities—for example, wearing black armbands and the often silent occupation of segregated spaces utilized by civil rights activists—as expressive conduct.[29] The decade also saw an expansion in the modes and manner of dissent, so that by the beginning of the 1970s the emotional tenor of profanity was protected as well as the general sentiment in a statement such as "Fuck the draft!"[30] Yet, as progressives note, this liberalism stopped short of addressing one of the deep problems of power of the era: the economic barriers of entry to the public sphere created by the dominance of commercial media systems and infrastructure.[31] Even in recognizing the right of the public to receive information in broadcast communication, the Court stopped short of attempting to create opportunities for the public to speak via the airwaves (a right of access). For some progressive legal scholars, the civil libertarian tradition had ossified into a formalism that was not only impartial (content neutral) but also impassive in the face of what many argued was the structural unraveling of the conditions necessary for democracy.[32]

This historiography renders the fact that the major beneficiaries of free speech law today are corporations as a hijacking of the freedoms of free speech. It follows that the answer to today's pressing problems resides in shifting the articulation of our expressive freedoms: new ways of articulating rights or new ways of invoking older traditions (e.g., forgotten progressive legal arguments, overlooked strains of liberalism or republicanism).[33] While the dominant historiography and prescriptions such as these teach us much about how we got to where we are today—and I find the "old" materialist arguments about the decoupling of speech and economics very powerful and persuasive—they overlook a significant portion of this history. Legal and media histories have been so focused on the "free" in free speech that changes in the deployment of free speech arguments as antiregulatory tools (or "weapons") naturally appear as political realignments— as in the idea, current at the moment, that conservatives have taken over free speech arguments, or liberals have abandoned them. In these arguments, the speech being fought over is a neutral ground, around which political affiliations shift. What these analyses miss, or even occlude, is that the ground is not stable; what counts as expression has changed in ways that have fundamentally altered what freedom of expression means. Take, for example, the expansion of speech rights in the 1930s and 1940s to include picketing and displaying or saluting a flag. These were not just expansions of existing expressive freedoms. Marching in the streets with or without signs and bending one's body to salute the flag are all activities (conduct); in being classified as expressive, these actions were turned into utterances.

This is not so much the expansion of an existing freedom as a transformation of the terrain on which a freedom is enacted, a right claimed.

If we ignore this history, we miss the broader stakes of contemporary battles over free speech—and the tools necessary to address the future of free speech. To bring into focus these stakes, and the technocultural forces shaping free speech law today and into the future, we need to change the scope of our analysis. Discussions of legal theory, precedent, or even liberalism are not sufficient to understand the vagaries of free speech law and opportunism. To understand or respond to the deep contradictions and corruptions of free speech law and discourse today, we need to understand the terrain on which the law is made: how different objects and actions are or are not read as expressive—and the normative considerations underpinning this categorization.[34] And in order to grasp this history, we need to attend to another set of material and discursive circumstances: those that constitute media history.

Toward a Media History of Free Speech

In 1789, when the First Amendment was drafted, the matter of mediation was not so diverse as it is today. The scope of freedom of expression was clear: the free speech clause of the amendment specifically guaranteed that Congress would not abridge "freedom of speech, or of the press." I argue that these were not vague sentiments at the time, but rather highly specific references to the primary technologies of publicity of the day: oratory and the printing press. In the eighteenth and nineteenth centuries, the law was quite clear and specific about the mechanisms of communication it covered. The meaning of speech and the press only became abstract, subject to debate and redefinition, after the means of mediation multiplied. It was only after these different, competing media opened up questions about whether communication in these different fora—or channels—counted as speech that the lay and technical meanings of speech diverged.

I argue that the First Amendment has always been shaped in subtle and overt ways by technology. It has, in other words, *always been a technocultural artifact*. This becomes clearer in the twentieth century. It was already true, however, in the eighteenth. In particular, the US guarantee of free speech bears the imprint of the printing press. The US Constitution was not crafted as a rare artifact, in which authority is invested in the original, but rather as a public, print document. It was printed and disseminated via newspapers so that everyone could hold a copy. In this way, it circulated as a symbol of public sovereignty and governmental transparency.[35] Both the logistics and the logic of print were essential to the founding and to the legal culture it inaugurated. As scholars such as Michael Warner, Benedict Anderson, and Jürgen Habermas have argued, the printing press and circulation of printed matter have played a central role in defining the culture and norms of publicity that have defined democracy in the United States and Western Europe.[36] The First Amendment was crafted in this context, defining expressive liberties in terms of print technology and practices of public oration.[37]

The scope of the First Amendment was clear, a given, for many years. It was not until the proliferation of new technologies of communication—in particular, new technologies of mass communication—that the categories of speech and the press became matters of concern, the subject of deliberation and debate. In the late nineteenth century, developments like the buildout of a communications network via the telegraph and the introduction of media such as silent film and the radio were changing the experience of communication and also providing alternatives to the written or spoken word. Telegraphy turned words into invisible electrical signals by transferring words into a code and transmitting them via pulses of electricity—a seeming dematerialization of the word, a reversal of the work of writing and print.[38] Phonographs and photographs created systems of inscription to rival print (in which not only words but also sounds and images constituted "the record").[39] Telegraph and then radio networks physically and culturally connected the nation.

The newness and plurality of such media and their cultural ramifications made communication more visible and more curious. Communication became something to think about. In the late nineteenth century, communication became a rallying cry for public figures and politicians (religious figures, mentalists, and utopians alike) and an object of study for scholars trying to understand the changing society around them. From Charles Horton Cooley to George Herbert Mead and Robert E. Park, turn-of-the-century philosophers and sociologists placed communication at the center of their analyses of society, as would the generation of communication scholars that followed them, breaking away from fields such as sociology and political science to forge the new field. In the bodily metaphor for society common at the time, communication and the technologies that enabled it became the nervous system (the transportation system was the skeleton): the mechanism for coordinating the social body and public action, from voting and writing to more abstract notions of social unity and peace.[40]

For law as well, communication became strange. What once was a simple matter, taken for granted, became ambiguous. The proliferation of the means of communication, coupled with a proliferation of discourse on communication (especially as an essential component of politics and social organization), denaturalized old assumptions and created the necessity for thinking through and defining "speech." New modes of transmission, sending electrical signals or the human voice great distances over a wire, and new modes of inscription, recording ocular and aural data for posterity, sat alongside the old. These new media of inscription and transmission, by virtue of operating parallel to the spoken and printed world—and at times superseding it—highlighted the particularity of each. With print as only one of several means of publication of the news, it became necessary to ask whether the press referred to the act of publishing or to a particular social institution (the news). The rise of mass media like film and radio changed what it meant to speak, but it also increased the distance between speakers and audiences. With these changes to the means and meanings of public communication, a question opened and became pressing that would have, before this period, seemed too obvious to merit consideration: What is speech?

Plan of the Book

In the chapters that follow, this book investigates the ways that this question has been posed and answered at various moments in the history of free speech law. The question first appears in a 1915 case involving the censorship of film. There are no doubt many reasons for this. The fact that a case made it to the Supreme Court, that the claim that moving images should be protected under freedom of speech was credible, no doubt had to do with several sets of factors. As detailed in chapter 1, free speech claims were on the rise at the beginning of the twentieth century, both in popular discourse and in court. And businesses were turning to the law, and to the Constitution in particular, for protection from regulation. But this fact also had to do with the way that the medium raised questions about what it meant to speak. Film presented a new method and manner of conveying ideas that was difficult for judges and justices to place or classify. If moving pictures spoke, they did so largely without words. In this, the new medium raised many questions. Did the mute gestures of the actors communicate the same types of ideas as words? What types of thought or ideas must be conveyed in order for a communication to be considered speech? What exactly were the organs of public opinion?

The book is arranged around such legal encounters, moments in which judges and justices engage in the work of defining and bounding the category of speech. Film and then radio, computer code, and algorithms have presented examples of communication that have troubled what legal scholars Jack Balkin and Reva Siegel define as the "regulatory scene": the background understandings (here, about the nature and purposes of communication) that provide coherence and meaning to legal principles.[41] These encounters provide the organizing structure of the book. In these cases, questions are raised and the legal category of speech solidified or revised—often with repercussions that are evident later in other areas of speech law (e.g., union organizing, as in *Hague v. CIO*).[42] Analyzing the ways that speech is defined—and redefined—across such cases brings to the fore a set of concerns and questions that are invisible within histories focused on the "free" in free speech. For example, how does one draw the line between speech and action (whether silent embodied gestures or processes carried out by computers)? How should we recognize the interests of listeners within a freedom of speech defined around individual acts of expression or publication? And how do we locate and define speakers in instances of distributed communication (whether via radio or in algorithmic processes and publications)?

The book opens with the first of these encounters, over whether silent motion pictures could be considered speech. Famously, in *Mutual v. Ohio* (1915), the Court answered no. Motion pictures were not speech. Examining the decision in *Mutual* and the legal briefs submitted by each side in the case alongside two other early film cases, the chapter examines how and why film was placed outside the category of expression. The reasoning employed to explain why films did not count as expression or opinion sheds light on how judges and justices of the day defined speech. It was not only that films were commercial entertainments that made them unfit for the category. They were also, more fundamentally, of a different order: copies rather than original publications, and closer to action or physical conduct than to ideas. It was a form of communication associated with the body, likened to the work of influence on crowds, as figured in turn-of-the-century social psychology and elite political fears of the crowd (which was understood to be composed of immigrants, workers, African Americans, and other less than fully formed citizens, such as women and children). Speech, in contrast, was defined in terms of an idealized rational and "civilized" discourse and public opinion, associated at the time primarily with the medium of print. Speech was, in many ways, defined in terms of a particular technology (print) and a population (educated white men).

Almost thirty years later, the Court would expand this definition of speech to include forms of expression formerly associated with crowds. In a 1943 case involving compulsory flag salutes in schools, the justices argued that (some) embodied gestures or actions could be considered speech. This seeming reversal, I argue in chapter 2, was the result of the debates about propaganda and the new mass media in the interwar years. The experience of propaganda highlighted the fact that the written and spoken word operated through irrationality and illegitimate vectors of influence, much like those attributed to film. The experience of propaganda taught elites that the frailties of reason formerly projected on "primitive" peoples were endemic in the public. In this context, it was unreasonable to think that only rational ideas merited protection. The legal conception of speech, borrowing from academic and popular discourse on communication, expanded to include the vague relays of connotation, suggestion, symbols, and embodied gestures. The case changed the terms and terrain of expression, laying the ground for later articulations of "expressive conduct" as well as for the inclusion of more sensational communications (including film) within the scope of free speech.

Chapter 3 takes up a different set of cases being decided in the 1930s and early 1940s. In these decisions, the justices were pioneering a parallel conception of speech as the dissemination of information, in which individual intent and authorship were no longer central or even essential. In cases dealing with the seemingly disparate problems of how to address the interests and rights of radio operators and the listening public and cases involving the rights of workers and religious minorities to distribute literature, the justices focused on freedom of speech as a right to distribute information or ideas, reconceptualizing speech rights in the shape of radio transmissions. In thinking about speech, the justices in these cases focused on messages and their distribution more than speakers and their individual rights. The chapter locates the conditions of emergence for this message-centric approach to speech not only in the social good theory of speech (political understandings of freedom) but also in the technical and cultural problems of radio (and to a lesser extent newspapers) in the 1930s. Radio in particular "spoke" via a technological and commercial structure that troubled the traditional link of speech to the mind of a particular speaker. Technically, radio broadcasts required the operation of several different people.

Rather than a deep analysis of a case or two, this chapter traverses a range of cases in order to demonstrate the development of a broad new conceptualization of speech without speakers.

Chapter 4 focuses on how this articulation of speakerless speech was taken up and used in the 1970s, to argue for the protection of messages created by corporate actors (who were not natural persons or holders of First Amendment rights), in decisions involving advertisements and corporations' involvement in elections. The chapter argues that these legal holdings were a logical extension of the earlier formulation of speech as the distribution of information, with a twist. By the 1970s, it was common in fields from communication to economics to conceptualize communication as a flow of information or data, from producer to recipient, thanks to the rise of both information theory and computation. In these cases, the posthuman conception of speech as an abstract, systems phenomenon, is realized. The locus of analysis of such communication was less the intent or sentiments of its producer and more the circulation of the message itself. In the hands of conservative justices in the 1970s, messages became the locus of equality and of the analysis of free speech claims. In other words, the freedoms of speech were not articulated to persons but rather to messages, artifacts of human communication.

While the Court has been happy to classify money as speech and to recognize corporate speakers under this posthuman conception of speech, the judicial approach to computational communication has not been so expansive. Chapter 5 examines how lower courts (where these cases have been heard to date) have responded to claims that computer programs and algorithmic outputs are speech. In cases involving the First Amendment status of computer code and algorithmic outputs, judges have returned to questions about speech and conduct and human will. At the dawn of the twenty-first century, in other words, we see a reprise of some of the debates that were current at the turn of the previous century: action versus expression and a definition of speech as the expression of human agency and intention. Yet much has changed in the way these debates play out in the legal decisions, the rationales employed, and the conclusions drawn. The notion of expressive conduct has been radically disembodied, and the subjectivity associated with speech has become technical and even perhaps mechanical. The terms of speech and speaking subjects in the law have, in other words, undergone a fundamental revision. The book concludes with a discussion of the political and social implications of this revision.

Media Technologies and Law: A Note on Method

In proposing a technologically driven history of free speech, I mean to highlight that media are not epiphenomenal but more foundational, even infrastructural, to freedom of speech; freedom of speech is not just applied to media but exists in and through media technologies. Other key drivers of legal change—wars and national politics; the activities and agitation of workers, dissidents, religious minorities, and social movements; and broader cultural shifts—have been described well elsewhere.[43] They become background in this book to bring to the fore the way changes in the means of communication—in the development of media technologies and industries—have shaped the legal category of speech through which speech rights are defined and exercised.

This is not just technological determinism. These communication technologies did not arrive on the scene autonomously, separate from society and politics. Yet, the shape of the technologies we devise and adopt matters. In adopting new communication technologies, we say yes to a host of implications, social roles, dynamics, and protocols. The affordances and implications of these media, in turn, enable different forms of social organization, politics, and knowledge.[44] When media are new, these implications are remarkable. The social roles favored, or in some instances created (as in the telephone), are evident and often subject to debate. The particularities of mediation—the social roles of communicants, ideas about perception or the archive, the divide between public and private—are subject to discussion, evaluation, and adjustments. Protocols and habits of use must be defined and adopted. That is, new media draw attention to or reflection on communication: the processes via which we engage in it, the social roles and power dynamics involved.

In making an argument along these lines, Lisa Gitelman compares media to scientific instruments. Both must be made to work or to represent. Once adopted, the particularities and partialities of each form of instrument are normalized and we see only the matter measured, the idea conveyed—the content. The mechanics of representation fade from view. It is only when such instruments are new, broken, or antiquated that we attend to the particularities of their instrumentality.[45] Similarly, the implications of mediation—the way that novel means of communication transformed the act of speaking, the social roles and dynamics of communication—were once subject to debate and discussion. My focus in this book on early legal cases in which judges and justices confront and categorize media technologies when their means of mediation and communication were new, their codes and protocols remarkable, builds on this approach to technology.

As this focus suggests, my approach to legal decisions and texts is more cultural than legal in the strict sense of the discipline. My methods are discursive and archaeological. I understand legal documents and decisions as historical documents or texts. In analyzing these texts, I am less interested in their specific outcomes (their holdings) than in the arguments employed and the reasons given. Rather, I am interested in the law as discourse, which both archives historical conceptions of communication and, given the instrumentality of law, puts them into practice. I work to excavate these understandings, or statements about "speech," within the discursive and material context of their use. To do so, in the chapters that follow, I draw on the history of media technologies and infrastructures, the way they changed everyday acts and experiences of communication, and the way they shaped the knowledge created about communication.

The cases assembled here show that media technologies are central to free speech law in that they provide the experience and models that help populate and concretize the category of speech. The creation of symbolic speech, or the recognition that some actions can speak, is found in the experience of mass-mediated propaganda, the rise of radio, and concerns about latent meaning in communication research of the 1930s. And the notion of speech as the flow of information—a concept central to the free speech formalism that has in recent years expanded the speech rights of corporations—has its origins in the debates over radio in the 1930s and the mathematically inflected theories of communication that gained popularity after World War II. These concepts shape the application of the First Amendment today. If our speech rights today are shaped by past media and the debates that surrounded them, what will the future of free speech law and discourse look like? What current mediated interactions will offer new ways of defining speech in future legal cases? Computers literally speak for us in call centers and speak to us in "personal assistants" like Siri and Cortana; they petition for us via programs like Resistbot; armies of simple bots troll for various interested parties online in political campaigns and culture wars alike. As our choices of news, books, music, and other cultural artifacts become more algorithmically driven, the authorship and intent of our preferences blur amid a hive of collective taste and the processing of machines.

This genealogy of the "speech" in free speech can give us new tools for talking about the First Amendment and for intervening in current and future legal debates. In unearthing a different set of sources that have shaped the legal category of speech—from technology to the production of knowledge about communication—I suggest a different way of talking about contemporary and future First Amendment decisions and a different set of precedents to anchor these arguments. In demonstrating the influence of technology and discourse on communication on free speech law, I point to an important area for media and legal historians and theorists to explore. In showing the historical variation of a category that is in practice either treated as technically settled or too evident to merit rigorous definition, I hope to make "speech" strange.

1. Moving Images and Early Twentieth-Century Public Opinion

> Very little is required to enable a person to speak; and since a certain inequality of capacity is observable among animals of the same species, as well as among men, and since some are more capable of being instructed than others, it is incredible that the most perfect ape or parrot of its species, should not in this be equal to the most stupid infant of its kind or at least to one that was crack-brained, unless the soul of brutes were of a nature wholly different from ours. *And we ought not to confound speech with the natural movements which indicate the passions, and can be imitated by machines as well as manifested by animals*; nor must it be thought with certain of the ancients, that the brutes speak, although we do not understand their language.
>
> —**René Descartes**, *Discourse on Method* (emphasis added)

On February 8, 1915, D. W. Griffith's notorious black-and-white silent film *The Birth of a Nation* premiered in Los Angeles. The film was hailed as an artistic masterpiece and has since been aligned with the maturation of film as a narrative form by film historians. It boasted its own musical score, a longer running time, and a larger budget than any previous American motion picture.[1] It used melodramatic pantomime and intertitles, and it perfected new methods of visual storytelling such as continuity editing (to "naturally" propel the narrative), parallel editing (to show different events taking place simultaneously), and establishing shots. It pioneered new levels of artistry in filmmaking. It also undeniably conveyed a strongly racist political message. The film, whose narrative revolved around the birth of the Ku Klux Klan, lionized the Klan and pandered to racial stereotypes and fears of miscegenation, famously portraying Reconstruction-era Black politicians as corrupt and dangerous, and depicting the rape of a white woman by a Black man (as the event that spurred the creation of the Klan within the film's fiction). The film was controversial from the start. Black and white citizens rallied to press cities and states to ban the film, and the National Association for the Advancement of Colored People (NAACP), then six years old, rose to the level of a national organization coordinating local protests of the film.[2] The reception of the film, by reviewers and political organizations alike, makes it clear that many at the time saw film as a medium via which ideas were spread, even as a mode of political discourse.[3]

The film was in fact banned in Kansas and Ohio and in a handful of cities, in part out of fear of the impact of the message of the film: that the ideas dramatized in the film would incite riots and racial violence.[4] In Ohio a group that included Black citizens deeply upset by the film's content drew on press reports of riots and violence against African Americans in response to the film in other cities in order to pressure the governor to ban the film.[5] The Ohio ban came shortly after such prohibitions had been decreed constitutional by the US Supreme Court, in a case precisely involving the state's censorship board.

For contemporary readers, this anecdote most likely brings to mind many complex debates around censorship and even hate speech. In beginning this chapter with *The Birth of a Nation,* I want to highlight a different set of issues. I want to use the example of *The Birth of a Nation* to demonstrate that already by 1915 films were a means of conveying ideologies and addressing public issues. They were, in other words, political expression. I mean as well to highlight the strangeness of the Court's reasoning about film as a medium of expression, its distance from contemporary understandings. *The Birth of a Nation* was released while the Supreme Court was deciding *Mutual v. Ohio* (1915), a case about the status of film under state and federal guarantees of free speech. The Griffith film, while not part of the case, was most likely on the minds of some of the justices, as it was gaining much press attention both as a political provocation (and cause of violence in many communities) and as an innovation in filmmaking. At least one of the justices, Chief Justice Edward Douglas White, had seen the film at a special screening at the National Press Club on February 19, 1915, the day after it was infamously screened in the White House for an approving President Woodrow Wilson.[6] As he watched the film, the justice was no doubt aware that the film advocated ideas and opinions (political ones at that). Yet, only a few days later, Justice White signed on to a decision in the *Mutual* case that argued that freedom of speech did not apply to—in fact was irrelevant to—film as a medium. No matter their content, the decision argued, films were simply not a form of speech or publication.

To contemporary sensibilities, this was a very strange decision and rationale. It is now a commonplace sentiment that banning a film is akin to banning a novel or suppressing the publication of news.[7] Looking back from this perspective, some have argued that the Court simply misunderstood the nature of film or did not understand that film could be used as a means of advocacy. That the Court simply failed to understand the capabilities of film is one common way of narrating the case in legal history.[8] In line with this narrative, *Joseph Burstyn, Inc. v. Wilson* (1952) has been credited with belatedly recognizing the discursive and political nature of film as a medium.[9] Yet, as the context of *The Birth of a Nation* demonstrates, at least some of the justices were well acquainted both with film's ability to convey ideas and with the political debates surrounding the ideologies, political and otherwise, expressed in film. Film historians have pointed out that one of the factors driving the censorship of film was exactly this capacity to advocate and to educate the young; films, it was feared, were replacing legitimate educators, including teachers and religious leaders.[10] In fact, the justices explicitly acknowledge in the text of the *Mutual* decision that film was a "medium of thought" and had educational value. Yet they argued film was not like speech or opinion. There is something paradoxical in this assessment to the contemporary reader. If films can convey ideas and sentiments and be considered a medium of thought, even used to advance arguments, how can they not be speech or opinion within the law?

This chapter explores this question, through an analysis of the language and reasoning employed in the *Mutual* case and in two closely related decisions that bookended *Mutual*. A close examination of the statements made in legal documents about the nature of film and the legal category of speech and opinion unearths a dramatically different way of thinking and talking about the category of speech (and of thinking and talking about film) than those common today. The statements on speech and film in these cases betray an iconophobia and a distrust of the commercial status of film. But more than this, close analysis of these documents reveals that the judgment rested on an ontological argument about the nature of the medium as a physical more than mental one: an exercise of physical (embodied) action rather than the mental work of opinion and expression. As an activity closer to conduct than expression, film was subject to regulation. This little-noted argument, that films were more akin to regulatable conduct than to the expression of opinion, reveals a host of ideas about speech and opinion, mind and body, originals and copies, and the ability of different populations to speak that were operative in the law in the early part of the century. Like *The Birth of a Nation*, these ideas were steeped in racial ideology and civilizational hierarchies prominent in some strains of turn-of-the-century social science.

The likening of film—or, in the terminology of the day, motion pictures or moving pictures—to physical action, alien to contemporary understandings of film as an expressive medium, owes much to the social and intellectual context of the first two decades of the twentieth century in the United States. Film was the revolutionary new medium of the day, understood and promoted as a new technology and a way of being modern.[11] Motion pictures were an electric, commercial mass medium accessible to anyone, inviting in the illiterate, the poor, immigrants, African Americans, women, and children. These factors ignited social and political concerns about motion pictures that took discursive form through ideas, supplied by social sciences, about technology and machines, social order, and mind and influence. These ideas in many ways structured the distinction that legal practitioners drew between film and speech. Speech, protected under the law, was aligned with expression, mental action, rationality, and self-governance. Motion pictures, in contrast, were treated as mimetic, a mere (mechanical) copy of an action or idea that originated elsewhere. Such mimesis was associated with "primitive" thought (more motor than cognitive, more imitative than original) and emotion, foregrounding the idea that film both shows and acts on bodies. Like theater and other spectacles, film was associated with physical arousal and sensations of direct experience (rather than the distanced deliberation and reflection associated with aesthetic and political judgment). To many elites, it seemed a potentially dangerous stimulus to "primitive," excitable urban masses.

In a way, this should come as no surprise. The most sensational aspects of film were its kinetic and visual nature and its speed. The kinetics of film were particularly salient to early twentieth-century understandings of the medium, as many of the terms for "film" at the time attest: kinetoscope, motion picture, moving picture, and even "movie" all reference physical action.[12] (In the documents analyzed here, the preferred term was "motion picture.") Any motion picture was, at heart, a form of re-animation. The movement "captured" in these pictures was frequently that of bodies, from Eadweard Muybridge's studies of animal movement and human nude studies to the focus on people on the move in Thomas Edison's shorts (another top contender is transportation machines, in the multiple shorts showing the arrivals of trains, streetcars, and ships that populate the early film archive).[13] Even stranger, the reanimation of this bodily movement was accomplished by an electrical machine. Various technologies of projection drew on electricity, a still new and somewhat mysterious force, to re-animate these bodies at a distance, on a screen, for paying audiences. It is difficult to disentangle the technological and cultural connotations and concerns surrounding bodies, electricity, and machines at the turn of the twentieth century from the discussion of motion pictures as a social force and the regulatory debates around them. In discussions of crowd psychology and media effects, stimulation might animate the bodies of the masses in a manner similar to the way electrical currents powered machines. The movement of bodies was not only the subject matter of many early motion picture shorts but also the stuff of early twentieth-century theories of crowd influence that were deeply entwined with both racial science and the power of the urban masses evidenced in the labor movement. Such theories and concerns shaped the legal classifications of both film and speech, in which judges and justices drew a hard and fast line between speech and film: speech was the representation of ideas, and motion pictures were a form of conduct.

Mutual and the Legal Ontology of Film

In *Mutual* the Supreme Court directly addressed the question of whether the new medium of motion pictures, characterized by silent, animated images, could "speak." The case, in which the distribution company Mutual Film challenged the institution of censorship boards in Ohio on free speech grounds, was the most noted and binding encounter between legal definitions of speech, the press, and film in its early years.[14] The case centered on the question of whether motion pictures could be considered the same as speech or publications and thus could be protected from censorship. It was one of many legal challenges to the local censor boards but the only one to make it to the Supreme Court. The Court's decision had long-lasting effects, excluding film from free speech protection until the case was overturned in 1952.[15] In these thirty-seven years, *Mutual* withstood a sea change in legal interpretations of the First Amendment and several changes in the role of film in American culture.

In 1913, the motion picture industry was new and in transition. The short spectacles of the first decade of the century, what Tom Gunning has called the "cinema of attractions" for their emphasis on spectacle, sensation, and performativity over narrative and continuity, were giving way to the longer narrative films we associate with classic Hollywood.[16] This shift was in part an effort to appeal to a more middle- and upper-class audience. In the first decade of the twentieth century, movies had been associated with poor and immigrant audiences, and most urban movie theaters, or nickelodeons, were located in working-class neighborhoods (movies were screened not only in such theaters but also for audiences at churches, community centers, vaudeville theaters, fairgrounds, and other traveling shows).[17] By the 1910s, motion pictures were a popular pastime for many Americans and nickelodeons were being replaced by elaborate movie palaces, meant to attract a more upscale clientele. Many movie producers, eager to increase their respectability, and their bottom lines, emphasized the educative and moral messages of their films under the label of "campaigns" (e.g., temperance films).

Despite, or perhaps because of, these efforts, religious leaders, politicians, and other reformers began to worry about the potential negative effects, or influence, of the medium. Motion pictures were popular, a competition for church and other wholesome pastimes, in particular for children and city dwellers. (In New York, religious leaders worked to try to shut movie theaters on Sunday, so as not to distract the populace from churchgoing.) As film and media historians have argued, the fact that movies offered moral lessons was a source of concern for traditional gatekeepers of culture. Religious leaders worried that movies, an emerging form of commercial culture, produced for profit more than progress or the "civilizing" process of moral uplift, might replace more legitimate sources of tutelage: religious and civic leaders, teachers, and parents. Concerns about the influence of motion pictures were thus part of emerging concerns about the development of commercial mass culture and the ways that mass cultural products and production would replace local culture and erode the control of local civic and religious leaders. These concerns about commercialism were, by the 1910s, enmeshed with xenophobia and anti-Semitism. As patterns of immigration shifted, more immigrants were coming from Eastern and Southern Europe, and more immigrants were Jewish. As these new Americans became involved in the emerging film industry, concerns about the influence of film as a new technology commingled with concerns about the influence of immigrant Jewish filmmakers.[18]

In this context, and the broader one of Progressive Era reform, many community leaders began to exert their power to curtail the influence and power of film. Cities and states began to pass laws requiring that films be licensed before they could be screened within their jurisdiction. Censor boards were established to prescreen and license films, withholding licenses from films thought to be immoral or otherwise dangerous. Licensed films would display the seal of the censor board in their first frames, a visual that directly echoed the practice of affixing "Published by Authority" on the front pages of printed books in England under seventeenth-century licensing laws, denoting that the work had been licensed by the Crown. Chicago was the first city to establish such a board, in 1907. In 1913, Ohio and Kansas followed suit.[19] These censor boards established local moral and political control over film. They also made it difficult for those in the business of making and distributing films to regularize their business.[20] (Smooth national distribution circuits were essential to the rise of the film industry, a rise underway in the 1910s.) This was a problem for Mutual Film Corporation, a distributor of films in Ohio and other states. The company turned to the courts to protest this disruption of business, attacking the censor boards on a variety of grounds, including that they restricted interstate commerce. One of their more novel claims was that the boards were an unconstitutional prior restraint on the freedom to speak and publish.[21] It was on this argument that the company found the greatest traction in the lower courts, giving rise to the legal case *Mutual v. Ohio* (the full name of the case was *Mutual Film Corp. v. Industrial Commission of Ohio*).

The Legal Context: Freedom of Speech in the 1910s

The idea that film forwarded arguments and might be used to sway the minds of audiences was already circulating in film-reform campaigns and in efforts to ban films, as exemplified by the debate over *The Birth of a Nation* (in particular, Griffith's reply to the film's critics that suppression of the film was a violation of freedom of speech).[22] Legally, however, the idea was a novel one. As John Wertheimer details, the fact that the lawyers for Mutual Film developed a free speech argument was surprising to many legal professionals at the time, who were puzzled at the idea that "the product of a mechanical device on a curtain in a motion-picture theater" might be considered protected speech.[23]

Motion pictures differed substantially from the vision of speech that most legal practitioners had at the time. In the early years of the twentieth century, speech was a much narrower category; the types of expression protected were much fewer and free speech was not as robust a right as it is today. Interest in free speech as a political right and cases invoking speech rights were on the rise, but in the period before World War I there were fewer Supreme Court cases involving free speech claims than there would be in the 1920s and 1930s.[24]

To begin, until 1925, the First Amendment was interpreted as applying only to federal laws, so it did not bar states from restricting speech.[25] Free speech legal challenges were more often based in state constitutions' guarantees of free speech (as in the cases analyzed in this chapter).[26] When free speech cases were heard, state and federal courts were not particularly expansive in their understanding of either "speech" or the freedoms granted to it under state and federal constitutions. State guarantees of freedom of speech were often understood to primarily protect speakers from prior restraint and often included reminders that speakers were responsible for the effects of their speech. Damaging speech (e.g., libel but also speech that might interfere with business or judicial processes) could be prosecuted after the fact.[27] And "dangerous" speech could be suppressed by local, state, or federal authorities under the "bad tendency" test, in which speech that was deemed to have a vaguely articulated "tendency" to encourage lawlessness or immorality could be limited or suppressed.[28] The idea that political speech was particularly central to the First Amendment, and that dissent must be protected, was not yet a pillar of mainstream legal thought.

The courts gave local authorities broad leeway to license and control their public spaces and the moral hygiene of their citizens; such orders were often given precedence over individuals' speech rights. For example, the Supreme Court was willing to countenance restrictions on the ability of political protestors (often socialist, anarchist, abolitionist, and/or union speakers) to use public spaces to make their cases; the court also enacted penalties on publications for contempt or libel after the fact. Immigration law targeted and excluded people with socialist or anarchist political views (and eventually would enable the deportation of immigrants with such leanings) without raising First Amendment questions.[29] Even a later champion of free speech, Oliver Wendell Holmes Jr. (while serving as a judge on the Massachusetts State Supreme Court), said in 1894 that freedom of speech did not provide citizens the right to speak on public issues on city streets, upholding the conviction of the Reverend William F. Davis for preaching against racism in Boston Common.[30] Local authorities regularly barred public speeches or pamphleteering about labor conditions, unionization, birth control, and antilynching campaigns. And publications could be barred from calls to boycott businesses with bad labor practices.[31] Such instances would not be considered violations of the First Amendment until the late 1930s and beyond.

The dawn of the civil libertarian transformation would come a few years after *Mutual* (and roughly contemporaneously with *Pathé Exchange v. Cobb* [1922], also discussed in this chapter). The suppression of dissent in World War I would lead scholars like Zechariah Chaffee Jr. to craft arguments about the importance of dissent—and the need to protect all political speech, no matter how unpopular—and jurists like Oliver Wendell Holmes and Louis Brandeis to deploy these arguments in influential dissenting opinions.[32] These arguments and organizations, combined with the linkage of liberal tolerance to American exceptionalism in the 1940s, would help move the civil libertarian approach to free speech into the mainstream. At the time of *Mutual*, however, the justices were not so friendly to free speech claims; they would determine only a few years later that jailing workers for criticizing the president and the war effort was not a violation of the First Amendment.

While the Court was not particularly receptive to free speech arguments in the 1900s and 1910s, there were various popular invocations of the idea. During these years, many advocacy groups and radicals began to couch their activities as freedom of speech. Feminists, anarchists, socialists, and others made claims that activities as varied as boycotts, labor rallies, strikes, nudity, and information about birth control should all be understood as forms of free speech. (Businesses, too, began to look to free speech as an antiregulatory tool; one man tried unsuccessfully to argue that a state law that prevented him from practicing medicine without a license was a violation of his freedom of speech.[33]) The Free Speech League, the more radical predecessor to the American Civil Liberties Union (ACLU), was formed in 1902 and worked closely with the labor movement, advancing labor issues, picketing, and strikes as free speech issues. Labor activists saw boycotts, demonstrations, and more generally agitation as forms of free speech.[34] These types of expression were frightening to elites, who feared not only the anti-industry and anticapitalist messages but also the physicality of these demonstrations, that is, the massing of crowds, often made up of immigrants and members of the working class. Their claims of free speech fell on deaf ears among the judiciary (and local governments), who saw their agitation as unruly conduct.

The contrast between the lively vision of speech claimed by radicals and that accepted by the Court is stark. In the cases where the Court accepted

First Amendment claims, the acts of speaking were decorous oratory (and the press referred to printed publication).[35] These acts—speaking, writing, and printing—were discussed in Supreme Court decisions of the time as the representation of thoughts or ideas, tied to individual minds and autonomy. Whether or not freedom of speech was best understood as an individual right, the speech of free speech was understood in personalized terms.[36] Speech was a representation of the thoughts or ideas of particular persons.

Analogies and the Ontology of Film

Given this legal and cultural milieu, the lawyers for Mutual Film faced an uphill battle in attempting to secure free speech protection for film. They asked the Court to see the projection of animated images as essentially the same sort of representation and expression as the output of the labor of human authors in the news, books, and other print publications.[37] As noted earlier, the free speech claim was as much about the marketplace of goods as ideas, an effort to invalidate local regulations that impinged on the business of film distribution. As such, it was in line with the turn-of-the-century tactic in which commercial interests drew on constitutional law to protect themselves from governmental regulation (today, this tactic is again common and the First Amendment one of its most useful levers).[38] The free speech argument may have been novel, but it was the one that got the most traction with federal judges in the district court, suggesting that, in the 1910s, while the idea that films were speech was not a winning one, it was a legible, even reasonable, one.

The lawyers for Mutual Film underscored this legibility, arguing that the new medium was a form of publication and that motion pictures were thus like the press. Such analogical reasoning is commonplace in law. Justices often assimilate new technologies into the law through comparisons to an existing technology or practice. Such analogies serve to define the body of precedents that "control" the case, dictating which existing laws apply.[39] In law, these analogies are acts of explicit and implicit categorization with particularly substantial consequences: how a given object is regulated; whether an act will land you in jail. The analogies employed, particularly the successful ones, offer insight into the discourses and sources of knowledge that the justices were drawing on to define the new medium of film. In this case, the justices weighed competing analogies: was film like a publication and the press (protected from censorship) or like the theater and other shows (subject to regulation)?

The comparison of motion pictures to publications was controversial, though not unheard of—one of the names forwarded for movies in their early days had been "visual newspapers."[40] If the justices accepted this analogy, the body of law that would apply was that which guaranteed the freedom to speak or publish. Specifically, the Ohio Constitution said, "Every citizen may freely speak, write, and publish his sentiments on all subjects, being responsible for the abuse of the right; and no law shall be passed to restrain or abridge the liberty of speech, or of the press."[41] If film was a form of publication, then the censor boards were a form of prior restraint that violated this guarantee. The comparison of film to print media, rather than to oratory or public speech, is worth noting. Given the connections to embodiment, it might seem logical that the lawyers for Mutual Film would have drawn on analogies to public speakers. There are several reasons that this analogy might have been less persuasive—or useful—at the time. First, motion pictures were clearly a record, archive, or re-creation of events, whereas oratory was live and thus an original act.[42] Second, legal protections at the time were much stronger for printed material than for oratory. There were many means of regulating street speakers and other public speech (as threats to public order or health), and so such analogies would not have been as useful a tactic.[43]

To make this comparison, the lawyers for Mutual Film pointed out that film presented adaptations of current events and literature. Building on this, they emphasized the similarity of the content and uses of film to those of the press. First, they argued that motion pictures about current events often employed the same images that were used as still photographs in newspapers; second, they offered an extensive list (twenty pages) of "Mutual Weekly" current events films in circulation in Ohio as an exhibit of the newslike qualities of film; and third, they included a typology of movies in circulation that emphasized those geared toward education and shaping public opinion (e.g., temperance films, women's suffrage, and other "propaganda" campaigns).[44] The brief went on to say that the definition of a publication did not only refer to those means of publication available at the time of the writing of state and federal constitutions, arguing that it applied to communication via "the medium of speech, writing, acting on the stage, motion pictures, or through any other mode of expression now known or which may hereafter be discovered or invented."[45]

In the end, the justices rejected this analogy, finding that films were more like the theater (as argued by the lawyers for Ohio) than publications— and thus films were, like theatrical performances, subject to licensing. Theatrical performances, being physical and spectacular and being the types of "shows" and "spectacles" associated with mixed and rowdy crowds, were already subject to licensing in many states.[46] Such performances, the justices granted, could express ideas (as "mediums of thought"); they even accepted that films had educative potential and use.[47] The justices, then, did not deny that films represented ideas, or could be used to persuade. This much was clear in the context of the day. Here it is useful to remember the controversies surrounding *The Birth of a Nation* occurring as the justices were writing their decision. In the nation's newspapers, the film was being both lauded as an artistic expression of its director, D. W. Griffith, and denounced as a distortion of history and provocation of racial hatred and violence. Newspapers reported on riots and individual violence, such as the story of a white man who had shot a Black man on the street after seeing the film.[48] Motion pictures, the justices were likely well aware, were effective at communicating ideas as well as provoking action.[49]

Yet these were not the terms of the decision. The justices did not ground the decision in the "bad tendencies" of film (they referenced the "evils" of film, a more plastic term used as well to characterize the physical and social dangers posed by trains). Rather, the justices focused on the nature of the communication, and perhaps even the type of idea or thought conveyed in filmic communication. Motion pictures might convey ideas, but the manner in which they conveyed them was suspect. It was a communication not of mind, but of sensation, like the theater or spectacles or, as I will argue, the potentially rowdy and disruptive physical conduct of crowds or mobs.[50] It was a physical more than mental form of communication, akin to lower, mimetic thought and behavior—a type of stimulus that might provoke automatic emotional and behavioral responses. Motion pictures, they said, were more like theater. Theater might convey ideas, but the physical conduct of actors on the stage was subject to the police power of the state, and states had the legal right to make laws to guard the safety, health, welfare, and morals of their residents. (*The Birth of a Nation* was based on a play, *The Clansman*, which had been denied a license in several cities.[51]) Thus, licensing was not a repression of ideas or opinion (censorship) but the mere regulation of bodies, public health, and safety.

Considering whether films were like publications, Justice McKenna in the unanimous decision first rehearsed and accepted Mutual Film's arguments about film's educational and moral uses. He then turned to whether this artistic and educational merit indicated that film was equal to the expression of opinion, stating that "opinion is free and that conduct alone is amenable to the law" (regulatable). He continued: "Are moving pictures within the principle, as it is contended they are? They, indeed, may be mediums of thought, but so are many things. So is the theatre, the circus, and all other shows and spectacles, and their performances may be thus brought by the like reasoning under the same immunity from repression or supervision as the public press—made the same agencies of civil liberty."[52] He answered his question with a resounding no: film was not the same as opinion or speech. To grant motion pictures protection as a form of speech or publication would open the door to conceiving of other unruly and commercial performances as civil liberties, something the justices clearly were not prepared to do. The alignment of film with the physical medium of theater provided a ready body of precedent (in which licensing was allowed) and more broadly allowed the justices to distinguish film from the press and the written word, which were associated with the mental labor and original ideas of individual authors—and the mental labor of reading and reasoned judgment or deliberation on the part of audiences. The public sphere and public opinion, per the justices' reasoning in *Mutual,* consisted of original ideas produced by individuals as well as reasoned responses to them. (These ideas were original in that they had their origins in the mind of an individual who had newly exteriorized those ideas, not in the sense that they were without precedent.) Enactments and spectacles were not part of this sphere. The publication of a book was speech, but the reproduction and staging of that book by a theatrical company was not. Likewise, the reproduction of the book before a camera and its projection at a later point by a machine was not speech.

In this distinction, the justices suggested that there are different modes of thought, or at the very least, of its conveyance: some high and some base. The communication considered speech was the realm of reflection, discerning judgment (as an ideal vision of public opinion), and originality. Any "thought" conveyed by motion pictures, theater, and other spectacles was associated with sensation and physical arousal.[53] These formats did not provide the proper voice for democratic communication.

These sentences separating high and low forms of thought, more and less legitimate ways of communicating ideas, set the stage for the rest of the decision, in which the justices laid out why regulating film was not a violation of free speech: "It cannot be put out of view that the exhibition of moving pictures is a business pure and simple, originated and conducted for profit, like other spectacles, not to be regarded ... as part of the press.... They are mere representations of events, of ideas and sentiments published and known, vivid, useful and entertaining no doubt, but as we have said, capable of evil, having power for it the greater because of their attractiveness and manner of exhibition."[54] This much-cited passage is densely packed with allusions both to the political concerns animating regulatory efforts and to the justices' conception of the nature of film. It is clear that the idea that film was a business, "pure and simple," was important to the decision that film was not speech. The justices noted that theater (to which film was analogized) had never been considered speech, in fact that it had not occurred to anyone that requiring performances to be licensed in advance was censorship or an impediment to the expression of opinion. It was, they said, simply a matter of property regulation.[55] There were ample legal and discursive grounds for this classification. As Lee Grieveson demonstrates, in the years leading up to *Mutual,* film had been increasingly classified as commerce, closer to the trade in lumber, cheese, cattle, and turpentine than to the social functions of the press or art.[56] This classification is operative in *Mutual,* helping to distinguish film from the press, which was an organ of opinion. It is somewhat remarkable that the justices were able to see such a clear distinction between the press and the business of shows and spectacles. The press was clearly already in 1915 a big business, ruled by "press barons" (named after the reviled oil and railroad barons) like William Randolph Hearst and Joseph Pulitzer and trading in sensation as much as information (i.e., the yellow press). The justices, it seems, saw a clearer line separating organs of opinion and those of commerce than did many contemporaneous critics.[57]

Yet, as noted above, there is more to the decision than this classification of film as commerce. The status of film as commerce alone would not have dictated a need for regulation; as Wertheimer has pointed out, the decision was a rare restriction on business for the era, a reversal of the Court's laissez-faire leanings.[58] That also may have been linked to the fact that film was an upstart business rather than an established industry—one associated with shoddily constructed nickelodeons in poor, immigrant neighborhoods and often owned by Eastern European Jewish immigrants who were targets of anti-Semitism and xenophobia.[59] The passage cited here, however, points to more than this. As important as the social and commercial status of motion pictures are the statements about them as a medium.

In explaining why film—which, it should be remembered, had been called by some a visual newspaper—was not like the press, the justices referred to two statements about the medium: it was "mere representation," and it was capable of "evil."[60] That movies were mere representations suggests that they were qualitatively different from publications as a means of communication, a mere copy rather than an original. That they were capable of evil suggests that movies could be used in harmful ways—an idea, I will argue, that was rooted in conceptions of crowd psychology steeped in eugenics and fears about the makeup of the public.

What is clear in this passage, among others, is that the justices were basing their decision in part on contemporaneous ideas about the nature and distinction of film as a medium. In this, a set of culturally and historically contingent ideas about the ontology of a new medium provided the grounds for the imposition of a particular regulatory regime. In *Mutual*, the justices drew on two sets of ideas about motion pictures: film was a form of mechanical reproduction, like photography, and it was capable of more direct or dangerous influence than the spoken or written word. Both ideas are helpful in elucidating the distinction the justices are drawing between film and speech—and what ideas about the political community, or the contours of full citizenship and political order, authorize this distinction. In order to draw out these different ideas about the distinction of film from other media, I turn to two closely related decisions that articulate these two different theses about the power of film: first, it was mere representation, and second, it had a special form of influence.

"Mere Representation": Film and Mechanical Reproduction

One of the core separations that the justices drew between film and the press and other organs of opinion was that films were "mere representations of events, of ideas and sentiments published and known."[61] This way of talking about film as "mere representation," and thus distinct from publication, differs from contemporary understandings. Today, we use the terms "expression" and "representation" almost interchangeably; representation is a form of expression. In the rhetoric of *Mutual,* in contrast, representation was distinct from expression and opinion. Expression and opinion were aligned with both publicity and originality (as in having its origin in a unique mind, personality, or even spirit of the author), and representation might be merely a copy of an original expression.[62]

In talking about film as mere representation, the justices were contrasting film to their definition of publication, as "a means of making or announcing publicly something that otherwise might have remained private or unknown."[63] This definition clearly draws on ideas of publicity key to modern liberal democracies: that the sovereignty of the people is best guaranteed by bringing what were once secrets of state, the workings of state power, to public light, for the people to deliberate on and judge.[64]

This bringing to light is most frequently associated with the press or the newspaper. Here, however, the justices were defining all publications in such terms, drawing not only from political ideals of publicity and transparency but also from ideas about originality and authorship versus mere mimesis and copying.[65] Copying did not evidence significant mental work. It was not the exteriorization of some idea, thought, or belief—the mental work of a particular person. As in contemporaneous discussions of authorship, writing or speaking were understood as representations of ideas, thoughts, or beliefs produced by individual minds. Photography and cinema, which captured an image of the world as it was, were often considered closer to mechanical copies of the original event than the products of human creativity or authorship. This can be seen in nineteenth-century discussions of photographs as evidence and as intellectual property. In the former, photographs were often attributed to being authored by nature (they "let nature speak for herself" or were called "heliographs," suggesting that they were written by the sun).[66] In the latter, they were most often discussed as mere copies.[67]

Similarly, it was not clear to turn-of-the-century courts whether or how to recognize intellectual property—or authorship—in film. Legal practitioners debated whether celluloid was part of the machine, covered by patent law, or an artifact of human creativity, covered by copyright (in Peter Decherney's analogy, whether film was hardware or software[68]). And as producers increasingly sought to copyright films, there was no immediate consensus on how to do so: as one photograph, as a series of photographs, or as a screenplay.[69] Such confusion testifies to the lack of certainty about where creativity and originality resided in the new medium.[70] It also shows how it was possible to view film as not quite original at all, as a mere representation of things written elsewhere, a visual enactment of written material or a re-creation of actual events.

One of the cases cited by Mutual Film in its brief and by Justice McKenna in his decision helps to elucidate this view of film. *Kalem Company v. Harper Brothers*, a case decided by the Supreme Court in 1911, revolved around whether a film adaptation of the book *Ben-Hur: A Tale of the Christ* amounted to copyright infringement.[71] In order to determine whether or not a film could infringe a book's copyright, the justices had to determine whether a film could tell the same story and communicate the same ideas as a book or a theatrical performance (as, under copyright law, theatrical adaptations were copyright infringements). As the decision put it, the case considered whether drama could be "achieved by action as well as speech"—in other words, whether silent film could through gesture alone tell the same story as the words in a book.[72] Of course, *Ben-Hur* did not rely only on gesture or pantomime to tell the story. Like most films of the day, its narrative also relied on editing and intertitles, which were usually black screens between scenes that contained words establishing spatial or temporal location, identification of characters, narration, or dialogue. While these intertitles meant that films did employ words as part of their narration, the focus in the popular and legal discourse of the day was on their pictorial and embodied communication; in the legal arguments and documents analyzed here, film is discussed as a purely nonverbal form of communication.

The lawyers for Kalem, the production company that produced the 1907 film of *Ben-Hur*, had argued that a film was not a dramatization of the book, which would have been a copyright infringement, but a mere mechanical animation of photographs illustrating the book, which was not. They stressed the difference of pictures from literature and the mechanical nature of motion pictures, which were understood as merely a way to animate still photographs. They compared film, thus defined, to the perforated sheets of a player piano and argued that, like such sheets, it was not a copy but part of the machine.[73]

The Court did not accept Kalem's definition of film as the mechanical animation of photographs. Instead, it took the mechanical nature of film to mean something else: that film was a mechanical copy of a silent performance or pantomime (the pro-filmic event). The decision of the Court, written by Oliver Wendell Holmes Jr., found that

> Action can tell a story, display all the most vivid relations between men, and depict every kind of human emotion, without the aid of a word.... [I]f a pantomime of *Ben Hur* would be a dramatizing of *Ben Hur,* it would be none the less so that it was exhibited to the audience by reflection from a glass and not by direct vision of the figures—as has been sometimes done to produce ghostly effects. The essence of the matter in the case last supposed is not the mechanism employed but that we see the event or story lived. The moving pictures are only less vivid than reflections from the mirror.[74]

What distinguished film from photographs and made film an infringement on the author's intellectual property, per the decision, was the ability of film to tell the story. The key point here is that even without the words of the actors, the gestures and movements of the performers dramatize the story and compete with the written version. Notably, within this passage, neither the theatrical performance nor the filming of it is legible as a source of originality or authorship—each simply repeats or re-presents the story in a new format.

The incompatibility of film and ideas of authorship is clearly telegraphed in Holmes's choice of analogy: that film is like a mirror, merely reflecting what is before it. In using the analogy to the mirror, Holmes evoked his father's famous discussion of photography as the perfect instrument for reflecting and copying life: "mirrors with memories."[75] This allusion referenced a whole set of ideas about photography as objective, scientific inscription (that existed alongside and competed with a set of ideas about photography as art). In this discourse, the objectivity of the camera depends on its status as a machine that bears no subjectivity or imprint of personality.[76] It merely records or copies the world before it. This set of ideas, of course, overlooks all the ways that the creators of film put their own imprint on a dramatization: from composition of a shot to lighting, to editing.[77] All of these are ways in which films demonstrate the subjectivity and ideas of their creators. Yet, in the legal and cultural context of the early twentieth century, as this case shows, it was possible to judge film as an automatic (objective) reproduction of events or the ideas of others.

In many ways, it is easier to see how this idea of film as mere reproduction or copy would apply to the short films popular in the first decade of the twentieth century than to narrative films with more complex staging and editing such as *Ben-Hur*. This take on film was nonetheless what enabled the justices to view the film version of *Ben-Hur* as an unauthorized copy of the book, by way of dramatization. This infringement was all the worse due to film's mass-communication capabilities, enabling the same dramatization to be shown to many different audiences at the same time.

The *Mutual* decision followed the logic of *Kalem* to define motion pictures as mere copies, like reflections, of ideas and events already published or known. Films did not evidence the mental work or subjectivity of their creators, who were merely the operators of machines that captured the world as it was. Films, in other words, were not speech, but a mere echo or parroting of the speech of others.[78] As with photography before it, the justices initially saw film as a medium of mechanical reproduction rather than human expression, with the subjectivity and originality associated both with conceptions of authorship (in which the imprint of the unique personality or character of mind inheres in the work) and in liberal conceptions of freedom, where the mind is the ultimate site of autonomy and liberty.

The rejection of the press analogy in *Mutual* hinged in part on this set of ideas about the camera and film. This approach to film as less a producer of opinions and knowledge and more a replica of things known was no doubt enabled by the fact that Mutual Film filed suit as a film distributor rather than producer. It does not fully explain, however, the way that the justices distinguished film from opinion and the press. The *Mutual* decision rested just as much on the idea of film's unique powers of influence.

"A Force That Could Not Inhere 'in the Words Themselves'": Film as Influence

If the status of film as "mere representation" was key to why it was not a publication protected by freedom of speech, what the justices called its capacity for "evil" and its unique power of "attractiveness" were why it merited censorship.[79] In this rationale for censoring film resides an idea about the difference between film and the written or spoken word, in particular that communication or advocacy via film was more forceful and powerful than communication or advocacy via the word.[80]

In *Mutual*, this evil was vaguely referenced but never clearly defined. In order to better understand the nature of the evil imagined by the justices, it is helpful to look into the arguments made for regulating film in the briefs submitted in the case. The lawyers for the Industrial Commission of Ohio, the regulatory body within which the censor board was housed, argued that film differed in important ways from the written word. Indeed, they said that if a film were made that consisted entirely of written material (words projected on a screen), it would not be subject to censorship. The realistic visual reproduction of human activity, however, was a different matter: "the liberty of displaying life-like reproductions of human activities [would be] an unrestrainable privilege to use a force that could not inhere 'in the words themselves' with which human activity might be communicated or published in speech or upon the printed page; a force that if used to effect a libel of a person could approach assault and battery in effects."[81] It was easy enough to argue that the ability to "display immorality and vulgarity in nearly all its nakedness" might have a bad effect on the morals of the citizenry, especially children and other particularly malleable individuals.[82] However, asserting that film had a greater force than words went a step further. Assault is a key example of the type of conduct that is subject to regulation. In arguing that cinema had a force that took on physical dimensions, the brief contended that filmic communication had a particularly material dimension that likened the effects of film to physical ones. Film might merely re-present ideas or events already known, but in so doing it gave them a material force beyond the power of written or verbal representation.

This understanding of film as a powerful form of influence is further evidenced by the fact that film censorship was housed in the Industrial Commission of Ohio, which oversaw the physical safety of industry. Like trains or factory machinery, film was subject to regulation in order to protect the physical and moral health of the citizenry. (It was not only the content of film that might endanger citizens but also the substance of celluloid itself; projectionists needed to be trained and licensed in the handling of the highly flammable material.) In its core argument that film was conduct, the decision of the Supreme Court in *Mutual* indirectly embraced this argument about the physicality of motion pictures, assimilating them to the realm of conduct rather than the more mental realm of expression. To the contemporary observer, this may seem an odd way of thinking about film, but it was not idiosyncratic. It was also a key logic in a later court case on the legal status of film (this time, newsreels) that solidified the hold of *Mutual* in the coming decades.[83] In addition, as I will show, it was situated within a broader set of ideas about the corporeal effects of film. As one of many lower (kinetic) forms of thought and communication, film was understood by some turn-of-the-century social science and film reform campaigns to work as much or more on the body as on the mind, stimulating actions as well as ideas.

The association of film and conduct was solidified further in 1922, in *Pathé Exchange v. Cobb*, which cemented the status of the *Mutual* decision and determined that the ruling in *Mutual* applied to newsreels as well as to fictional film. *Pathé* drew heavily on *Mutual*, interpreting the earlier decision to rule that newsreels were no different from other films and thus were subject to censorship. The case began when a New York censor board refused to license a newsreel containing images of a female bather in a one-piece suit, which the censors found too revealing.[84] Pathé Exchange, a producer and distributor of newsreels and other films, argued that the newsreel was news and the censor board had thus engaged in censorship of the press. It argued that it did not matter whether the news was expressed in words or pictures; its status as news should guarantee protection under freedom of speech and the press, no matter the medium of its conveyance. Pathé Exchange and its lawyers went on to argue that protecting only the written word would drastically reduce the meaning of publication and the state constitution's free speech guarantees. They even made an argument about pictorial language, stating that the written word was only a permutation of hieroglyphs, so making a strong distinction between writing and images was spurious.[85]

The Supreme Court of the State of New York did not accept these arguments. Rather, it picked up on and extended *Mutual's* discussion of film's ontological distinction from print and opinion (no matter the messages conveyed). The court ruled that newsreels were no different from other films, also subject to censorship. The decision, written by Justice Harold J. Hinman, dismissed the argument that newsreels were protected because they were news (and thus part of the press). Hinman argued that no matter the content, film as a medium was too powerful, even coercive, to be considered a form of speech or part of the press.[86] The court's read on freedom of the press was that the law protected a particular *type of exchange and mental activity* rather than a particular type of information.

Hinman agreed that newsreels conveyed news; after the role of newsreels in providing information about World War I to those at home, it would no doubt have been difficult to argue otherwise. He argued, however, that news had little to do with freedom of speech. What was protected in legal guarantees of freedom of speech and the press was not news per se but rather the "freedom of expression of thought, involving conscious mental effort, not mere action."[87] That is, it was not the content or substance of the news that was protected but a certain type of mental activity. Thought, the decision explained, involved mental effort, deliberation, reasoning, and judgment. Print news relied on these. Motion pictures offered none of them:

> We cannot say that the moving picture is not a medium of thought but it is clearly something more than a newspaper, periodical or book and clearly distinguishable in character. It is a spectacle or show rather than a medium of opinion and the latter quality is a mere incident to the former quality. *It creates and purveys a mental atmosphere which is absorbed by the viewer without conscious mental effort. It requires neither*

literacy nor interpreter to understand it. Those who witness the specta-
cle are taken out of bondage to the letter and the spoken word. The au-
thor and the speaker are replaced by the actor of the show and of the
spectacle.[88]

As in *Mutual*, the decision in *Pathé* emphasized the idea that films did not have authors. The actor and the spectacle, it said, replaced the author and the speaker. Film thus did not engage in the creativity and thought associated with literature and oratory but only displayed (re-presented) physical and aesthetic performance. The linkage of film with the body of mind/body dualism was made explicit here. What distinguished the actor from the author or the speaker was the centrality of the body as the object of attention and display. Whereas authors communicate via words, actors communicate via bodies. While both authors and speakers, of course, have bodies, in the liberal tradition writing and even more so printing (synonymous with publication in the legal discourse analyzed here) have frequently been technologies of abstraction, means of appearing in the guise of abstract reason rather than embodied particularity.[89] In Anglo-American law, the body is not often thought of as the site of mental work like authorship. (For example, think of how copyright law applies to dance: choreography can be considered a form of expression, but the actual work and interpretation of the dancers cannot.[90]) In proposing that the actor replaced the author and speaker, the decision worked to undercut the expressive capacity of film, its ability to *say* anything meaningful, original, or *reasonable*. In the logic of the decision, films do not say but rather do.

What films do, per this decision, is not only re-present events but also impose messages and meanings on the minds and bodies of audiences. That is, the justices drew another line of distinction between the reception of speech and the reception of film. Speech was associated with mental reflection, processing, and reasoned judgment on the part of its audiences. Film, on the other hand, seemed to automatically evoke ideas and actions, without reflection or authentic will on the part of the audience.[91] Justice Hinman elaborated on the way that films worked on their audiences: "The moving picture attracts the attention so lacking with books or even newspapers, particularly so far as children and the illiterate are concerned, and carries its own interpretation. It needs no other illumination than the bright light behind the film which moves so rapidly that it reproduces the life of the world as it in fact exists and as it is portrayed in fiction, the evil as well as the good. Its value as an educator for good is only equalled by its danger as an instructor in evil."[92] He is here particularly concerned about children and the illiterate (generally, the poor and immigrants) and the ability of film to reach and influence them. He is, as well, concerned about the way films do so—that is, without any conscious mental effort on the part of the audience. If the film carries its own interpretation, in the words of Justice Hinman, then the audience need not do any work to decipher or decide their own views on what is being presented to them. They need not engage in judgment, or mental activity. This is the evil of film: whom it may educate, the matter it may educate about, but even more, the manner in which it does so, which leaves the audience defenseless, without the powers of counterargument. The latter points to an idea of filmic influence as particularly insidious and powerful, able to deliver messages or ideas as if by a hypodermic needle. As such, it was not part of the expression of ideas, debate, or other means of legitimate persuasion. It was closer to coercion, changing minds or behavior without enlisting the viewer's mind or will.

This understanding of film and its influence made perfect sense within both the contemporaneous discourse on film's ill effects and the broader discourse on crowds and crowd psychology that informed the discussion of film's effects. Film, as noted, was particularly popular in its early years in urban centers among immigrants, youth, and women (the very same populations that might engage in discussions of birth control, mass demonstrations, strikes, or other uprisings) at a time when industrialization and urbanization were changing the contours of social life. In these transformations, traditional sources of social order and influence (e.g., the family, church, local community leaders) were eroded or replaced. Film's popularity, location in urban centers, technological character, and commercial status made it a flashpoint for such concerns about influence.

While some Progressive Era reformers and politicians saw positive potential in film as a technology (most thought this promise depended on film being dislodged from the profit motive), many saw film as a source of antisocial influence and disorder.[93] Such concerns about disorder were most famously discussed in the 1920s and 1930s in the Payne Fund studies but were already forming during the first decades of the century, precisely in the years leading up to *Mutual* and *Pathé*.[94] By 1910, William McKeever had argued in *Good Housekeeping* that films were an insidious form of influence, likely to incite criminal activity due to their "flesh and blood" appeal to the senses.[95] In a 1911 address to a popular educational group, the People's Institute, film regulation advocate Reverend Herbert Jump decried film's ability to work, via "psychologic suggestion," like hypnosis.[96]

These statements had the force of truth or knowledge in part because they reflected the intellectual, institutional production of knowledge about film and about psychology of influence. Authoritative sources like Jane Addams suggested that film led audiences to copy in body and behavior what they saw on the screen, and she called film the "mimic stage" in her 1909 book, *The Spirit of Youth and the City Streets*.[97] Similarly, the *American Journal of Sociology* likened cinema to hypnosis and portrayed audiences as being "under the spell" of the cinema in 1912.[98] Hugo Münsterberg's popular and influential 1916 work, *The Photoplay*, formalized and offered a scientific explanation for how film conveyed ideas and produced behavior, or mimicry, in its audiences, offering a particularly clear distillation of ideas about the power of filmic influence.

Münsterberg's articulation of filmic influence and his language are particularly similar to that employed in *Pathé*; tracing the genealogy of these terms helps to uncover the discursive context and coherence of the legal judgments in *Mutual* and *Pathé*. Münsterberg argued that motion pictures were a "penetrating influence" that "force[d] themselves upon" the mind of the viewer.[99] This ability was located less in their pictorial nature and more in movement, or editing—he argued that film techniques such as the close-up and the crosscut so closely mirrored physical perceptual processes in the brain that they directly evoked them in the body when the spectator watched them on the screen.[100] The penetration of motion pictures, then, was not on the cognitive processes, or higher order thought, but rather on more basic motor responses, automatically eliciting attention, excitation, and imitation—even potentially eliciting involuntary physical movements. The projection of the image on the screen was thought to animate not only the images of the film but also the bodies of the audiences. It no doubt helped that film projection ran on electricity; the flickering of the image on the screen and the speed of the projection were reminders of this fact. The messages on the screen reached the minds of the audience like electricity, in the form of a stimulus (absorbed by the mind and body). The consonance between electricity in film and the electrical currents of the body suggested a relay between screen and body in which the excitations of the screen might be transferred to (and overstimulate) the bodies of the audience.[101]

If the electrical properties of the medium were transferred to the bodies of its audiences in this discussion of media effects, the idea of media effects itself transferred fears about the social body onto the new technology of film. The imputed effects of film (quickening of the pulse, enervation of body and emotions) mapped exactly onto the fears associated with the social groupings that film addressed. Film audiences, like the audiences of vaudeville and burlesque theater, circuses, and other turn-of-the-century shows and spectacles, were commonly labeled "crowds" by journalists and elites.

"Primitive Communication":
Filmic Influence and Crowd Psychology

In the late nineteenth and early twentieth centuries, crowds were a particularly problematic social formation; like mobs, they were seen as dangerous congregations that might erupt into riots and other activity that undermined social order and stability.[102] Communication that might conjure a crowd was thus the antithesis of what free speech law ought to protect within the turn-of-the-century intellectual and cultural context: orderly democratic discourse.

Elite concerns about crowds as a threat to the social order (and democratic discourse) had evolved as a reaction first to the revolutions in France and then to industrialization, urbanization, and the labor, anti-immigrant, and race riots in the late nineteenth century.[103] By the 1910s, these concerns were particularly associated with unionization and radicalism in the United States. The first decades of the century saw many bloody confrontations between labor and industry. For radical labor organizers, strikes and boycotts were a form of advocacy and expression, part of freedom of speech. Employers and most courts disagreed. In what came to be called the "free speech fights," union organizers, socialists, and anarchists organized in the streets, often in the face of police and vigilante violence. (Local ordinances commonly forbade using the streets in this way without permission from local authorities, who were free to act as censors, refusing access to those with whom they disagreed.[104]) One of the most famous of these took place in San Diego in 1912–1913, not long before *Mutual* was decided. Police jailed many speakers and vigilantes physically assaulted others, going so far as to kidnap and tar and feather organizer Ben Reitman (a physician and, more famously, Emma Goldman's lover). These fights were not only over labor and unionization but also over citizenship; many members of the Industrial Workers of the World were recent immigrants with few formal rights in the United States.[105]

There is an important parallel between the advocacy of radicals and the way courts decided films were not speech. Both have to do with the

Figure 1.1 Emma Goldman, an anarchist and feminist, addressing a crowd of workers in New York in 1916. Goldman was an advocate of birth control, free love, and workers' rights, and she was involved in the "free speech fights" of the 1910s. She was eventually deported to Russia for her views under the anti-anarchist provisions of the Immigration Act of 1918.

relation of bodies and passions to speech and opinion. The freedom of speech claimed by labor was not staid discourse or only pamphleteering (though it included these). Rather, they claimed agitation and advocacy that were embodied and impassioned—what elites saw as the unruly activity of crowds—were part and parcel of freedom of speech. Worried about the gathering of bodies, perhaps especially about the gathering of bodies of immigrants and the poor (see fig. 1.1), the courts for the most part categorized strikes not as advocacy or expression, but unruly conduct. The courts' discussion of film as a form of conduct than expression drew on similar lines of demarcation between legitimate speech and the excitation or agitation of the masses.

This connection was in fact explicit in the Industrial Commission of Ohio's argument that libel via motion pictures was akin to a physical assault. In making this argument, the commission's brief cited a 1911 case (*Gompers v. Buck's Stove & Range Co.*), in which the Supreme Court had classified calls to boycott as "verbal acts."[106] Verbal acts, the Court argued in that case, had a "force not inhering in the words themselves, and therefore exceeding any possible right of speech which a single individual might have"; such acts were a form of conduct and could be restricted.[107] It was the fact that the boycotters acted in concert (like a mob) that gave utterances a force greater than could inhere in the words of an individual.[108] In the argument against Mutual Film, it was the nature of the representation (the sensation and stimulation of motion pictures) that gave the ideas presented a force greater than could inhere in words alone. Concerns about urban masses were quite explicitly transferred from labor disputes to the medium of film in the adaptation of "verbal acts" to define motion pictures as closer to conduct than to speech or the press.

These political and social concerns about the agitation (or advocacy) of crowds were addressed and rationalized and given the stamp of the authority of science and esteemed academic institutions via the work of sociologists and psychologists. In particular, influential work by Gustave Le Bon and Gabriel Tarde defined crowds as modern social formations susceptible to irrational influence, prone to erupting into riots or other disruptive activity. These ideas about the crowd and communication of the suggestible masses would be formative in early US sociology and later mass-communication research, as well as in the political discourse about film's effects.[109] In this work, images, emotion, and physical gestures or behavior were vectors of suggestion and influence; crowd psychology offers a rich trove of turn-of-the-century ideas about nonverbal communication.

In this discourse, communication in crowds (e.g., workers demonstrating on city streets) or movie theaters was said to operate differently from more orderly forms of discourse. It worked like contagion, a physical process of imitation or transfer that did not involve higher mental processes. The visual and gestural spectacle of the theater, the street speaker, and, later, the movies evaded the "logical bond of analogy or succession" that rational (verbal-linguistic) communication required.[110] Images and gesture worked, rather, by a logic of suggestion and imitation, in which the bodies and behavior of members of the crowd conformed to one another. Members of the crowd acted, as Tarde's early emphasis on imitation as a simple (immature) form of social learning suggested, as copies repeating and replicating emotions, slogans, or simple ideas. Such imitation and suggestion, especially when in excess of other forms of abstract mental activity, were seen as "primitive" and "feminine." Once lured in by charismatic speakers or images, an individual became part of the crowd, like a puppet or sleepwalker, guided by forces other than her or his will.[111] While Tarde saw imitation in all social life, he argued that in primitive societies such imitation was more gestural and behavioral (more physical), whereas in more advanced societies, imitation was more often an idea or utterance (more linguistic and mental). Tarde was more nuanced in his evaluation of crowds than Le Bon, who saw only irrationality and primitivity in the masses. Le Bon asserted, "By the mere fact that he forms part of an organised crowd, a man descends several rungs in the ladder of civilisation. Isolated, he may be a cultivated individual; in a crowd, he is a barbarian—that is, a creature acting by instinct. He possesses the spontaneity, the violence, the ferocity, and also the enthusiasm and heroism of primitive beings, whom he further tends to resemble by the facility with which he allows himself to be impressed by words and images."[112] He was quite explicit about who these primitive beings were: "Latins" and other non-Anglo subjects, women, and children were particularly suggestible, or ruled by the body.[113] As in Münsterberg's discussion of filmic influence (and older discussions of mesmerism), suggestion impressed itself not on the brain but on the body. For Le Bon, both images and oral communication in crowds worked irrationally, via a process of connotation and suggestion, rather than the linear processes of logic. This is not the psychological vision of the subconscious we have inherited from Sigmund Freud but rather the unconscious of the motor system, which might animate bodies without any mind.[114] To be a primitive or barbarian was to be ruled by emotion and impulse, in which suggestions triggered actions without reflection.

Not only was the unconscious understood in more physical terms, associated more with the spinal cord than the mind, but emotion was as well. The discussion of crowd psychology was rooted in late nineteenth-century scientific discourse on emotion (i.e., that produced in the work of Charles Darwin, William James, and Carl Lange). While today we often talk about emotions as mental, psychological states, in this late nineteenth-century discourse, they were understood as more embodied physical responses to the world, defined and enacted through particular configurations of body (gestures or poses) and of facial muscles.[115] These bodily dispositions and facial expressions conveyed feelings, even basic ideas, without language— a form of communication available to both animals and primitive peoples.[116] (The work of civilizing, or educating and uplifting, so common in early twentieth-century discourse on culture, was in large part to learn to override or harness these impulses and expressions.) In the case of crowds, the gestures and expressions of a speaker were thought to add a viral sensational and emotive force beyond the meaning of the words uttered.[117]

Not only the streets but also theaters and film screens were prime sites of such primitive communication. The bodies of actors on stage or on screen communicated in a manner only a few steps removed from the communication of animals. Particularly in silent films, where words were not necessary, those watching only had to recognize the attitude, physical pose, or gesture of the actors to get the gist. This was one of the key problems of the visuality of the theater for late nineteenth-century crowd psychologists: that the mode of spectatorship involved in the theater worked via recognition and repetition—whether this was expressed as a sort of hypnotic suggestion or as imitation, it meant that communication transpired without any need for logic or reflection. Rather than relying on the "logical bonds of analogy and succession," the flickering images on the screen aroused emotions and motor responses in the bodies of viewers.[118]

The particular bodies that made up crowds and urban movie audiences were, I want to highlight, central to this discourse. Crowd psychology was deeply entwined with eugenics, and some groups of people were considered more passionate and less capable of deliberation. These groups included women, children, "Latins," and other non-Anglos in Le Bon's work (he presumed British crowds were more rational than Italian or African ones). Such passionate people were thought to be more likely to be held in thrall to the suggestions of either an impassioned live speaker or the direct sensory and motor stimuli of motion pictures. The judges in *Pathé* (and *Mutual*) were less concerned with the effect of films on their peers (who moved in a different media environment); their concern was with the ability of film to take viewers with limited literacy—whether by virtue of age, education, ethnicity, or nationality—out of the "bondage to the letter and the spoken word" to a realm of direct and potentially unruly influence.

The Publics of Public Opinion

In both *Mutual* and *Pathé*, the way that film was denied the status of speech contains clues as to the constitution of the categories of speech and public opinion implicit in the legal discourse. Film was not a form of mental activity: it did not use words or reason, it did not express new ideas, and it did not articulate or contribute to public opinion. It was the latter that was repudiated in 1952 when films were given First Amendment protection in the *Burstyn* decision, in which the justices argued that films were covered by the law because they were organs of public opinion.

In the early legal discussions of film and free speech, then, the speech protected in freedom of speech was equated to public opinion. Yet this was not exactly the public opinion of today. In the first decades of the twentieth century, the idea of public opinion was invoked by intellectuals concerned with mass media and urbanization to distinguish legitimate practices of popular expression from illegitimate ones—an alternative to the impulsivity and suggestibility of the crowd. The ideal of public opinion, as a basis of democratic governance, implied a deliberate form of reception in which ideas were received and considered, subject to at least internal debate if not actual discussion with others.[119] In opposition to the work of suggestion, the formation of public opinion was a "cooler" and more drawn-out process of judgment—akin to the mental work of well-read men.[120] This model of reception, in many ways the opposite of that popularly imagined to describe film reception, was also transferred onto a social formation: the public. Tarde, in particular, offered the idea of the public as an antidote to the crowd, a model of how media might bring people together in a functional way, through thought and conversation, even deliberation. In this articulation, the public offered a vision of the masses and mediated mass persuasion that was legitimate and in which the masses were not a source of disorder.

The idea of the public as a "civilized" version of the crowd (or as a mass on the model of the middle class rather than the working class) took hold in early US social science, in the work of sociologists Robert Ezra Park and Albion Small, and intellectuals like Walter Lippmann. Publics deliberated and discussed whereas crowds acted, moving and overthrowing.[121] Importantly, the communication of publics was more mental than physical. The medium of exchange, and persuasion, that brought publics together was not the body but the word—more specifically, the printed page of the newspaper. Publics need not be brought together via proximity and co-presence. They could be convened via reading and discussion, aligning them with mental processes and with the use of, or at least the aspiration to, reason.[122] Publics might not always employ reason, a point Tarde and later Lippmann were quite clear about, but as collectives they were held together through reading and responding to news and thus associated with some level of cognitive engagement, reflection, and deliberation.[123] Reading back through the racial science at the heart of crowd psychology, it seems that in many uses publics were defined in part by whiteness and class. The modes of reception and comportment associated with publics were those assigned to Anglo-Saxon peoples (particularly in the work of Le Bon) and to the middle and upper classes.

This raced, gendered, and classed distinction between crowds and publics, in which crowds were embodied and emotive while publics were enjoined through reading and conversation, was encoded into the legal decisions analyzed here. Film was positioned as the display of bodies and events, a stimulus for emotions, "lower" mental processes, and even physical reactions. Speech, in contrast, required mental activity, creativity, and interpretation—a form of mental judgment that involved deliberation and opinion formation. In *Mutual*, the justices argued that film was a spectacle and not a form of public opinion. In *Pathé*, the justices argued that film, even if it was used to convey news, was not a form of speech or the press because it did not involve mental activity. In the discourse on crowds and publics that was operative at the time, there is an association of publics and print. Public opinion, as the opposite of crowd activity and the (illegitimate) work of suggestion, was distinguished as a form of mental activity that engaged the mind and will. The proper medium of such opinion was the subdued printed page. Reading required mental work to decode, and ideally, to stop and evaluate the words just read, engaging in an internal if not external dialogue.[124]

This way of drawing the parameters of speech as a legal category had political and pragmatic implications. The legal reasoning and categorization in *Mutual* and *Pathé* formally subsumed collective action to the use of reason (the latter would be protected, the former not). Further, the focus on reason and literacy had an exclusionary bent. Reading was the substrate for public opinion, but reading not only required mental activity but also formal education, not available to all. In this sense, the classification of some modes of expression (like film) as more akin to action, and thus subject to regulation, was an indirect way of regulating the speech of those populations less able to employ or participate in decorous forms of public opinion. Unable to regulate the actual thought processes or intimate behaviors of the populace, the Court enabled the censorship of a form of communication that stood outside the recognized bounds of deliberation. The idea of the sensory, direct influence of film enabled this displacement of concern about the bodies of the masses onto a technology of projection and mode of communication.

Conclusion

In the cases analyzed here—early encounters between film, as a new medium, and free speech law—we see the beginnings of speech becoming strange (and the eventual evolution of "speech" as a term of art in legal discourse). In the claim that films were a form of publication, the justices were faced with the question of whether images projected on a screen were the same as either a story told in words on a printed page or a description of events and ideas in a newspaper. The questions posed about communication and the law in these cases could have been asked earlier, as they apply to pantomime and the stage as well as to the screen. Yet it was the intersection and arrangement of technology and commerce into a new form of mass culture that made the questions meaningful and prompted the consideration of film as a form of speech.

Also, the way in which the judges and justices defined filmic communication as distinct from, and outside of, the legal category of speech tells us much about how this group of specialists defined and policed the boundaries of the legal category of speech. Circa 1920, they conceptualized speech largely as words, and words as representations of thoughts, ideas, or beliefs. There was always implicitly a human mind (or spirit or personality) behind such words; in this sense, there is always an author—an author whose mind and intent animated those words and made them speak. The flickering images and bodies of film did not speak in part because the judges and justices did not see minds at work behind the images. Instead, they saw mechanical projections on the screen, spectacular displays or the repetition and imposition of ideas that had originated elsewhere (in words and other minds). They saw an illegitimate and dangerous source of influence. And, of course, they saw commercial transactions.

The justices' conception of speech in these cases, which excluded film (but also embodied forms of protest), is what I am describing as a liberal humanist approach to speech (to be distinguished from a liberal approach to speech rights).[125] Speech was animated by, and important because of, its tie to particular persons and their minds. Ideas, thoughts, and beliefs were properties of—originating and grounded in—the minds of individuals, as a site of freedom. In reasoning about what constitutes speech, why it is special, the justices looked behind the words for liberal individuals, wills, beliefs, or souls.

Yet this liberal humanism was steeped in exclusion and not all individuals were recognized as fully "human" or in possession of the proper sort of mind or will. The passionate—or even deliberate and organized—agitation of crowds did not register. Speech was equated with the linguistic representation of ideas or beliefs and their rational and reasonable articulation. Embodied actions, gestures, and expressions like those used so eloquently by early silent film actors like Charlie Chaplin or Lillian Gish were too primitive. They were a form of communication to be sure, but it was a form of communication that one might grant to animals, plants, or the "savages" of turn-of-the-century racial and social science. In this discourse, what distinguishes speech from the communication of animals (e.g., the utterances of parrots) or machines is the spark of intellect or spirit that inheres in the mind of "man."

To be clear, this liberal humanist vision was not separate from or prior to technological intervention. It is an application not of a liberalism that existed independent of the mechanisms of publicity, but of a liberalism defined in relation to that technology. While the mechanical nature of film projection argued against its classification as speech, the meat of the problem was in the primitivity, physicality, and irrationality associated with the medium. The legal category of speech, as I have argued, was defined in reference to techniques of publicity and interpretation derived from the medium of print. That is, the ideal of speech at the heart of early twentieth-century free speech law was crafted in terms of the mechanisms and materiality of printing, which implied a set of social relations. Motion pictures did not fit within legal conceptions of speech, press, or opinion precisely because making them and watching them did not fit within the techniques of publicity that implicitly structured these categories: those of printing. As the technological means of communication proliferated and the public sphere transformed, the justices would change their conceptions of what it meant to speak.

2. "A Primitive but Effective Means of Conveying Ideas"

Gesture and Image as Speech

Like children and neurotics[,] man as a political animal lives in a world riddled with bugbears and tabus [sic] — a dream-world of symbols in which the shadows loom far larger than the realities they represent.

— **Max Lerner,** "Constitution and Court as Symbols"

Because of its power to siphon emotion out of distinct ideas, the symbol is both a mechanism of solidarity, and a mechanism of exploitation. It enables people to work for a common end, but just because the few who are strategically placed must choose the concrete objectives, the symbol is also an instrument by which a few can fatten on many, deflect criticism, and seduce men into facing agony for objects they do not understand.

— **Walter Lippmann,** *Public Opinion*

In *Burstyn v. Wilson* (1952), a case dealing with Italian neorealism, church efforts to suppress sacrilege, and changing mores, the Court recognized moving pictures as an "organ of public opinion" deserving of First Amendment protection. In the majority decision, the justices stressed the social similarity of film to newspapers and magazines—a seeming about-face from the legal depictions of film as distinct from news (as discussed in chapter 1). In the *Mutual v. Ohio* (1915) and *Pathé Exchange v. Cobb* (1922) decisions, the Court had argued that moving pictures worked via mechanical and sub-rational processes: image, mimesis, and gesture. Print media and debate, in contrast, presented ideas—some good ideas, some bad. Print afforded educated audiences the ability to discern and make judgments about the value of these ideas. It was the stuff of public opinion. From *Mutual* to *Burstyn*, then, the Court appears to have radically changed its view of film, elevating it to the level of print publications.

While a change in the status of moving pictures was certainly part of this history, to focus only on the social status of film is to miss the bigger picture.[1] The more important change between *Mutual* and *Burstyn* was the constitution of "speech" and "opinion" in the law. Between the early 1920s and 1952, the objects and actions that had been legible as utterances within legal discourse changed to include visual, nonverbal communication: images and physical gestures (actions that conveyed meaning).

So, while typical accounts of the history of media and the First Amendment follow the trajectory from *Mutual* to *Burstyn,* I trace a different route.[2] In this trajectory, the key reversal is not *Burstyn* but rather a 1943 case (*West Virginia State Board of Education v. Barnette*) in which film does not show up at all: in the *Barnette* case, the flag salute was rendered as speech. In drawing a line between cases that do not at first glance seem connected— early film cases and a case concerning religious minorities and the flag salute—I offer an alternative genealogy of speech rights and media regulation. In this genealogy, film is not so much assimilated to a preexisting legal category (through a judiciary that only belatedly understands that film does indeed fit) as the category of speech itself is recast to fit shifting conceptions of the public mind, language, the printed word, and influence. Within this revised understanding of speech, the visual and kinetic features of film were a much easier fit.

In *Barnette*, which was about the ability of religious minorities to abstain from requirements to salute the flag, the justices staked new ground for speech. The decision is best known for its stirring expansion of civil liberties in wartime, as signaled in the oft-cited line, "If there is any fixed star in our constitutional constellation, it is that no official, high or petty, can prescribe what shall be orthodox in politics, nationalism, religion, or other matters of opinion or force citizens to confess by word or act their faith therein."[3] However, it is also the case in which the Court held that "symbolism is a primitive but effective way of communicating ideas" protected under freedom of speech.[4] Picking up on the latter, I show how *Barnette* expanded legal conceptions of speech in a consequential direction. No longer primarily the publication of original, linguistic (logocentric) messages, the *Barnette* decision redefined speech to include visual symbols and physical (bodily) gestures or acts. In this decision, communication that had previously been understood to operate via mimesis, connotation, and suggestion—subrational mental processes excluded from speech in the cases examined in chapter 1—was commingled with discourse, deliberation, and opinion.

In the discussion of the flag salute in *Barnette*, we can see the emergence of a legal articulation of speech that is more akin to the expansive notion of expression we see in today's law. *Barnette* expanded the legal conception of speech beyond the written or spoken word and the rules of rational argumentation. In this more expansive conception, *Barnette* upset established legal dichotomies and opened the door for classifying as speech for First Amendment purposes actions as varied as flag burning and wearing black armbands (such actions were later termed "symbolic speech") as well as works of classical music and abstract art that do not make a clear or coherent "statement."[5] The decision eroded the line not only between word and gesture, or speech and action but also between sense and non-sense, idea and sensation, opinion and entertainment. It paved the way for other "primitive" communications, from lurid magazines to movies to pornography and profanity, to be included within the category of speech. In this chapter, I show the material and discursive conditions under which these forms of communication came to "speak" within the law.

Barnette and the Contested Flag Salute

The story of *Barnette* began in January 1942, just after the US entry into World War II, when the West Virginia State Board of Education adopted a compulsory flag salute. All teachers and students were to be instructed to salute the flag in the "commonly accepted" way (the Bellamy salute), with the right arm stiffly extended forward at an angle, palm up (see figures 2.1 and 2.2). Failure to do so was considered insubordination and was punished by expulsion. As the war heated up in Europe and fears of fascist sympathizers at home percolated, many states passed such laws.

In a small schoolhouse outside of Charleston, West Virginia, the policy led to the expulsion of two sisters, Marie and Gathie Barnett, who refused to salute the US flag. The girls refused the salute out of religious conviction; Jehovah's Witnesses understood the flag itself to be a graven image and the salute a form of idolatry.[6] The girls were not alone in their predicament. Across the United States, Jehovah's Witnesses understood the compulsory salute laws as the state asking them to violate the Second Commandment. Many Witnesses, caught between the Bible and the state, refused to obey the state.[7] In return, they were expelled from school.

The Barnett family, backed by the American Civil Liberties Union (ACLU), fought the board, on the grounds that the policy violated their religious liberties. The case quickly made its way up to the Supreme Court. It came only two years after the Court had controversially denied that a compulsory salute in another state was a restriction of Witnesses' religious liberties.[8] That decision had quickly been repudiated in liberal circles and was decried by many journalists as intolerant and illiberal—and linked to a rise in violence against the Witnesses. *Barnette* thus offered the Court a do-over of a controversial decision.

Surprisingly, though, *Barnette* was not decided on grounds of freedom of religion but rather on grounds of freedom of speech. In declaring the compulsion to salute an infringement of speech rather than of religion, the Court decided the case in sweeping terms that would directly affect not only religious worship but also other walks of life. Today, we might call such a decision judicial activism.[9] The decision, penned by newly appointed Justice Robert Jackson, expanded freedom of speech in several ways. It held that compelled speech was an abridgment of speech; that actions as well as words could be considered utterances; and that symbols were a form of speech.[10]

That the Court upheld freedom of speech in wartime may at first glance seem surprising. Yet freedom of speech was ideologically freighted. It was one of the "four freedoms" Franklin Delano Roosevelt promised to export from the United States to the rest of the world in his 1941 State of the Union address. It was, more broadly, one of the core markers of liberalism that distinguished US democracy from totalitarianism abroad.[11] Justice Jackson's rhetoric in the decision drew on such discourse, making the line of distinction between "our totalitarian enemies" and the United States as precisely the latter's commitment to individual liberty and freedom.[12]

Further, the decision was articulated in the heat of the civil libertarian transformation of free speech law. The Court was, by the late 1930s and early 1940s, endorsing an interpretation of free speech more attendant to the protection of dissenting points of view (and less concerned with maintaining public order). This civil libertarian theory of free speech, as legal scholars emphasize, was a reaction to the suppression of dissent and immigrant speech during World War I. At the outset of the next war, some members of the Court were eager not to repeat the same mistakes of World

War I (censorship and suppression). Legal scholars and practitioners argued that it was important to protect minoritarian speech, even despised speech such as that of the Witnesses, in order to protect democratic debate and foster a diversity of views. And legal protections for speech, especially political speech, were increasing as the First Amendment was reinterpreted in a more civil libertarian vein. The *Barnette* decision came on the heels of others that struck down local ordinances restricting the distribution of leaflets, peaceable assembly, picketing, and proselytizing.[13] Between the changes in legal thought and the political context of combatting authoritarianism abroad, it is not so surprising that the Court endorsed civil liberties and expanded freedom of speech in wartime.

More remarkable is the substance of the civil liberties the decision endorsed. The antitotalitarian political context and civil libertarian transformation explain the impulse toward strong protection, even expansion of freedom of speech. They do not, however, explain the direction of the character of this expansion or the direction of this expansion. Jackson included not only individual conscience and opinions in his description of the scope and nature of speech but also acts and attitudes.[14] The decision brought images, gestures, symbols, and vague, affect-laden states of mind within the purview of free speech. It did so through a complex theory of signification and polysemy, in which meaning was not direct or easy to discern. A flag salute, Justice Jackson noted, did not necessarily signify fealty or love of country but might be "a simple gesture barren of meaning."[15] Not only gestures but also words might be empty. Neither guaranteed the presence of belief or ideas they symbolized, Jackson noted. This was a significant change in how both words and symbols had been discussed in earlier decades of First Amendment law.

For many observers operating within the visual and political context of the early 1940s the symbolism of the flag salute would have been fraught. The West Virginia policy required students to salute the flag using the Bellamy salute, which was commonly used before World War II.[16] The salute began with a "right hand lifted, palm downward, to a line with the forehead and close to it."[17] However, by the late 1930s, this gesture resonated with unwanted connotations. Most Americans had seen images of Nazi rallies full of visually similar salutes in newspapers, magazines, and newsreels (see figure 2.3).[18] What had once signified loyalty, love of country, and democratic ideals now disconcertingly conjured images associated with the enemy: totalitarian leaders and enthralled masses that seemed to abandon freedom and individuality.

Figure 2.1 (*above*) Children using the Bellamy salute in a New Jersey classroom, 1943. Source: Photograph by Ralph Amdursky for the Office of War Information.

Figure 2.2 (*opposite above*) A crowd of children using the Bellamy salute outside a school in Connecticut, 1942. Source: Photograph by Fenno Jacobs for the Office of War Information.

Figure 2.3 (*opposite below*) A crowd of supporters greet Adolf Hitler using the fascist salute in Germany. Images such as this circulated in American publications in the late 1930s and early 1940s. Source: Library of Congress.

The National Parent Teacher Association, Boy Scouts, Red Cross, and the Federation of Women's Clubs objected to the new policy on such grounds; the Bellamy salute looked too much like the Hitler salute.[19] Arguably, the policy was similar to the German one in content as well as optics. The West Virginia policy's requirement that children perform a physical act as an expression of fealty to the state echoed the requirement that German citizens employ the Nazi salute in their daily lives. For many critics, though, it was the visual resemblance and symbolism that rankled. The West Virginia State Board of Education responded to the controversy by changing the requirement to the more modern hand on the heart, a move with fewer unfortunate connotations.[20] Somewhat ironically, this "improvement" forced students to move their bodies in line with a more intimate gesture of feeling. This change satisfied the majority of the objections—though not

those of the Jehovah's Witnesses, who continued to find the salute a form of idolatry.

That the salute conveyed meaning was crystallized by the political context and proliferation of visual media (newsreels, photojournalism, and photo magazines increased in number and reach in the 1920s and 1930s). The way the salute conveyed meaning, via connotation or the evocation of a set of similar images and ideas, was the subject of heated intellectual debate and popular concern in the 1930s—a debate about symbols and their role in politics and public opinion. In order to contextualize the *Barnette* decision, it is necessary first to sketch out some of the broader cultural and political context, in particular the changes in the media and in the way that public opinion was understood and discussed in the 1930s and 1940s (as compared to the 1910s and 1920s).

I turn to the transformation in how social scientists and intellectuals talked about public opinion between 1920 and 1940 in the next section. Building on this, the section that follows focuses in on the role of symbols and symbolism in public opinion and attitudes in the intellectual discourse of the 1930s and 1940s. In that section, I argue that new media and interwar communication research (often preoccupied with the propagandistic capacities of radio), in combination with the psychologizing of public opinion, constitute the grounds for the equivalence the justices drew between bodily gesture and linguistic utterances. The chapter concludes by considering the legacy of the theory of communication imported into and sedimented into the law in *Barnette*, drawing a line from *Barnette* to the inclusion of film and sensational publications with the ambit of speech. This legacy, I suggest, was one reason that the justices began to recuse themselves from making judgments about the meaning or value of any given text or act of expression. Such interpretations were a matter of individual psychology, attitude, and liberty, not the jurisdiction of the Court.

From Mind to Psyche:
Transformations in Public Opinion

In the cases analyzed in chapter 1, the justices declared film beyond the bounds of public opinion. However, in the 1952 *Burstyn* case, the justices would reclassify films as organs of public opinion. In the intervening years, not only the cultural status of film but also understandings of the nature of public opinion had changed. Public opinion became less deliberative, more psychological, and subject to manipulation (and measurement). It became a matter of drives and personal attitudes as well as reasoned judgments. Justice Jackson alluded to this shift already in 1943, in his decision in *Barnette*, when he argued that the choice of whether to salute the flag was part of the liberty of self-determination in "matters that touch individual opinion and personal attitude."[21] That Jackson had included attitude along with opinion was a marker of the intellectual and political context of the late 1930s and early 1940s, a context laid out in this section. That he codified gestures, or actions, as representations of attitude or opinion was predicated on the blurring of word, image, and bodies under the aegis of symbols, explored in the next.

Public opinion, as mentioned previously, was in the 1910s and 1920s understood as a product of elites: the output of educated dialogue and dispassionate judgment. It was the opposite of the passions of the crowd. In this early twentieth-century elite discourse, public opinion was associated with the newspaper and the distanced judgment associated with reading (elite) newspapers.[22] Public opinion was thought to be created via the reception of cognitive-linguistic messages, a lag time for intellectual work (the "decoding" of linguistic parsing of the message and also considering the content of the message), and judgment. Newspapers were aligned with publics because they "brought" dispersed people together in a safe fashion and because reading embodied a decorous set of affects that aligned with predominant ideals of political order. Motion pictures did not fit within this understanding of public opinion or order. The effect of film on its viewers was more motor than mental, more collective than individual. Visual and visceral spectacles like film and the theater were likened to primitive communication, implanting impulses and ideas via bodily sensation, evading the "logical bond of analogy or succession" that verbal-linguistic communication required and instead moving the bodies of their audiences in unison.[23] In the words of the *Pathé* decision, films carried their own interpretation, leaving no room for disputation, doubt, or interpretation.[24] Further, as already described, the discourse on influence in the 1910s and early 1920s suggested that filmic impressions operated as much on the body as on the mind. Filmic influence was a form of excitation or stimulus closer to physical coercion than to the mental work (and bodily reserve) of opinion formation.

By the time the West Virginia State Board of Education passed its compulsory flag salute and the case made its way up to the Supreme Court, elites were talking about public opinion differently. By the 1930s, elite discussions of public opinion had taken on a more psychological cast. Public opinion was no longer held out as an ideal of rational deliberation to which the public might aspire. Rather, public opinion was increasingly, in the 1930s and 1940s, coterminous with attitudes, a shift registered in the words of the *Barnette* decision. Attitudes, a mix of psychological drives and cognitive processes, were an amalgam of reason and reaction, higher and lower forms of thought.[25] In this shift, the nature of suggestion and irrationality changed; by the 1930s, suggestibility (and emotionality or irrationality) was discussed as more mental than physical, and it varied with individual history or psychology. The Freudian-inflected language of drives, psyches, and personalities that came to occupy a central place in discussions of influence emphasized subterranean mental processes, attachments, and ideas that varied with personal history. This was a very different understanding than that which dominated the discourse of influence in which unconscious responses were suggested by the influence of the motor system.

This discussion of public opinion as a set of attitudes further suggested that everyone was in part irrational (not just the less educated or "primitive" peoples). We were all, as Donald Fleming describes, "organism[s] oriented by cravings and aversions ... neither purely cognitive nor purely affective, but an indissoluble compound of thinking and feeling, knowing and wanting."[26] As Fleming also argues, demographic shifts were as important as Freudian influences in this shift: importantly, immigrants, women, African Americans, and youth were gradually included in elite descriptions of the public. As these groups of people formerly labeled "primitive" or "passional"—irrational, poorly suited to the conditions of modernity by virtue of race/ethnicity, sex, or youth—were included in the categories of the public and the human, these categories underwent a revision. "Man" and the public were described in less loftily rational terms. Some intellectuals even wondered whether this "man" was even capable of pure rationality. As a contemporaneous historian of ideas, James Harvey Robinson, put it, even using the term would arouse reader suspicions as modern scholars would all know that "pure reason seems as mythical as the pure gold, transparent as glass, with which the celestial city is paved."[27]

This shift in how public opinion was characterized and studied is tracked in the work of Walter Lippmann. In the late 1910s, in *Liberty and the News*, he diagnosed the problem of journalism and public opinion as one of gatekeeping. Informed public opinion was possible in the absence of governmental censorship or the corruption of commercial interests. By

1922, when he published *Public Opinion*, his diagnosis had changed. No longer was the problem of public opinion one of access to more accurate facts or information. Rather, it was a problem of the minds of the public, who comprehended the world through stereotypes, the simplified and distorting "pictures" in people's minds (his use of imagery to explain irrationality echoes Gustave Le Bon's description of crowd mentality). He came to see news less as the uncovering of truth and more as the deployment of symbols, which worked not to convey information but rather to activate not fully rational associations and prejudices through which the public formed attitudes.

As others have argued, this loss of faith in public reason was based not only on the influence of Freud but also on the daily experiences and practices of a highly mediated society. Concerns about influence, propaganda, and conformity were deeply rooted in media change. Commercially operated media that traded in sensation and image (and made use of increasingly psychologically driven advertising) became the norm in the 1930s. At the movies and listening to radio, people found themselves addressed less as individuated readers and more as members of the mass.[28] Such experiences—and their disruptive newness—were constitutive of the mass society thesis proffered in 1930s social science. The thesis was that members of modern society were shorn from tradition and ties to locality and, thus unmoored, were subject to manipulation (e.g., by mass media). The experiences of attending to and being immersed in new media (radio, film) were central to the descriptions of social change that emerged during this period. That commercial mass media—especially radio and film—held many people's attention in the same way (that their "attention [was] held in the same way at the same time to the same stimuli"), that people went ritually en masse to the movies or listened to the same shows at the same time, seemed to prime them for conformity or worse (succumbing to charismatic leaders and demagogues).[29]

Such concerns were inflamed by the rise of authoritarian dictators in Europe—and their use of radio and film to address and, in the eyes of many observers, manipulate the masses. For many on the left, the examples of totalitarian media systems abroad provided dystopian visions of how the US media system might become a tool of mass influence at home. News reports in the 1930s commonly attributed Adolf Hitler's rise to power to his mastery of symbol and spectacle and his total control of the channels of communication.[30] For many leftist intellectuals, the concentration of ownership of the means of information and culture production in the hands of a few industrialists paralleled the German media system in deeply unsettling ways. The centralized industry structure of film and radio meant that a handful of powerful organizations were producing one-size-fits-all messages to the many (the "culture industries" critique). If Hitler's stranglehold on German media produced masses in thrall to his charisma and political ideology, then the mass media in the United States might as well propagandize either illiberal politics (e.g., populist authoritarianism at home like that of radio demagogues Father Coughlin or Huey Long) or consumerism and the passivity of "narcotized dysfunction."[31]

These were the conceptions and concerns about the public operative at the time of the *Barnette* decision: that is, the public was an atomized, semirational social formation held together via commercial mass media. In contrast to the crowds that had so concerned elites in the 1910s and 1920s, the mass media audience was open to suggestion not through the body and co-presence, but rather through the mind and psyche.[32] Importantly, elites were part of the same audience as the masses. No longer part of separate media spheres, elites such as the Supreme Court justices were by the late 1930s part of the same semirational, affective public or mass. As Justice Felix Frankfurter acknowledged in his dissent in the *Barnette* decision, "Even the most sophisticated live by symbols."[33] No one was immune to psychological appeals and the pull of suggestion.

The *Barnette* decision in many ways addressed this new vision of the public. As I will show, the decision formalized a new constellation of opinion, minds, bodies, and media. The First Amendment no longer protected only communication associated with reasoned (i.e., elite) audiences and informed judgments but also chains of suggestion and potentially irrational influence. Attitudes, as well as opinions and ideas, were the stuff of democratic decision-making.

Symbols were central to this shift in how public opinion and politics were understood. Rather than logic, reasons, or ideas, symbols were the mechanism by which minds were turned and attitudes formed. The proliferating references to symbols in intellectual discourse of the 1930s (discussed in the next section) were a way of approaching communication and influence that did not happen primarily through logic or reason, but rather through hidden drives, personal histories, and psychology. In other words, the discussion of symbols was a way of managing communication and influence within a public defined by psychology as much as by reason and critical judgment. Notably, as I will show, these symbols were not only or primarily associated with visual (pictorial) communication or other suspect forms (like embodied communication, or mimesis) but also included the word and print media. This is the context for Justice Jackson's focus on the status of symbolic communication in *Barnette*—and the inclusion of bodies and actions within freedom of speech.

Images, Words, and Symbols in the Law

The *Barnette* decision famously determined that states could not compel students to salute the flag. In order to get there, the Court had to argue that bending one's body in salute to the flag was a form of expression (and that compelling someone into such an expression was as much an abridgment of that expression as suppression). This required drawing a line of connection, if not equivalence, between language and physical gesture—the latter of which had, circa 1915, been associated with unthinking action and irrational impulses. To draw this connection, Justice Jackson drew upon a term, and discourse, operative in the late 1930s and early 1940s: that of symbolism.

Justice Jackson, writing the majority decision in *Barnette*, argued that the salute and the flag were symbols and that such symbols were equivalent to linguistic expression ("utterances"):

> There is no doubt that, in connection with the pledges, the flag salute is a form of utterance. Symbolism is a primitive but effective way of communicating ideas. The use of an emblem or flag to symbolize some system, idea, institution, or personality is a short cut from mind to mind. Causes and nations, political parties, lodges, and ecclesiastical groups seek to knit the loyalty of their followings to a flag or banner, a color or design. The State announces rank, function, and authority through crowns and maces, uniforms and black robes; the church speaks through the Cross, the Crucifix, the altar and shrine, and clerical raiment. Symbols of State often convey political ideas, just as religious symbols come to convey theological ones.[34]

In earlier drafts of the decision, Jackson had been more precise about the substance of the symbols at issue, noting that a hand on the heart or an upraised arm was a type of "utterance."[35] Such gestures conveyed simple ideas in an effective manner. They were symbols, a form of communication that operated at a lower register—a "short cut from mind to mind."

Symbols, in other words, were a form of communication that operated with a different level of mental engagement, much like the description of film in the legal discourse of the 1910s and 1920s. In this discourse, such symbolic communication was excluded from the category of speech precisely because it operated at such a "lower," or less cognitive, register. Moving images had been excluded from the category of speech—and public opinion—precisely because they were a shortcut from mind to mind, a primitive form of communication that did not involve the higher mental faculties. In the words of the *Pathé* decision, the pictorial communication of films carried its own interpretation.[36]

A key change between *Pathé* and *Barnette* was that in the *Barnette* decision, primitive communication no longer carried its own interpretation but rather was open to interpretation. Symbols, in Jackson's reasoning, in fact required the mental activity of interpretation—although it was a different sort of mental activity than that imagined and idealized in the legal decisions analyzed in chapter 1, which emphasized dispassionate judgment. Jackson's decision presumes, in fact, that interpretation and judgment are necessarily inflected with psychological drives and hidden, "latent" attitudes or beliefs. The decision went on to explicitly reference both duplicity in the deployment of symbols and variability in interpretation of symbols, asking whether the compulsory flag salute required students to actually adopt an attitude or merely fake its adoption. The salute, he argued, might be an empty gesture, with no conviction behind it. Efforts to regulate fealty to the nation were thus naive and ineffective. No law could require a person to read a particular meaning or faith from a flag or other symbol; such interpretations varied with individual disposition and commitment. Or, as Jackson put it, "A person gets from a symbol the meaning he puts into it, and what is one man's comfort and inspiration is another's jest and scorn."[37] One person might see in the salute an expression of faith in liberal democracy while another saw an act of acquiescence to proto-authoritarian rule. In such cases, legislation that attempted to inculcate unity or moral hygiene via control of symbols was doomed to fail (per Jackson, such efforts would only lead to the "unanimity of the graveyard").[38]

In Jackson's decision, then, symbols are open to interpretation (and failure) in a way that they were not before. Although it would become more common in future decisions, it was a controversial assertion for some justices at the time. Notably, Justice Frankfurter's dissent in the decision rails against this understanding of symbols. Frankfurter, too, saw symbols as an integral part of social life.[39] In Frankfurter's telling, however, symbols were more linear and less polysemic, as evidenced in his critique of Jackson's comparison of the flag salute to the fascist one: "And surely only flippancy could be responsible for the suggestion that constitutional validity of a requirement to salute our flag implies equal validity of a requirement to salute a dictator. *The significance of a symbol lies in what it represents.* To reject the swastika does not imply rejection of the Cross."[40] For Frankfurter, the swastika and the cross (or the Hitler salute and the flag salute) had clear and uncontested meanings. Symbols had simple, stable referents. A swastika was a swastika, and a cross a cross.

Frankfurter was, it should be pointed out, no enemy of civil liberties.[41] His dissent was complex and involved ideas about the public-private divide and the imperatives of national unity, as well as the nature of symbols. His approach to symbols, was, I want to point out, not unusual. It was in fact in line with earlier decisions involving symbols (mainly, the flag). In these cases, symbols were not open to interpretation. Justices commonly assumed that a symbol conveyed a single message and that they could assess its meaning, often literally writing that meaning into law. So, for example, in 1907 and 1920, the Court found that states could restrict commercial uses of the US flag, at least in part on the grounds that states had the right to protect the meaning of the flag from desecration.[42] The 1907 decision included a particularly precise definition of the meaning of the US flag, asserting that it "signifies government resting on the consent of the governed; liberty regulated by law; the protection of the weak against the strong; security against the exercise of arbitrary power, and absolute safety for free institutions against foreign aggression."[43] Frankfurter, in his dissent in *Barnette*—and in the earlier flag-salute decision that *Barnette* overturned (*Minersville School District v. Gobitis* [1940])—drew directly on the word and logic of this decision. Even when the justices reached a more civil libertarian decision, as in the 1931 ruling that a California law forbidding the display of a red flag was unconstitutional, they did so on the assumption that the red flag signified communism.[44] There was no haggling or hedging over interpretation.

Barnette, then, was a turning point in the way the Court talked—and ruled—about symbols. In the cases that came before *Barnette*, symbols were assumed to be inert and were associated primarily with expressions of religious faith and nationalism—forms of expression rooted less in reason than in belief and conscience.[45] Jackson's decision in *Barnette* made symbols like the flag dynamic, slippery, and fallible. Per *Barnette*, it was not easy for the Court (or anyone else) to determine a single, stable meaning of a symbol; it might not mean what it appeared to at first glance, either in terms of intent or interpretation. We get out of them what we put into them; they may even be devoid of meaning entirely. (Jackson mused whether the West Virginia policy required the students to internalize a particular feeling or just "simulate consent" via empty words or gestures.[46]) A symbol might be, as he said, a primitive shortcut from mind to mind, but that shortcut could easily fail.[47]

Symbols and symbolism were important elements of the decision. Jackson worked on his articulation of the salute as a symbol and symbols as sites of interpretation in various drafts as he prepared and circulated the decision to come up with the winning articulation.[48] In doing so, he drew on an academic and popular discourse on symbols circulating widely in the 1930s. While the term "symbol" had a technical meaning in semiotics already at this point (as a particular type of sign that conveyed meaning through an arbitrary system or "code"), in popular parlance, it had a more general use, highlighting the irrational, psychological aspects of communication (borrowing as much from Freud's work on dreams as from semiotics).[49] Already in the 1920s, Walter Lippmann and John Dewey were discussing the problem and uses of symbols in democratic, mass-mediated politics.[50] Journalists began discussing people and politics as symbols in the late 1920s and 1930s.[51] By the 1930s, legal and political scholars were increasingly framing governance and the law itself as symbolic practices: Thurman Arnold published an influential and controversial book, *The Symbols of Governance*, in 1935, and James Marshall published *Swords and Symbols: The Technique of Sovereignty* in 1939. In sociology, Martin Blumer famously placed symbols and symbol exchange at the heart of social relations (replacing and refining the conception of communication in turn-of-the-century sociology) in his theory of symbolic interactionism, which highlighted the variability of interpretation and meaning.[52] Max Lerner and other Freudian-inspired legal realists defined the law as an enterprise concerned with ephemeral and manipulable symbols.[53] In all of these uses, "symbol" is invoked to suggest that meaning is conveyed, or influence gained, via connotation or affective relay. Symbols, in this discourse, referenced communication that worked via processes associated with habit, feelings, or drives more than reason-giving or logic. This is the type of communication referenced in the *Barnette* decision when Jackson defined a symbol as a "short cut from mind to mind"; the shortcut is around lengthy description and deliberation. The work of association, like insight, happens in a flash.

This general discourse and a more specific set of social scientific research on communication and propaganda were resources for Jackson's discussion of symbols. While communication research in the 1930s and

1940s was deeply imbricated with public policy goals in many ways, the author of the *Barnette* decision had a particular point of contact with this knowledge.[54] Jackson had, prior to his appointment on the Supreme Court, headed the Special Defense Unit (SDU) at the Department of Justice, charged with evaluating and containing espionage, treason, and enemy propaganda. As Brett Gary details, the SDU in this era relied heavily on communication research, in particular that of Harold Lasswell and his students.[55] Jackson employed many of Lasswell's students to gauge the potential effects of alleged propaganda. Jackson was committed to a civil libertarian approach to propaganda that would balance the social import of free speech and wartime security concerns. As Gary demonstrates, resisting simple notions of the direct ideological effect of words was an important component of this project, and social scientific research on communication was a key tool.[56]

Reading Symbols and Attitudes in Interwar Communication Research

Lasswell's method of symbol analysis had been a tool in Jackson's efforts to craft an approach to propaganda that fit the civil libertarian ideal of free speech at the SDU. Symbol analysis, later renamed content analysis, was developed by Lasswell as a means to rigorously pinpoint and dissect propaganda and persuasion across different media.[57] The method was intended to be employed to study images as well as words—newspapers as well as radio, advertisements, and posters—focusing on hidden or "latent" meaning. (Lasswell also applied the technique to interviews, in which body language like biting fingernails was recorded and read as symbols of such latent meaning.[58]) In this focus on latent meaning, content analysis borrowed from Freud's work on dreams (and images). Just as Freudian dream analysis plumbed beneath the manifest content of the dream to the latent, symbolic meaning, content analysis sought to peel back the literal meaning of media texts to uncover the "latent" work of connotation, association, and arousal within a text. While often used on linguistic representation (in radio and print), one of the aims and purported strengths of the method was its transferability across media, from print, radio, and posters to film (and so was an example of the shift from assessments of the effects of specific media to attempts to assess effects more broadly, across different media). In its flexibility as to medium and its focus on hidden vectors of influence, symbol analysis was a tool attuned to contemporaneous concerns about communication, namely that some texts or messages worked via hidden, psychological mechanisms—a concern directed by the experience of propaganda in World War I and postwar changes in the media environment.

The experience of propaganda in World War I, combined with the massification of media that collapsed the distinction between the media of elites and masses, heightened concerns about illegitimate influence. These concerns crystallized in a reaction against propaganda in the 1920s and 1930s. Chronicles and exposés after the war, like former Committee on Public Information (CPI) head George Creel's *How We Advertised America* and George Seldes's *You Can't Print That!*, detailed the work of the Wilson administration's CPI to manage the news (largely through encouraging self-censorship) and to sway public opinion. Intellectuals and journalists in the 1920s and 1930s noted that the same techniques used by the government in World War I were being used in public relations and in commercial mass media, from newspapers to radio broadcasts.[59] Propaganda took on a pejorative meaning, connoting not so much public education (as it had in the 1910s) as manipulative communication for hidden ends.

In the postwar period, references to symbols evoked just this sort of manipulation; they became central to explaining the effectiveness of propaganda. Symbols replaced logic or reasons as the mechanism by which minds were changed and opinions swayed in much social science. For Lippmann (in *Public Opinion*), symbols were what stood between the average citizen and reality (they constructed the images in our heads). Lasswell thought that the power and potential of propaganda was in its ability to manage opinion through suggestion rather than through direct instruction or coercion; the father of American public relations (and nephew of Sigmund Freud), Edward Bernays offered a similar definition and defense.[60] While there was a split among academics as to whether such opinion management could be put to democratic use, especially as World War II heated up in Europe in the 1930s, there was a fair amount of consensus on how propaganda worked: the mechanism of propaganda, and the source of its power, was the use of symbols, which harnessed emotions or the subconscious.[61]

If wartime experiences with propaganda suggested to many that communication could be weaponized, or used to engineer public consent, the new technologies of communication highlighted for contemporaneous intellectuals that this engineering took place via suggestion, association, and sentiment—the work of symbols.[62] In the changing media environment of the 1930s, the differences between illustrated magazines, radio, and cinema did not seem so great. All had a similar political economy and deployed both ideas and suggestion or subtle invocations of feeling or association (connotation). All were perfect media for the deployment of messages to subtly, subconsciously persuade toward hidden ends. As educational materials from the Institute for Propaganda Analysis—founded in 1937 to combat the perceived threats of propaganda—attested, "[Propaganda's] persuasive appeals are geared to the century's streamlined channels of communication—the newspaper, the radio, the motion picture, skywriting, blazing neon and electric signs, and innumerable other media such as picture and editorial magazines and handbills and conventions and parades."[63] There is little difference among the channels here; there is a similarity in the appeals of *Triumph of the Will*, the tirades of radio demagogues (or, for that matter, FDR's fireside chats), and soap commercials. Given this and given that newspapers and the speeches of the four-minute men (volunteers who gave four-minute talks in gathering places such as movie theaters before screenings) had been the primary media for governmental propaganda in World War I, it had become harder for elites to imagine that print or oratory was more rational than other forms of publicity. They all seemed to operate via suggestion and connotation as well as denotation and logic. And, given the political economy of mass media, they all might be governed by hidden (private) interests.

The term "symbol" nicely flattened the distinction between media formats and suggested that they all worked via a similar mechanism. This is in part why Lasswell's method of symbol analysis became the most favored and famous method for analyzing media—in fact it is still discussed today as the only method devised specifically for the analysis of modern mass media. It was adaptable to multiple media formats: newspaper articles, magazine stories, radio addresses, or movies, promising to analyze the irrational aspects of not only radio but also the printed page. In its focus on latent meaning, symbol analysis also offered to explain the most troubling aspects of the new means of mass communication—the way it seemed to communicate in the libidinal and viral register associated with hypnotism, hucksterism, and the crowd. This vision of communication animated much communication research in the 1930s and broader discussions of the power and abuse of symbols that grew out of it (e.g., the idea that Hitler's rise in Germany was due to his successful use of symbols).

I want to emphasize that in this discourse, the printed and spoken word was a symbol, as much as icons, pictorial representations, or other suspect forms of communication (e.g., gestures).[64] In propaganda studies and in Lasswell's content analysis, and, to varying extent, in communication research more broadly, words as well as pictures operated through suggestion and emotion.[65] It is helpful to remember that many Americans' experiences of propaganda in World War I were defined by spoken and printed words. People had been misled, betrayed even, by words via the propaganda efforts of the CPI in World War I. We may most easily remember the posters (many of these relied more on informational text than on pictures; see fig. 2.4), but much of the propaganda effort was in shaping and curating news coverage and spoken-word campaigns on the radio and in person (as with the four-minute men).[66] After the war, such examples came to show that words, language, and meaning could be used as weapons of a sort, deployed strategically to manipulate the hearts and minds of enemies and those on the home front alike.[67] In addition, ads and public relations campaigns increasingly deployed words to inculcate insecurities and desires; in other words, they attempted to harness subconscious drives in order to achieve either specific actions (purchases) or to mold attitudes (public relations). Voices in the ether, or radio transmissions, were by this period engaging audiences for commercial or political purposes. Advertisers spoke directly to consumers in their homes, hoping to sway them into purchases. Political speakers followed suit. FDR's fireside chats capitalized on the reach and intimacy of the new medium, using direct address and vernacular idioms to speak to and reassure the nation during the banking collapse that ushered in the Great Depression. Opportunists and ideologues also made great use of the airwaves. In the United States, Reverend Bob Shuler, Huey Long, and Father Coughlin made careers out of fearmongering and populist appeals over the airwaves.

While the nonlinguistic aspects of radio, for example, the emotive content of the speaker's voice (which Marjorie Fiske and Paul Lazarsfeld called the "surplus value" of the voice), were important, much of the concern of academics, journalists, and regulators focused on the way that radio amplified the words of speakers.[68] From Cantril and Allport's work on the psychology of radio audiences to the Federal Radio Commission's denial of radio licenses to speakers who used the radio to spread unwelcome or irresponsible ideas, the ability of radio to amplify and lend legitimacy to the words of dangerous speakers was the target of concerns over radio's influence.[69]

The elite suspicion about radio and its ability to influence the public was brought to life in the reaction to Orson Welles's 1938 *War of the Worlds* broadcast. After the airing of the radio play, which made excellent use of

Figure 2.4 World War I propaganda poster produced by the Committee on Public Information (CPI). As with many works of the CPI, the poster relied on words as much or more than images to influence morale. Source: Library of Congress.

emerging radio formats to stage a fictional alien invasion, newspapers printed reports of mass panic and people filling the streets. We now know these reports to be untrue; perhaps they were even an attempt on the part of newspapers to discredit a rival medium.[70] Yet it was at the time—and continues to be—a popular myth. It inspired academic study and elite handwringing about the vulnerability of audiences. In other words, discussions about the ways that communications might derail or betray democratic politics were not, by the 1930s, focused only on movies, theater, or visual communication. These were still points of concern, from the Payne

Fund studies on how movies molded behavior and morals to popular out-rage at what were seen as the excesses and immorality of movie stars. (The rigorous self-censorship of movies via the Hays Code in the 1930s was, among other things, an effort to manage such concerns.) But the types of messages that ignited popular and elite concern were as often verbal or printed ones as pictorial or gestural ones—and they were not limited to the emotional appeals that inhered in use of the human voice but also leveled at newspapers and the printed word.

Fittingly, then, the critical response to wartime propaganda in the 1930s focused on the failures of language, more than on the abuse of images. Public intellectuals and educators worked to inculcate a new form of lit-eracy in a public they (now) saw as prone to being duped or betrayed by the duplicitous use of language in governmental propaganda or in public relations and advertising. The situation was seen as pressing enough that two institutes, the Institute for Propaganda Analysis and the Institute for General Semantics, were founded in the 1930s to educate the public about the potential abuses of the printed word. Both were driven by academic research, and both were aimed at a public imagined as linguistically naïve, liable to confuse words (signs) with things (referents). This was particularly acute in the interventions of the Institute for General Semantics, inspired by work in linguistics and philosophy.[71] General semanticists in particular aimed to lift the wool from the eyes of laypeople, revealing that language and words were symbolic processes that worked not only via logic and definition but also through connotation and implication.[72] (They worked to create a version of English—Basic English—in which such connotations did not apply and words mapped simply and unequivocally to their refer-ents.) Taken together, these different initiatives attest to a felt need both to educate the public about the latent influences present in verbal-linguistic messages and to craft tools with which members of the public could de-fend themselves.

In this interwar discussion of symbols, the distinctions among media formats were flattened (or bracketed) and the process of reading and inter-preting sober discourse (not just spectacle) was rendered as less than fully rational. In discussions of propaganda, written and spoken words were un-derstood to operate not through logic or procedures of reason but rather via connotation and subconscious influence. Just as in *Barnette*, in which a physical gesture was likened to both a visual symbol and an "utterance," in the interwar use of symbols to discuss and analyze propaganda, words, gestures, and images were substitutable. This is in sharp contrast with the distinction between visual and linguistic communication and the suspicion of visual and embodied expression present in *Mutual, Pathé,* and the fears of the crowd at work in the 1910s.

The leveling of various media formats (spoken word, print, photographs, and film) under a theory of latent influence was linked not only to proliferation of media technologies and their messages in the public sphere but also to changes in the way that the receipt of these messages was understood. The influence of messages was seen as less direct in part because it was more psychological. In the intellectual context outlined above, and within the discourse of symbols, it was hard to argue pure and direct effects (i.e., that words, no less than images, impressed one uniform meaning upon their viewers). As a case in point, when a group of noted researchers convened to discuss the use of print, radio, and film to influence public opinion at the University of Chicago on the eve of World War II, one of the speakers noted that all communication is "the process by which a symbol, originating within an individual or a group, is transmitted to other individuals or groups. The extent to which the symbol has the same connotation to both the communicator and the communicatee is dependent upon the extent of their background common experience."[73] Just as Lasswell's method highlighted, the speaker argued that meaning could not be found purely in the bounds of a text or message, but was subject to vagaries of individual interpretation. Further, if all communication works via association and if (as many Americans had come to discuss by the 1930s) there were many competing cultural contexts and value systems, then communication would invariably be dogged by noise, gaps, and miscommunication.[74] We see this way of talking about and conceiving communication imported into free speech law in the *Barnette* decision, where communication as an uncompleted circuit shows up in Jackson's assertion that symbols do not always carry the same meanings. We get out of them what we put in. This was, as I have argued, as applicable to the printed word as it was to the output of the new, electronic media.

Coming back to the *Barnette* decision and the way that it expanded the category of speech to include visual icons such as the flag and physical gestures such as the salute, I want to emphasize that by labeling both as symbols, the decision argued that both operated like language. This connection was made even more explicitly in an early draft of the decision, in which Jackson elaborated:

Apart from the commanded oral expression of adherence to the present political system, there can be no doubt that *the salute itself, the lifted arm, the hand on the breast, in this connection is a form of utterance.* Symbolism is a primitive but always dramatic way of communicating ideas. Meaning of dramatization is grasped by minds that would not follow a lecture. The salute in forms that vary but little from this have been found capable of utilization as a form of influence in mass psychology. But little modified, it becomes the counterpart of the Nazi, Fascist, or Falangist salute; clench the fist and it would resemble the communist salute to the hammer and sickle.[75]

No doubt this comparison of the salute to those of totalitarian regimes did not sit well with many of Jackson's colleagues. We see here, though, both a more explicit articulation of gesture as utterance and a discussion of how this action operates as drama and symbol, as a vector of psychological influence especially on the unsophisticated. Democratic commitment to free speech and civil liberties, Jackson was arguing, includes such influence (when there is no evidence of clear and present danger).

The discourse on symbols that I have outlined here enabled Jackson to say that the gesture and flag were "utterances." It was not only, then, that gestures (physical actions) could speak but also, and perhaps more importantly, that they could be subject to interpretation, or read. In the early twentieth century, as I showed in chapter 1, intellectuals viewed embodied forms of communication (like that of film, theaters, circuses, and crowds) as a lower, more primitive form of communication in large part because it operated via recognition and repetition (mimesis). It did not require any higher order abstract mental processes or logic to decipher (but rather carried its own interpretation). Twenty years later, in *Barnette*, the gesture of the flag salute and the flag itself, while still highly emotive, were open to interpretation and misreading—not only to mental processing but to individuated mental work. Understood as symbols, gestures, like words, require abstract interpretation—what we mean when we say we read a room, or the writing on the wall. This complication of communication, in which the line between linguistic and pictorial and embodied communication was blurred, would have lasting effects for freedom of speech.

From Bad Tendencies to Limited Effects:
The Legacy of *Barnette*

In propaganda, as in many other things, one man's meat is another man's poison. This may lead to boomerang effects, when arguments aimed at "average" audiences with "average" reactions fail with Mr. X.
—**Paul Lazarsfeld, Bernard Berelson, and Hazel Gaudet,** *The People's Choice*

In the years after *Barnette*, more objects and actions spoke. But judges and justices also increasingly refrained from determining the value of such expression. This was, in part, an outgrowth of the fallibility of symbols and of even expert (judicial) opinion, outlined in the previous sections. If the meaning of symbols was indeterminate, then determinations of high or low social value were fraught, as was the line between political and other forms of speech. In the face of this indeterminacy, the justices' interpretations or judgments about value looked less objective or universal and more subjective. Like other experts seeking to overcome their subjectivity in order to render more or less objective results or analysis—notably, social scientists and journalists—judges and justices needed to work to keep their personal taste and aesthetic judgments out of their professional judgments about the value of any given expression.[76]

In the late 1940s and early 1950s, the justices began to argue that they could not distinguish between highbrow and lowbrow expression or between entertainment and politics. Such abstention from judgment about cultural or political value was at the heart of rulings that sensational descriptions and illustrations of crime and war deserved protection, no matter how salacious, beginning with *Winters v. New York* (1948). This ruling paved the way for the Court to determine that film was an organ of public opinion, like the press, in 1952 in *Burstyn*. The core argument of *Winters*, cited by *Burstyn*, and many cases after, was that "what is one man's amusement, teaches another's doctrine."[77] This argument, emergent in the wake of *Barnette*, that judges and justices cannot or should not make judgments about the cultural, aesthetic, or political value of speech, has reverberated through First Amendment law since—for example, in the idea that determinations of obscenity should be made by reference to community standards rather than judicial evaluation or that what is "one man's vulgarity is another's lyric" (in a case involving a jacket emblazoned with "Fuck the draft!").[78] Or that we cannot distinguish between commercial and political speech or between corporate communications and the news.[79]

This new orthodoxy, what we might call an attitude of agnosticism about expression, is often conveyed in the one-liner about amusements and doctrines above. This line, which often stands in for the *Winters* decision as a whole in legal citations of the case as a precedent, is embedded in the original in a larger statement about the substance of speech and judicial evaluations of expression: *"We do not accede to appellee's suggestion that the constitutional protection for a free press applies only to the exposition of ideas.* The line between the informing and the entertaining is too elusive for the protection of that basic right. Everyone is familiar with instances of propaganda through fiction. What is one man's amusement, teaches another's doctrine. Though we can see nothing of any possible value to society in these magazines, they are as much entitled to the protection of free speech as the best of literature."[80]

The very substance of speech (and publication), notably, was no longer simply the exposition of ideas. Rather, it covered a range of sensation and excitation.[81] And the justices were no longer in a position to judge whether even the most lurid sensationalism might influence or inform public opinion for good or for ill. In this, *Winters* and many of the decisions it authorized as precedent carried on and expanded the legacy of *Barnette*'s theory of speech (without expressly citing it as precedent).[82]

This agnosticism was a sharp departure from earlier judicial approaches to expression. In the 1910s and through the 1920s, justices were quite comfortable in their ability to assess the meaning and likely impact of a message or symbol. The ability to make such judgments was at the heart of the "bad tendency" test, common in the early years of the twentieth century, in which justices upheld regulations of speech they believed had a tendency to harm public health or morals. It was on display as well in legal decisions prior to *Barnette* protecting the flag and all that it symbolized.

By the early 1940s, as we see in *Barnette*, this comfort was dissipating. There were other reasons that the courts moved away from the bad tendency test that had to do with the rise of civil libertarianism and decisions that reduced the government's ability to suppress speech.[83] But I argue that ideas about communication as well as civil liberties were part of this change. By the late 1940s, justices were loath to distinguish ideas from sensation, education from entertainment, in part because it was too difficult to do so. The lines between ideas, information, and entertainment were becoming too blurry to police. (The invocation of "information" is of note here. As information, the "best" literature and a lurid publication are flattened; both may have the same informational content—the consequences of this are discussed further in the next two chapters.) It was a short step from Jackson's assessment that we get out of symbols what we put into them to the declaration that "what is one man's amusement, teaches another's doctrine" to the emerging orthodoxy that the Court could not draw a line between entertainment and public opinion or political speech.[84]

This shift in the way that mass communication and persuasion was being talked about in academic circles and in the wartime and Cold War policies this research often informed had lasting effects for free speech law. Not only could judges and justices no longer universalize their judgments about the aesthetic or political value of texts (e.g., sensational magazines, films), but also the mechanisms of mass persuasion were brought within liberal freedoms. If symbols are subject to reading and individual interpretation, then the determination of meaning, significance, and value is enmeshed with the mind, will, and conscience of the individual, part of his or her democratic liberties. This was one of the upshots of Jackson's argument that the interpretation of symbols such as the flag and the flag salute were core individual liberties (part of freedom of conscience and thought). That is, it became more difficult to argue illiberal or illegitimate influence. As the site of influence had become the mind, rather than the body, and influence was understood to involve individual psychology and the mental work of interpretation, mass influence (for good or for ill) was squarely within the bounds of "speech" (rather than, say, coercion). Questions of how to limit such influence would have to shift to different terrain—such as the creation of new categories of speech like "fighting words" that merited less protection from "pure" speech, a development that Genevieve Lakier points out emerged at this moment and replaced judicial distinctions of good and bad speech (i.e., the bad tendency test) as a means of limiting the scope of the First Amendment.[85]

In this line of reasoning, and in these legal cases, the central issue that needed to be defended (in the pursuit of freedom of speech) was not consensus around some issue, idea, or symbol (as Frankfurter's dissent in *Barnette* and much earlier free speech jurisprudence had held), but rather the process of arriving at the decision. Democratic communication was not, as in the visions of Charles Horton Cooley and George Herbert Mead at the turn of the century, a means of coordination in the sense of a way of tuning and turning the social body toward a utopian consensus or community. Rather, it was about the ability of individuals to make choices—albeit, often these choices were delimited by a menu of predetermined options (whether by technocratic experts, mass-media gatekeepers, social scientists, or advertisers).[86] While the rhetoric of choice posits intellectually and morally active citizens evaluating and engaging in decisions about meaning and about feelings, by the 1940s, this rhetoric applied equally well to consumer choices as to political ones.[87] The exercise of agency in reading and interpreting symbols, whether the flag or a film, was thoroughly enmeshed with the mass psychology that Fred Turner describes as "a mass individualism grounded in the democratic rhetoric of choice and individuality, but practiced in a polity that was already a marketplace as well."[88]

Conclusion

I began this chapter by noting that the conventional narration of the history of how film became speech jumps from the Court's denial that moving pictures were a form of speech or publication in 1915 to their determination that they were a form of publication, even an organ of public opinion, in 1952. In closing this chapter, I return to film and its incorporation into free speech law. This incorporation both highlights the historiography that I have put forward in this chapter and introduces themes addressed in the following chapters.

The Court's 1952 reversal on the First Amendment status of film in the *Burstyn* decision is often attributed to a belated recognition of the political functions of film or to the Court's change of heart on matters of entertainment. In this chapter I have argued that changes in the Court's conception of communication were a more fundamental reason for this reversal. The objections to film in 1915 had not been that it was a form of entertainment; the justices recognized its educative function. Rather its status as copy, its form of its influence, and its status as commerce had placed film beyond the scope of speech or publication. I have argued that we should understand *Barnette* as an important intermediary point in this history, in which speech became less verbal-linguistic in scope and in which public opinion was linked to attitude and psychology. (Indeed, the Court argued in *Burstyn* that films were organs of public opinion because "they may affect public attitudes and behavior in a variety of ways, ranging from direct espousal of a political or social doctrine to the subtle shaping of thought which characterizes all artistic expression." This line of reasoning drew on the skepticism established in *Winters* but also and explicitly on communication research.[89]) The importance of *Barnette* as an inflection point in legal conceptions of speech, it should be clear by now, extends far beyond film. Yet coming back to film completes the story I began and highlights the issue of commerce, not addressed in this chapter.

I argue that *Barnette* elaborated a vision of speech that could in theory encompass the kinetic, spectacular, and emotive aspects of film. Yet it took a decade after *Barnette* for films to be included within the scope of free speech. (Though the Court signaled in the 1948 antitrust suit that broke up the vertical integration of the major film studios that it was ready to reconsider the First Amendment status of film.[90]) While there are no doubt many reasons for the delay, I'd like to suggest that one central one was the commercial nature of the "speakers" in filmic communication; films were equally the product of directors as artists and of film studios as businesses. As such, they were both organs of public opinion and commercial products, or transactions.

Indeed, one of the key points of discussion in *Burstyn*, the case that changed the First Amendment status of film, was the commercial nature of film. In arguing for film as speech, the justices first argued that it did not matter that films might be frivolous, "lowbrow," or mere entertainment and diversion; per *Winters*, such considerations of aesthetic or cultural value were beyond the scope of the First Amendment. Second, they argued for the inclusion of film despite the fact that movies were economic products as much as artistic or ideological messages: "It is urged that motion pictures do not fall within the First Amendment's aegis because their production, distribution, and exhibition is a large-scale business conducted for private profit. We cannot agree. That books, newspapers, and magazines are published and sold for profit does not prevent them from being a form of expression whose liberty is safeguarded by the First Amendment. We fail to see why operation for profit should have any different effect in the case of motion pictures."[91] What stands out in this reasoning is that all outlets for expression are considered commercial. Newspapers (and books), in particular, were no longer idealized cultivators of elite public opinion (as implied in *Mutual* and *Pathé*) but also profit-driven outlets for the dispersal of symbols and even, at times, manipulation. Both the medium of print and the institution of the press (increasingly discussed as a commercial entity as much as a civic one) were difficult, by the late 1940s, to distinguish from the medium and institution of film.

The inclusion of film within freedom of speech (in *Burstyn*) was, then, made possible by the revision of the category of speech that took place in *Barnette*—and by extension, by the rise of psychology as a paradigm for understanding social and individual behavior, changes in elite discourse on communication and persuasion, and changes in the media environment that I have argued underpinned this revision. But the consideration of film as a form of speech also involved commerce, or the relation of political and aesthetic choices to consumer ones—the overlap of the decisions that form public opinion and those that inform the purchase of cultural products, like tickets to a movie or which newspaper to purchase. This complex relation of commerce and speech, publics and markets, is taken up in the next two chapters.

3.   **Transmitters, Relays, and Messages**

Decentering the Speaker in Midcentury Speech Law

Speech is natural and inseparable from the human person, the breath of his social existence, and so intimate a tool of all mental life that without free speech thought itself could not be fully free. The press, by contrast, is an institution of developed society, a machine-using institution, and one whose role tends to enlarge as new instruments are developed.... It is incumbent upon us to inquire whether the traditional groundwork of principle which has inspired our existent law and our social attitudes is adequate to the period we now enter.

—**Commission on Freedom of the Press,**
A Free and Responsible Press

At the same time that images and words were undergoing reevaluation in the events and cases analyzed in chapter 2, a very different set of questions circled radio and, to a lesser extent, newspapers. Concentration of ownership in newspapers and radio, political sentiment, and the distinct technological characteristics of radio as a medium combined to provoke questions about the nature of speakers within the law. In the 1930s and 1940s both newspapers and radio stations were increasingly becoming part of vast media chains. No longer a local mom-and-pop production, the typical newspaper or radio station was, by 1940, an outlet for a larger organization, operating via economies of scale in which the production of content—a commodified form of the utterances, thoughts, and ideas of speech law—was centralized. These media outlets became less like authors or speakers and more like mouthpieces of a larger industry or, in the words of the report cited above, a "machine-using institution."[1]

How to fit such media outlets within the existing models of speakers (and speech) within First Amendment law is the question that animates the history and legal cases assembled in this chapter. The questions of how to deal with media outlets as speakers and how to fit the mass-produced messages of big media into existing models of speech surfaced in public political debates about freedom of speech and the press in the 1930s. In the pro-regulatory climate of the Depression and New Deal, progressive advocates and regulators proposed curbs to the excesses of media industries, sparking a debate about the meaning of freedom of speech and the best means of achieving it.

These regulatory efforts—and the broader set of critiques in which they were embedded—were initially aimed at newspapers and radio, which were both inescapably industries by the 1930s, with all that the term implied. The messages, or ideas, they circulated were not the products of a small set of owner-operators, but rather the product of highly segmented and specialized labor. The words "printed" or "spoken" via these outlets did not necessarily reflect the ideas of the reporters or announcers who gave them shape and form. Instead, they might reflect the ideas of publishers and owners—or simply be the product of a cold economic calculus. In other words, both industries presented "speech" as the product of alienated labor and distributed the intent and agency behind these utterances—the function of the speaker—across a set of job descriptions and economic relations. The distance between these media messages and the ideas, intents, and beliefs of any particular speaker presented the conceptual and legal question at the core of this chapter: how to apply a body of law and democratic norms based on notions of individual speech—understood as an activity anchored in individual minds and experience—to a mechanized, industrial-scale system of communication? This question was posed by reformers, academics, policy makers, and lawyers. It was among the questions that the Commission on Freedom of the Press, also known as the Hutchins Commission, tackled. Formed by *Time* magazine publisher Henry Luce in 1941, the commission brought together experts, from philosophers to poets, bankers to legal scholars, to evaluate the role of the changing press in society and politics and to make recommendations on how best to ensure freedom of the press.

These questions arose against the backdrop of industrialization and concentration of the press, the Depression, and the New Deal. They reflected a sense that the concentration and industrial scale of the press had restructured the public sphere and might no longer serve democracy or the people. The Court attempted to resolve these tensions not only by re-negotiating the relation of speakers to the state (the oft-recounted debate between positive and negative liberties) but also and more foundationally by reenvisioning what it meant to speak, the forms of expressive agency enshrined in speech law.[2]

Beginning in the late 1930s, the Supreme Court began to state that free-dom of speech included not only the production or publication of utter-ances, ideas, or beliefs but also the distribution of ideas and information. While this may at first seem a subtle distinction, I argue that it was a signifi-cant one. It enabled a shift in legal reasoning away from analysis of speaking and writing as the expression of personally held beliefs or ideas and toward an analysis of speech in terms of the bits of information (or data) conveyed or exchanged—and the best systems of distribution for such speech—a conceptualization of speech befitting institutions, aggregates, and systems more than specific speakers. It was, in this sense, an impersonal under-standing of speech.[3] Ultimately, this line of reasoning would make speech into something that was not connected to individual persons or their minds but rather might flow through a mechanized system—or a market.

In the cases examined in this chapter, particular speakers became less central to the law than questions about the transmission or distribution of information. I argue that this era saw a reconceptualization of speech less in terms of personal communication (or mind) and more in terms of ab-stract systems. Speech was, in these cases, not so much the expression of a particular person's thoughts, ideas, or beliefs as it was the transmission of messages that might or might not originate with the sender. No longer was it a problem if an utterance was a re-presentation or copy. The act of pass-ing along a message of information became legible as a sign of agency and site of freedom, in the model of radio relays or consumer choices.

This chapter highlights the way that the technology of radio signifi-cantly shaped this reconceptualization. The emergence of a legal concern and discourse around the distribution of information was an artifact of the clashes between emergent industrial media, in particular radio, and the existing body of free speech law. In the following sections, I outline the ways that radio disturbed the background assumptions about public com-munication embedded in speech law of the day—radio was an instrument of commerce as well as an organ of public opinion, it was more a medium of distributed speech than direct expression, and it was a powerful plat-form controlled by a concentrated industry—and then analyze how these technical and political economic aspects of radio communication clashed and combined with contemporaneous free speech debates. In the second half of the chapter, I examine how this clash shaped the terms in which the Court justified the regulatory regime applied to radio. I conclude by showing how this line of thinking, developed around the technical and political challenges of radio, was employed to characterize citizen speech rights, or, how a machine-made theory of free speech was applied to instances of citizen dissent.

The Problem of Radio

The first serious consideration of how radio would fit within the First Amendment came in a case involving a popular preacher's radio license. In 1932, the Federal Radio Commission (FRC), the regulatory body administering the use and provision of the airwaves, denied Reverend Bob Shuler's application to renew his radio license. Shuler, the pastor of Trinity Methodist Church in Los Angeles, operated a radio station out of his church.[4] He was one of the entrepreneurs of the new medium, using the radio to influence a broad audience and to enrich himself. Shuler's broadcasts were filled with charges of corruption and incriminating accusations aimed at local officials and private individuals alike; common targets included the California judiciary, local officials and civic leaders, Catholics, and Jews.[5] While some of his allegations were accurate, many had no basis in fact; before one of the hearings regarding renewal of his radio license, he blustered on the air that he would not get a fair consideration because one of the commissioners was biased against him due to the commissioner's Catholicism. In fact, there were no Catholic commissioners.[6] Given his track record and complaints lodged with the agency, the FRC denied the license renewal request. Shuler and his lawyers responded that the denial was an infringement of his freedom of speech and appealed the decision in court.[7]

The case illustrates the uncertain legal status of radio in the 1930s. Radio broadcasts were not, as we might think, self-evidently "speech." That the first free speech claims came so late in radio's history is telling on this account. The first regulation of radio had come in 1910, yet challenges in the name of free speech did not appear until 1930. There were other legal challenges to radio regulation before 1930; they just centered on radio as a form of commerce and on the legitimacy of radio regulation and its enforcement.[8] Litigants and regulators alike were not certain of which classifications, or areas of law, would be most successful in attacking regulation. This was in part due to the legal climate: First Amendment claims were not common in the 1920s but were becoming more common as the civil libertarian transformation of First Amendment law got underway in the 1930s. It was also due to the technical nature of radio. The FRC, in making its case against Shuler, argued at the district court level that radio transmissions were not speech at all for the purposes of the First Amendment, but rather mere electronic reproductions of speech at a distance, echoing one of the arguments used in *Mutual* to deny film the status of speech (that film was merely a reproduction of ideas originating elsewhere).[9] This line of reasoning did not work, but the fact that it was forwarded, I argue, highlights the tension between the existing body of law and its embedded assumptions about public communication—the existing "regulatory scene"—and the sociotechnical system of radio.[10]

In order to understand this and other early encounters between radio and the law, we need to understand the formation of radio as a technology and as an industry and the free speech debates of the 1930s. By the end of the 1930s, as this history shows, radio was understood as a mix of commerce and opinion and as a highly concentrated industry—the epitome of the problem of the industrialization of communication.[11]

The Evolution of Radio in the United States

The peculiarity of radio owes much to the way the medium developed as an industry. Before 1920, most users of radio were hobbyists, many of whom built their own receivers and transmitters. Hobbyists used radio sets and technical expertise to tune in distant signals, gaining pleasure from their ability to connect with other radio users across great distances. A user in Maine might exchange salutations and location with one in Arizona or play chess over the air. Before World War I, these messages were primarily in Morse code (the vacuum tubes required for the transmission of voice or music were not widely available until after the war). Radio was both a dialogic medium and a highly technical one. Hobbyists had to be able to assemble a radio set, know Morse code, and be adept at tuning and transmission.[12]

After World War I, manufacturers like RCA and Westinghouse began producing easy-to-use home radio receivers. As receivers, they enabled people to receive messages but not transmit them, shifting radio from a dialogic use toward dissemination, or broadcasting. This, and the design of many of these receivers in the form of furniture suitable for the living room (rather than a machine more suited to the garage or attic), was a key step in domesticating radio as a consumer technology. In order to provide more regular content and drive sales of the receivers, some of these manufacturers began producing regular broadcasts, initially a mix of music, talk, sports scores, and other bulletins.[13] By 1922, the nation was in the midst of what commentators called the "radio boom" of rapid radio adoption. By 1930, the US Census Bureau deemed radio an important-enough social trend to measure. In the first census tally that year, 39 percent of homes reported owning a radio receiver. By 1940, 73 percent of homes would report owning a receiver.[14]

Speaking or Selling? Radio and Commerce

Americans buying radio sets in the 1920s and 1930s increasingly encountered commercial stations on the air.[15] Earlier legislation had determined that the electromagnetic spectrum was public property and that use of the airwaves would be administered by the government (initially the Department of Commerce). In order to send radio transmissions, a user had to apply for a license and would be assigned a frequency. Responding to crowding of the limited spectrum in 1922, the Department of Commerce sidelined amateurs, forbidding them to transmit "weather reports, market reports, music, concerts, speeches, news or similar information or entertainment."[16] While many of the new stations both provided their own talk and entertainments and allowed other local talent (e.g., musicians) or politicians on the air, AT&T's New York station WEAF pioneered "toll broadcasting." Taking toll phone calls as a model, WEAF sold airtime to whoever wished to address its audience. (The first such broadcast was an ad for a suburban housing development in Jackson Heights, New York.) Overt ads were soon replaced by sponsored concerts, variety shows, talks, and radio dramas.[17] Rather than simply speak about the product over the air, sponsors would pay for or, increasingly, create content to be aired on radio. From merely announcing sponsorship of a musical performance (e.g., *The Firestone Hour*) to actually writing and producing radio serials (most famously, many of the daytime serials that would become known as soap operas), sponsors and the advertising agencies they hired created a large percentage of what was on the air in the 1930s. By 1929, advertising agencies produced 33 percent of programs aired on networked radio stations and single sponsors produced another 20 percent. The networks themselves produced only 20 percent of programming. In the ensuing years, advertising agencies would take over production of nearly all network content.[18] While there were a variety of other business models in the 1920s and a strong coalition of supporters of nonprofit, educational radio into the 1940s, this commercial model became the norm, institutionalized in legislation.

This model of broadcasting normalized a commercial and polyvocal form of address, in which it was hard to pinpoint just who was speaking: the local station owner, the sponsor, the network, or the writers and actors. Commercial entities, however, were not the only third parties that might speak via a radio station. It was common as well for political candidates to buy airtime in order to address a larger segment of the population. Voices combined and commercial and political appeals mixed easily over the airwaves. Radio was never simply entertainment or edification but an often-confusing blend.

Here it is worth remembering that in the early decades of the twentieth century, commerce and opinion were conceptually and legally separated. Part of the rationale in the *Mutual* and *Pathé* cases was that filmmakers were commercial actors, in the pursuit of private profits rather than (public) ideas and opinions. By the 1930s, commerce and opinion were beginning to blend together in popular culture. As scholars like Jackson Lears and Gary Cross demonstrate, buying and displaying goods was becoming a form of expression and a way of asserting individual identity outside of the traditional strictures of family, class, and shop.[19] While the beginnings of what would become known as the consumer society were visible, it was not yet a settled matter—and in fact there was much resistance to the intrusion of commerce on politics and the home. The very strong popular resistance to the commercialization of radio was one example of such resistance. In the 1930s, one of the strongest voices of resistance came from a coalition of advocates for educational radio.[20] These advocates argued that the commercial use of radio was a debasement of a scientific advance that should be harnessed for the betterment of society and nation.

The desire to separate commerce and opinion and the difficulties of doing so as radio developed into a commercial medium are on display in early radio regulation. The dual nature of radio as commerce and opinion was written into the Radio Act of 1927, which established the FRC to administer the electromagnetic spectrum and which set the course of radio as an industry and medium for most of the remainder of the century.[21] The status of radio as a political platform was so important to the legislators who wrote the bill that they included an entire section specifying that license holders should not discriminate among political candidates who wished to speak via their stations.[22] Yet the act is credited with sedimenting the commercial structure of broadcasting in the United States.[23] A similar balancing act is evident in the Supreme Court's decision in the Shuler case detailed above. In denying Shuler's claim (and upholding the FRC's denial of his license), the Court argued that free speech did not include the right to use, or abuse, radio as "an instrumentality of commerce."[24] In this and in other legal cases, speech meant that which contributed to public opinion, not commerce. And radio was often labeled explicitly as a technology or a medium of commerce more than of ideas. Challenges to regulation before *Trinity Methodist Broadcasting v. FRC* (1932) were made in the name of commerce rather than freedom of speech. And even in *Trinity*, the judges continued to characterize radio as an instrument of commerce (and science) and opinion, warning that if Shuler were allowed to continue his broadcasts, then "this great science, instead of a boon, will become a scourge, and the nation a theater for the display of individual passions and the collision of personal interests. This is neither censorship nor previous restraint.... [Shuler] may continue to indulge his strictures upon the characters of men in public office ... but he may not, as we think, demand, of right, the continued use of an instrumentality of commerce for such purposes."[25]

Who Is Speaking? Radio as a Medium of Distributed Speech

The practice of "toll broadcasting" typifies another way that radio did not fit within the parameters of freedom of speech. In the media that preceded radio—newspapers, books, pamphlets, and oration—freedom of speech was equivalent to the freedom of a speaker or author(s). The content of a book, pamphlet, or speech was assumed to be the product of the mental activity and the specific sentiments of an author or authors; the publication or oration of these sentiments was the exercise of the authors' expressive freedom.[26] Newspapers were more complicated but still seen through this conceptual prism. It made sense to think of a newspaper as the expression of the sentiments of the editor-publisher up through the mid- to late nineteenth century. Newspapers in the eighteenth and early nineteenth centuries had often been the output of an individual or small group: the editor-publisher, who often also manually operated the printer. The output of many newspapers reflected the views and wisdom of the editor-publisher, or the party to which he owed his affiliation (especially in the partisan press).[27] By the early twentieth century, the link between newspaper content and the views or opinions of the editor or owner was more complicated. Newspapers were a concentrated and industrialized industry. Yet the historical association of the newspaper with the voice and views of an individual or small group continued to color much public discourse on the newspaper and legal understandings of the industry.

Radio had no equivalent figure, no individual to whom the role of speaker could be assigned. While the license holder would be the closest analog, there were a number of differences in both the way that radio transmissions were received and the way that radio was understood that militated against a simple association of the output of radio with the license holder. While in some cases, like that of Shuler, the speaker and the license holder were one and the same, in many cases this was not so. The messages broadcast by any individual station might be attributed to the license holder, to an announcer/speaker employed by the station, to a third party who paid for airtime (frequently, as noted above, a politician or a commercial sponsor), or to the station owner. By 1933, Franklin Delano Roosevelt was using radio to deliver his famous fireside chats to the nation (see figure 3.1); in such examples, radio seemed to exist more as a platform for the speech of others than as a megaphone for a station owner (or license holder). License holders might "editorialize" over the air or simply allow others to do so. In the early 1930s, examples of both could be found around the dial. This meant that the association of radio license holders, or owners, and the messages they transmitted was more tenuous than the cultural association of the content of print with the publisher's opinions.[28]

Legal cases from the early 1930s show that the question of who the speaker was in radio transmission was fraught. Discussions of who was responsible for libel over the air illustrate the confusion on this point.[29] When a paying speaker libeled another over the air, who was responsible? This was the question raised in *Sorensen v. Wood* (1932). In the case, a proxy for a candidate in a Senate race in Nebraska (Richard Wood) criticized the morals and character of the state attorney general (C. A. Sorensen) in a radio broadcast. The deliberations of the case considered whether the engineers should have cut off the offending transmission, whether Wood alone was responsible, or whether the station owner should take responsibility for speech transmitted using his equipment and through authority of his license. The final decision found that both Wood and the station

Figure 3.1 FDR using radio to address the nation in a "fireside chat," September 1934. He needed only access CBS's and NBC's networks to address the nation. Source: FDR Museum.

owner were liable, or the responsible speakers. In his decision, the judge rejected the owner's argument that radio was a common carrier—not an extension of his speech, but rather a platform for the speech of others (i.e., Wood)—and thus he was not responsible, though the judge noted that there was some confusion on this point in the courts.[30] This confusion extended further than the courts; legislators in the 1930s went back and forth on whether radio should be a common carrier, and the requirement in the Radio Act of 1927 that radio operators could neither discriminate among political candidates nor censor their speech seemed to imply that, in some instances, radio operators were to act like common carriers.[31] (Similarly, in the 1940s, the FRC prohibited radio owners from using the airwaves to promote their opinions or views, or "editorializing.") Between these two sets of expectations, radio operators found themselves in a bind. Understanding themselves to be both obligated to carry the speech of political candidates per the Radio Act and responsible for what they said per *Sorensen*, operators took to requiring candidates to submit written copies of their radio addresses ahead of time, for review. Operators could refuse to allow a speaker whose remarks might prove damaging. They could also cut off the transmission if a speaker appeared to be veering into libelous territory, ultimately contributing to the sense, common in the 1930s, that radio operators allowed only a very narrow range of opinion and discussion on the air.[32]

As these examples show, radio was already by 1930 treated as a polyvocal medium in law and policy, a medium in which there was more than one speaker and in which different speech rights might conflict. This would become even more complicated as the decade progressed and national radio chains became more dominant. In the beginning, radio stations were primarily local, and the license holder for a station was the operator of that station, overseeing programming. In the late 1920s, this began to change as AT&T used its phone lines to link stations in different cities together in a "chain" to allow simultaneous transmission of programming (e.g., a musical act, talk).[33] Such chains, or networks as we know them today, enabled economies of scale in programming. Only one program had to be produced to be aired in multiple cities or regions. Taking over from AT&T, the National Broadcasting Company (NBC) began contracting with smaller stations to carry a certain amount of NBC's programming and sponsors. Local station owners (license holders) went from acting as producers of content and gatekeepers for acts and speakers who wished to address their local or regional audiences to being relays in the distribution of content aimed at a national audience. As local stations affiliated with networks, they became links in a chain of distribution of messages created elsewhere, often by companies wishing to sell goods and the ad agencies that worked for them. Increasingly, people across the United States in rural communities and urban ones were listening to the same programming at the same time (inspiring the concerns about homogeneity discussed in chapter 2).

Networks thus further complicated the question of who the speaker was over the air. Programming might be the product or choice of the local station owner, the network (e.g., quality or sustaining programming that was not sponsored), or a sponsor. Networks also simultaneously increased the reach, or power, of broadcasting and decreased the influence of individual station owners. Local radio stations had a reach similar to or only slightly larger than a successful newspaper.[34] In contrast, one network could reach a majority of Americans, dominating the public sphere. Networks were able to blanket the nation with the messages that they, or their advertisers, or other third parties who could afford to buy the time, chose. It was this centralized industry arrangement, as much as radio's technical capacities to reach beyond the territorial bounds of tradition distribution circuits, that made radio seem so powerful. Radio networks were credited with the power to bring the nation together and to homogenize and degrade culture through their scale and centralization.[35] In discussions about opinion and information over the air, this homogenization was understood by some critics of the day to be a form of censorship—a censorship by private actors and interests rather than governmental ones. Such homogenization or censorship was at odds with the articulation of freedom of speech as a means to ensure a diversity of ideas and views gaining ground in the 1930s.

Defining "Freedom of the Air": Censorship and Freedom of Speech in the 1930s

Freedom of speech—at least in the realm of radio—is in the ear of the listener.
—**Morris Ernst**, "Radio Censorship"

Who has this freedom of the press? The answer is: those persons who own the press. Nobody else. Freedom of the press is a property.
—**Lowell Mellett**, cited in Sam Lebovic, *Free Speech and Unfree News*

Intellectuals and a segment of the public responded to the concentration of media, in particular radio, with alarm. Not only radio but also newspapers were becoming concentrated in "chains" in the 1930s. For many on the left, this meant a concentration of power in the hands of a few (the captains of industry, or in George Seldes's terms, the lords of the press)—a concentration that in the anti–big business atmosphere of the Depression seemed to require regulation. This was a conundrum. These critics argued that democracy required regulation of the press, yet democracy also required freedom of the press. How to square these two requirements opened a set of questions about the meaning of freedom of speech and the press. Was freedom of speech the same as freedom of the press? Were freedoms of speech and of the press about individual rights or broad, social interests? Did freedom of speech and of the press mean a freedom from regulation or freedom to speak (or access information)? Whose interests—or freedoms—were central: owners or audiences?

These questions may have been catalyzed by concerns about the concentration of media ownership—and the censorial powers of these owners—but they were made possible by the civil libertarian re-interpretation of free speech that was becoming dominant in legal circles in the 1930s. In particular, these questions were made possible by the way that this theory grounded freedom of speech in democracy and a set of social interests, or the social good, rather than solely in individual rights.[36] Speech was protected as a means of ensuring collective self-determination; as such, it required a diversity of ideas and opinions in public discourse. This view was influentially articulated by Zechariah Chafee Jr. as a response to governmental suppression of speech in World War I and in order to protect minority viewpoints; it was made the context of a Progressivism suspicious of individual rights as property claims.[37] It was adopted via famous dissents by Holmes and Brandeis and formed the foundation for later legal theory such as that of Alexander Meiklejohn and many contemporary media reformers. Understood as a social good, the measure of free speech (or press) was less the ability of any one individual to have his or her say and more the diversity or quality of viewpoints expressed in public.

This social good theory of free speech was forged in response to a different set of political pressures and constraints: governmental suppression of minority viewpoints and the prevailing distrust of individual rights rationales among Progressives. Yet it became a useful lens and tool for media reformers in the 1930s, who sought a way of understanding freedom of the press outside of the individual liberties of its owners. Prioritizing the individual liberties of owners meant that freedom of the press, as the old adage says, belonged to those who owned one. Such an approach, in which freedom of speech hinged on property ownership, was common in nineteenth-century thought about the First Amendment.[38] There may have been political economic and ideological reasons for this alignment. As Sam Lebovic points out, nineteenth-century freedom of the press reflected the craftlike political economy of the mid-nineteenth century, revolving around the image of the editor-publisher, in which the content of the newspaper was tied to his or her personal thought, conscience, and opinions (even though it might contain the words or ideas of others). In this way, there was little reason to distinguish between the right to speak, write, or print.[39] Any member of the public might, with luck and a bit of capital, be the operator of a press. That this depended on ownership was no different from public speaking, which depended on access to (often ownership of) a platform on which to do so.

Changes in the political economy of newspapers and the advent of radio threw such popular and legal assumptions about freedom of the press into question. By the 1930s, news was big business. Radio networks, as the previous section outlined, provided a mouthpiece for politicians, entertainers, and advertisers to reach a majority of Americans—and the networks were controlled by a very small handful of people. Similarly, newspapers were increasingly not local outfits owned and operated by an individual or small group, but rather incorporated into large "chains" like Hearst, Gannett, Cox, and Scripps-Howard. These chains concentrated ownership of newspapers in the hands of a few wealthy industrialists who were not connected to the communities the papers served; called "absentee" owners, they attracted some of the same critiques as absentee landlords.[40] Further, the content of large newspapers clearly did not represent the views or opinions of an editor-publisher. Rather, it was the product of many different people's labor: the specialized beat reporter, the copyeditor, the editor in chief, the advertising desk, and the printers.[41] And, increasingly, it was content produced afar (by other newspapers or by wire services) and distributed throughout the chain. In these ways, newspapers were much like radio: polyvocal and industrial. And gatekeeping power resided in the hands of a few powerful men.

For many on the left, the model of speech rights as rights of individual expression did not seem applicable to the industrial communication of mass media. In such industrialized communication, speakers like journalists or radio hosts might be engaged in a form of alienated labor, forced to express the political views of owners rather than their own. The social good theory of speech provided a way of thinking about freedom of speech outside of the rights of owners and more fitting to this arrangement. It also allowed them to argue for regulation in the name of democracy: in order to protect or foster a diversity of views, it might at times be necessary to regulate the press. While media owners argued such regulation was an infringement of their freedoms (of speech, of the press), reformers argued that regulation was necessary in order to secure freedom of speech as a social good.[42]

Reformers argued that this regulation was required because of the evils or corruption of the industrialized commercial press. The press no longer operated in the public interest, but rather in the private interests of a small set of owners and advertisers.[43] The massification and concentration of ownership in newspapers and radio—and the physical scope of radio networks—seemed to be working in concert to capture and transform the public sphere. No longer a "space" for the formation and sharing of organic opinion, it seemed to many to be a site of domination and coercion by industry and commerce.[44] Critics like Seldes detailed the different topics and events that large newspapers failed or refused to cover (from allegations of rape made against an advertiser's son to evidence of the danger of smoking) due to personal interests and broader commercial pressure.[45] Others looked less to publisher decisions and more to structural forces of homogenization as a form of censorship (reducing the diversity of ideas and voices in the public sphere). For example, when Marlon Pew surveyed the content of newspapers in 1933, he found alarming homogeneity, which he attributed to both a reliance on wire services and the concentration of newspaper ownership.[46] In radio, advocates pointed out that not only were advertisers quite literally running the show (at least in scripted series) but also that network and industry policies seriously limited what on-air announcers and third parties could say, for fear of upsetting advertisers.[47] Among the taboo topics were criticism of advertising or of the power and utility companies and any discussion of labor disputes, birth control, anti-lynching crusades, and other issues deemed "controversial."[48]

Leftist advocates pointed out that radio restrictions meant not only that there were fewer ideas and viewpoints in circulation but also that the voices and opinions of labor, communists and socialists, African Americans, and women's groups were being systematically shut out by the most effective and powerful channels of discourse. This restriction of voices and views amounted to a form of private or commercial censorship distinct from governmental censorship. This articulation of censorship, it should be noted, focused on distribution more than production. Media acted as brokers on ideas and restricted the diversity of views not through keeping people from speaking, but by refusing to distribute or amplify existing speech. This critique of how media restricted discussion of important matters developed in the pages of publications like the *Nation* and the *New Republic* (and later *PM*) as well as in more academic publications like *Public Opinion Quarterly* and *the Annals of the American Academy of Political and Social Science.* Some on the left, like media critic James Rorty, lawyers Clifford Durr and James Fly, and the ACLU argued such commercial censorship was as serious a threat as governmental censorship. These arguments had purchase in the newly renamed Federal Communications Commission (the FRC was renamed the FCC in 1934); both Durr and Fly were FCC commissioners.

But commercial censorship was not a threat that existing law and policy was ready to address. A new articulation of free speech was required in order to diagnose and combat such private censorship. Toward this end, advocates drew on the social good theory of speech to argue that "freedom of the air" meant the freedom of American audiences to hear the diverse viewpoints of African Americans, labor, communists, women, and religious minorities.[49] And freedom of the press was better understood as a public *right to* a robust press than as an individual *right of* its owners. Understood this way, regulation might be required in order to achieve the ends of freedom of the press. As Archibald MacLeish, a poet, radio playwright, Librarian of Congress, and key figure at the Office of War Information during World War II, put it:

> What we have now been brought to see is this: that the press is not by its essential nature an instrument of illumination and of freedom; that it is not necessarily a weapon which is sharp only in the hands of the partisans of freedom; that it is an instrument which ignorance can use against truth as well as truth against ignorance, which superstition can use against science as well as science against superstition, which tyranny can use—and effectively use—against the dearest freedom of the people. And learning this, we have learned that our duties toward the press are not now the negative duties they may once have been. It is no longer enough to provide the negative guarantees of a bill of rights. It is necessary to take action.[50]

Regulation, advocates argued, was necessary in order to reform the public sphere and promote a healthy exchange of diverse ideas—the measure of a free press in the social good theory. There were a number of suggestions about how government might step in and do so. Press critics, and a few government officials, suggested a variety of tactics: passing laws prohibiting vertical and horizontal integration in media; taxing large media outlets; imposing federal rules about pricing and production practices; nationalizing media outlets or regulating them like public utilities (with less editorial discretion and a duty to convey views from all sides of an issue); and, specific to radio, allocating more radio stations (up to 25 percent of existing stations) to nonprofits and educational interests and to create governmentally owned radio stations to compete with commercial ones.[51]

These calls for regulation were aimed at newspapers and radio alike. Newspapers were able to effectively deflect such proposals, despite intense public suspicion and criticism (with some important exceptions: newspapers were subject to some labor and antitrust regulation in the 1930s and 1940s).[52] Industry lawyers and associations, most frequently the American Newspaper Publishers' Association (ANPA), were able to position newspapers as the mouthpieces of individual publishers, who were both individual speakers and proxies for the publics they served—any form of regulation might suppress both sets of rights.[53] This positioning was aided by the specter of totalitarian control of media abroad. But it was also strongly indebted to a residual cultural and legal association of newspapers with an obsolete nineteenth-century political economy of printing. The continuing ideological link of newspapers with the views of editor-publishers is a key reason that ANPA lawyers were able to so successfully conflate the individual freedoms of newspaper owners with freedom of the press. With this tactic, the newspaper industry had by the end of the 1930s effectively harnessed liberal individualist defenses of speech to an antiregulatory politics—a coupling that continues to have ramifications today.[54]

The radio industry was not so successful in its attempts to use expressive liberties as an antiregulatory tool.[55] There were a number of reasons that radio was not able to do so (and thus was more tightly regulated). Radio used a scarce public resource as a medium of transmission; both scarcity of frequencies and public ownership of the airwaves were important rationales for why radio had to be more aggressively administered (in ways that might infringe the liberties of license holders or station owners). Also among these reasons was the fact that the social good theory enabled the FCC to argue that these regulations were a means to ensure a more diverse field of voices and ideas. However, another factor was that the radio industry could not mount the same defense as the newspapers, calling on the individual speech rights of owners. As noted above, radio was understood to be more polyvocal; the content of radio broadcasts was less clearly linked to station owners or license holders. Radio, in this way, simply did not fit within existing conceptions of speech in free speech discourse. Or, more precisely, radio changed the dynamics of speaking. Radio programs could not be directly attributed to a (single) mind, conscience, or person. And the political economy of radio—more than of newspapers—highlighted the fact that most rights-holding citizens were not potential speakers, but rather listeners, or audiences, in this new medium.[56]

In the rest of this chapter, I will explore how the inability to align radio broadcasts with a single speaker and the progressive impulse to protect not only media owners but also the listening public in and through the First Amendment led to a new conceptualization of speech, which prioritized editorial choices and acts of dissemination over the production of utterances, or even opinion formation. The FCC's efforts to regulate chain broadcasting, and the legal battles that ensued, illustrate the challenges that both industry and regulators had fitting radio within existing free speech discourse and presumptions. Out of this clash, a new way of talking about speech emerged—one that focused not on locating one among the many competing rights-bearing individuals, but rather on identifying and protecting messages or information itself. In this, the legal approach to freedom of speech expanded from a focus on the production of messages (in acts of speaking and publication) to include—and at times prioritize—their distribution. This expansion was the beginning of a broader transformation in the way that communication was imagined within free speech law, away from the specific human context of the production of meaning and toward a more industrial-scale distribution of preconstituted messages.

Speech as the Distribution of Messages

Alarmed by the growing reach and power of the radio chains, in 1938, the FCC convened a commission to investigate chain ownership and "determine what special regulations applicable to radio stations engaged in chain or other broadcasting are required in the public interest, convenience, or necessity."[57] The commission's *Report on Chain Broadcasting*, issued in 1941, detailed the development and scope of radio networks. NBC and CBS controlled more than 40 percent of the nation's radio signals through ownership of local stations and restrictive contracts with affiliates; together, they controlled more than 96 percent of the high-powered clear-channel stations, whose broadcasts could reach much farther than regular radio stations (see figures 3.2 and 3.3).

While both NBC and CBS were presented as engaging in monopolistic practices, the report expressed particular concern about the scope of NBC's parent company, RCA (which controlled both NBC's radio networks and also radio manufacturing, music, and motion pictures). This one commercial entity, the report noted with some unease, was in a "premier position in fields which are profoundly determinative of our way of life."[58] The report concluded with a set of new rules, which were issued in the name of breaking the hold of such powerful companies by crafting a more competitive and diverse field of radio programming.[59] The rules, among other things, barred networks from establishing contracts that made it difficult for affiliates to reject network programming they deemed unsuitable, prevented

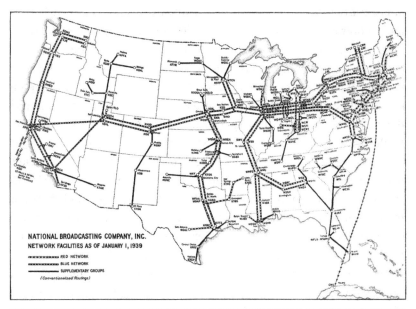

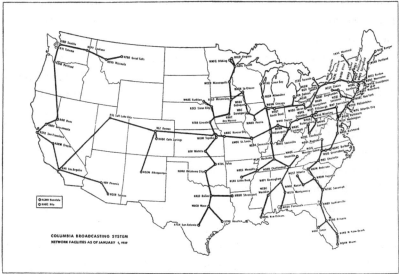

Figure 3.2 (*above*) Map of the physical infrastructure of the NBC network, circa 1939. The lines are the phone lines that the network used to distribute programming to affiliate stations, which then broadcast them to the public. Published in *Broadcasting Yearbook*. Washington, DC: Broadcasting Publications, 1939.

Figure 3.3 (*below*) Map of the physical infrastructure of the CBS network, circa 1939. Published in *Broadcasting Yearbook*. Washington, DC: Broadcasting Publications, 1939.

affiliates from airing programming from other networks, or established too much control over affiliates scheduling. These rules also effectively barred one company from operating two networks, which in the end forced NBC to get rid of one of its networks. The company would sell the Blue Network to Edward Noble in 1943, creating the American Broadcasting Company (ABC). Initially, however, NBC contested the FCC's rules, arguing in part that they infringed freedom of speech and the press, resulting in a case that made its way to the Supreme Court: *NBC v. United States* (1943).

In the arguments submitted to the Supreme Court, both the debates over the meaning of free speech and the difficulty of determining who the speaker was in radio were operative. Whereas newspaper publishers had in the prior decade pioneered arguments equating freedom of speech with the freedom of publishers to make decisions about how to run their businesses, NBC could not adopt the same rhetoric. There was no single person who could fill the role of editor or publisher at the corporate level. And radio was seen as too commercial a medium to presume that the choices of network executives would in any way coincide with the public interest. There was too much confusion about who was behind the messages on the radio—both who produced or scripted them and whose (private) interests they served. NBC and its lawyers opted instead for a broad argument, focusing on the technology of radio as an instrument of speech analogous to the printing press, arguing that any regulation of the operation of such an instrument was an unconstitutional governmental intrusion on the expressive function of the press.

The lawyers for the FCC, in contrast, focused on the actions of a particular set of agents as speakers, though the freedoms of these agents were different from those envisaged in much contemporaneous free speech discourse. In their brief to the Court, the lawyers for the FCC argued that the chain ownership rules were about protecting the freedom of local station owners to make choices about what programming to air and protecting the public sphere (via ensuring competition among speakers). The FCC, in other words, framed its defense of the rules by reference both to the idea that the regulations protected the diversity and circulation of ideas—an idea that runs through the 1941 *Report on Chain Broadcasting* containing the rules—and to the idea that the regulations protected the choices of the operators of affiliate radio stations.[60] The brief pointed out that the rules had nothing to do with "program content and in no way attempt to regulate what may or may not be said on the air." In fact, the agency argued, the rules enhanced the ability of a local station owner to "broadcast what he [*sic*] prefers."[61] The rules would not only restore the freedom of choice of the station owner but also maintain a competitive system in radio (as a vehicle for speech as a social good).[62]

In many ways this paralleled the rhetoric and logic that connected the freedoms of newspaper editors with the public interest. The choices of the station owner, however, were articulated differently. (And, whatever the FCC's legal arguments were in the case, it did not endorse a strong vision of editorial freedom for broadcasters; the same year, the agency established the Mayflower doctrine, which forbade operators from using their stations to amplify their own views.) The FCC did not argue for the station owners' freedom to form and express their own ideas or opinions, but rather the freedom to choose from among various programs presented to them by third parties (other networks or other producers). If the freedom of station owners looked a lot like consumer choice, the discussion of free speech also relied on metaphors of the economy. In its emphasis on establishing a competitive playing field as a vehicle for—or, arguably, a proxy for—a diversity of ideas, the FCC was forwarding an approach to freedom of speech and the press that bracketed questions of production (the generation of messages), relying instead on competition at the level of gatekeeping and distribution (selection and transmission of a message).[63] In this, the regulatory conversation was moving away from particular speakers and the acts of speaking or publishing—which had been the focus of antipropaganda criticism, critical literacy programs, advocates of educational media, and other press critics in the 1920s and 1930s—to encompass a focus on how messages were or were not passed along.

Legally and politically, focusing on measures to foster editorial choices about messages was easier than choosing from among the competing claimants seeking speech rights. Rather than deciding whose rights were primary in radio transmissions—station owners, third-party advocates or salesmen, the networks themselves, or the audience—regulators and judges could simply focus on maximizing messages. This contrasts with the logic of the circuit court decision the Court was reviewing, in which Judge Learned Hand had based his decision on a clear delineation of whose speech was at issue. In radio broadcasts, Hand declared, freedom of speech was hierarchically distributed among the interested parties: it lay first and foremost with the audience, and then with the local stations, and only lastly with the networks.[64] (The Supreme Court would not engage in such ranking until *Red Lion v. FCC* [1969], when the Court declared that the rights of listeners were paramount.[65]) In the *NBC* decision, the Supreme Court dodged such explicit considerations by focusing on technical, and thus seemingly neutral, issues of administration of spectrum and on the distribution of messages. A focus on messages and their distribution, rather than on speakers, recognized new ways in which speech might be restricted. It was also, however, a hedge, an indirect way of recognizing the rights of the audience (or public) to receive information without explicitly ranking the rights of competing claimants.

An economic logic was at this moment becoming embedded in policy and legal discourse. The very logic of diversification on which the 1941 *Report on Chain Broadcasting* was based, and which NBC v. *United States* upheld, drew together and conflated a way of talking about free speech and a way of talking about the economy. The rules, and the FCC's defense and discussion of them in later years, equated more independent channels with greater diversity of ideas or information. Restriction of unfair trade practices would, from this perspective, bring us free speech. Competition was a proxy for freedom.[66] More channels and more information indirectly meant that the public had access to diverse ideas. The freedoms, or speech rights, of the public, were becoming, in this logic, less the right to engage in advocacy, or even dialogue, and more a right to choose which ideas and information to consume. Even in the hands of a relatively progressive Court, the social good theory of speech was already beginning to be re-articulated in the language of the marketplace: a trend that would increase in the 1960s and 1970s. Coupled with specific technologies of transmission, the industrial economy was becoming a model for speech, and the rights associated with it, within the law.

If the debates in the 1930s over the nature of censorship and whether or how to regulate the press were centrally about the industrialization of communication and news, the response by state agencies embodied in the chain broadcasting rules and the legal debates about these rules was typical. The solution to industrialization and corporatization in the twentieth century had been one of curbing the excesses of economic gigantism. Administered markets reined in the excesses of concentration, maintaining some level of competition.[67] What was distinct in the trajectory outlined here was the fact that speech and the press were being subject to this discussion and solution.

Distribution as an Industrial Metaphor

In common parlance as well as the law, "speech" even more than "communication" is human scale and human made. While we often think of mass communication and massified communication, it is much more difficult to think of speech in these terms. Rather, in discussing speech in mass media, we refer to metaphors of amplification, in which a human voice is given superhuman scale. As the Hutchins Commission put it, in attempting to disambiguate human speech and the mechanized press, "Speech is natural and inseparable from the human person, the breadth of his social existence."[68] This act of speech dominates our metaphors and ways of conceptualizing speech (as something uniquely human, distinct from plant and animal or machine communication). As this chapter has suggested, the speech in free speech had, through the 1930s, evoked a specific mode of production, in which messages were created by individuals or small sets of individuals and in which those messages reflected the ideas, beliefs, or desires of their producers (e.g., the nostalgic vision of the newspaper as a mouthpiece for an individual editor-publisher).

The massification of communication, from the industrialized and highly concentrated newspaper to movies to radio networks, upended this association. Messages were produced like widgets. The people crafting them did so in significant part for wages or profit; messages might or might not reflect the judgments and beliefs of their creators. The communication of mass media was, like so many other mass-produced products, alienated. Such an idea of speech, or communication, unsettled the romantic notion of expression internal to so much free speech discourse. Even more, it called into doubt much of what freedom of speech had previously been presumed to protect: ideas, conscience, attitudes, and beliefs.[69]

What did it mean that utterances—or even ideas and beliefs—might be produced on an industrial scale more typical of machines than "men"? What did freedom of speech mean in such a world? This was the dramatic transformation that free speech law and discourse faced in the 1930s and 1940s. While these are not the terms that legal actors used, they are the words that a different set of analysts pondering the same conjunction would. That the production of ideas, the formation of conscience, attitudes, or beliefs, might be massified or industrialized was a core concern of a set of sociologists, psychologists and philosophers, most notably of the Frankfurt school.[70] It is no accident that the Frankfurt school, which coalesced in the 1930s in the mix of concerns about totalitarian politics and the growth of mass media, focused on exactly the problem sketched here: the industrialization and alienation of human thought and expression. For Frankfurt school theorists from Theodor Adorno to Erich Fromm, industrialization of culture produced a mechanized automaton of a subject, programmed to step to the tune of capital.

The legal response to the industrialization of communication was different from these scholars' responses. In the face of alienated and mass-produced messages, legal discussion shifted to distribution of these messages. While this shift was a way of addressing the interests of the public as the audience in receiving messages, it also became a way of envisioning the speech rights of individuals in terms of those of machine-using institutions. In the move toward discussing speech rights in terms of distribution, an economic and technical model for thinking about freedom of the industrialized press would become a model for thinking about freedom of speech for individuals. Rather than distinguishing freedom of speech and freedom of the press and elaborating two distinct sets of rights or ways of making judgments about freedom of speech for the institutional press and for individual speakers—as some advocates had suggested—the two were conflated.[71] In the 1940s, speech rights for individuals as well as for the press would often be articulated as both rights of distribution and access to a mass audience. In a subset of legal decisions in the 1940s, individual speech rights, especially the right to protest, were envisioned *in the image of* the "machine-using institution" of the press.

From Utterance to Transmission:
The Waning of Interiority in "Speech"

The questions around radio and free speech, as I have suggested, were fundamentally about the ability of ordinary citizens—the masses—to engage in public discourse and advocacy: to have a voice. The decisions in NBC v. United States and in a set of related cases involving strikes and affordable means of amplification (record players and sound trucks) were progressive efforts to rethink speech rights in a context where the mechanism of publicity and amplification was available only to those with means and in which most people were structurally positioned as listeners more than speakers. In such cases, the courts worked to recognize the rights of the audience or to give the masses a voice in the new public sphere. This voice was not, however, articulated in the humanist rhetoric of intent, will, and interiority that had pervaded the legal discourse of the first decades of the twentieth century. It was, rather, articulated in industrial terms: as a right to distribute or relay messages.

This industrialized vision of speech and speakers shows up in what might be a surprising set of cases, having little to do with media in the strict sense of the word, cases involving strikes and religious minorities' rights to speak. In these cases, the justices similarly focused on the distribution of messages as a component of freedom of speech, whether or not these messages were the words or ideas of those seeking to pass them along. In these cases, as in *NBC*, the justices focused on distribution of ideas or information as distinct from the articulation, or production, of these ideas. The very need to consider production and dissemination of ideas as distinct was an artifact of the conditions of communication (increasingly characterized by mass media rather than what might be termed "artisanal" speech and publishing). In the cases involving film in the 1910s and 1920s, the courts had classified only those communications that involved originality and mental activity as speech or publication. Films and newsreels, which the judges and justices argued did not really employ authors (being mere re-productions or copies of ideas already known), did not count.[72] In shifting to a concern with distribution, authorship or newness was less important. The "speakers" in the cases below did not need to be expressing an interior state, bringing to light a new idea or creation, or even using their own words. They might merely be passing along (re-presenting) the words and ideas of others, events and issues already known, or facts that belonged to no one.

While these cases were not directly about media, they were shaped by changing means and practices of communication. In a series of cases in the late 1930s and early 1940s, the Supreme Court ruled that strikes, protests, and the distribution of literature in public places were protected under the First Amendment. In 1938, the Court declared that not only laws that restricted publication but also ones that restricted dissemination violated freedom of speech.[73] Local officials could not use restrictions on distribution to censor minority views. The right to distribute information was furthered in *Schneider v. State of New Jersey* (1939) and *Hague v. CIO* (1939) and extended to picketing and sign-bearing in *Thornhill v. Alabama* (1940) and *Carlson v. California* (1940)—and later, in 1948, to the use of sound trucks; sound trucks were cheap and portable means of amplifying and disseminating a message, a sort of poor man's radio.[74] In *Hague v. CIO*, the Court argued that the city streets and parks were public forums, venues for citizens to address a broad audience, making it harder for local authorities to restrict the advocacy of labor activists and other radical speakers.

The creation of the public forum reflected decades of pressure from radicals, the evolving consensus that debate about working conditions was a matter of public concern (rather than a private matter between employers and employees) and the civil libertarian turn in free speech law. It was also, as Samantha Barbas shows, deeply enmeshed with concern about the effects of media concentration, in particular in radio.[75] She shows how the label of public forum traveled from efforts to democratize radio broadcasts to the recognition of the streets as a channel or venue for popular speech—in the words of the Third Circuit Court, "the platform[s] of the poor."[76] In *Hague* and the cases involving amplification, from phonographs to sound trucks, that defined public forum law in the 1940s, many of the jurists (in appellate courts as well as the Supreme Court) expressed a concern to redress systematic economic (and political) bias by opening up new channels for citizen speech, an attempt to balance the effects of the rise of commercial mass media and create supplementary platforms for citizen advocacy and agitation. Arguments about the efficacy of the streets for radical speech long predated these debates about radio, but in when and how they were decided it is hard not to see the influence of media and concerns about the way commercial mass media created an unequal playing field.[77] Decisions like *Lovell, Schneider, Hague, Thornhill,* and *Saia* contain efforts to create new venues or opportunities for those without the means to buy access to commercial media.

Yet the influence of contemporaneous mass media and media criticism on these cases, and the legal doctrine they created, goes deeper. The speech rights accorded to individuals, in particular dissenting individuals, were crafted in the image of the mass media of the day. The activities that were classified as speech in these cases were less authorship or production (publication) and more mass distribution and the transmission or relay of messages that might originate elsewhere. In *Lovell,* the Court explained that individual speech rights were not limited to acting as producers (e.g., printing pamphlets) but extended to the act of distribution—in the face of legal arguments that a local ordinance banning the distribution of pamphlets as a public nuisance was not a violation of freedom of speech or the press because it did not restrict the publication of any material.[78] The Court's ruling made plain that this was no longer sufficient. Like the media of the day, individuals had a right to distribute messages—their own or others'—to their own "mass" audiences. The need to specify that individual speech rights covered not only publication but also distribution tracks the expansion in public concern about censorship from a focus on restrictions on publication to restrictions on dissemination. *Lovell* was the first of a series of decisions that recast individual speech rights through the lens of industrialized communication. Individuals were given rights to distribute or transmit to a broad, anonymous audience. Even when the messages were not their own, as distributors of information, such individuals were now legible—and open to classification—as speakers.

This reasoning was extended in *Hague v. CIO*. While the most consequential outcome of *Hague* was the creation of the public forum as an open platform for speech, I want to suggest that the terms in which the case was argued and justified are worth noting for the way they helped craft an emergent conceptualization of speech less as an activity and more as a good, subject to distribution. The case involved labor organizers who sought to publicize the provisions of the National Labor Relations Act (NLRA), detailing workers' rights to unionize and strike in Jersey City. The efforts of the CIO to distribute pamphlets containing information about the NLRA and their attempts to hold a public meeting in Jersey City were clearly a form of advocacy, attempting to persuade workers to form a union and to confront anti-union mayor "Boss" Hague (who had wooed industry by promising to quash union efforts in Jersey City).[79] But the terms in which this right was articulated and justified diverged from the humanist terminology of earlier decades. The CIO argued that all they were doing was distributing, or passing along, information—not unruly advocacy or disorderly crowd activity (no doubt a tactic to push back against the mayor's argument that they were engaging in disorderly conduct). In other words, the argument shifted attention from the clashes of bodies—in the ongoing labor battles—toward a clash of ideas and pamphlets.[80]

The CIO and its lawyers argued that the members of the group had a right to "carry their message to the public by means of the written word, by circulars and placards," emphasizing distribution (the ability to reach an audience) over creation or advocacy.[81] The Court's decision in the case followed suit, describing the use of pamphlets and placards as vehicles of transmission rather than artifacts of expressive agency. Focusing the case narrowly, the majority argued that members of the CIO enjoyed the "freedom to disseminate information" about the NLRA under the First Amendment.[82] Declaring that CIO members enjoyed the "freedom to distribute information" created a homology between the distribution of information and the other activities covered under the First Amendment, such as the freedom to speak, publish, or advocate beliefs. This right to distribute information would be extended to pickets, placards, and sound trucks in the

1940s.[83] This homology is of interest, I argue, because of the qualitative differences between distributing information and these other invocations of expressive freedom. Information, unlike utterances, opinions, and beliefs, is not necessarily the product of an individual mind, or the expression of thought. (The particular information at issue in the case, as in *Lovell*, was not the product or creation of the "speakers" who brought the case.) Rather, information had already by midcentury taken on an objectified and quantified set of implications, suggesting facts or data.[84] There may have been impassioned advocacy in Jersey City, but its protection as speech was rationalized in terms of a right to distribute information rather than a right of persuasion.

Cases like *Hague* and those establishing the right to amplification in the public forum (e.g., sound trucks, phonographs) that immediately followed may have been attempts to create opportunities for face-to-face communication and discussion as an alternative to the restricted channels of mass media.[85] However, the way that the justices imagined speech in these cases was informed more by visions of broadcasting, and dissemination, than by visions of dialogue.[86] In Supreme Court decisions in the 1910s and 1920s, the justices had described the substance of free speech in terms like "idea," "thought," "deliberation," "advocacy," and "critique."[87] These terms all prioritize the production of ideas or opinions by a unique human mind and reference an exchange, or dialogue, among interlocutors. The model here is conversation, either face-to-face, or a back-and-forth of ideas experienced when reading printed matter.[88]

In *Hague* and the public forum cases involving sound trucks that followed (and even *Lovell* before them, to a lesser extent), speech is no longer so dialogic. In these cases, the justices debate how best to enable dissenters to disseminate ideas to a broad audience. Not only do speakers become likened to other transmitters (say, the electronic ones of radio), but speech itself is mechanized. Speech need not be the expression of individual opinion, the product of the mental activity of the speaker. It might also be merely a relay or re-presentation of ideas that originated elsewhere. In this, the speech of dissenters is figured in the terms used to describe the work of the projector and motion picture in the 1910s and 1920s. Even more so, the justices describe dissenting speech (newly becoming the heart of free speech law) in terms that echo the technological and industrial workings of radio: speakers may relay or transmit ideas—or that less personal substance, "information"—to a mass audience.[89] In these cases, individuals and groups were granted rights to communicate in a manner parallel to mass media: to disseminate and amplify, to relay, and to choose which messages to amplify. In the case of sound trucks, in which a truck with an amplification system would drive through cities advocating for a politician or reading out religious literature, the amplification of the speaker (as a holder of opinion or as a transmitter of information) was literal.[90]

In this way, the Court addressed the question that this chapter begins with: in the context of industrialized communications, what are the distinctions between freedom of human speech and freedom of the (machinic) press? The Hutchins Commission concluded that the press had a responsibility to act not as the extensions of individuals (publishers) but rather as essential democratic institutions. The report suggested that newspapers and the radio should act, of their own accord, more as public trustees than as advocates or mouthpieces of their owners.[91] To act as a public trustee was to operate not as a speaker but as a gatekeeper (or editor), deciding what information and analysis to let through to the audience-public. Or, to draw on the metaphors of circulation and flow cited above, newspapers and radio should regulate the flow of information and analysis.

The conceptualization of freedom of speech as the distribution of information suggests a remarkably similar set of ideas about the role of communication in a democracy, in which production and distribution of ideas are distinct and in which the key threats to public discourse reside in censorial power at the level of distribution rather than production. However, this conception of speech was applied to individuals and groups as well as to institutional speakers. Rather than distinguishing between individuals or groups and institutional speakers—between freedom of speech as a form of social interaction and freedom of the press as an institutional form of communication—the Court crafted a new articulation of speech in the image of "machine-using" institutions.

Conclusion

In the late 1940s, Alexander Meiklejohn published his famous normative theory of free speech. His argument, often summed up as what is essential is not that everyone shall speak but that "everything worth saying shall be said" (we might add, or be passed along—or even be heard, though Meiklejohn does not go there), is one of the more famous articulations of a social good theory of speech.[92] It was, as well, informed by the technological and political economic concerns of his day. From the vantage point of the

1940s, with its concentrated newspapers, radio speakers, and striking workers, Meiklejohn looked back to an earlier, often idealized, public sphere in which the town hall and face-to-face discussion were central.[93] The town hall, he argued, was not a wide-open, free space for discourse. Rather, the idealized town hall was already highly regulated and administered by rules of procedure and order, necessary because there was inevitably less time than participants. In other words, public speech was always already subject to limited bandwidth and subject to some form of regulation. The important thing was to get this regulation right. Meiklejohn's historical argument, and the normative theory he built on it, I would suggest, is filtered as much through the technological and political economic characteristics of communication in the 1930s and the 1940s as it is an example of his positive liberties stance on the role of the state in securing democratic discourse.[94]

In Meiklejohn's theory as in the legal decisions, we can see the traces of the technological concerns of transmission and the political economic concerns that dominated the 1930s and early 1940s. Notably, both Meiklejohn's theory and the cases discussed in this chapter were efforts to rebalance the public sphere, reducing the power of mass-media giants and empowering minority speech (at the time, most often labor, socialists and communists, religious minorities, and racial and ethnic minorities). These legal texts bear the imprint of a historically contingent vision of the substance of speech: the distribution of information. This vision was formed by a set of technologies—radio, and also the machinery of mass-produced newspapers— and an industrial economy. The imprint of these technologies in legal discourse left behind an internal contradiction. The public good theory of free speech aimed to increase public debate and dialogue. Its articulation in case law as the distribution of information, however, was shaped by the one-to-many communication that characterized both broadcasting and chain newspapers, and which dominated public discourse and concerns about mass communication. In this, from its inception, this line of legal rhetoric and reasoning has been troubled by a contradiction between ends (public discussion, or dialogue) and means (dissemination).

Certainly, the conception of freedom of speech as the dissemination of information had some progressive outcomes in the 1940s through the 1960s. In cases involving media industries in particular, it was a way of pushing back against the ability of large media outlets to use free speech claims to rid themselves of troublesome regulation. In *Associated Press v. United States* (1945), the Supreme Court famously pushed back against the newspaper industry's claims that the First Amendment exempted them from antitrust regulation. As in *NBC v. United States*, rather than trying to parse the rights of different claimants, the decision focused on messages and their distribution. The majority decision did not argue that freedom of speech protected the speakers of the newspaper industry, or the potential audience, but rather that it protected "the widest possible *dissemination of information* from diverse and antagonistic sources" and the *"free flow of ideas."*[95] Thus, the diversity and flow of ideas was valued above the economic interests of media owners, without granting explicit rights to the audience (e.g., a right to receive information as had been suggested by Judge Hand in the lower court decision in *NBC v. United States*).[96]

Focusing on information, or ideas, and their circulation rather than their creation allowed the Court in *Associated Press v. United States* and similar cases to redress what many people in the midcentury thought was a contortion or corruption of the public sphere. Freedom of speech was not the protection of privileged speakers (as newspaper industry groups and some liberal theories of free speech would have it) but the creation of a diverse and fertile field—or market—of information available to the public. In this way, the shift in legal rhetoric and reasoning away from speakers and their ideas or minds toward messages and their channels of distribution enabled the Court to find a limited, largely implicit, place for listening within freedom of speech.[97] In the cases from the 1940s, protecting the flow or distribution of messages was a means of protecting the interests of a public largely structurally barred from opportunities to speak within the public sphere and a means of fostering a diversity of viewpoints in this public sphere. It was, importantly, a way of protecting the interest of the mass audience without recognizing formal rights for its members or weighing their interests against those of the owners and operators of media industries. It was, thus, also a way of avoiding the conflict in free speech law and theory brought on by the transformations in the public sphere in the early to mid-twentieth century. It would not be until 1969 that a particularly liberal Court would formally recognize that members of the public had any speech rights in mass media—a right to receive information in broadcasting. In *Red Lion v. FCC* the Court finally addressed the conflict between the interests of media owners and the interests of the audience, concluding that the audience's "right to receive information" merited some limits on the expressive freedoms of broadcasters to choose what content to air.[98] (This recognition would be walked back in the more conservative judicial climate of the 1970s.)

The way that speech rights were articulated in this legal reasoning, though the activity of distribution and the substance of objectified messages (epitomized in the term "information"), also eroded distinctions between human speakers and institutional ones. Both the rights of industrialized media outlets and those of groups and individuals were understood to serve the public interest in a diversity of ideas. Individuals and groups were granted rights to communicate in a manner parallel to mass-media outlets: to disseminate and amplify, to relay, and to choose which messages to pass along.

The legal discourse tracked in this chapter demonstrates a concern with massification of communication, or the incorporation of the press and culture into an industrial economy. In such an economy, communication is subject to mechanization, rationalization, and monopoly. Yet, already, the actual technologies and economy of communication were less industrial and more ephemeral electronic ones, what James Carey called the economy of the signal.[99] In contrast to the use of machines to extend or enact physical labor in the industrial economy, in the economy of the signal, electricity is used to convey information. Human language and messages are encoded as manipulations of current for rapid and wide dissemination, whether by broadcast technology or, in the postwar era, by computers. In this shift, and especially in the development of computers, the very tasks that are mechanical, automated, and rote (not requiring human ingenuity or mental activity) are increasingly those previously associated with human mental processes.[100]

In the following decades (the 1950s to the 1970s), the economy of the signal became part of everyday experience and discourse, in the guise of information theory, cybernetics, computers, and the "control revolution." As chapter 4 demonstrates, the discursive articulation of control and information that proliferated in this context would have profound consequences for the way that legal practitioners would reinterpret the "distribution of information" and the forms of communication it covered. Messages, objectified and disassociated from speakers, could flow or circulate on their own. They could, as well, compete in a marketplace without reference to or consideration of the conditions of their production.[101] In shifting the focus from speakers to the flow of information or messages, the legal discourse of this chapter unwittingly paved the way for legal recognition of speech without speakers.

4. Speech without Speakers

How Speech Became Information

> We can no longer speak, for how can we guarantee the
> value of a proposition, if not by offering another proposition
> which, however, no one can answer for?
>   In this world without speech, we recognize the West. From
> Socrates to Hegel, it moved towards the ideal of language,
> in which the word counts only because of the eternal order
> which it manages to bring to consciousness. At the end-point
> of this itinerary, the speaking man feels part of a discourse
> that speaks itself. The meaning of language no longer de-
> pends on the intentions placed on it, but on a coherent Dis-
> course to which the speaker merely lends his tongue and
> lips. Not only Marxism, but the whole of sociology and psy-
> choanalysis bear witness to a language whose principal
> feature lies not in what words teach us, but in what they hide
> from us. We have a closed language, and a civilization com-
> posed of aphasiacs. Words have once more become the mute
> signs of anonymous infrastructures, like the implements
> of dead civilizations or the abortive acts of our daily lives.
>
> —**Emmanuel Levinas**, "Freedom of Speech"

In the first half of the twentieth century, as detailed in the previous chapters, the parameters of speech were being tested, redefined, and defended
in relation to the body. The expressive capacity of bodies, whether inclined
in deference to the flag or gathered in the streets to picket or protest, was
a recurring concern from the cases dealing with film through those dealing with flag salutes and striking workers—and beyond to the various embodied forms of protest of the 1960s (some of which took place under the
banner of the free speech movement), discussed further in chapter 5. By

the 1970s, perhaps not coincidentally, legal discourse on free speech was moving in a different direction.[1] Beginning in the late 1960s and 1970s, speakers and their bodies began to recede in discussions of free speech, replaced by a focus on messages themselves, as information. In a series of decisions analyzed in this chapter, the justices began answering questions about whether freedom of speech applied to a given case by looking for messages, or artifacts of human communication, rather than for speakers or acts of publication or distribution. In this, the legal conception of speech was abstracted and disarticulated from particular speakers and their bodies, interests, and rights.

This shift, I argue, underwrote some of the more contentious First Amendment expansionism in recent decades, namely the incorporation of commercial activity (i.e., advertising) and corporate communication. Since the 1970s, the typical beneficiary of Court rulings about free speech has been a business or industry group (rather than ideological or other minorities, as envisioned in the popular romance of freedom of speech).[2] A key moment in this expansionism was the decision in *First National Bank of Boston v. Bellotti* (1978), which struck down a Massachusetts law restricting business expenditures to influence the outcome of ballot initiatives on First Amendment grounds. In their decision, the justices defined freedom of speech as not just about the freedom of speakers to voice their intentions or beliefs but also about messages and the freedoms that attach to them. This was the beginning of a set of legal decisions that would bring us to the infamous *Citizens United v. Federal Election Commission* (2010) decision, in which the Court said corporations have speech rights akin to those of natural persons.

In the *Bellotti* decision, speakers were displaced, and artifacts animated.[3] Speech became less a social activity and more the activity of a set of objects or artifacts (messages) subject to exchange, circulation, and measurement.[4] The locus of analysis of freedom of speech shifted from the interests and activities of social actors (subjects) to the movement or availability of artifacts of human expression (texts and other products of communication).[5] This was a disembodiment of speech, but it was also something more, a revisioning of expressivity in terms that downplayed consciousness or mind, which were earlier liberal humanist hallmarks of personhood. It is, in this sense, a *"posthuman" conception of speech*. By this I mean that speech was abstracted and disarticulated from both actual individual speakers with specific contexts and drives (and potentially competing rights claims) and from the aforementioned traditional properties of personhood. In this conceptualization, expression was less a property of agents with intentions and complex—and conflicting—interests and more a property of artifacts (messages, texts, bits of information) and their circulation.[6] Agents were decentered in favor of objects. This shift in terrain opened up the field of freedom of expression, once reserved for natural persons, to corporations and other artificial entities. To be clear, not all reasoning about free speech has followed this route; the posthuman conception of speech has not replaced older (and more traditionally humanist) conceptions of speech but rather exists alongside them—producing tensions examined in chapter 5. Yet this route has been consequential, leading to the inclusion of money, databases, and more generally data as speech.

In this chapter, I show how this came to pass. Speech, once distinguished from mere communication through reference to the human mind, soul, or some other such grounds of exceptionalism (e.g., "primitive" vs. "civilized"), was in a series of legal decisions in the 1970s detached from particular minds or bodies. These decisions "recognized" commercials and corporate advocacy as speech, admitting the communications of one set of artificial entities as speech. (The courts' reticence about the speech of another set of artificial entities, technological agents, is discussed in the next chapter and conclusion.) But the conditions of possibility for this enfranchisement of commercial speech and corporate speakers go back much further, to the progressive legal decisions of the 1930s and 1940s and to the growing ubiquity of "information" as an immaterial good and means of quantifying communication in the following decades. From the 1950s onward, it became common for social scientists and commentators to conceptualize the substance of communication less as ideas, beliefs, opinions, or intelligence and more as abstract and immaterial information. The abstraction and capaciousness of the concept of information have, in part, eroded older distinctions between opinions and advertisements, advocacy and expenditures, and commerce and communication.

There is a deep irony here. What began as an effort to combat the corporate takeover of the public sphere became a tool for enfranchising corporations. The rearticulation of freedom of speech as the distribution of information in the 1930s and 1940s, described in chapter 3, was a way of wresting speech away from a handful of powerful speakers and recognizing the public interest in the circulation of a variety of ideas, opinions, and facts. These decisions disarticulated freedom of speech from the rights of particular speakers in order to enfranchise the audience (and marginal speakers)—an impersonal conception of speech. Within the logic of the

1930s and 1940s, freedom of speech meant not only the freedom of individuals (e.g., media owners) to speak but also, and more importantly, the availability of a diverse set of ideas. By the 1970s, the implication of the separation of speech from speakers had changed. It came to focus more on artifacts of communication (speech as an artifact or object—or bits of information). The protection of information, and its ability to flow freely, has since become a powerful deregulatory tool, used to protect the investments and operations of corporate actors; the protection of information has provided grounds for striking down public interest regulations, from limits on corporate expenditures in elections to consumer and patient privacy laws.

In both the linearity presumed of communication when its content is understood as information and the convergence of different types of message under the term "information" provided key background conditions and assumptions that enabled the justices to accomplish the reversal outlined in this chapter: a 180-degree shift in the deployment and usefulness of the conceptualization of speech as the distribution of information. This historical context helps to explain how in legal discourse information went from a social good subject to distribution (and calls for distributive justice/redistribution) to a more fluid good that could or should flow on its own—and was best left unimpeded by regulation. Here we see a set of ontological assertions about the nature of communication camouflaging the politics and ideological commitments of legal judgments. Even more, though, we can see a shift in the terrain on which freedoms of speech are discussed, extended, or restricted.[7] Rather than distributing speech rights among (competing) individuals, the legal decisions analyzed in this chapter seek to protect information itself, as a site of agency and freedom; the freedom of information to flow on its own comes to stand in for the expressive freedoms of the public.

I trace the implications of this change of terrain across this chapter and the next. They are political in the sense that they serve specific (mainly commercial) interests. But they are also political in a broader and more abstract sense; this shift in terrain was a shift in the very grounds and meaning of expressivity in the law. Legal reasoning migrated from questions of meaning, access, and whose rights were paramount in a given medium or situation to a drier, more technical set of questions: Is there a message (or signal)? Is information transmitted? This shift is posthuman not only in that it provides the grounds for granting expressive rights to "artificial" entities but also in that it marks a repositioning in how speakers—and the subjectivity and agency associated with expression—are defined. Rather than the authors, advocates, and creators (and attendant concerns with intent, psychology, and belief) that animated early twentieth-century legal discourse, the posthuman strains of late twentieth-century legal discourse are more concerned with artifacts (is it a message?), proof of transmission or receipt, and discussions of utility.

Free Speech in the 1970s

The 1970s marked an economic turn in free speech law, in which the First Amendment was used to protect corporate spending to influence politics and advertisements and to invalidate campaign finance laws. This turn came after the liberalism of the 1960s, during which the Supreme Court, especially under the leadership of Justice Earl Warren, further expanded expressive civil liberties, in response in part to the civil rights movement and antiwar activism on college campuses. (The 1960s are generally regarded as the second great expansion of civil liberties, after the 1930s.[8])The eventful decade is at the center of more typical historiographies of free speech, with good reason. The political and cultural context presented cases that reshaped First Amendment law, expanding academic freedom and student speech rights, relaxing libel law, and further limiting the ability of the state to restrict speech due to the danger of its content (from a "clear and present danger" standard to the more difficult "incitement" standard).[9] Perhaps most notably, the decade saw an expansion of symbolic speech to a number of types of protests (and then its circumscription)—a trajectory I discuss at greater length in chapters 2 and 5.[10] And the Court determined that the audience's right to receive information in broadcast communication was more important than the broadcasters' editorial rights in the 1969 decision *Red Lion v. FCC*.[11] Yet the broader claim that free speech might mean a right of access to the meaningful platforms for speech of the day—so key to progressive decisions in the 1930s and 1940s—never gained a foothold in this otherwise famously progressive era.[12]

The 1970s saw a rightward shift for the Court, pushing back against some of the liberalism associated with the leadership of Justice Warren in the 1960s.[13] In particular, the Court moved toward a more economically conservative, neoliberal outlook, in which the First Amendment was used to protect businesses from regulation. Attempts to use the First Amendment to further the workings of business were not new; the film case described in chapter 1, *Mutual v. Ohio* (1915), was one early example of this. But the 1970s marked an increase in the success rate of such attempts. It was the decade in which, Cass Sunstein notes, the typical free speech beneficiary in Supreme Court decisions became not a dissident, a minority, or an individual but, rather, a corporation or other institution.[14] The decade saw a series of Court decisions in which free speech was expanded in ways that greatly reduced the ability of state and federal legislatures to regulate advertisements and the role of money in elections. (More recently, similar decisions have restricted state efforts to protect consumer privacy.[15]) First, the Court ruled that monetary expenditures were not conduct but rather expression in a decision that invalidated campaign finance provisions put in place in part in response to allegations of serious financial abuses by the Nixon campaign in the 1972 presidential election: *Buckley v. Valeo* (1976).[16] The *Buckley* decision overruled the lower court's determination that campaign contributions and expenditures were a form of conduct, subject to regulation. The decision ruled that monetary expenditures were a necessary part of political speech (needed in order to secure a medium for that speech, whether that be a physical hall or broadcast airtime), and thus, that restricting campaign expenditures was a restriction on political ideas.[17]

The decisions that came after *Buckley*, however, were qualitatively different. The same year, the Court granted advertisements limited First Amendment protection, overturning precedent set in the 1940s defining advertisements as commercial transactions rather than speech. In doing so, the Court created a special kind of (less protected) speech: "commercial speech." Two years later, the Court struck down a state law restricting the ability of corporations to attempt to sway the outcome of local elections, on the grounds that these restrictions were a violation of free speech. In these decisions, the speech in question was not necessarily tied to a particular person, as in *Buckley*, or any particular ideas. Rather, speech was coterminous with information, which could be produced by individuals, institutions, populations, or objects. These decisions—*Virginia State Board of Pharmacy v. Virginia Citizens Consumer Council* (1976), and *First National Bank v. Bellotti* (1968)—define the shift traced in this chapter. They provided both the logic and formal precedent that has propelled recent corporate expansionism in free speech, from *Citizens United v. FEC* (2010) to *Sorrell v. IMS Health* (2011) (finding that privacy laws preventing the sale of patient information to pharmaceuticals had violated freedom of speech). In *Virginia*, the Court ruled that advertisements, even those that did not convey any substantial political message or idea, but merely posed a commercial transaction, were a form of speech that deserved some protection. (Ads, or "commercial speech" can be regulated, for example in laws restricting false advertising or requiring health warnings.) The decision aligned the freedom of messages (ads) with those of the audience, specifying that the public had an interest in a robust flow of information, no matter the source or content. In *Bellotti*, the Court used a striking rhetoric to frame its decision. Rather than making the case about whether or not corporations had First Amendment rights, the decision was articulated around the freedom of information itself—the freedom of messages to flow, irrespective of their origins. The decision, notably, did not define the bank as a speaker or discuss its intent or its rights. Nor did it reference protecting the rights or interests of the audience or public as a rationale. Rather, the decision protected messages, or speech itself, abstracted from any particular speakers (or listeners). Messages stood in for the social interests of the public, whose actual interests faded from view.[18]

The move toward protecting economic activity as free speech is perhaps obviously motivated by politics: the rise of economic conservatism and the Court's rightward shift. But the means and mechanisms of this shift, I argue, were in conceptualizations of communication external to these political shifts. In order for messages, rather than people, to become the subjects of free speech law and for individual and corporate speech to be equated, the individual units of speech had to be conceived of as undifferentiated and objectified: exchangeable tokens. In this transformation, a social action is treated as an object, which can be measured or traded. As utterances became tokens, a legal concern with speakers (those who hold rights) gave way to a search for messages or information (artifacts of expression). And more messages, or information, could stand in for a diversity of ideas or debate; quantity could be assumed to guarantee diversity and quality. The conceptualization of communication that enabled this shift, I argue, had its origins in the development of efficient, automated communication systems, where communication was described as the transfer of information. Information was a unit of measurement that allowed the telephone company to quantify and compare communications across various media, from telephone conversations to the Morse code of telegraphy to radio and television signals.

To provide the background that explains how a discourse on information emergent in the postwar era shaped the legal trajectory outlined here, I now turn to a comparison of the discourse on information circa 1940 and the discourse on information tied to information theory that emerged in the postwar era. Founded in historical problems of communication technology and defense (namely, compression and encryption), a more abstract and technical conception of information proliferated and became central to American social and political thought in the postwar era, with implications for the way speech was conceptualized and agency was attributed to speakers in both social theory and, as I show, the law. I then show how this discourse on communication as information transmission became a key pillar in the reasoning of the corporate and commercial speech cases of the 1970s outlined above.

The Rise and Influence of "Information" in Twentieth-Century American Thought

The late twentieth-century career of information is closely entwined with that of communication. In the postwar discourse on information theory that I argue is central to the legal reinterpretation of free speech (in which speech becomes autonomous and the subject of the law), information was alternately the measure or the content of communication. The production of knowledge about communication no longer revolved around questions of influence and psychology or even interpretation, but rather around the transmission of information (e.g., the sender → message → receiver model of communication). To highlight the shift in the stakes of such conceptualization, remember that in the 1930s (as described in chapter 2), human communication, institutional management, and international relations fields had been described in terms of human psyches and psychologies. In some of the most famous and influential work of the time, solutions to political and social problems were framed in terms of psychopathology and personalities. By the 1970s, these fields and problems were more often described and studied (in institutional sites like universities and government) in terms of information flows and exchange.[19] Similarly, by the 1970s, symbols were discursively constituted less as products of human psyches (as they had been in *West Virginia State Board of Education v. Barnette* [1943]) and more as data or signals to be manipulated by human or machine.[20] This shift was driven in large part by information theory and its adoption—and transformation—in the social sciences.

Information as Official, Public Communication

The term "information" took on its modern meaning of objectified and quantified knowledge (facts or data) in the late nineteenth century.[21] By the 1930s, information as factual and objective (as opposed to the subjectivity of individual perception) had become an ideal in not only governance but also social science and journalism, in the guise of objectivity. Information promised knowledge beyond the viewpoint of the individual, a viewpoint from the institution. To paraphrase John Durham Peters, it suggested knowledge with the human body (and subjectivity) taken out, a statistical-institutional point of view.[22]

Such meanings are clearly referenced in the naming of governmental publicity offices. In World War I, the large-scale tasks of communicating about the war—both in an effort to persuade the populace to support the war and in defining what news was fit for public consumption and what was secret—were undertaken by the Committee of Public Information. The committee's name was aspirational; George Creel, the director, saw his job as one of providing needed facts and figures. In World War II, the Office of Facts and Figures tellingly became in 1942 the Office of War Information (OWI) (information and facts and figures overlapping considerably). The Office of Facts and Figures and the United States Information Service had been the primary organs of domestic government publicity in the 1930s.[23] (Notably, in World War II, in an effort to bolster public trust in the office, the OWI was in charge only of the dissemination of information. Censorship was the job of the Office of Censorship.) Similarly, in journalism, references to the news as information—rather than some of its earlier descriptors such as intelligence, knowledge, or opinion—were a way of claiming a dispassionate reserve, in which individuals crafting the news attempted to put aside their subjective perspectives and views, to keep themselves out of the story.

In the 1930s and 1940s, when the justices were including information within the conceptual category of "speech," it was this set of institutional meanings they were drawing on.[24] In *Hague v. CIO* (1939) and *Thornhill v. Alabama* (1940), the justices expanded the category of speech from the articulation of personally held views, beliefs, and ideas to include facts that did not originate with any of the participants and were not externalizations of their own feelings or ideas (e.g., distributing pamphlets containing facts about labor laws or signs with slogans) under the rubric of information. The former prioritized the will and mental work and beliefs of individuals, or the production of utterances (it is worth remembering that one of the arguments against considering films as speech is that they were not such original utterances). The latter made speech more impersonal, prioritizing the distribution, or even copying, of ideas or statements that might originate elsewhere (the act of expression was understood here as selection and repetition or amplification rather than creation). Arguing that freedom of speech encompassed the distribution of information included both the institutional discourse of the press and the marginalized communication of striking workers and religious minorities within the law. Not incidentally, it also helped define activities like picketing as being more speech than action.[25] The Court recognized in *Carlson v. California* (1940) the right of picketers to carry signs, banners, or badges on the grounds that they all conveyed information to passersby. The idea of information also delimited speech in the 1940s and 1950s. "Fighting words" and racial epithets were given lesser protection under the law on the grounds that they did not convey ideas or information (the substance of "speech"); they were categorized as closer to a form of conduct than a form of expression.[26] Similarly, in *Valentine v. Chrestensen* (1942), the Court upheld a local prohibition on distributing advertising pamphlets by drawing a distinction between an advertisement and informational material on the same handbill — that is, advertising was not speech because it did not convey meaningful information (rather, it proposed a commercial trans*action*). In all of these decisions, information is used to refer to facts, and other raw materials for public opinion, or to a sort of official knowledge distinct from individual opinion.[27]

Information as an Engineering Problem

At the time that these decisions were published, however, there was already a different way of defining and using the term "information"—one that would become more popular and pervasive in the 1950s through the 1990s and would provide the architecture for both ideas of the information society and the posthuman definition of speech in legal reasoning. This approach to information had its origins in the work of engineers and mathematicians like Claude Shannon, Warren Weaver, and Norbert Wiener.[28] It would substantially shape the construction of artifacts and knowledge, social and economic activity, in multiple fields. The model of communication as information transmission that was developed in the communication engineering context fatefully abstracted communication as a set of logical processes (amenable to computer processing) in order to apply to transmission of messages in multiple channels. The specific ways in which communication was abstracted—as a sort of disembodied logic that could be accomplished by persons or machines—proved immensely useful for a number of projects, from military to managerial. It has also, N. Katherine Hayles argues, been instrumental in the erosion we see in many facets of late twentieth-century science and culture of understandings and experiences of self and "the human" in terms of not only embodied experience but also ideas of self-ownership and individual will so central to liberal visions of freedom of speech.[29]

This trajectory began in efforts to construct a more robust and efficient communication network. As early as the 1920s, engineers working for Bell Labs were trying to quantify and maximize the number of messages that might be sent over the telephone and telegraph wires and the airwaves. (The content of these messages was, in the 1920s and 1930s, not only the voices of people speaking to one another but also the music, variety shows, and other "plays" that comprised network radio programming.) For engineers as well as for government bureaucrats wishing to quantify the output of the new communications industry, the invisibility and immateriality of the electronic communication of telephony and broadcast made it particularly difficult to pin down, or to quantify just what it was that was sent via the different material conduits of telephone, telegraph, and radio communication.[30] The desire to specify and measure communication was thus located within a technical and economic problem of maximizing transmission and value from existing telephone lines and bandwidth and within a bureaucratic impulse to quantify innovation and economic activity. In the latter, there is a direct line from the invention of information as a unit of measurement for communication at Bell Labs in the 1920s to the later conception of the information society.[31]

In 1928, a Bell Labs engineer, responding to these concerns about maximizing and quantifying transmission, published a paper proposing a way of defining and measuring the communication sent over their lines. Deviating from prior efforts to quantify the "intelligence" (also a common cognate of speech in early twentieth-century legal discourse), communicated via wire and air, Ralph Hartley suggested, it would be helpful to think of the stuff they trafficked in in less subjective and complicated terms: as information. While in lay usage "information" suggests the content or even meaning of a message, the engineering definition bracketed meaning in order to "eliminate the psychological factors involved and to establish a measure of information in terms of purely physical quantities."[32] For communication engineers, information meant the amount of indeterminacy in any given message. In order to calculate this indeterminacy, Hartley offered a highly abstract definition of communication as a set of selections, or bounded choices:

> As a starting place … let us consider what factors are involved in communication; whether conducted by wire, direct speech, writing, or any other method. In the first place, there must be a group of physical symbols, such as words, dots and dashes or the like, which by general agreement convey certain meanings of the parties communicating. In any given communication, the sender mentally selects a particular symbol and by some bodily motion, as of his vocal mechanism, causes the attention of the receiver to be directed to that particular symbol. By successive selections a sequence of symbols is brought to the listener's attention. *At each selection there are eliminated all of the other symbols which might have been chosen. As the selections proceed more and more possible symbol sequences are eliminated, and we say that the information becomes more precise.*[33]

Communication—at the time in other intellectual circles a fuzzy concept, suggesting the manipulation of the subconscious and the exercise of power through personality or spectacle (symbols)—could thus be pinned down, measured, and optimized.[34] In this sense, the information contained in a message is not the meaning of the message, but rather a function of the degree of possibility (or uncertainty) in any utterance, or transmission. And various forms of communication are rendered similar by defining disparate physical phenomena—from the movement of vocal cords to the depression of a teletype key—as indications of a choice, or a selection of available symbols. Such a conception was general and abstract enough to describe multiple formats of communication that might be conveyed through the Bell system. Such abstractions were, as Hayles notes, a central component of the discourse of disembodiment that would later characterize information theory. (Ironically, this abstraction was premised on studies of acoustic perception constructed around particular hearing, bodies, instantiated as the norm within the Bell system.[35])

Central to the abstraction and quantification in the theorization of communication at Bell Labs (that would become a keystone of information theory) was the articulation of symbol selection as discrete choices.[36] Understanding communication in terms of discrete choices emphasized the mental work—choices—over other aspects of communication (i.e., the different physical means of registering or communicating that choice detailed in the quote above). This abstraction was, as noted above, key to the generality of the model; it also made it amenable to computer processing. Shannon built on the work of Hartley and others to further abstract communication, defining these choices in the binary logic of yes/no, representable in 1s and 0s, or closed or open circuits, to produce what he called a general theory of communication. The generality of the model transformed the evaluation of communication. Understood in terms of discrete choices, successful communication depended not on understanding, persuasion, or a meeting of the minds, but on deciphering or replicating these choices at a distance. And reception was not a question of interpretation (with all the complications of shared knowledge and language), but rather a question of whether the choice of symbols instigated at one end of the transmission could be discerned at the other—a point famously articulated by Shannon:

> The fundamental problem of communication is that of reproducing at one point either exactly or approximately a message selected at another point. Frequently the messages have *meaning*; that is they refer to or are correlated according to some system with certain physical or conceptual entities. These semantic aspects of communication are irrelevant to the engineering problem. The significant aspect is that the actual message is one *selected from a set* of possible messages. The system must be designed to operate for each possible selection, not just the one which will actually be chosen since this is unknown at the time of design.[37]

The question of meaning might be fundamental to the communication system (its raison d'être), but the system had to be agnostic, or indifferent, to the specific meanings of any particular message in order to operate as a system. The system had to be designed not for a particular message (or user) but for all. The basic theory or model of communication had to be general enough to optimize them all.

In this way, the theory of communication produced by communication engineers was fundamentally different from how their contemporaries and those who had come before them saw communication: *it defined communication not in terms of the perspectives of the communicants, but in terms of the system itself.* The conceptualization of communication as information was, in essence, a theory of communication in systems or institutional terms more than individual, human ones. It was developed around the technical and economic imperatives of communication systems: interoperability, efficient use of lines, the minimum signal required to reproduce an intelligible signal, and automation. Defining communication in terms of discrete selections allowed a variety of different forms of message to be similarly encoded and decoded (and sent along the same conduits). If successful communication was defined by the ability to reproduce these selections at a distance, any extra data beyond that required for this replication was inessential and could be eliminated from the transmission; as Mara Mills documents, many of the acoustic characteristics associated with the "human" quality of the voice, and body, of the individual on the other end of the telephone line were downplayed in favor of the fidelity of the content of the message.[38] And if successful transmission of messages did not depend on—or was analytically distinct from—the meaning of particular messages, then there was no need for operators to understand the messages (e.g., to speak the same language as the customers). In fact, there was no need for a human operator at all. The replacement of a human operator with an automated system was among the political economic goals at Bell Labs.[39]

This formulation, in which communication—from telegraphy to the spoken word—is modeled and encoded as a process of selection and replication, suggests a different role for the minds, will, and agency of sender and receiver than the understandings of speech defined in earlier chapters.[40] While this was true of the work of early communication engineers (who wanted to avoid the psychological aspects of communication), it took on new resonance in Shannon's contributions to and popularization of the general theory of communication. Shannon analyzed the particular choices involved in message selection (and reception) in terms of probability. His statistical analysis of the level of redundancy in English calculated that language itself structured many of our messages—the probabilistic patterns of letter and word succession were such that the number of choices individuals made in composing a message were fewer than assumed (so less information was required to successfully send a message). A significant number of the seeming choices involved in message composition could be explained by the patterns of language structure. To some extent, probability and statistics replaced intentionality, will, or psychology as the source of messages.[41]

The implications of this theorization of communication as a field of structured choices will be familiar to any reader versed in structuralism. There is a suggestive similarity in the way that engineers and structuralists conceptualized language as a constraint on agency. In many ways, Shannon's model echoed Saussure's turn-of-the-century work on language, in which the structure of language constrained any particular utterance (*parole*). In structural linguistics as well as in Shannon's model, the agency of the speaker was reduced by the system of language. While many social theorists defined the structuring forces of language in less mathematical terms, scholars like Lydia Liu and Bernard Geoghegan have shown that practices of computing, compression, and encryption were powerful provocations in what we call the linguistic turn. We can see the direct imprint of computation and information theory in many thinkers' work, from Roman Jakobson's adoption of Shannon's terminology (in which the engineering terms "code" and "message" replaced Saussure's *langue* and *parole*), to Jacques Lacan's description of the unconscious as a circuit, to Jacques Derrida's famous critique of the metaphysics of presence, in which he draws on computing and cybernetics to argue that writing has been "liberated" from the subject, that it no longer requires a human individual (but, rather, can be accomplished by a cell or a computer).[42] In these examples, the mathematical theory of communication (and the closely linked probabilistic model language offered by Shannon) and computational "decisions" suggested the need to rethink the human sciences and the role of human agents in the social world.

Shannon's model would have broad implications for the way communication was conceptualized not only in media systems but also in sociology, social theory, communication, economics, and, as I will argue, law. The epistemic consequences for the legal conceptualization of speech as information are not unlike those of structuralism and poststructuralism.[43] Up until midcentury, utterances were the basic unit of speech in legal discourse; utterances were vehicles for advocacy, dissent, and providing intelligence or news. In its reference to the physical act of speaking, the term "utterance" linked words/symbols to the activity (verbal, scriptural, or typographic) of a particular speaker or author. In contrast, the general theory of communication emphasized systems and messages over speakers (or speech as a social activity). As Geoghegan notes when discussing the conception of information in this engineering discourse, "Thus even spontaneous, ostensibly noncoded and nontechnical *communications situations lost their apparently expressive kernel and were replaced by a series of alternating, differential selections.* Telegraphy was no longer an information medium for transmitting speech and meaning; speech and meaning became a medium for the production of telegraphic information."[44] Geoghegan points out the inversion of human and machine here, in which speech and meaning become raw material for the technical apparatus. The expressive kernel of communication is what is at the heart of early twentieth-century free speech discourse; this kernel is the expression of a uniquely human interior (the source of this kernel might be creative genius, the mind, the psyche). Information theory posited a very different model of communication, in which this kernel was no longer essential; it might exist, but it was irrelevant to the problem at hand. This way of talking about, ordering, and, as we will see in this chapter, regulating communication, is what I have called a posthuman conception of speech, in which communication is not defined or tied to particular persons or traditionally humanist forms of subjectivity.

In the decisions analyzed below, the speaking subject is not only decentered but also replaced by abstracted information or autonomous messages.[45] In Geoghegan's phrasing, the typical relationship of human and machine is inverted, one becoming the medium for the other. Such formulations were one implication of information theory—one that was propagated by some of the popularizers of Shannon's model and by those involved in the Macy conferences and the ripples of this work out into various social scientific disciplines (and the natural sciences). This inversion challenged social theory, provoking a rethinking of its objects of knowledge.[46] It also changed the terms of social scientific discourse and study, from the study of mass communication (in US contexts) to economics and sociology. In the next section, I discuss in further detail the way that the popularization of information, as both a quantifying and animating substance, changed both conceptions and practices of social and economic life. In discussions of communication, information reified messages; in other fields, it rendered social relations as signaling.

The Social as an Informational (Engineering) Problem: The Popularization of Information Theory

In the 1950s and 1960s, the general theory of communication began to take on a life of its own. It was popularized and used to explain phenomena from genetics to human communication (interpretation or meaning-making) and reasoning. In this, a conceptualization of communication as a purely physical, quantifiable process crafted expressly to avoid the problems of intent and interpretation became a model for understanding both. This was in large part because the abstraction and immateriality (communication modeled as a set of choices or acts of logical ordering) of communication in

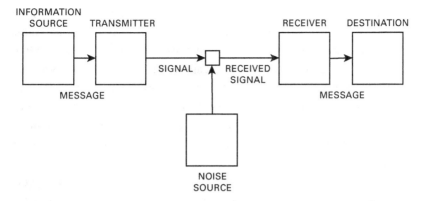

Figure 4.1 Claude Shannon's diagram of a general communication system. A 1949 *Scientific American* article explained: "A communication system may be reduced to these fundamental elements. In telephony, the signal is a varying electric current and the channel is a wire. In speech the signal is varying sound and pressure, and the channel the air. Frequently things not intended by the signal source are impressed on the signal. The static on the radio is one example; distortion in telephony is another. All these additions may be called noise." Source: Warren Weaver, "The Mathematics of Communication," *Scientific American* 181, no. 1 (1949).

information theory enabled its application to many different domains, an application encouraged by popularizers such as Warren Weaver.

Claude Shannon published "A Mathematical Model of Communication" in 1948, building on his wartime work on cryptography and earlier work at Bell Labs to articulate what would become his influential model of communication (see figure 4.1). Like Hartley before him (and Nobert Wiener's contemporaneous work), Shannon sought to remove the human problems of psychology (the unpredictability of human behavior) as well as the differences among sign systems (languages) and channels (media) from his schematic model.[47]

The very generality and abstraction of the model, the way it made different signals interchangeable and information fungible, was key to its influence. The potential sweep and application of the model captured the attention of Warren Weaver, then a natural science program officer at the Rockefeller Foundation. Weaver translated the article into a coauthored book for a more popular audience and also a 1949 article in *Scientific American*.[48] The book and article encouraged a general application of the model to multiple domains, not only the workings of media systems. This encouragement is clear in the first paragraphs of the *Scientific American* article:

How do men communicate, one with another? The spoken word, either direct or by telephone or radio; the written or printed word, transmitted by hand, by post, by telegraph, or in any other way—these are obvious and common forms of communication. But there are many others. A nod or a wink, a drumbeat in the jungle, a gesture pictured on a television screen, the blinking of a signal light, a bit of music that reminds one of an event in the past, puffs of smoke in the desert air, the movements and posturing in a ballet—all of these are means men use to convey ideas.

The word communication, in fact, will be used here in a very broad sense to include all of the procedures by which one mind can affect another. Although the language used will often refer specifically to the communication of speech, practically everything said applies equally to music, to pictures, to a variety of other methods of conveying information.[49]

In this opening, Weaver encouraged the use of the general theory of communication designed for technical systems to understand interpersonal and artistic communication and advocacy.

Weaver invited the reader to use the mathematical theory of communication to evaluate a nod or a wink, music, smoke signals, pictures, and ballet in terms of their conveyance of meaning—the very thing that the engineers originally sought to bracket with the choice of the term "information." He went on in the article to note that such communications need to be approached from three levels: the technical one of transmission, the level of semantics, and finally that of influence. Weaver, in his zeal to popularize, projected the technical aspects of communication onto the semantic ones, not to mention issues of power/influence (a blurring of the line between lay meanings of information, in which it can mean the content of a message and the technical, quantitative meaning that was also furthered by Wiener's even more popular discussion of information in his work on cybernetics).[50]

It is worth noting as well that Weaver here listed and made equivalent a set of communicative practices that had only recently been recognized as equivalent to speech in the law: namely, bodily gestures from a nod to the complex moves and meaning of ballet. In chapter 2, I showed how legal conceptions of speech broadened in the early 1940s to include symbols, conveyed through physical gestures or images (e.g., saluting the flag) as well as words, in the *Barnette* case. While symbols were understood in

Barnette to be a primitive and direct route from mind to mind, Weaver described them in 1949 in highly technical and immaterial terms: a process of abstract signaling akin to the blinking of indicator lights or the transmission of messages in a media system. In fact, in many ways, Weaver and the field of information theory more broadly would transpose conceptions of communication drawn from devices onto the workings and conveyance of meaning from mind to mind.[51]

As highlighted by the expansion of legal conceptions of speech in *Barnette*, more realms of interaction had been becoming legible as communication in both social science and law in the 1930s and 1940s: actions such as the flag salute and picketing.[52] As I argued in chapter 2, physical gestures were legible as speech to the justices deciding *Barnette* because they could in the early 1940s be "read" as externalizations of inner mental states (e.g., belief, conscience). In some ways this is similar to the rhetoric of Weaver in his 1949 *Scientific American* article, where symbols as diverse as the physical gesture of a wink, television, drumbeats, and the human voice are variant methods of signaling. Yet, in the legal rhetoric of 1943, symbols had been more closely tied to the minds and bodies of their creators. While the salute was open to interpretation, and misinterpretation, and symbols in general were fallible, their status as speech was closely tied to their ability to convey the ideas and desires of specific speakers.

Weaver's technical description of communication as signaling differs in that the intent or internal state of speakers (the thoughts or ideas behind communication) was no longer central to communication. To unpack this difference, it is useful to look at the way that the Shannon-Weaver theory of communication was used to describe nonverbal communication at the time. In what appears to be the first textbook on nonverbal communication or body language, *Nonverbal Communication: Notes on the Visual Perception of Human Relations,* psychologists Jurgen Ruesch and Weldon Kees drew on the mathematical model and cybernetics to analyze gestural communication, from the pantomime of early silent cinema to Native American sign languages.[53] In their analysis of such communication, Ruesch and Kees (in collaboration with the anthropologist and cyberneticist Gregory Bateson) dismiss questions of whether such gestures express inner states and whether such states were higher or lower forms of mental activity, arguing that what was important, instead, was the transmission of information: "certain actions convey information about the person who performs them."[54] It did not matter whether this information was an accurate representation of an internal state or whether what was conveyed was complex or primitive. What mattered was the legibility of a signal, or the ability to read a gesture. In the book, body language, nonverbal conduct, and material culture (e.g., dress, objects, customs of eating and drinking, glances and facial expressions, and pictures) were equivalent in their ability to convey information.[55]

The work of Ruesch and Kees is illustrative of the popularization of information theory more broadly, particularly the way in which technical issues of signal transfer were being used in the 1950s and 1960s to explain human communication and social relations. In this transfer, information was no longer a physical measure of uncertainty (or entropy) but rather came to refer to the semantic content of messages. Weaver's work, Wiener's use of information theory in his articulation of the initially promising and influential field of cybernetics, and the Macy conferences translated the mathematical model of communication into a variety of other fields, but with a twist. The model was no longer a means of quantifying discrete choices or selections but was now a way of apprehending the social activity of communication—or even a broader range of human behavior and relations—as immaterial transmission (and feedback), with wide-ranging applications across disciplines.

In the postwar era, the idea of communication as information transfer shaped various disciplines, from linguistics to biology.[56] In biology, genes became carriers, or media, for information used by cells in development; their messages were "expressed" in physical features or phenotypes. In psychology, individual behavior became a source of information, or feedback. In economics more broadly, information theory provided models for describing and calculating individual economic decision making as well as a new form of value production.[57] By the 1960s, mass communication scholars articulated human communication and ideology in a direct flow of S → M → R, in which communication (and influence) was fashioned as a linear process of transmission, and messages were conceived of as containers for meaning or ideas.[58] The continuing influence of this model can be seen in even its critics; for example, Stuart Hall's "Encoding/Decoding" essay (which is known precisely for pushing back on the way communication and control were paired in information theory and cybernetics) drew on communication engineering metaphors of encoding and decoding to name the critical moments of meaning-making.[59] Taken to an extreme, talking about communication as information transfer enabled a kind of synecdoche in which messages, artifacts of communication, came to stand in for the whole of social (and industrial) communication processes.[60] (Put differently, in this discourse communication was more often a noun—as in the plural, communications—than a verb.) Marshall McLuhan's famous line that the "message was the medium" was likely in part a response to this over-emphasis on messages.[61] Such ideas will show up in the legal discourse analyzed in the next section. Their presence may be in part due to the ubiquity of the formulation of communication as information flows or transfers—a result of the popularization of information theory. But it may as well have come from the specific translation of information theory into economics, which by the late 1960s and early 1970s was a source of influence in the law, both ideologically (in the coalescence of an economically conservative legal movement in reaction to the liberalism of the Court in the 1960s) and procedurally (in the law and economics movement, which sought to import methods of analysis and efficiency from economics into legal reasoning and practice).

The conceptualization of communication in terms of information had at this point traveled far. What had originated as a problem of quantification, compression, and encryption (and, in the wartime context, prediction) had become a tool or metaphor for understanding social relations and the economy.

The Information Economy

While the information of information theory was vague enough to encapsulate phenomena from genetics to propaganda, its specific origins in electronic communication, and perhaps particularly in the development of digital computers, inflected its usage and popularity. So many fields began to draw on models and theories of communication as information transmission in part because of the promise of disembodiment, or immateriality, that it suggested. This immateriality offered powerful fantasies of transcendence, from transcendence of social inequalities to economic transcendence of the material limits of production. At a moment in American life where the link between embodiment (in particular, race and gender) and social inequalities was becoming difficult to ignore, mocking the promises of democratic equality at the heart of US political culture, disembodiment seemed to promise a way around or above the messy power entanglements of bodies as sites of difference. This fantasy of virtual equality would reach its peak in the digital utopianism of the 1990s but was, as Fred Turner shows, incipient in the uptake of cybernetics and information theory in countercultural utopianism in the 1960s.[62]

In economics, the fantasy of transcendence was over physical scarcity, from labor to raw materials used in manufacture. From Wiener's prediction that there would be a second industrial revolution in 1950 based on information to the mainstreaming of discourse about the information society in the 1980s, the idea of information as the foundation of a new economy took shape. By the early 1970s, as Ronald Kline shows, the idea of a mode of economic organization built not on the processing of raw materials or manufacture but rather on the ordering and processing of information had taken hold.[63] Academics like Peter Drucker and Daniel Bell—and more popular futurists like Alvin and Heidi Toffler—argued that, increasingly, economic growth was predicated on the communication and manipulation of information, a process in which a potentially limitless production of immaterial informational goods might be produced out of limited materials.[64] Similarly, policymakers inside the Washington, DC, beltway were arguing that we were moving from an industrial to an informational economy and society in which the production and manipulation of information (rather than the production and distribution of goods) fueled economic growth—and, implicitly, structured social relations.[65]

The debt these ways of measuring and managing the economy owed to the engineering discourse on communication outlined above was clear in the US government's uptake of the concept of the information society. In the early 1970s, the Department of Commerce launched a study of how much of the US economy comprised informational activity.[66] In quantifying and calculating this activity, the report offered a definition of information as primarily a product of organizational activity and communication, in terms derived from cybernetics and information theory: "Information is *data that have been organized and communicated.* . . . To organize data into information, one needs to superimpose order: a system of logic, a system of thought, a system of measurement, a system of communication. *To communicate these organized data, one requires three elements: a communicator, a channel of communication, and a receiver.*"[67] Communication is here figured as the use of information to manage and control, in an echo of cybernetics. And the process of communication draws on Shannon's mathematical model, in its focus on logic and in its use of the sender-message-receiver schema.

The link of communication to information and information to the economy placed communication more centrally within economic calculations and discussions. The incorporation of computers and computation into business was one element of this shift. Computers were able to store and process much more information (organizing data into information). As information became central to the production of wealth—and was treated as a form of property—industries looked for ways to protect that property. Intellectual property law was an important site of protection, but so was the First Amendment. Information, advertisements, and the right to lobby the government were increasingly understood as important sources of value in the 1970s; this was an important impetus for free speech claims for commercials and corporate advocacy.[68]

One early advocate of using free speech claims to protect informational property was Martin Redish. In 1971, he published an article outlining a set of arguments for the protection of commercial speech.[69] Key to his argument was a discussion of advertisements as a form of information. In an argument that echoed contemporaneous discourse on communication, Redish contended that ads were messages, or containers for information, like any others. The primary difference between ads and other speech was that ads were crafted for personal gain (but then, so were political messages; it was increasingly difficult to draw sharp lines between the two). These messages performed a valuable function for the audience, increasing their access to information (say, about prices and competing products) and their ability to make informed choices. That the information contained in advertisements might be used by individuals to make choices meant that a greater flow of such information would improve individuals' decision making (make it more rational)—a means for improving the ability of citizens to self-govern, either in private decisions as an end to themselves or as practice for decision making in public matters. Further, if the Court allowed such sensational messages as crime magazines (citing *Winters v. New York* [1949])—he might have added "and film"—then why not also recognize that advertisements were speech deserving of protection?[70]

This argument would be picked up and elaborated in the cases examined below. In this line of argumentation, we can see a number of the conceptions of communication as information transfer described above. Specifically, the legal discourse analyzed here borrowed from the popularized version of information theory a focus on messages, independent from senders and receivers or social context; the idea that communication was a process of information transfer and management; and that the unit of communication was the message, as a container of information—which could be extrapolated to suggest that messages were expressively equivalent in their ability to convey information. In this borrowing, a set of engineering problems replaced the problems associated with the speaker and the author. In other words, "the problem of communication" in legal discourse became one of transmission, much as Shannon's mathematical theory promised to turn the "problem of communication" into one of accuracy of signal reproduction at a distance, rather than the more intractable problems of interpretation, agency, presence, and ethics that dogged many philosophical and sociological discussions of communication from the late nineteenth through the mid-twentieth century.[71]

Information Replaces Speakers in the Law:
Commercial and Corporate Speech in the 1970s

This approach to speech was a key mechanism for the deployment of speech rights for commercial entities. The decisions introduced at the beginning of this chapter—*Buckley, Virginia,* and *Bellotti*—were instrumental in this deployment. In these cases, speech was increasingly figured as information and freedom of speech became the unrestricted flow of information (an extension and variation on the conception of speech as the distribution of information discussed in chapter 3). Conceptualizing speech as information untethered from particular speakers or contexts enabled the justices to reconfigure the regulatory role of the state in the public sphere. Rather than regulating the distribution of ideas or information (or engaging in redistribution), the state could step back and allow information to flow on its own. With no speakers with conflicting rights claims, the state need not interfere.

The commitments behind this rightward shift were ideological, the product of the development of the modern conservative movement in reaction to the leftism of the 1960s and in concert with the Cold War (namely, aligning pro–business policy arguments with anticommunism and the more prosaic material interests in wealth accumulation at home). Nixon appointees on the Court had a more neoliberal view of the law and the state than had those on the bench in the previous decade, under Earl Warren. And more broadly, politics was being expressed as and in economics on both the right and the left. In the wake of the rise of the Chicago school of economics in the 1960s, the rhetoric of the marketplace as an efficient and rational system was becoming dominant. By the 1970s, the marketplace and economic logic were being incorporated in law via the law and economics movement. Further, in the mainstreaming of the consumer rights movement, consumer practices were increasingly the subject of political debates. And in the early 1970s, corporations and corporate actions became the target of leftist protests from antiwar and environmental groups (e.g., protests against Dow Chemicals, attacks on Bank of America).[72] All these made businesses and business decisions the terrain of politics at the level of popular protest and legislative action.

The discourse on communication as information transmission would, however, provide the mechanism for the rightward move. But more than this, it made this rightward move one that more liberal justices would sign on to. In the years to come, it reconfigured the substance, and stakes, of free speech law. In the landmark decisions of the 1970s analyzed here, justices focused on messages, often to the exclusion of speakers or listeners, in their determination of what constituted speech. Further, in discussing messages as fungible carriers of information, they equalized political and commercial transactions. These two tactics enabled the justices to argue that it was untenable to distinguish between commercial and political messages and that it was unconstitutional to restrict the former: information was information, which could and should flow freely on its own.[73]

Messages without Meaning

In 1976, the Court struck down parts of a federal law limiting campaign expenditures, as a violation of freedom of speech, in *Buckley*. It was clear in this case whose speech and interests were at stake. Restrictions on campaign expenditures, the justices reasoned, might limit the different groups of individuals who could enter politics and thus curtail the types of ideas and proposals that make up political discourse. Thus, the law would limit both the individual speech of politicians and the broad social interest in a diversity of ideas. Similarly, the rights and interests of both consumers (the audience) and advertisers were central to a decision the Court handed down later the same term in *Virginia*. The decision neatly conflated the two in a way that enabled later decisions to simply rule in favor of the producers of information on the (implicit or even forgotten) rationale that the audience (consumers) would benefit.

The case concerned a Virginia law that banned pharmacies from advertising drug prices, in order to keep the practice of professions "above the morals of the marketplace."[74] A group of consumers and consumer advocates, including Ralph Nader's group, Public Citizen, sued, arguing that the law interfered with the ability of citizens to access information about drug prices, information that was especially important to low-income elderly or ill citizens. As such, they argued, the law violated freedom of speech; they were explicitly concerned with the ability of the public, or audience, to receive information. Only a year before *Virginia*, the Supreme Court had decided that restrictions on advertisements of legal abortions were an unconstitutional violation of free speech.[75] *Virginia* was different, however. Where abortion ads were arguably political, and so, for the legal practitioners involved, closer to "pure speech," the drug ads at stake in *Virginia* did not enter into a political argument or even really propose an idea (see figure 4.2). It was a trickier question of whether a message that did "no more than propose a commercial transaction" could be considered speech.[76] As Justice Harry Blackmun put it in the majority opinion: "Our pharmacist does not wish to editorialize on any subject, cultural, philosophical, or political. He does not wish to report any particularly newsworthy fact, or to make generalized observations even about commercial matters. The 'idea' he wishes to communicate is simply this: 'I will sell you the X prescription drug at the Y price.'"[77] The terms of this passage are telling. The utterance in question eschews the lofty realms of opinion and higher thought so central to earlier legal discourse (e.g., the discussion of film as speech). It even distances itself from the proposition that the advertisement in question is an idea, through the use of quotation marks. Ideas, it should be noted, had been at the heart of early twentieth-century free speech jurisprudence. Speech is often uderstood in legal discourse as a representation of thoughts or ideas. In other words, one reason speech has been special is that it has been understood as the representation of ideas or thoughts tied to the working of minds—but not here. The quotation marks distance the content of communication from any romantic visions of mind, thought, or psychic interiority. What is presented is less an idea and more a commercial proposition—what would, in an earlier decade, have been dismissed as commercial activity.[78]

The majority argued for the inclusion of such propositions that did not quite merit the label of ideas based on the equivalence of the commercial transactions to other facts. If freedom of speech protected the dissemination of facts about labor disputes, as in *Hague* and *Thornhill*, which were, after all, economic, then it was not clear why commercial facts would not be included.[79] Drawing on the earlier *Buckley* decision, the justices argued that the commercial, or monetary, nature of the speech was not sufficient to place it outside First Amendment consideration. The majority argued that even the most basic of commercial appeals was a form of informa-

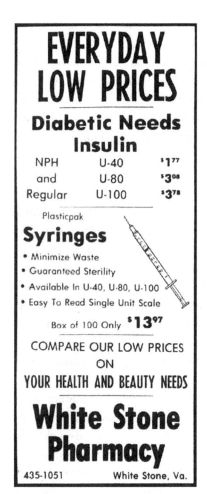

Figure 4.2 The types of ads in question looked something like this pharmacy advertisement. Source: *Rappahannock Record* 61, no. 43 (August 4, 1977).

tion transfer and, thus, speech. The decision thus drew on the definition of speech articulated in *Hague, Thornhill,* and *Carlson,* which included the transmission of information, or ideas that originated elsewhere.

In practice, however, the outcome of *Virginia* reversed the power dynamics of these earlier decisions. *Hague* and the other 1940s decisions discussed here had attempted to provide outlets for relatively powerless citizens (i.e., workers) to speak to a broad audience, rights of individual publicity on the model if not the scale of radio and industrial newspapers. In *Virginia,* in contrast, the right to disseminate information was granted to those with wares to sell, in the name of the listener's, or public's, interests. This move weds liberal public interest rhetoric to an economically conservative application of the law—a recipe that has been repeated successfully many times since. The outcome of the decision benefited businesses by protecting them from state and federal efforts to set restrictions on advertisements (and thus was a win for the business-minded wing of the conservative movement). The justices did so on the logic that these freedoms for advertisers would benefit the public, as more advertising would provide this public with more information on which to base personal, political, or economic decisions.[80]

Extrapolating out from the details of the particular case, the justices constructed an image of advertising as primarily the dissemination of information and built a category within speech law based on this extrapolation: "commercial speech." In doing so, they re-categorized advertisements from a form of action (commerce)—as they had been in the 1943 case involving advertisements (*Valentine v. Chrestensen*)— to a form of expression, though a notion of expression removed from the humanist associations of its everyday use. The expression of commercial speech was information, facts, and data. This moved the needle further away from the humanist concern with minds, meaning, opinion, and reasoning in early twentieth-century discourse and ratcheted up the abstraction and formalism of legal conceptualizations of speech.

While the ads in question in *Virginia* were simply information about prices, the decision existed in context and a line of other decisions about commercial communication and was part of the evolution and elucidation of the legal category of "commercial speech." Notably, *Virginia* came close on the heels of a more complicated case, *Bigelow v. Virginia* (1975). In *Bigelow*, the Court struck down a Virginia law restricting ads about abortion (in other states in which the procedure was legal). *Bigelow* was in some ways like *New York Times v. Sullivan* (1964). The latter case, more famous for its change to libel laws, was also a key step toward the inclusion of advertisements and other commercial communication. As in *Bigelow*, the advertisement in *Sullivan* was clearly political. It was paid for by supporters of Martin Luther King Jr. and constituted a full-page editorial criticizing the police in Montgomery, Alabama, for their treatment of civil rights protestors. The chief of police had sued the *Times* for libel, in response to some factual errors in the editorial (such libel suits were a tactic of segregationist officials in the South to block critical coverage of the civil rights struggle in other states); the case was contentious enough to be appealed up to the Supreme Court, where the justices decided that the ad was covered by the First Amendment (and that libel of public figures required actual malice).[81]

What I want to highlight here is how *Sullivan* and *Bigelow* offer an alternate example and potential set of rationales for protection of advertisements, when they are also advocacy. Instead, the Court took a different course, creating a legal category of "commercial speech" that would include many more commercial communications, including simple publication of prices (without idea, opinion, or need for interpretation).

Labeling advertisements as information was not the only way the justices could have argued for their inclusion. In addition to basing protection of advertisements on the advocacy or political ideas they advance, the Court could also have argued for categorizing advertisements as speech because of their artistry, rich meaning, or symbolic content. By this point, advertising was understood as a creative industry. As many others have pointed out, the vast majority of advertisements are not primarily informational but rather focus on psychological appeals, the evocation of affective states, and the association of affective states with products or brands. (The ad about drug prices at the heart of *Virginia* and the elaboration of the category of "commercial speech" were in some ways more typical of nineteenth-century advertisements.[82]) Rather than providing information about products that can help rational actors work in the marketplace, ads draw on cultural conventions (codes) to associate feelings and ideas with the product or brand or even to suggest these feelings or ideas dwell in the products themselves. By the 1970s, such psychological appeals and semiotics were within the scope of the stuff recognized as speech—in the inclusion of expressive conduct (e.g., saluting the flag, burning a draft card, or wearing a black armband) and emotive speech (e.g., that replacing "fuck" with some other word in the phrase "Fuck the draft!" would substantively and unconstitutionally change the meaning of the message).[83] The justices could, then, have focused on the symbolism or emotional appeal of ads, or cast them as a form of political persuasion, in order to include them in the law.

Rather than making any of these arguments or assertions, however, the justices built their defense of commercials on information. The justices in *Virginia* argued that there was no way of drawing a hard line between commercial messages and those concerning public issues—one might slide into the other at any moment. This was a continuation of the restraint in judgments of political and aesthetic value that emerged in judicial decisions of the 1940s and 1950s; just as it is not for the justices to decide what is entertainment and what is propaganda, it is not for the justices to decide what is political information and what is crass commercialism. Both offer information that might aid audiences individually and in the aggregate. As in the earlier cases (e.g., the inclusion of film as speech in 1952), this restraint was a way of expanding the boundary of speech (or utterances)— that is, it was a way of transforming the law performed through a rhetorical act of abstention. Before *Virginia*, commercials had been treated as a form of commerce. *Virginia* suggested that justices should not be making judgments about when and whether an ad was purely commercial or political. Rather, as messages containing information, ads were part of the free flow of information essential to democratic decision making:

> Advertising, however tasteless and excessive it sometimes may seem, is nonetheless dissemination of information as to who is producing and selling what product, for what reason, and at what price. So long as we preserve a predominantly free enterprise economy, the allocation of our resources in large measure will be made through numerous private economic decisions. It is a matter of public interest that those decisions, in the aggregate, be intelligent and well informed. To this end, the free flow of commercial information is indispensable.... And if it is indispensable to the proper allocation of resources in a free enterprise system, it is also indispensable to the formation of intelligent opinions as to how that system ought to be regulated or altered. Therefore, even if the First Amendment were thought to be primarily an instrument to enlighten public decision-making in a democracy, we could not say that the free flow of information does not serve that goal.[84]

Restrictions on advertising, the argument went, were likely to infringe on the rights of the audience (public) to receive information. The Court should not attempt to decide for the public whether or not that information was useful.

Defining commercials as carriers of information equalized ads with other messages; they were all equivalent as sources of information. Just as in the engineering discourse, the term "information" abstracted messages away from the conditions of their creation (or receipt). The rhetoric of information in legal discourse rendered National Labor Relations Board pamphlets (as in *Hague*), picket signs (*Thornhill* and *Carlson*), and commercials effectively interchangeable.[85] In the coming years, the rhetoric of information would make it easy to argue that efforts to curb commercialism or the influence of money in elections were as objectionable as efforts to restrict advertisements for abortion, or the use of libel laws to censor paid messages by civil rights advocacy groups—all were equally restrictions of the flow of information. The way that the generality of communication as information exchange enabled an equation between efforts of relatively disenfranchised citizens to combat inequalities based on embodiment (gender and race) and efforts of commercial entities to influence politics and evade regulation is a theme that returns in the gradual "recognition" of corporate speech in the law.

Speech without Speakers

This recognition began two years after *Virginia*, in 1978, in *Bellotti*, and again relied heavily on the discourse of communication as information transfer. The case concerned a Massachusetts law forbidding businesses from spending money to attempt to affect the outcome of ballot measures (unless the ballot measure directly affected some aspect of the business's interests, in which case it was free to spend). First National Bank of Boston and several other corporations in the state wished to air commercials arguing against a ballot measure proposing the introduction of a graduated personal income tax (to replace the state's flat tax). The corporations sued the state, arguing that the law infringed their freedom of speech. The case was first heard by the state supreme court, which decided against the corporations on the grounds that, as corporations, they had only limited speech rights and the law did not infringe these. When the case made its way up to the Supreme Court, something interesting happened.

In the majority opinion, Justice Lewis F. Powell reframed the case and reversed the lower court's judgment. He argued that the legal question was *not* whether corporations could speak, or "had" First Amendment rights, but, rather, "whether [the statute] abridges expression that the First Amendment was meant to protect."[86] The lower courts—and amicus briefs—had, in other words, framed the case in terms of "who": speakers (and which speakers had rights).[87] In contrast, Powell framed the case in terms of "it": messages or information. The case, he argued, was not a matter of who the speakers were, and whether they had rights, but of whether there was a restriction on messages; in terms of deciding the case, then, the justices did not need to look for persons or other rights holders, but simply look for messages and determine whether these were unduly restricted. What might have been a thorny political and normative question was, superficially at least, transformed into a simple, technical one. Was there a message? If so, free speech was involved. (In particular, as in this case, if it was a message concerning politics, or public issues.[88]) On this logic, because the Massachusetts law restricted the flow of messages—or information—it was a violation of the First Amendment.

If free speech law has been captured by business interests, as some contemporary scholars argue, then this is the moment it happened.[89] The decision was a major victory for the conservative legal movement. Not only did the decision make it more difficult for legislatures to restrict corporate advocacy, but it also demonstrated the utility of the First Amendment as an antiregulatory tool. This was exactly the type of outcome the movement had convened to bring into being: the movement aimed to counter the influence of liberalism (symbolized by the ACLU and the Warren Court) and embed values of free enterprise (and, later, socially conservative political values) in the law and legal institutions. *Bellotti* had been on the movement's agenda; First National Bank and the other corporate appellants were supported by several new organizations of the movement: the Pacific Legal Foundation, Mid-America Legal Foundation, and Northeastern Legal Foundation filed amicus briefs on their behalf.[90] Justice Powell was an early advocate of the ends of the conservative legal movement. Before joining the Court, while still a corporate lawyer in Richmond, Virginia, Powell authored the now-infamous Powell memorandum. The memorandum, titled "Attack on the American Free Enterprise System," urged corporations to turn to Congress and the courts to fight back against the perceived attack from the left, specifically by working together to craft legal cases that would advance business interests and engaging in legal advocacy in order to sway legal decisions in their favor.[91]

In the mid-1970s, this position was much more radical than it is today (the conservative legal movement has won many victories in recent decades). Justice Powell would have supported explicitly granting corporations speech rights. Yet few of his fellow justices would have signed on to such an idea. In order to win a majority in the *Bellotti* case, and effectively achieve this end, he had to craft an argument that would court the sympathies and commitments of his liberal colleagues. Freedom of speech fit the bill.

Powell won over more liberal members of the Court by shifting the locus of analysis from debate over who was a rights-holding speaker to a question about the suppression of speech itself. In this framing, speech was imperiled and the Massachusetts statute was an attack on the most sacrosanct type of speech per modern free speech theory: political speech. In casting the statute as an attack on speech, or a specific set of messages, the case made these messages the subject of the law: "The question in this case is, simply put, whether the corporate identity of the speaker deprives this proposed speech of what otherwise would be its clear entitlement to protection."[92] Notably, in the grammar of the sentence, the message is the target (or victim) of discrimination based on the identity of the speaker.[93] While elsewhere the identity of the speaker had been downplayed, here it became a target of discrimination—a discrimination that had negative implications for democracy, or the public (not the corporation). The politics of this passage are striking. Powell borrowed the rhetoric of civil rights, casting artifacts (messages) in the place of minoritarian subjects, in order to protect corporate actions, in the name of democracy. In this, the decision hijacks the legal protections against discrimination to provide gains for corporations. In a historical irony, the disembodiment of information that some hoped would help transcend discrimination against embodied subjects replaces them as the targets of legal protection.

The rhetorical reversal—that the case was not an issue of whether corporations had speech rights but of whether speech was restricted—had implications beyond bringing more liberal justices on board with a decision that arguably elevated corporate interests over those of citizens. It created a playbook for making free speech arguments that obscure their beneficiaries. The rhetoric in the decision placed messages—artifacts of communication— on equal footing with the humans who presumably create and use them. Such artifacts cannot, of course, claim rights. When speech or messages become the center of legal discourse, the question is no longer about whose rights or interests are at stake (or are paramount). Rather, the questions become, is there a message, and is that message free to flow where it will? In other words, when speech becomes the subject of free speech law, other subjects recede from view. Protecting the freedom of messages or information to flow can substitute for discussions of the audience's rights, or the public interest; it can also obscure the substantial matter of whose rights are in fact being protected. In *Bellotti*, the case may have been reframed away from the question of whether corporations have rights, but in the end, it has answered exactly that question. Justice Anthony Kennedy's *Citizens United* decision in 2010 claimed as much: corporations already had speech rights, per *Bellotti*.[94]

If in *Virginia* (and in the amicus curiae filed for First National Bank and others in *Bellotti*) the freedom of information is a proxy for the interests of the audience, in *Bellotti* the freedom of information is a substitution for the freedoms of the public. What was once a mechanism for diversity of ideas and the public good became an end in and of itself (something that could stand in for the public good or for members of the public). Ideologically, the freedom of information is still supposed to enable human freedom and enhance democratic processes. But in the letter and the practical outcomes of the law, the freedom of information in fact substitutes for human rights and freedoms—speech (which manifests in concrete terms as messages or information) becomes, as I have argued, the subject of the law. Free speech arguments in this vein become arguments that social theorists might term posthuman. This was literalized in *Citizens United*, where Justice Kennedy stated, "The First Amendment protects speech and speaker, and the ideas that flow from each."[95] Speech and speaker, and the ideas that flow from them, are equal under the law. Justice Antonin Scalia, in a concurring opinion, took this further, to stipulate that, for originalists, the law protected messages rather than their creators, specifying that the First Amendment "is written in terms of 'speech,' not speakers."[96]

It is worth dwelling on the political inversion here. In the 1930s and 1940s, defining freedom of speech in terms of speakers' rights was a conservative move, used to argue that the First Amendment protected media owners' expression, essentially allowing for an oligopolization of the public sphere. Contemporary efforts by the left to draw on the progressive rhetoric of the 1930s or 1940s cannot assume that current regulatory battles line up in the same way. Today, the corporate takeover of free speech is accomplished less by endorsements of owners' rights over the collective good, or even protection of information as a means of addressing the interests of the public, and more by the substitution of information for the interests of the public.

This substitution of information for the interests of the audience-public entails a shift in the locus and uses of equality. The legal decisions of the 1940s sought the equality of citizen participation associated with normative understandings of democracy, an equality rooted in notions of fairness or justice. References to a right to distribute information were employed to equalize a distorted public sphere, providing new "channels" (i.e., the city streets) for disenfranchised speakers and their own, embodied perspectives. In the years that followed, this right to distribute information was articulated as a marketplace of ideas; it was a rowdy and agonistic marketplace (like a public square) in which hawkers competed for shoppers' attention.[97] Ultimately, the reasoning went, the public's interest would be served, just like the shopper's, by this competition. In *Virginia* and *Bellotti*, in contrast, it is not speakers (or even listeners) whose equality is essential, but rather the equality of messages that matters. And the equality of messages is an equality of interchangeability (more than of justice). Whereas the desired outcome of the 1940s cases was a competitive and diverse field of ideas, in *Bellotti*—and to a lesser extent in *Virginia*—it is an undifferentiated "stock" of information available to the public.[98] Any utterance was equal to or interchangeable with any other, and all are equally available to members of the public who wish to draw on them.

The term "information" works in the 1970s to render different sorts of messages equal in this sense. Whether the message is commercial or political or whether it is produced by a corporation, politician, newspaper, or individual, it contains an idea, bit of information, or data.[99] To distinguish among messages based on whether they are issued by a corporation or an individual is, in Powell's argumentation, tantamount to discrimination. This interchangeability (and usurpation of civil rights rhetoric) works best when we think about messages in the abstract, divorced from social context—as in the technical discourse on communication as the transmission of information.[100] As in the cyberlibertarian rhetoric that would become popular two decades later in the 1990s, economic conceptions of fungibility are here converted into political ideals of equality. The job of the state was to step back and allow for the flow and exchange of information, in a marketplace that was understood less in terms of the exchange of physical goods and more in terms of the exchange of seemingly immaterial information (the market is no longer imagined as a physical space of haggling and intermixing, or even a supermarket of boundless consumer choices, but is rather the stock market).[101]

Making speech, or messages, the subject of the law, then, did several things. Under the guise of protecting messages, it occluded the rights and interests at stake in legal decisions. It shifted the locus of equality from democratic participation to informational fungibility and mobility. And it inverted the typical description of censorship as restrictions on a speaker/person based on the message, or content, of his/her speech. This last reversal was one of the great rhetorical—and legal—innovations of *Bellotti*. Per Powell's rhetoric, the Massachusetts law unconstitutionally restricted the message (and its freedom to flow) due to discrimination against certain speakers: corporations ("the corporate identity of the speaker deprives this proposed speech of what otherwise would be its clear entitlement to protection"). The suggestion of discrimination was subtle within the text of *Bellotti*. It becomes explicit in *Citizens United*. In the majority decision, Justice Kennedy summarized the outcome of *Bellotti* as a prohibition on the government from "distinguishing among different speakers, allowing speech by some but not by others," as not only censorship but also discrimination.[102] By implication, to place restrictions on corporations and their expenditures in elections is tantamount to a civil rights violation.[103] In this, *Bellotti* and *Citizens United* continue the long tradition of corporations bending legal guarantees of equality crafted for racial and other minorities to their own benefit; just as corporations and business owners drew on the Fourteenth Amendment (which had extended citizenship to formerly enslaved African Americans) to craft antiregulatory arguments in the late nineteenth and early twentieth centuries, legal arguments and doctrines established to protect racial and ideological minorities (e.g., Jehovah's Witnesses, socialists, and labor) are now being leveraged by corporations.

Conclusion

In the legal discourse examined here, speech as information becomes disembodied and disarticulated from particular social actors or even particular minds in the 1970s. What flows in this discourse is not so much (human) ideas as the information of systems, indiscriminate about the identity of the sender. In *Buckley* both political expression and money flow together; in *Virginia* the two are condensed and the public is found to have an interest in the free flow of commercial information; and in *Bellotti* information should be left free to flow on its own. Information and flow go together not only in their ties to computation but also in the way they suggest circuits or systems of speech that seem to exist without any individual interlocutors.

Even before electronic bits of information wanted to be free in the digital utopian discourse of the 1990s (also fueled by libertarian visions), then, information wanted to be free in speech law. The idea that the First Amendment protected a "flow of ideas"—as well as the more embodied acts of advocacy and avowal—built on the foundations of the 1940s, in which speech was disarticulated from particular individuals. While in the 1940s this depersonalization allowed the Court to define speech as a social good, it became just another good in the metaphorical marketplace of ideas within the neoliberal political context of the 1970s.[104] By the 1970s, as well, this disarticulation had taken on more posthuman implications: legal reasoning could focus on messages and their freedom, more than or instead of speaking subjects and the distribution of rights among them.

In the cases examined here, a posthuman theory of speech is utilized in the service of a neoliberal political agenda in which questions of political equality and distributive justice are obviated. Messages came to substitute speakers just as the protection of minority speech at the center of the civil libertarian tradition was extending to racialized minorities as well as to ideological ones. And just as legal protections were being crafted for the subjects of racial (and to some extent gender) discrimination, the abstraction and depersonalization of speech opened these protections to corporations. The disarticulation of speech from speakers—and conditions of production in general—has enabled justices to combat discrimination against ideas more than discrimination against disenfranchised groups of people. This is the logic underpinning legal decisions in recent decades that have prioritized the rights of businesses and organizations (e.g., the Boy Scouts, the South Boston Allied War Veterans Council) to discriminate against gays and lesbians over local antidiscrimination measures meant to protect their civil rights.[105]

In the same move, the quantity of information comes to stand in for the quality of information. The formal, logical link between protecting the flow of information and protecting the rights or interests of the public is the idea that the public will have access to this information, and that more information will enable better decisions. If the Court should not be the judge of the quality of the content of messages, then the focus would be on the amount of information—more information would presumptively be better information. The ideal of the public sphere suggested here is then defined not by channels to which access is variable, but rather as a general repository ("stock") of information that anyone in the public may access at any time.

These political outcomes aside, the posthuman supplanting of speakers in favor of information, data, and systems has posed challenges for free speech law. It has broadened "speech" to include the distribution of facts, formulas, and messages (irrespective of the speaker and their intent) and to include messages that did not originate with a discrete speaker (messages produced by the government or by a business to sell goods or ideas). "Speech" within the law, as I noted at the beginning of this book, is a subset of communication that is closely tied to conceptions of human will, freedom, and creativity. Legal conceptions of speech were further focused around political advocacy and liberty in the 1920s through the 1940s, as the civil libertarian interpretation of freedom of speech (forged in response to the suppression of World War I and Progressivism) gained dominance in US courts and legal theory. In the speech and commerce cases of the 1970s (and their echoes in the 2010s), we see the category expanding to the point that these parameters seem set to collapse.[106] If speech is equated with information, what is not speech?[107]

This question haunts the contemporaneous questions before the Court, about communication via and between computers. If speech is the flow of information, then much of the work of software, the outputs of programs and algorithms, is classifiable as speech and the hardware, software, and networks that define much contemporary economic, intellectual, and social life are beyond regulation. Yet, as chapter 5 details, to date, judges and justices have been hesitant to follow this reasoning in the technological realm. In cases dealing with computer-mediated communication, they have chosen not to apply the arguments they happily adopt when faced with economic issues. Instead, in cases involving the extent of free speech when computers are involved, judges and justices have looked for evidence of human speakers, will, and intent.

5. Speaking Machines

The Uncertain Subjects of Computer Communication

Late twentieth-century machines have made thoroughly ambiguous the difference between natural and artificial, mind and body, self-developing and externally designed, and many other distinctions that used to apply to organisms and machines. Our machines are disturbingly lively, and we ourselves frighteningly inert.

—**Donna Haraway**, "A Cyborg Manifesto"

In chapter 4, I show how speakers were decentered in free speech law and how it became possible to protect speech without consideration of whether there was a speaker (or whether that speaker was a natural person, able to claim rights). The protection of corporate speech was built on such abstracted speech, disarticulated from specific rights holders or speakers. As computer networks became ubiquitous, along with the heady libertarian discourse of the 1990s in which information "wanted" to be free, a new set of implications for these decisions became clear. If it did not matter who—or what—the messages were for in order for them to be granted protection, then why not protect communication via—or by—machine? As legal scholars like Toni Massaro and Helen Norton have shown, automated utterances like Google Maps directions and the queries of assistants like Siri or Alexa could easily be classified as speech based on the line of legal reasoning in which messages or texts take center stage.[1]

While it makes perfect sense within the line of legal reasoning traced in the last chapter, judges and justices have to date recoiled from the implications of computer speech.[2] While the Supreme Court is yet to rule on the issue, lower courts have balked at the implications of extending speech to computer-mediated, much less computer-created, communication. In cases involving claims that computer code and algorithms and speech, judges have looked for individual speakers and then based their decisions on the judgments, desires, and values they attribute to these speakers. Judges and justices have, in other words, put individual speakers back into the picture. In these cases, decisions about whether or not computer communication counts as speech have not hung on the existence of messages, but rather on the ability to discern the intent of a speaker in algorithms or code, and on where to draw the line between the programmer's expression and the action of the computer executing the program.

Judges have to date been eager to make sure that computer-mediated communication involves natural persons before it can be defined as speech in cases involving technologies.[3] That this is so even as they abstract speech away from particular subjects in cases involving corporate persons suggests not only a political orientation toward corporate interests but also a profound uneasiness with the potential of computer actions and decisions to replace human ones. In many ways, the anxieties in these cases echo those evident in the cases involving film analyzed in chapter 1, *Mutual v. Ohio* (1915) and *Pathé Exchange v. Cobb* (1922). In these early film cases, the issue was whether silent films were a form of original expression (mental activity) or more like mere mechanical conduct. The mechanism in these early cases was corporeal: movement of the human body. In the cases involving computer code analyzed here, the mechanization is electronic, and the processing and automation of the computer stand in for the physicality and primitivity once associated with the body. Ephemeral electrons replace the body as the site of action (the limit or boundary of speech).

This chapter explores cases in which the boundaries between speech and computer action are being drawn: cases revolving around the legal status of computer programs, and those involving the outputs of algorithms. In the former cases, judges defined programming, which is commonly seen as an activity in which people write instructions addressed to a machine, as technical communication among programmers, or human-to-human expression. Yet the expressivity granted to programming in this definition is far more limited in style and substance than if they had considered programs to be computer actions, advocacy in and through execution of the program. The logic employed in this case shows what happens to expressive conduct—a legal category formed around examples of embodied human expression—when filtered through the disembodiment of speech as information. To show this, and the implications of this shift, I return mid-chapter to the 1960s and draft-card burning—a key precedent for defining the parameters of speech and action in computer programs.

The chapter ends with a review of cases involving corporate algorithms, in which district courts have argued that the outputs of algorithms are speech. In these cases, the judges read through the lines of code to find programmers making judgments about the value of various types of speech. In doing so, they present the output of algorithms, which rely on the speech of many people and the processing of both software and hardware, as the embodiment of the values and judgment of a defined set of individuals—grafting a simple vision of agency and speech onto an empirically complex one.

Taken together, the two sets of cases highlight present legal commitments. Different conceptions of the roles of humans and computers in communication are mobilized in each, but one outcome is similar: protection of the interests of large commercial entities (the motion picture industry over hackers, incumbent search engines over competitors and political dissidents). This is evidence of a political commitment to corporate and institutional speech, even over citizen speech. But it is also evidence of something more. The character of the expression at the heart of each of these cases is qualitatively different from the expression at the heart of First Amendment jurisprudence of the early twentieth century and midcentury. The expression recognized in the cases examined in this chapter is about procedure, definition of metrics, and efficiency—as opposed to the production or transmission of ideas, reason, interpretation, symbols and psyches, and advocacy analyzed in chapters 1–3. Further, the embodied communication that had been recognized in the 1940s (with flag salutes) and extended in the 1960s (to sit-ins, armbands, and other forms of physical protest) was re-articulated through the lens of information, to separate messages from medium.[4] Bodies, minds, or machines are, in this line of thinking, substitutable media.

Speaking in Code: How a Set of Instructions to Machines Became "Speech"

When the FBI asked Apple to open up the phone of one of the shooters in the San Bernardino, California, mass shooting in 2015 as part of its investigation, Apple refused. Among other things, Apple and its lawyers argued that computer code was speech and hence forcing the company to write code to break into the phone would be compelling the company to speak in a way that ran counter to its values. Apple did not need to bring the First Amendment into play, but it was a dramatic and popular argument, taken up in simplistic terms in much of the news commentary. Invocations of code as speech ran through many of these articles.[5] While the face-off between Apple and the FBI fizzled when the FBI hired hackers to crack the phone, and the Department of Justice had largely rejected Apple's First Amendment claim, legal scholars noted that Apple's argument drew on solid precedent: legal decisions that in effect argued that code is speech. In this section, I unpack how the legal category of speech came to encompass code, the rationales on which this inclusion rests (a story of coverage), and the way that these rationales pose limitations on what computer communication counts as speech. The legal cases I analyze here define code as speech in an immaterial and depoliticized way. I argue that this is the culmination of the disembodiment of speech as information described in chapter 4.

The argument that computer code is speech emerged in the 1990s in a series of publications and legal cases involving the publication of decryption code on the web.[6] In many ways the argument culminated in the 2001 case *Universal City Studios v. Corley*. The case brought together debates about private ownership of culture, the ethos of coding as a liberatory political and creative act (hacking), and the regulation of decryption programs (in the name of national security). While there were earlier cases involving the publication of decryption code in academic contexts, the *Corley* case presented more basic, general questions about the status of code as speech. The decision articulated the most detailed reasoning and rationales for classifying code as speech to date. It has, further, become a common reference point for the legal status of code, operating as a precedent for a number of cases.

The case pitted a set of hackers sympathetic to the free software movement—which opposed the enclosure of software within legal and property regimes, some proponents of which used the slogan that software ought to be free as in free speech, not free beer—against the movie industry. (The full name of the case is *Universal City Studios, Inc., et al., v. Eric Corley, also known as Emmanuel Goldstein, and 2600 Enterprises, Inc.*) At the center of the case was DeCSS, a program developed to "unlock" the copyright protections on DVDs. DeCSS was a simple program created in 1999 by a young Norwegian computer programmer and two anonymous collaborators to unscramble the content scrambling system (CSS), an encryption program that polices where DVDs can be played (both in which geographic regions and on which devices). Movie studios and other major copyright holders—often referred to as the "content industry"—adopted CSS to protect their intellectual property against what they saw as the threat of digital piracy. This move toward digital rights management, underwritten by the passage of the Digital Millennium Copyright Act (DMCA) in the United States, was controversial. A chorus of legal and media scholars and computer programmers, among others, argued that the DMCA did not so much update copyright law for the digital era as extend it, greatly increasing the scope of culture owned by the content industry and eroding or eradicating rights of use that the public had previously held in copyrighted material.[7] One key point of contention was that digital rights management—like CSS—made it impossible for users to save or copy a small segment of a movie for comment or criticism (typically, a fair use). It also made it impossible to watch a DVD that you had bought in a different geographic region on your DVD player at home—a problem for cinephiles of obscure foreign movies—or to watch any DVD on a nonapproved device, say, a computer running UNIX. Another key complaint was that systems like CSS, in which the movie studios only shared the "key" that would decrypt their DVDs with device makers who agreed to their restrictions on end use, moved the regulation of copyright from public law to private negotiations, contracts, and technologies (device design).[8]

In this context, the DeCSS decryption program was both a pragmatic tool for unlocking DVDs and a way of figuratively giving the finger to the content industry: a protest of changes in the balance of power between copyright owners and the public—or, as some put it, in the balance of ownership of culture. It also allowed users to decrypt DVDs, whether to watch purchased content on unapproved devices or to "rip" (or copy) movies. The major movie studios moved to block the program, which had been distributed internationally via various websites. The studios demanded that all websites in the United States stop posting or linking to the DeCSS program; they also pressed Norwegian authorities to prosecute the young man who had created and posted the program.[9]

In December 1999, eight movie studios issued an injunction against the owners of three websites that continued hosting and/or linking to non-US sites hosting the program: Eric Corley, publisher of the online magazine *2600: The Hacker Quarterly*; Shawn Reimerdes, owner of the website dvd-copy.com; and Roman Kazan, owner of krackdown.com and escape .com. In their defense, the men and their legal teams argued that posting

DeCSS was protected speech because computer code was a form of speech and the act of posting the DeCSS program was political speech (they also argued they had acted in a journalistic capacity). In particular, in his appeal of the district court ruling, Corley, who was an activist hacker libertarian and also went by the name of Emmanuel Goldstein (after the fictional dissident leader in George Orwell's dystopian novel *1984*), argued that posting—and running—the program was a form of civil disobedience, a critique of what Corley and others saw as an illegitimate encroachment of intellectual property management into arenas of creativity and innovation. Corley and like-minded programmers in the free software movement saw themselves in a David-and-Goliath struggle with a massive industry that wanted to monopolize creativity, culture, and, increasingly, software.[10] Posting or linking to the DeCSS program was, in this frame, an expressive political act critiquing the extension of corporate control of the means of creativity—and arguably a critique of corporate capture of the legislative bodies who extended copyright law.[11]

Two sets of judges found for the movie studios: first at the district court level in *Universal City Studios v. Reimerdes* (2000) and then, when Eric Corley appealed (Reimerdes and Kazan dropped out of the case after the district court decision), in the Court of Appeals for the Second Circuit as *Universal City Studios v. Corley* (2001). The studios' injunction against posting or linking to DeCSS was valid, the judges argued, because code had distinct expressive and functional aspects, and the penalties for posting DVD decryption online were aimed only at the functional aspect: cracking the CSS code that kept users from running DVDs on unauthorized devices. Thus, they argued, the injunction—and the anticircumvention provisions of the DMCA on which it was based—was content-neutral (that is, not based on the expressive content of the code). From Corley's perspective, of course, the anticircumvention provisions of the DMCA were precisely this: the suppression of a decryption key, which is information. Further, he argued, the publication of this key was a critique of the copyright law. From his perspective, the DMCA was a content-based restriction on programmers' ability to critique what they saw as the enclosure, or privatization, of the digital public sphere.

In many ways, the decision was hardly surprising. *Reimerdes* and *Corley* were not just about the publication of decryption code in online journals or academics' websites (as in earlier legal cases dealing with decryption) but also about the public posting of code to decrypt copyrighted material; DeCSS could be used to access copyrighted material for either fair uses or illegal ones. That is, it could be used to perform an illegal action as well as a critique. Further, it presented an extension of the idea that decryption code was speech into a particular practice that threatened property regimes. Given the tendency of the courts to uphold private property rights, it is not surprising that the judges sided with property claims. What is interesting is the rationale they used to do so.

The legal rationales in the decisions revolved around the relation of speech and action. A program not only expresses an idea but executes an action. For Eric Corley and like-minded programmers, this would have made sense. For critics of the DMCA, sharing (or executing) DeCSS was akin to refusing to salute the flag or burning a draft card: political critique in the form of an action. What was different here was the site of action was not the body but the machine.

Yet the judges saw it differently. The understanding of expressive conduct that they used was not the same one used in the earlier flag-salute case or most discussions of picketing in the 1940s, in which the action and the expression were inseparable. Instead, the judges applied a standard of "speech plus" developed in a draft-card burning case in the late 1960s (*United States v. O'Brien* [1968]). The test involves distinguishing the action from the expression; if a law or regulation targets only the action (and only incidentally restricts expression), it may not infringe freedom of speech.[12] To make this separation, the judges described code as expressive only when it existed as lines of symbols on a screen, and as pure action by a machine when it was executed. In doing so, they inscribed a dichotomy between, to borrow Lisa Gitelman's terminology, programs as text (purely representational) and programs as instrument.[13]

The way that this dichotomy is drawn illustrates changes in the way expression is conceptualized in the law. In many ways the discussion of code as both speech and action echoes the discussion of film at the beginning of the twentieth century. As in the early twentieth century, the speech-conduct distinction remains one of the key mechanisms for excluding actions and objects from the category of "speech"; the way the line between speech and conduct is drawn, however, has changed, as have the normative rationales and commitments underpinning the distinction.[14] The policing of the boundary of speech and action in the early twentieth century had been about defining the subjects of law as rational and civilized persons. The terms of disembodiment were about a liberal conception of legal subjects, in which speech represented interior workings of individual, autonomous minds: ideas, beliefs, and reasoned judgments. Such mental work was the site of freedom. By the late twentieth century, in *Corley*, the policing of the boundary of speech has shifted to identifying human agents as sites of agency and will, in the face of computer automation. However, the agency and mental work, if not minds, at issue were not described in terms of intent, ideas, sentiments, or beliefs, characteristics central to liberal humanist understandings of subjectivity. In *Corley*, a different character of subjectivity was associated with speech.

The Language of Computer Code / Computer Code as Language

In *Corley*, we can see a disembodiment, or dematerialization, of speech and expressive conduct. One important place where this happened was in the focus on programs as a form of writing. In an influential amicus brief, a group of computer scientists led by David Touretzky argued that code was expressive (protected speech) because it was like any other form of writing. "At root, computer code is nothing more than text, which, like any other text, is a form of speech. The Court may not know the meaning of the Visual BASIC or Perl texts ... but the Court can recognize that the code is text."[15] The argument that code was "speech" because it was a form of text (written or printed media) highlighted the fact that speaking and printing have merged in legal discussions of "speech."[16] It also had a strong impact on the judges. The district court judge (Judge Kaplan) who first heard the case reportedly went in to the case thinking that code was "no more expressive than an automobile ignition key."[17] (In this, he followed the State Department, which had classified decryption programs as objects: "munitions" subject to restrictions on export and publication.[18]) The testimony of Touretzky and others changed this stance, to the extent that in his decision Kaplan stated that "[t]he path from idea to human language to source code to object code is a continuum. As one moves from one to the other, the levels of precision and, arguably, abstraction increase, as does the level of training necessary to discern the idea from the expression."[19]

The equivalence asserted between media was central to the lower courts' understanding of code as expressive. On appeal, Judge Newman echoed Kaplan's equation of code, text, and speech, beginning his discussion of the First Amendment issues in the case with the following:

> Communication does not lose constitutional protection as "speech" simply because it is expressed in the language of computer code. Mathematical formulae and musical scores are written in "code," i.e., symbolic

notations not comprehensible to the uninitiated, and yet both are covered by the First Amendment. If someone chose to write a novel entirely in computer object code by using strings of 1's and 0's for each letter of each word, the resulting work would be no different for constitutional purposes than if it had been written in English. The object code version would be incomprehensible to readers outside the programming community (and tedious to read even for most within the community), but it would be no more incomprehensible than a work written in Sanskrit for those unversed in that language.[20]

As in the brief cited above, code was equivalent as a medium to English or Sanskrit, or math, or music. Computer code and natural languages were simply different ways of representing ideas; the same message could in theory be encoded in and conveyed by any. (This equivalence works best if you are focused on transcoding different characters or words, but not as well if you are attempting to convey or conserve nuances of meaning, tone, or effect, as any translator can attest.)

Positing an equivalence between mathematical equations, musical notation, computer code, and the English language, however, elides important functional distinctions. It also elides the different normative grounds for protecting the different types of expression brought together in this argument. Novels are not protected because they are written in words. (Many things written in words, like contracts, instructions on products, or the exchange of information about prices among competitors, are considered irrelevant to the First Amendment.[21]) Rather, novels and poetry are protected because they convey ideas and sentiments of political and social value and because they express the ideas of their authors. Likewise, mathematical formulae are protected not because they can be analogized to language, but rather because they further knowledge production. Music is a trickier example; musical scores are covered out of a vague sense of the aesthetic and cultural value of the music they represent.[22]

Touretzky and the judges emphasized both code's ability to convey messages and its textuality. (For the judges, computer code seemed to exist primarily on screens.) Yet, as a number of scholars have pointed out, computer code has a double life, as saying and doing, text and instrument.[23] Touretzky and the other computer scientists asserted it was illogical to draw a distinction between a computer program hosted on a computer or printed on a T-shirt, or between these examples and a description of the program in English, a spoken-word poem, or print publication of the program. Yet it is not clear that this is so. There are meaningful differences between a program on a computer and one printed on a T-shirt, or between one on a piece of paper and stored on a computer as an executable file. This is not only because of the way meaning depends on context but also because of differences among media.

Code, as a system of representation, can be used to do a number of things. Code can be used to display words or images on a screen or print them on a piece of paper. It can store images, poetry, and more in computer memory. It can also be used to calculate, to operate complex machinery (like your car), to crawl and index websites, or to creep into and hijack or corrupt other computers. In the latter examples, programs operate as instruments, used to accomplish tasks. This duality, in which code is both representational and functional, makes code interesting for media theorists as much as legal scholars. Yet the ability of code, or a program, to do these things is determined not only by the choices of programmers but also by the machines on which it runs, complicating the dynamics of address. In comparison to the DeCSS haiku, or the novel written in 1s and 0s, the legibility of the program is less determined by other people. The hardware and operating system of the computer it runs on are integral to the program's legibility and usability.[24] A program written for one operating system may not run on another; a program with a bug might likewise be illegible and inert. (Such a failed/illegible program would be readable text to other programmers, but would not be recognizable or operable by the machine.[25]) The English description of the DeCSS program and the program itself may represent the same idea in a logical sense, but they function and communicate quite differently in practice. As was the case with Shannon's general theory of communication, the equivalence depends on a high level of abstraction: bracketing the medium as well as the social uses, meanings, and value of the communication.

The judges deciding the DeCSS case did not ignore the nontextual, functional aspects of code. Rather, they grappled with them, trying to parse programs within the speech/action distinctions of speech law. In discussing what computer programs expressed and how, Judge Newman noted that programs were a set of instructions, like recipes or blueprints. The level of protection granted to such instructions, he argued, varies: the First Amendment protects recipes and instructions on how to engage in dangerous sex acts, but not instructions on how to violate tax laws or build an explosive device.[26] Yet he also noted there was an important difference between these examples (precedents) and the case at hand. Blueprints and recipes are instructions to other human beings, who must then make the independent decision to actually undertake the tasks and even make judgments about how to carry them out, which, as actions, may be subject to rules and constraints. In computer programs, the instructions are to machines. And machines do not have minds. Programs might require a click of the mouse from a person, but this "momentary intercession of human action" was, according to Newman, not a significant enough decision to shift the locus of regulation from publishing a program to running it.[27] (The question of whether the click of a button is an indicator of human will or is more like a "mechanical" action has recurred in cases involving Facebook likes and other forms of computer communication.[28]) That someone must click a button did not change the idea that computer programs were not simple (inert) instructions but also a form of incipient action: blueprint and assembly, all rolled into one.

How the First Amendment would apply to DeCSS hung on this executability, or excitability—the ability of symbols to flip into action at any time. Because the distance between text and action was so attenuated, simply publishing the program was tantamount to running it.[29] And regulation of the functional aspects of the program could be justified. In the case of DeCSS, which could be used to perform an illegal action (copying), the judges decided that this regulation did not violate freedom of speech. Per Judge Kaplan in the first ruling, the expressive element of code did not "immunize" it from regulation any more "than the expressive motives of an assassin immunize the assassin's action."[30]

The way the decision distinguished programs as text and action might at first glance seem to be a return to jurisprudence centered on traditional speakers, what I have called a liberal humanist approach to speech. The reasoning did argue that speech was the product of individual human agents. Yet the tone and capacity of the communication at stake in the decision is different from that which characterized earlier descriptions of speech and speakers. In particular, the type of thought and qualities of mind referenced are distinct. To see what I mean, consider the way the decision described communication and reading. Programs were expressive because they carried information—a carriage that was described in terms reminiscent of the engineering discourse analyzed in chapter 4: "The fact that a program has the capacity to direct the functioning of a computer does not mean that it lacks the additional capacity to convey information, and it is the conveying of information that renders instructions 'speech' for purposes of the First Amendment."[31] Programs might "tell" the computer how to perform a task. They can also, the decision argued, tell other programmers how to efficiently write a program, just as mathematicians might learn to do math by reading the equations of others. In this description, the expressivity of programs diverges from more classically liberal free speech theory, in that it was not centered on the intent, beliefs, or ideas of the speaker/writer. In the logic of the decision, the reader does not get from the program the idea or message intended by its programmer creator(s), but rather a secondary, perhaps inadvertent, message about the craft of programming. This is not the same type of reading or communication discussed in the normative theories of free speech or in early to mid-twentieth-century legal cases. It is not communication as a transfer from mind to mind, or as a psychologically inflected work of interpretation, or even an attempt to follow a set of instructions. Rather, it is reading as a form of reverse engineering.

To be clear, this was not the understanding of code as text and programming as writing forwarded by Corley or his supporters. Their comparisons of code to writing defined programming as an act of classical authorship in the liberal humanist tradition, endorsing a view of programming as a site of mastery in which symbols make the machine run. Eric Corley, aka Emmanuel Goldstein, had argued that posting the DeCSS program was an act of political protest, and that the studios' actions and the DMCA were illegitimate usurpations of fair use and the commons. His supporters had re-posted the program, printed it on T-shirts, performed it as spoken-word poetry, and translated it into music and visual art projects as political theater. They expressed a shared vision of programming as a creative and potentially political act.[32] Programs were, in their arguments and advocacy, an extension of the vision and agency of individual programmers.

In contrast, the judges' description of the textuality of programs did not recognize the artistic or political implications asserted by the programmers. Rather, it offered a vision of programs as texts that are only ever read for grammar or form. As a form of writing, this is one shorn of associations with traditional conceptions of interpretation and authorship. It is, I would argue, a vision of writing filtered through the precedents and legal logic around speech as information—and their implications. Unlike the cases examined in chapter 4, the judges in this case said that there must be persons behind the speech; however, these persons do not exhibit many of the hallmarks of subjectivity—belief, sentiment, even thoughts or ideas— associated with earlier (humanist) articulations of personhood. Rather, they offer a different vision of personhood and perhaps mind: one more centered on procedure, calculation, or accounting—a set of activities that had been deemed inexpressive, lacking the investment of passion or conscience of advocacy and other forms of pure speech in earlier decades of legal discourse. In fact, the normative rationale and precedent for the case did not rest on the liberty or autonomy of the programmers, or their conscience or belief. Rather, as Judge Newman noted, speech need not show conviction or even convey an idea (citing *Virginia State Board of Pharmacy v. Virginia Citizens Consumer Council* [1976] as precedent). If even the dull and "dry" economic proposition to sell X drug at Y price constituted speech, why not this vision of technical communication?[33]

I do not mean to invoke nostalgia for the earlier definition of speech—and subjectivity. It had, as discussed in chapter 1, its own set of exclusionary consequences. Rather, I want to draw attention to the shift in how expressivity, subjectivity, and personhood are being articulated in these cases—and its implications. In this particular case, the subjectivity associated with speech as information worked to depoliticized the free speech claim made by the publishers of DeCSS. By defining code as communication among programmers—rather than communication by programmers to a broader public—and by excluding the functionality of code (what the program "tells" the machine to do) from their evaluation, the judges limited what can be said via code. Defining code as writing on the screen, the judges saw programmers reading each other's work like mathematicians, learning from each other about how to more efficiently and effectively program computers—a process the judges imagined as dry, technical expression (a characterization that I imagine many programmers and mathematicians would take issue with). They did not leave room for artistry, or using programs to create experiences or interfaces. Nor did they see the advocate, passionately attempting to intervene in politics and policy and public opinion (how Corley appeared to see himself).[34] Far less is at stake in the communication the decision attributes to programming.

The decision also evaded one of the more interesting implications of the claim that programs were speech. That is, whether the functionality of a program might in some cases be expressive. *Corley* classified programs as expression and conduct, but it did so in a way that divorced expression from function. The case had raised the question of whether programs might be a form of expressive action: that the action of the machine, like giving the finger or burning a flag, might convey a message. In doing so, it raised the question of whether the action of the computer might substitute for the body as a site of expression. After all, the expressiveness—in the usual sense of the term—of programs like Resistbot (which partially automates users' communications to their representatives) or computer-generated music and art lies not in the lines of code that make the machine run, but in the uses or interactions of the program in the social world of users.[35] In terms borrowed from the cases dealing with film analyzed in chapter 1, such meaning-making is the mental activity of users.

The focus on programs as writing, and the illegibility of the expressivity of their functionality is, I argue, rooted in the discursive configuration of communication as an ephemeral transfer of information (or signals) based in telecommunications and computation, discussed in the previous chapter. This way of thinking and talking of speech in many ways replaced more embodied notions of rhetoric and persuasion, in which the presence (or absence) of a physical speaker had been so important. In the new discourse, such concerns took a backseat to information, often understood as "pure" idea. The implications of this shift are particularly pointed in the trajectory of the legal category of expressive conduct from the 1940s to the 1970s. In the initial cases involving flag salutes and strikes, actions and meanings were tightly bound.[36] By the 1970s, expressive conduct could be abstracted from the body, with actions like saluting a flag and burning a draft card disarticulated from the message they conveyed.

The Disembodiment of Expressive Conduct

In many ways, the logic of the *Corley* decision drew on that of an earlier, precedent-setting case, *United States v. O'Brien* (1968), in which the justices pushed back against the inclusion of more forms of conduct within the purview of the First Amendment. They did so by talking not of inherently expressive conduct but rather of "speech plus," in which the expression and the action could be easily distinguished—and the action subject to limitation. *Corley* drew on *O'Brien* as the basis for thinking about how to distinguish the speech and nonspeech elements in computer programs. The *O'Brien* decision, in which the justices decided that a law banning the burning of draft cards was not aimed at suppressing speech, outlined a new way of approaching embodied symbolic speech in which messages were not only stripped of context but also unmoored from their material basis and expression in embodied action. This dematerialization of expressive conduct was echoed in the *Corley* decision.

O'Brien was about the constitutionality of a law enacted in 1965 to criminalize burning—or other means of mutilating or destroying—draft cards, the public spectacle of which was at the time becoming a symbol of op-

Figure 5.1 David O'Brien burning his draft card in front of a Boston courthouse in 1966. Source: Bettmann.

position to the Vietnam War. It was, many argued, an attempt to quash a particular form of dissent.[37] Not long after the law was passed, a young Catholic pacifist, David Miller, climbed on top of a sound truck—a prior generation's site of First Amendment struggle—at an antiwar protest and burned his draft card in front of a crowd.[38] He was arrested and sentenced to two years in jail under the new law. Others followed suit in protest of the war and in defiance of the new law. Among them was David O'Brien, who in 1966 burned his draft card in front of a crowd on the steps of a South Boston courthouse (see figure 5.1). The tactic of draft-card burning, it should be noted, had to do with both its symbolic resonances and its use as an instrument of surveillance and coercive induction into the army.[39] Like the computer punch card IDs vilified by college students in the free speech movement as symbols of the machine, draft cards represented a large bureaucratic "machine" and rationalization run amok; the 1965 law's directive not to "fold, spindle or mutilate" the punch card IDs seemed to provide a piece of paper with more protection than the bodies of the young people both fighting and protesting the war.[40] These connotations of the draft card as an instrument of an increasingly inhumane machine were an important part of the performative and interpretive context of draft-card burning. O'Brien pointed out that he had not burned his card to evade the draft. He did not seek to evade the law but to confront it, burning the card before a crowd on the steps of the South Boston courthouse. Burning his draft card, he argued, was not an act of evasion but of expression: a public, political statement, a visceral criticism of US policy. As such, it was an example of not only expressive conduct but also the sort of political speech at the heart of free speech law.[41]

The Court, in a 7–1 opinion, disagreed. The majority decision, written by the famously liberal Justice Earl Warren, argued that the law was not a restriction of O'Brien's speech but rather a legitimate regulation of his conduct; the law prohibiting draft-card burning, he argued, was not directed at draft-card burning as an expressive activity but rather at protecting government property and vital administrative procedures, especially in a time of war.[42] The law did not touch on the message, only the manner of its delivery. Foreshadowing the consideration of computer code in *Corley*, the status of the draft card as both symbol (or text) and instrument was an important consideration in the case, as Lisa Gitelman has pointed out. For O'Brien, the card was a symbol of the inhumanity of the war machine, and its destruction was a political act of critique of both an unjust war and an illegitimate law. For the Court, the card was an instrument of bureaucracy, and its destruction a material impediment to the workings of government.[43] Faced with this duality, the Court created a test to separate text from instrument, speech from action, message from medium—the *O'Brien* test. Under the test, if a regulation was understood to be aimed at the action involved in expressive conduct, it would receive a lower level of scrutiny than if it was understood to be aimed at suppressing the message.

I want to highlight that this move, the creation of the *O'Brien* test to separate message from action, came at a moment when radical political action was increasingly taking on an embodied form. Given this context, the decision and the test operated as a means of preserving the ability of the state to regulate such conduct. *O'Brien* was decided in 1969, at the end of a decade in which members of the civil rights, antiwar, and free speech movements had increasingly engaged in physical and dramatic forms of political expression and protest: in particular, Black bodies occupied segregated spaces as a performative critique and provocation of local laws that had designated some spaces off-limits to Black people. Further, bodies amassed in protest in antiwar demonstrations and marches on the capitol and in riots in cities across the nation. (It was in this context that Martin Luther King Jr. said that riots were "the language of the unheard."[44]) Putting one's body on the line was both a form of mass action and a symbolic move, trafficking in the visual imagery and drama necessary to gain access to media outlets and to shape public opinion.[45]

The idea that all these actions, and more, might be forms of speech protected by the First Amendment gained ground in the 1960s. It was also profoundly unsettling to many legal practitioners and theorists. In a context in which more and more forms of conduct were legible as communication, thanks in part to the formalized study and popular discussion of nonverbal communication and the application of the idea of communication to more and more realms of inquiry, from biology to economics, then where to draw the line?[46] As Justice Warren put it in his majority decision for *O'Brien*, the situation threatened to make an "apparently limitless variety of conduct ... 'speech' whenever the person engaging in the conduct intends thereby to express an idea."[47] This was a threat not just to First Amendment law but also to a broader segment of law. If lawyers and defendants could—as seemed possible at the time—argue that actions from rioting to vandalism were speech, and thus protected from regulation and restraint, large areas of criminal law would unravel.[48] The *O'Brien* decision was a way of putting the genie back in the bottle, resolving the legal crisis (and perhaps moral panic) caused by the recognition of embodied communication in cases involving symbolic gestures, or "expressive conduct."

O'Brien shifted the framework for approaching gestural or embodied communication in First Amendment law away from gestures that speak toward separating out messages, or signals, from the embodied actions that convey, or carry, them. In examples like saluting the flag, wearing an armband, and sitting or standing in silent protest, the Court recognized expression that inhered in physical acts.[49] There was no separating message from medium in such examples. In *O'Brien*, in contrast, the Court approached burning the draft card as speech plus action, in which the message (criticism of the draft) was distinct and could be disarticulated from the action (burning the draft card). This approach allowed the Court to argue that regulating draft-card burning was not censorship because it was targeted only at the action.[50] The Court argued that protestors like David O'Brien were free to convey their message—criticism of the draft—in editorials, speeches, songs, or a variety of other forms. Of course, this argument could have been made in any of the earlier symbolic speech cases; in fact, it was Felix Frankfurter's argument in his impassioned dissent in the flag salute case analyzed in chapter 2. The decisions in the 1940s had opened the door to the inclusion of inchoate symbols and gestures, akin to what Justice William Rehnquist later called "inarticulate grunts or roars" that did not so much express an idea as provoke or react.[51] *O'Brien* narrowed the scope of symbolic speech, limiting such speech to acts that could be rendered as a linguistic message. Unlike arm waving and bodily occupation of spaces, which may or may not be expressive, everyone could agree words were messages, without the need to demonstrate the intent of a sender or the interpretation of an audience.

I want to suggest the computer code presented a similar challenge to the law in the 1990s as did expressive conduct in the 1960s. As more and more activities took place on and through computers, computer code was already becoming the substrate for much of social life in the 1990s. Claims that code was speech not only took aim at the creep of copyright law but also threatened to undermine many other areas of regulation. The decision in *Corley*, and the logic behind the decision, in which the expressive aspects of code were carefully disarticulated from function, then, followed the logic of *O'Brien*. Where *O'Brien* had preserved the ability of the state to regulate embodied forms of protest, *Corley* preserved the ability of the state to regulate activities that took place on or via computers. Disarticulating messages from function in *Corley* allowed Judge Newman to argue that orders to take down the DeCSS program did not interfere with Corley's ability to critique the DMCA.[52] (Corley's political message, the judges suggested, existed solely in the commentary surrounding the program, as a sort of paratext.[53]) As in *O'Brien*, this parsing of message and function served to contain the potential of free speech arguments to undermine other areas of law (whereas in 1969 the area of concern was criminal law, in 2001 it was intellectual property law).

There are valid reasons to limit the creep of free speech claims (e.g., the use of free speech to undermine economic regulations, the need to protect the flow of traffic as well as the right to speak in demonstrations). However, in *Corley*, the political and legal complexities and values involved in this determination were underplayed via a focus on seemingly simple, technical definitions. As in *O'Brien*, where the details of the draft-card burning and the local meaning of the event had been overlooked in favor of discussion of the nature of the draft card and the separation of message from action, in *Corley*, the particulars of the case—those details that might distinguish expressive conduct from other forms of conduct not considered expressive—faded from view. The lawyers for *Corley* were not arguing that all programs, or even all decryption programs, were speech (though Corley and others in the free software movement most likely would have endorsed this argument). Rather, they were suggesting that this particular instance, in the context of the magazine *2600* and Corley's overall advocacy, was—like O'Brien's decision to burn his draft card on the steps of the South Boston courthouse in front of police and an angry crowd—an act of protest. The judges likely would have rejected the claim that the DeCSS program was expressive in its functionality and that limiting its circulation was a suppression of political speech or protest, but they would have had to supply reasons in order to do so.

In this way, a seemingly neutral act of categorization took the place of deliberation of more moral and political issues. Was Eric Corley engaging in a political protest? Was this an act that ought to be protected for its value to democratic self-governance, autonomy and liberty, or for its promotion of a diversity of ideas and discussion? Or was he merely engaging in digital disruption (or trespassing)? The question of when, if ever, the use of computers to accomplish tasks is expressive was decided by the technical parsing of computer programs devoid of social context (as if expressivity resided solely in the medium, divorced from context and use).[54] The result was a decision that was both too broad (suggesting the First Amendment may be involved in every regulation of computer programs) and too narrow (the functionality of a program is always subject to regulation).[55] In its overbreadth, the decision contributed to the First Amendment expansionism in which free speech operates as a tool to evade economic regulation and to shore up property rights. In its narrowness, it foreclosed an avenue through which individuals might engage in creative or political protest, arguably narrowing the usefulness of the First Amendment for computerized protest.

Moreover, the illegibility of the idea that computer action might be expressive (an extension of the ideas of the programmer) illustrates how the legal category of speech has become disembodied or dematerialized. The idea that some programs might be a form of advocacy or proselytizing or expressive conduct *in their functionality* harkened back to sets of arguments in the 1930s and 1940s around union organizing, flags, and sound trucks. In these cases, the Supreme Court recognized new formats of communication and, in some cases, recognized a wide range of possible meanings and interpretations. This symbolic complexity was replaced in both *O'Brien* and *Corley* by an understanding in which meaning and interpretation were less central, and expressivity was defined in terms of whether or not information was conveyed to an audience. This follows on the abstraction of speech discussed in the last chapter: the separation of message from medium, signal from carrier wave. Both cases relied on a rationale of dematerialization, in which speech is conceptualized less as a social activity and more as ephemeral information. This is an ideology premised on the experience of technologies of communication in which ideas or data seem to flow seamlessly from one machine to another—through clouds and air. But it is also based on a strategic forgetting of human social contexts and hardware infrastructures.

Information does not flow on its own. Information must be collected and ordered, data must be processed, words must be typed and formatted, encoded as bits, packaged and sent, reassembled and organized as letters on the screen or page. All that work behind the scenes is accomplished by agents we often fail to recognize: stenographers, typists, and assistants and increasingly algorithms and computer processes (the latter originally was, of course, the work of female computers who wired and rewired the original large computers, before computer programming became a job of symbol manipulation and status). There are a host of intermediaries whom we have tended to overlook as neutral conduits for the speech, decisions, and ideas of others: scriveners, clerks, typists, stenographers. At the turn of the twentieth century, these invisible assistants were often gendered female: from telephone operators to secretaries and human computers. More recently, these invisible human intermediaries have been replaced by algorithms, software, and computers themselves—all are treated as inert conduits for, or mechanical execution of, commands that come from elsewhere. As feminist scholars remind us, this execution is not necessarily simple; even typewriters and machines leave their mark, human stenographers and transcribers more so. They leave the mark of not only their embodied labor of inscription and transmission but also the different marks of interpretation, inflection, and format.[56]

This is what happens to a legal category built around bodies and gestures when filtered through the conception of speech as information. Not only can performativity and communicative surpluses be stripped out of legal considerations of speech, but the subjectivity involved in speech takes on a different cast—and the interests and potential rights claims of other subjects can be overlooked. Whatever the actual experience of programming is (many would describe it as rich and expressive, even artistic), the legal cases analyzed here describe the mental work of programmers in terms of efficient transfers and reverse engineering. This mental work akin to that once derided by Justice William O. Douglas as the quiet "tabulations of the statistician or economist," a pale and insufficient shadow of impassioned political and social speech.[57] In *Corley*, such tabulations form the mental work, or subjectivity, behind speech.

Further, the type of narrow technical argumentation in which the justices focus on the nature of the tool (ontology) to the exclusion of social uses and context has a tendency to evade issues of power. We see this in *Corley*, where the political use of a technology recedes in favor of analysis of its nature. This shows up as well in a different set of cases, involving algorithmic outputs. In these cases, the judges have defined the products of algorithms as the speech of their creators. In their discussions of algorithmic outputs as the expression of their creators pure and simple, judges have followed a similar logic of abstraction and demediation, overlooking the role played by both hardware and other speakers, in the distributed expression and judgments of other users that power many such outputs. This oversight both mis-characterizes the expressive agency of programmers in complex algorithmic systems and denies the agency and interests of users.

Algorithmic Outputs as Editorial Judgments

The output of the program in *Corley* (the decryption of a DVD) was not necessarily or intuitively expressive. In other examples of computerized communication, the output of programs is more intuitively expressive—the creation of a message, or the curation of the speech of others. Such is the case of search engines. In search engine results, the action of computers is both to make the words and images of others (third-party content creators) available to users and to organize these words and ideas. The websites assembled by search engines—the words and images of others—are generally accepted as the speech of their creators. But the assembly of these sites into ranked search results is a trickier issue. Are such results, which assemble the websites of third parties and rank them for predicted relevance, speech?

In a set of legal cases, search engines (companies like Google) have argued that their search results reflect corporate opinions about what websites are most relevant to user queries. In deciding these cases, the lower courts have so far defined algorithmic outputs as the embodiment of the judgments and values of their creators: software engineers and/or the companies they work for (e.g., Google). This creates a stark contrast with the logic in *Corley*. In that case, the judges declined to see the output of the program as the extension of the individual programmers' speech, political or otherwise. In the algorithm cases, on the other hand, the courts have argued that the outputs of the programs that perform searches, which also happen to be the products of companies like Google, are speech.

By analyzing these cases together, I mean to highlight the political commitments of the courts. The romance and ideology of free speech still center on the law protecting the lone dissenter, but increasingly the application of the First Amendment has not been to such individuals but rather to corporations and other institutional actors (to the judges making the decisions, no doubt, the most trustworthy actors). While the claims of Corley, aka Emmanuel Goldstein, that posting or linking to the DeCSS program was a political statement were not recognized, the claims of Google and other search engine companies that their products were speech protected by the First Amendment were recognized.

In pulling these cases together, however, I also want to show something more about the anxieties about automation and human agency and personhood that haunt discussions and legal decisions about how the First Amendment applies to computer communication. Despite the different legal outcomes for programmers and search engines in *Corley* and the search engine cases, they all demonstrate an anxiety about automation and an interest in recentering speech in liberal speaking subjects. Yet the gap between the legal rhetoric and the empirical phenomena at issue in the algorithm cases exposes the difficulty of such a recentering: the speakers' "authoring" algorithms are just one link in a broader assemblage of machinic processes and human judgments that go into producing search results. Empirically, I argue, the agency of such speech is qualitatively and quantitatively different from that attributed to speaking subjects in early twentieth-century speech law (and the regulatory paradigm that continues to be applied to print communication).

Before I go into the cases, let me briefly elaborate on the terminology involved. Search engines refer not to technologies but to companies like Google that create proprietary (and secret) algorithms to define the process of responding to a search query and ranking results.[58] While we often talk about search engines as technologies, conflating corporations with their products, we also often reduce the process of a search to a set of algorithms. However, processing a search involves more than just algorithms. It involves parsing a user query, collecting and indexing a sample of the web, determining which sites from this sample best fulfill the query, then ranking them according to metrics of "relevance."[59] So, while we often think a query on Google searches the entire web for the best answers, in reality Google searches an index that represents Google's take on legitimate websites (ones that are not junk, or spam—each search engine has a set of metrics it uses in its crawlers to separate the junk from the legitimate websites).[60] The engine searches this index for sites that match the search terms. At least some of the variation in the results among search engines comes from indexing—in particular, from differences among the metrics used to delineate legitimate content from "spam"—and query parsing techniques. The processes of collection and indexing may involve algorithms, but these are not usually what we refer to when we discuss the algorithms of search engine results. Rather, we usually are referring to the algorithms used to determine and rank the most relevant (top) results for a given search query. These algorithms, which involve proprietary proxies for quality, calculations of relevance, and so forth—and so involve a number of value judgments about reliability, usefulness, and legitimacy—are the ones at the heart of legal cases determining whether search engine results are speech.

In cases like *Search King v. Google* (2003), *Langdon v. Google* (2007), and *Zhang v. Baidu* (2014), lower courts have determined that search engine results are speech (the speech of the companies that operate the searches) but not because judges have made their peace with the idea that messages from computers to humans are speech. Nor have judges dodged the whole problem of human versus machine speech by simply determining that the outputs of the search engines on the screen are messages, regardless of origin. (As chapter 4 shows, judges do not need to locate human speakers in order to grant protection; they could have argued that search results were speech because they were messages or information.) They could also have argued that search engine results are protected because of the rights of users, or the public's interest in access to information.[61] Instead, judges and lawyers for search engine companies have worked hard to articulate search results as the speech product of specific subjects: search engine companies and their employees. As in *Corley*, in order to justify the status of algorithmically produced search results as speech, judges and lawyers have worked to define programmers as speakers and focused their discussion of expression on those speakers (to the exclusion of listeners, or the public). This has been a winning line of argumentation. In the case law to date, search algorithms have been defined as a simple extension of human judgments about content, often as a form of editorial decision.

To make this comparison and define search results as the speech of the companies who own and operate them, jurists have arguably inflated, or simply misconstrued, the work of individual human authors, seeing simple linear paths of agency and judgment in places where agency and judgment are not lacking but are either attenuated or complicated. As in *Corley*, the judges ground their decisions and reasoning in the agency and ideas of the persons behind the code. Yet the subjectivity associated with computerized expression is different in many of these cases. Whereas in *Corley* the judges downplayed traditional humanistic markers of subjectivity, suggesting that coding need not express ideas to be expression, in the cases involving search engine algorithms, the judges argue that the outputs of such algorithms reflect the ideas, values, and judgments of their designers. In this way, the judges based their decisions both on a liberal humanist vision of speakers and arguably on an idea of speaking or publicity grounded in print media. An analysis of these cases shows, however, that this liberal vision does not fit the expression at issue. It is not that there is no expression involved in these cases, but rather that it is qualitatively different, involving different agents, relationships, and responsibilities than the liberal model of speech and print publicity.

Authors and Algorithms

The *Search King* case involved a company that brokered ads for clients on websites that were highly ranked in Google searches and was thus competing with Google's own main revenue stream (selling ads). Google tweaked its ranking system so that Search King's clients' web pages were no longer highly ranked; Search King argued that Google was attempting to undermine competition and steal Search King's clients and so it sued Google for interfering with its contractual relations. Google responded that its search results were essentially company opinions and thus speech, protected by the First Amendment. In *Langdon,* a man who created and operated a variety of websites alleging local government corruption and human rights abuses in China accused Google and Microsoft of being duplicitous both in their refusal to run ads for his site and in general in their representation of their services. Google and Microsoft argued that the decision of which ads to run—whose business to accept—was part of their editorial prerogative under the First Amendment.[62] In *Zhang,* several US-based advocates of democracy in China alleged that Baidu, China's largest search engine (globally, Baidu was the third largest search engine at the time), was blocking pro-democracy content (theirs included) in US-based web searches. This blockage, they argued, was a form of conduct that violated their civil rights, essentially asking the court to see the work of search engines in terms of functionality.[63] The judge did not, arguing instead that Baidu was like a newspaper and that the company's decision to block some content for ideological reasons was the proof that search engines were not mere platforms or conduits (mute infrastructure) or tools (conduct) but rather mediums for judgment and ideology. Thus, Baidu had the First Amendment right to decide whose speech to carry, which viewpoints to endorse, and which to suppress. To decide otherwise, the judge declared, would be undemocratic, "[contravening] the principle upon which 'our political system and cultural life rest: that each person should decide for himself or herself the ideas or beliefs deserving of expression, consideration, and adherence.'"[64]

In these cases, then, the lower courts have ruled that the outputs of search algorithms are speech, that this speech is that of the search engines (Google, Baidu), which have full First Amendment rights (not to be balanced or shared with content creators or users). As the description of *Zhang* above might suggest, analogies have played a particularly important role in this argumentation, in particular the analogization of search engines to newspapers. This analogy is important because it carries with it precedents, in particular the precedent of *Miami v. Tornillo* (1974), in which the Supreme Court decided that for newspapers, the publisher was the only speaker who could make rights claims, and the public had no rights of access or reply; that is, newspapers could refuse to carry opinions (or events and issues) they did not like. Any regulation, including that intended to increase the amount or diversity of information available to the public, violated the First Amendment.[65] Lawyers for the search engine companies have been eager to secure the analogy to newspapers because it brings with it a host of protections from governmental regulation as well as protections from legal claims by website creators or users (though the Court in the 1940s did make clear that this protection did not extend to labor and antitrust law). In contrast, the public and content creators have some speech rights in broadcast and cable. Broadcasters, under the now defunct fairness doctrine, once were required to present more than one side of any controversial public issue in order to serve the public right to receive information.[66] (This was, as I note in chapter 3, in part due to anxieties over broadcasters' status and power as speakers, and in part due to the use of the airwaves as a public resource.) Cable operators have been required to carry local broadcast television stations and have in general been treated both as speakers in their curatorial role of selecting which channels to carry and as conduits for the speech of others (program creators). The effort to analogize search engines to newspapers is thus a fight over which body of law and regulatory regime will apply to search engines. Some legal scholars have argued that cable operators are a better analogy; still others have argued that the work search engines do is more of a purely economic activity, like the curation and ordering involved in stocking the shelves of supermarkets.[67] Ultimately, the effort by company lawyers to compare search engines to newspapers is not an attempt to find the most apt comparison, but rather an attempt to secure the most advantageous regulatory regime.

The analogization of search engines to newspapers, though, carries with it a host of other implications about agency and algorithmic expression. The analogy casts the output of algorithms as equivalent to editorial decisions, arguing that search algorithms are an embodiment or amplification of judgments made by engineers or corporations. This was in fact a major line of argumentation in the influential white paper that Eugene Volokh and Donald Frank wrote for Google. In the Google-commissioned white paper, Volokh and Frank repeatedly emphasized that search engine outputs reflect a set of human judgments equivalent to those made by newspaper editors: they compared or equated search engine results with editorial or other substantive judgments twenty-eight times in the paper (fifteen of these instances are in the first fifteen pages, priming the reader for the argument and precedents offered). To make their case, they argued that the output of algorithms, like the content of newspapers, represents choices about what content to include and how important that content is. Like editorial decisions about what news goes on the first page and what on the last, search engines rank their results, suggesting some results are more valuable or relevant than others. The ranking is important because it distinguishes the search engine from a passive filter. Rather, results are the product of a deliberate set of subjective decisions.[68] Seen this way, Google's decisions about how to define and hone search algorithms are similar to the *New York Times'* judgment about what constitutes "all the news that's fit to print."

The newspaper analogy highlights the algorithm (rather than indexing or parsing the language of user queries, rather than the judgments of the dispersed actors that provide some of the metrics of relevance) as the site of distinction and judgment in search results.[69] It highlights decisions about inclusion and exclusion and ranking of importance as points of similarity between newspapers and search engines. Yet analogies like the newspaper one obscure differences as much as they highlight similarities.[70] The analogy of search engines to newspapers in particular obscures differences in the social roles and the relationship of the media outlet to the speech of others. More central to my argument, the analogy obscures differences in the very types of judgments and decisions made by editors of newspapers and the designers crafting and maintaining search algorithms, among other things.

The Subjects of Algorithmic Decision-Making

The types of judgments that go into producing and fine-tuning search engine results and those that go into producing news are in some ways quite different. Historically, editorial judgments have been judgments about the quality and usefulness of a particular topic or piece of information or opinion on that topic. They are guided by substantial expertise, credentials, and reputational costs of getting something wrong. The legitimacy of editorial judgment and its authority, importantly, are premised on accuracy and fairness (metrics of journalistic objectivity).[71] The decisions and judgments that go into creating and maintaining search algorithms, on the other hand, are more about process than substance (though they are equally guided by investment in particular ends: maintaining user engagement). Search algorithms are, of course, created by humans, and they reflect their judgments and biases, but these judgments are not about the character or quality of any specific information or content served up in a search. Rather, these judgments are about what procedures will produce the most useful results for users and the best proxies for value, relevance, and reliability—it is in this meta-level determination of the proper parameters of public discourse and authoritative results that the judgments involved in ranking search results and journalistic norms most overlap.[72]

This is a consequential difference in what the judgments are *about*. Famously, Google's PageRank algorithm does not just match search query terms to terms on websites, but rather it defines a set of parameters and processes for determining what results are the most relevant. While the specifics of Google's search engine are closely guarded trade secrets, we do know some things about the basic outlines of its ranking system. Firstly, and most distinctively, Google's original PageRank system relied on the number and types of links to a particular website in determining its relevance. Links from more trustworthy or established sites translated into a higher relevance rating. In this, Google drew on proxies (the judgments of a distributed set of others) to determine relevance and authority, borrowing from the established academic practice of measuring citations as a proxy for quality of ideas.[73] These decisions inscribe into the algorithm judgments about what constitutes a good proxy for authority and what is useful, not decisions about the best information or even about what particular topics to include or exclude.[74] Human judgments—those of engineers, contract workers, and user preferences—about the actual content of the search results are used to test the algorithm; these are then inscribed into it as "tweaks" or adjustments. They are, also, increasingly being replaced or supplemented by machine learning, which helps identify new patterns and metrics for defining useful ("quality") search results. The output of search results is thus a reflection of these judgments *about* process and relevance in general, not substantive judgments *about* specific content. (Interestingly, Google's judgments about the quality of the content of websites is arguably clearest in the creation of its index; yet indexing—in some ways akin to stenography, filing, and invisible secretarial work—as an activity and an organization of information is absent from the legal debates surrounding search engines.)

To be clear, this does not mean that there is no bias in search engine results, or that the outcomes of search results do not reflect the values of those who designed them. But this reflection is less like the substantive editorial decisions referenced by Google and its lawyers and more like the way that the built environment and other infrastructures embody values and ideas about social hierarchies and organizations. Langdon Winner's famous example of how the mechanical tomato harvester led to tomatoes optimized for harvesting more than eating shows how the values embedded in the design of technological artifacts can produce unintended consequences—and biases. The tomato harvester was crafted to improve efficiency and yield for tomato farmers, not in order to produce a less tasty tomato. Nonetheless, that the harvester produced a less tasty tomato reflects the values and priorities of those who built the machine (efficiency over enjoyment, exchange value over use value).[75] Likewise, many of the current biases of search engines may be more a reflection of priorities than of direct intentionality. For example, Google's decision to draw on citation ranking as a proxy for authority and quality imported and sedimented a set of mathematical models of social hierarchy and power developed in the midcentury as the criteria for assessing and ranking content on the web today.[76] Further, decisions about what sites and sources are proxies for quality are often embedded with subtle racial, sexual, national, and religious assumptions that, as scholars like Safiya Noble and Ruha Benjamin argue, reproduce and naturalize such assumptions (biases) as neutral or objective.[77] Similarly, decisions about how to test the search engines (what types of searches to perform in order to determine whether and how the algorithm needs to be tweaked) reflect these same biases. Yet, there may not be a single Google employee that explicitly endorses these values or intends to promote them. There is a gap between the specific values and intent of the designers of the algorithmic system and its working, or outputs. To say that search engine results do not reflect judgments of programmers *about* topics or speakers does not get the designers off the hook for the biases embedded in their judgments about process and metrics. But it does create problems for imposing a framework for analyzing free speech claims based in the processes and mental activities involved in running and publishing a newspaper (not to mention the different social roles and uses of each).

As in *Corley* (and earlier cases involving decryption), the judges in cases dealing with algorithms define speech as an intentional act by particular human agents. Yet, in doing so, the judges both overinvest the programmers with agency and intent and mischaracterize the types of judgments that are involved in the design of search algorithms. The chain of causality from the "tweaks" that programmers make in order to fine-tune search results is not simple; they cannot just write a few lines of code to create a predictable outcome. Tweaking the algorithm is more like adjusting levers on an experimental basis; other changes—like a preference for Wikipedia results—can be coded in. It is true that the algorithms involved in searches reflect both individual and corporate values and judgments. But these judgments differ in important ways from editorial ones. Editorial judgments are most directly about the value of the content and packaging of a news item, whether that value is informational or more crassly economic (e.g., clickbait). The judgments and values in algorithm design are more procedural, about how to deliver results, generally in the absence of substantive knowledge about the content of any of the websites served up.[78]

The conflation of these two types of judgments has consequences. It projects one type of decision making and rights and responsibilities with strong normative rationales for legal protection onto a sociologically and politically different one.[79] It asks us to see judgments about the process of finding relevant information with judgments about the import or value of particular information.[80] Further, the conflation of these two types of judgments asks us to see the outputs of search algorithms as the product of a set of individuals or a corporation. The outputs express the values and opinions of the corporate persona of the company. Yet search engines do not always position search results as an expression of corporate values, or even as their own speech.

In the past, when Google results have prioritized websites featuring racist, anti-Semitic, or medical misinformation, or its autocomplete feature suggested an anti-Semitic, racist, or misogynist query, Google argued that these results were not Google's speech at all. Rather, the company asserted, such results reflected the speech and ideas of others.[81] In these instances, the company argued that the algorithm operated as a barometer of public sentiment or opinion, and the engine was a platform or conduit for the speech of others. If it was a conduit for others' speech, Google was not legally liable for the results it served up.[82] This was immensely useful for the company, which essentially had it both ways: claiming its search results were its opinions in one set of cases, in order to gain protection against regulation, and claiming such results were the speech of third parties in a different arena, in order to disavow responsibility for misinformation and harm. It is easy to see the equivocation as evidence of bad faith, that Google was cynically using free speech claims both as a strategic business tool to deflect regulation and as a public relations ploy. That Google has been strategic—and cynical—in when and how it has positioned itself as a speaker is almost certainly true. Yet, at the same time, rather than brushing off Google's efforts to have it both ways as the crass opportunism it undoubtedly was, we might also inquire into how and why Google was able to make both claims.

I would suggest that this ability to make both claims is instructive for thinking about the character and origin of "speech" in search engine results: in other words, about what in search results is speech, and who the speakers are. Search algorithms historically have not embodied their creators' substantive judgments about content—what topics or information are important and which are not, what ideas have merit. They have relied instead on (among other things) judgments about content by third parties. By drawing on linking, and other indicators of third-party vetting, as a proxy for value and by drawing on user data to tweak their algorithms, companies like Google rely on judgments by other content creators and users.[83] (In the words of industry, the utterances and decisions of these content creators and users are "signals" that search engines can use to help refine search processes.[84]) In this light, Google's search results seem to be the products of algorithms created by Google employees, and a set of judgments of a distributed mass of others, including users and content creators who make judgments about the quality and/or usefulness of content.[85]

In this way, search results are not really the speech of Google or any one person. (Most of the existing legal analogies are not, in this way, a good fit.[86]) Search engine results, as speech, are chimeras. They are part product of procedural judgments, part judgments by search engines about what constitutes relevance and quality in search results in general, and part judgments about the quality of particular websites on the part of webmasters and others—the crowd and institutional actors (both governmental and corporate). While Google may put a democratic spin on it—that the results reflect the interests or opinions of the searching public—search parameters are notoriously ripe for gaming, or optimization by savvy users, often organized groups.[87] Like other examples of emergent automated speech, search results are a highly distributed form of speech not reducible to the intent or idea of any one person or group (or, some might argue, to people at all). Increasingly, search engines are relying on machine learning, programs that adapt and change semi-autonomously, so that their function cannot be simply reduced or equated to the intentions or judgments of their programmers. This distribution, it should be clear, is neither random nor democratic.

The complexities of agency and power (not to mention harm) in these examples are ones the courts are not well equipped to handle; neither the existing legal conceptions of speech nor those of rights adequately capture the dynamics outlined here. Judges and justices have attempted to reinsert speakers on the model of liberal subjects where the agency and intent implied by this model are not to be found. Search engine results express judgments and values in a far more complex ways than that envisioned in legal descriptions of editorial decision making—or conventional legal descriptions of "speech" in general.[88] If algorithmic outputs are speech, they not only are a different type of utterance from editorial decisions and statements of opinion but also suggest a different type of legal subject. They suggest a subject that is less liberal, less the owner of its own ideas, and more part of a larger social and technological assemblage.

Conclusion

Whereas, in cases of corporate speech, judges in the 1970s classified transmission of messages without clear (rights holding) speakers, in cases involving computer communication in the 1990s and beyond, judges have insisted on speech as the product of specific sets of individuals. In focusing so much of their analysis on whether communication involving computers is purely the product of human agents, they have attempted to create a one-size-fits-all legal status for communication that is varied and complex (often, protecting both too much and too little communication).

Both *Corley* and the algorithm cases work to define different sets of individuals (programmers, computer scientists, Google engineers, Baidu executives) as the agents behind particular messages. This framing has consequences. The judges in the decisions analyzed in this chapter did not arrive at their decisions through normative discussions of competing rights or the way that programs and search engines create or restrict opportunities for citizen speech, or how they structure access to ideas and opportunities to speak. Had the judges approached these cases by focusing on social uses and implications, the reasoning, if not the outcomes, would have been different. The appeals court would have had to discuss, and most likely offer, reasons for dismissing the political claims of Eric Corley. The courts adjudicating free speech claims for search engines might have had to consider the rights or interests of the people who create the web pages ranked in search results (a bit like the content creators for cable TV); it also would be harder for search engines to use free speech arguments to defend against charges of anticompetitive practices.

That the courts have followed the path they have in search engine results is partly due to the types of cases that have been brought: many have been legal actions over interference with contracts, fraud, and discrimination in which ads run. In these cases, neither side is invoking the needs of the audience (most of the cases have been bounded by private commercial and contractual relations).[89] But, I would submit, this path is also a reaction to computation and automation, and to attempts to place automated forms of communication—or potentially communicative functionality—within the traditional bounds of the law.

The highly abstracted model of communication, in which messages (like signals) are divorced from context and medium, has played a role in this reaction. The notion of pure information, or content, that is the same in any medium animates legal reasoning on code and algorithms as speech. When attempting to answer questions of coverage—is this speech?—the justices look for natural persons as producers. Positing clear and short lines of causality between programmers and code, or algorithmic outputs, they overlook the mediating role of hardware, computational processes, and resources (from compilers to indexes), and the crowd of users whose judgments are so integral to search results.[90]

In these decisions, we can see a set of anxieties, and perhaps an ambivalence, around speech and the status of speakers as subjects in complexly computer-mediated communication. On the one hand, decisions around algorithms have ascribed a traditional liberal subjectivity (with ties to both printing and romantic notions of authorship). Perhaps ironically or perhaps tellingly, this ascription underscores not the rights of the individual designers or programmers but, rather, the companies they work for (one kind of artificial person). On the other hand, in the case where programmers had sought to assert liberal speech rights (in the image of political dissenters, as Corley's alias so clearly telegraphed), judges recognized the expressive capacities of programs in general as a procedural and technical communication that they described as dull and (like simple sales propositions) largely devoid of ideas or politics, or the type of substance and subjectivity once at the core of free speech law.

Both sets of decisions, around computer programs and around algorithmic outputs, involve human intent and decisions as well as computer processes. In either reducing these processes to mute machinic action (seen as distinct from ideas) or making them simple extensions of the values and ideas of programmers, the judges and justices sidestep the big issues and questions at stake, which are about what it means to speak in these sociotechnical systems. These are questions about the sites and types of expressive agency enabled via computers, the internet, and platforms. They are as well questions about how meaning is constituted and relationships established and maintained in these sites. These big issues include the work of mediation: how new infrastructures and technologies of communication mediate and distribute access to information and opportunities to speak.

Conclusion

The Past and Future of Speech

The rising importance and ubiquity of computers in communication, economy, and infrastructure from the 1990s onward have produced something of a legal conundrum. If signals and messages circulating on their own are speech, and much of the economy and infrastructure runs on electronic signals and digital information, then many economic relations and infrastructural edifices are legible as speech. Logically, this would include the outputs of search engines, recommendation engines (e.g., Amazon, iTunes), and personal assistants like Alexa, Siri, Cortana, and Jibo (very literally, the disembodied speech of machines), as well as the messages of bots seeking to influence consumers or voters.[1] It's worth noting that many of these examples are commercial products of large companies: Apple, Amazon, Google. If the outputs of these companies' products are classified as speech, they cannot be regulated, for example, to counter the spread of misinformation, protect the privacy of users, or hold companies liable for the outputs or recommendations of their programs.[2] This is part of the contemporary terrain, in which freedom of speech is a powerful tool to counter economic regulation—and antidiscrimination laws—as much as it is a tool to protect and enhance civil liberties and democratic discussion.[3]

The history of the "speech" in free speech helps us understand how we got to this moment. It is not only a betrayal of political commitments or an investment in the interests of corporations and the economy over citizens but also a transformation in the category of speech itself. While the move toward using the First Amendment as a deregulatory tool is clearly political and motivated by an organized conservative judicial movement, the move is taking place via arguments about just what speech is as well as via arguments about freedom. Viewed through the lens of the shifting contours of speech, this move is not surprising. It is the outcome of an often untheorized and unremarked-upon change in the way judges and justices have conceptualized speech and determined the bounds of coverage—changes that have broader and more foundational implications than deregulation.

As I have argued, this is a problem that inheres in the formulation of US freedom of speech around a technologically and socially specific concept masquerading as an abstract ideal. The speech of free speech has never really been abstract. It has always had a technologically and culturally specific structure, informed by technologies and techniques of communication ranging from the printing press through film, radio, and computer code. The genealogy of this conceptualization of speech highlights the terrain on which battles over civil liberties and speech rights take place—and it draws attention to the historical variations in the topography of this terrain.

"Speech" has in the last hundred-odd years gone from a rather literal conception of public oration that existed alongside freedom to print to a more general category. In this more general category, speech and the press have largely lost their distinction. In addition, the category has come to include forms of speechless speech, like bodily gestures, symbols, and images; it includes not only the transmission of thoughts or ideas but also the emotional and aesthetic effects of communication. Or it can include transmissions that have little subjectivity at all, the publication of facts and figures, or "dry" information (e.g., the prices of medicines, technical communication, receipts)—a conception of speech that is arguably fitted to most benefit the institutional producers of information at scale.

The Structure of Speech

In the preceding chapters, I argued that speech as a legal category has always had a technologically and culturally specific structure. This structure has implications for what it means to be a speaker—which, in this context, also means a holder of rights. Communication technologies, as the material means of communication, often sediment particular sets of relations among speakers, messages/text, and audiences in hardware, protocols, and common practices. These different sets of relations constitute what we might call the structure of speech. These relations get written into the law, often as assumptions.

From *Mutual. v. Ohio* (1915) to *Zhang v. Baidu* (2014), the cases analyzed in this book show different expressive possibilities—new sites, forms, or formats of speech—realized or denied in the law. In the early twentieth century, the justices defended "speech" against mechanical reproduction and nonverbal communication (the conveyance of ideas and stories via gestures and bodily expressions). Mimesis and mere re-presentation did not count. Speech was defined as the original production or presentation of ideas. The speaker or author was central, as the source and owner of ideas and sentiments. Just as freedom of the press is said to belong to those who own one, freedom of speech in this moment belonged to those who could lay claims of ownership to their words. One of the things that divided speakers from animals and the primitive communication not covered by the law (the cries of angry mobs, the idioms associated with women, children, immigrants, and racialized others) was a type of mental activity. In order to be a speaker, one had to be able to claim to be ruled by mind (rather than passions or body) and cultivated sentiments and beliefs (rather than a mere channeling of stimuli).

This is a vision of the speaker that is at the heart of much liberal discourse on free speech. It is an autonomous speaker, the owner of his (or her, but mainly his) ideas and conscience. This subject owes much to American strains of liberal political theory but also to gender and racial ideology, to class and Eurocentrism.[4] It is my contention that it also owes much to the technologies and infrastructures of communication that shape legal discourse on speech. Liberal expression has been imagined through a Romantic view of the printing press and the political economy of printing—a vision that remains anchored in the nineteenth century—and the power of rhetoric as the ability of an autonomous speaker to sway his or her audience through appropriate word choice and inflection. In other words, this subject is an effect of a particular structure of speech, one organized around the dominant means of publicity of the late 1800s: oratory and the printing press.

We see the way technology shapes the law—the way what Jack Balkin and Reva Siegel call the "scene of regulation" was ordered around print—in the refusal of filmic communication as speech in chapter 1.[5] The projection of images on a screen was, according to the justices, an activity without a speaker or an author, merely action or, at best, the representation of ideas that were published elsewhere. Film, a collective endeavor in which ideas were conveyed by means of pictures, editing, and acting, did not fit within the structure of speech implied by the printing press, in which the publisher-editor defined the content of a paper and printed it.[6] In contrast, to the extent that they presented ideas, films dramatized or copied (re-represented) preexisting ideas or events already in the public realm.

The different technologies of mass communication that have transformed public discourse in the twentieth century have challenged this vision of the speaker and reformulated the relationships among speaker, utterance, and audience. The ubiquity of visual communication and shifts in the conceptualization of the public as mass audience—and the boundaries of legitimate persuasion as containing both rational argumentation and subtle, connotative, and irrational nudges—opened up the definition of speech to include images and bodily gestures. This recognition marked a shift in the concept of speech from a lofty articulation of elites to the inchoate expressions of the masses. In this shift, what it meant to be a speaker was democratized, or massified. Minds were still central to defining what it meant to be a speaker—or listener—but these minds worked in a different way, moved by primitive desires and impulses as well as by rational argumentation and logical progression. People who had formerly been excluded from being speakers (because their expression was too tied to the body or was not rational enough) were given voice.

Similarly, the development of radio broadcasting and the industrialization of the press reformulated the relation of speaker to text to audience, spurring a new set of social concerns among academics, journalists, and policymakers. Most people (the masses) were structurally barred from actually speaking, or producing statements, in this medium. Rather than speaking or debating, the main act of engagement in the structurally transformed public sphere was receiving information and making choices about what information to receive: the work of audiences. Understanding freedom of speech in terms of the ability to distribute information was a way of addressing this new social arrangement, in which most people were consumers rather than producers of information. Protecting the flow of information was a way of indirectly protecting citizens as audiences; more information would, in theory, benefit them. The legal definition of speech was (eventually) expanded to include the act of listening and thus address the interests of the majority of citizens who were structurally positioned as audiences rather than as speakers or proto-publishers.

At the same time, this transformation altered the way that the act of speaking was understood in the law. Whereas earlier cases had hinged on protecting thoughts, ideas, and opinions (mental activity), as well as on making new ideas and events known (publishing), in the cases I examine in this era, transmission and amplification—what had looked like mechanical actions in previous decades—were legible as speech. "Speech" came to encompass not only uttering but distributing a message. In this process, speakers and speech were described in terms borrowed from technologies of mass communication (mass media) and industrialization. No longer did the speaker need to own his or her words. Rather, to be a speaker might mean repeating or relaying information or words that originated elsewhere or choosing from a menu of preset choices. In this way, the activities and attributes once at the heart of being a speaker receded, and a different set of activities—from consumerist choices to repetition and transmission—was recognized as meaningful expression.

By the end of the twentieth century, the material and situated act of speaking had been downplayed, mechanized, or replaced. Speaking was either less distinct from mechanical actions (e.g., amplification, transmission) or not necessary to discussions of freedom of speech (the original words of the Constitution, as Justice Scalia reminded in *Citizens United v. FEC* [2010], included no references to speakers as persons). In this shift, then, there was less concern or discussion about originality, mental activity, or intent. There need not be a mind or thought behind a message.[7] Speech included acts of repetition, amplification of messages that originated elsewhere, and simple statements of information (e.g., price). At the same time, computers were coming to do work once associated with human mental activity, from processing symbols to making decisions. This brings us to where we are today, with a set of precedents and legal theories in which there is less distinction between speaking and the work of computation and also less need for speakers at all in legal reasoning.

Legal theorizations of speech have direct implications for who can make free speech claims. When only erudite, "civilized" discourse counts, those who can make claims to this idiom (historically, mainly educated white males) are more likely to be able to make legible/successful free speech claims. The expansion of the category of speech to include primitive communication (symbols) and repetition in effect enfranchised both formerly "unreasonable" forms of communication associated with the crowd (from immigrants to women to racialized minorities). The shift to conceptualizing speech as the distribution of information granted indirect means of addressing the interests of the masses and the marginalized, now structurally defined as listeners rather than as potential speakers. Industrial metaphors of distribution and amplification recognized the right of people to combine to amplify particular messages (rather than simply to produce them). Yet the reconceptualization of speech as information and information as a dematerialized substance has enfranchised the messages and interests of organizations and corporations as much as those of—and perhaps at the expense of—individuals.

Information can be produced by bodies, gestures, or art. But it is produced par excellence by artificial entities, from corporations to government agencies. By virtue of being the biggest producers of information, institutional actors and interests have been among the biggest beneficiaries of this legal reasoning. Even when individuals produce information, it does not always flow in their favor.

It is possible for some bodies to unwittingly produce information by virtue of being read by others. This odd fact does not necessarily grant them extra rights, however, but can enable others to discriminate against them. By reading the bodies or presence of gay or lesbian participants as sending messages, the Court has ruled that groups like the Boy Scouts and organizers of parades can exclude gay men and lesbians from their activities. Such exclusion is an enactment of the freedom of speech of the organizations. For, to include queer participants would send a message that the organizations did not wish to send—antidiscrimination measures that force such inclusion, the Court decided, were a form of compelled speech.[8] Such decisions rest on a reading of the bodies of gay and lesbian would-be Boy Scouts or parade participants as always already saying something beyond their control. This speech is turned against them and, more broadly, against antidiscrimination laws and policies.

These examples point to an odd politics of speech as information. The protection of information began as a response to the structural transformation of the public sphere, a way of granting rights to citizens whose practical ability to speak was diminished via the technology and political economy of mass media. With the majority positioned more as listeners than speakers, the meaning of speech was stretched to include forms of engagement understood as more passive, rights of listening or consumption and repetition or retransmission (e.g., of slogans). This was a response, I have suggested, to the diminished agency of the legal subject (an imagined agency)—at least in terms of publicity. Yet, at the same time, this stretching of the definition of speech arguably worked to dilute other forms of legal progressivism. At the moment that the law began to protect more groups of people who are minoritized based on embodiment rather than ideology (racial and ethnic or sexual minorities rather than minority viewpoints), the protection of disembodied information took legal precedence over claims to protection or redress from such discrimination. And the decentering of speaking subjects in favor of information paved the way not only for recognition of diminished forms of agency on the part of consumer-subjects but also for the accumulation or hoarding of rights by powerful artificial entities who assumed rights in the name of the audience or consumers.

Speech without Speakers

The informationalization of speech has been more than a betrayal of the social progressivism it arose from. The disarticulation of legal conceptions of speech from particular speakers with interests and rights has provocative implications for the legal understanding of subjectivity and agency as well as for the scope of speech rights. In many ways, the legal discourse analyzed in this book engages questions that have captivated social and media theorists. What are the implications of the ability of media technologies to separate human voices or visages from human bodies for how we think about personhood and subjectivity? What are the theoretical and social consequences of the decentering of speakers from notions of speech, so long associated with agency, thought, and democratic politics? (To have or give voice is a pervasive and powerful metaphor for political agency.) Or, as media theorist Friedrich Kittler asked, what happens to our conceptions of consciousness (or soul) when we can have speech without speakers and writing without authors?[9] Such questions—and the disarticulation of speech from speakers—point to problems in the way Western philosophy has theorized the subject and suggest that we abandon old dichotomies of man and machine to understand that they have always been mutually imbricated (these questions, and the problems they point to, have been a central topic of both poststructuralism and posthumanism).

In the legal cases assembled here, we see one set of answers to these questions. Legal conceptions of speech have, as I have argued, always been shaped by the technical means of communication. So, too, arguably, have ideas about political subjects. These ideas have shifted with changes in the material means of communication that structure public speech. Legal practitioners have redefined speech implicitly and explicitly in response to media, though they have been consistently haunted by a print-based ideal of expression and publicity. Some media and social theorists see in transitions that mirror those detailed in this book a move away from subject-object, man-machine dualities—a decentering of subjects that attenuates agency and attends to nonhuman sources of this agency, from machines to nature, and in doing so opens up ethical possibilities.[10] In the legal discourse analyzed here, the decentering of the speaking subject has not so much offered a more ethical or empirically grounded vision of agency, but rather allowed some sets of artificial agents to claim standing, rights, and a subjectivity on the model of an autonomous liberal subject.

The way in which these questions have been answered in the law, then, offers some cautions for our approach to similar questions in social and media theory. The legal debates analyzed in this book have focused on speakers or messages—artifacts or the agents behind them. Less often have the ways technologies embody social relations or the ethics of communication been considered: the ways that media (as material means of communication) enable some groups to speak more than others, the impact of the act of speaking on others, the rationales for prioritizing speaking over listening, the differential distribution of the ability to speak (always also mediated by technology). As feminist scholarship cautions, the question of technology is not only one of ontology, but also always one of ethics and power. What gets left out, or forgotten, in many of our discussions of expression, politics, and freedom are those people (e.g., transcribers, translators, and operators) and material circumstances (e.g., ownership, affordances, infrastructure) that make speaking possible. Such ethical questions and concerns with social relationships are, in the archive of cases I have assembled, too often hidden behind—or buried under—seemingly technical (depoliticized) discussions of classification (e.g., asking, "Is this speech?"). These concerns are the hidden moral calculus involved in legal classification.

Attention to these dynamics and the framing of our questions (in terms of an ethics of speech as well as an ontology of speech) are particularly important at this moment. The structure of speech has changed greatly in the past century. While changes to this structure, as I have stressed, are not new, the specific changes involved in computerized speech have the potential to further shift the legal definition of speech in consequential ways in the future. Some of the examples and practices of computer speech suggest models of what it means to speak and the relation of speakers to both messages and audiences that blur fundamental principles and boundaries presumed in law.

Ghosts in the Machine: The Future of Free Speech?

Today, in many ways, computers can speak.[11] And their communication is likely to become more like ours; computer giants like Google and Apple (and many others in universities and industry) are working hard toward this goal. Already, personal assistants like Siri, Cortana, and Alexa engage in dialogue with human users and tell users when and which direction to turn to reach our destination (e.g., Google Maps) and complete simple social tasks like making an appointment for us—very literally via machinic utterances. Humans surely programmed the ability of these agents to speak but did not in a direct sense tell them what to say (most of the time, at least). The more flexible such assistants are, the more they are designed to reach "decisions" on the fly about what the user is looking for—and the less they are programmed to convey the priorities of their creator(s)—the more we might look at them as actual utterances of machines. Legally, this raises questions about whether or not such utterances count as "speech" for First Amendment purposes. As scholars like Toni Massaro and colleagues and Tim Wu have pointed out, existing precedents offer grounds to include such utterances as speech, without worrying about whether machines have consciousness, autonomy, or rights—on the basis that the information they produce should flow freely.[12] We may want to protect some computer utterances as speech. Yet, to unilaterally declare such utterances speech would expand the definition of speech in a way that disproportionately protects the firms developing this technology from economic and other forms of regulation (e.g., privacy, consumer protections, anti-trust).

The outputs of personal assistants and bots are certainly legible as speech. They also fulfill some of the social functions aligned with speech in the law, namely amplification. In this way, they can be likened to radio and to sound trucks. Chatbots and social bots (here, simply bots) are small programs designed to engage in seminatural conversations with humans.[13] Bots can be simple extensions of their creators' intent, for example, bots designed to call one's representative (Resistbot) or to counter climate change denial on social media or to create poetry. Simple bots that extend or amplify the ideas or aims of their programmers are amenable to classification as speech under the liberal humanist conception of speech (for example, bots programmed to counter climate change denial with information about climate change). The use of bots made stories about Donald Trump appear popular in the 2016 US election, and bots in Mexico "hijacked" a hashtag with nonsense or material that would trigger Twitter to shut down the hashtag, silencing efforts to publicize protests around the disappearance of forty-three students in Guerrero.[14] In such examples, a group of humans used machines to interfere with or game other machines in order to influence people—examples of persuasion that some will argue fall within the classic liberal understandings of freedom of speech. Complex bots, however, raise more questions for legal and lay conceptions of speech and agency.

With complex social bots, the issue of who is speaking is much more complicated. Take Microsoft's infamous chatbot Tay, for example. Microsoft released the chatbot, designed to mimic the personality of a teenage girl, on Twitter in 2016. Tay was a sophisticated chatbot, designed to interact with human users via tweets; in such interactions, Tay would improve its ability to engage in naturalistic conversation (social media was Tay's training ground).[15] Within a day, things had gone very wrong. Twitter users had figured out how to get Tay to spout racist, anti-Semitic, and misogynist tweets, and Microsoft took the chatbot offline, issuing an apology. The question of who was responsible for these tweets was not easy to resolve.[16] Tay's tweets may have been the product of programming decisions made by the bot's creators, but the content of the tweets (or the ideas they espoused) had little to no relation to the programmers' desires or intentions. What Tay said was largely a product of the dispersed network of interlocutors who trained Tay to emit hateful utterances, filtered through the affordances of both hardware and software (determined in turn by a dispersed set of designers). Like the search engine algorithms discussed in chapter 5, Tay's tweets were utterances not of a particular individual or machine, but rather the product of several, dispersed sets of actors: programmers and online interlocutors. The question of who the speaker is in Tay's tweets is, then, not a simple one. The chains of causality and influence are not straightforward.

Tay may be at one end of the continuum of bot speech, but even many simple bots are not entirely reducible to their programmers' speech. The programmer sets parameters within which the bot operates, meaning that a significant amount of the expressive capacity of these bots comes from the platforms or other technical systems within which they operate and from the other users they interact with. As Sam Woolley and colleagues show, many bot creators feel that their bots are not quite tools or extensions of themselves but also not quite separate. These creators experience their bots as having a limited independent agency, which the authors define as a proxy—something that acts on behalf of another but is not identical or reducible to their intentions, values, or point of view.[17] The utterances of such bots are a function not only of the programmers' directions—and code—but also of the systems and networks via which it communicates, and the other actors and dependencies within those systems. The authors argue this is not only a matter of perception but an accurate description of bots as sociotechnical systems.[18]

In these examples of bot speech, it is far from clear who is speaking to whom. Humans program machines to use language to communicate with other humans. Yet, as machine learning is used more and more, the programming of these machines is diffuse—it is not only accomplished via the programmers who define the parameters of operation and the training data but also by the many different users the entity interacts with online (the crowd) and, some would argue, by the machine itself (in that machine learning is supposed to involve autonomous computer decisions, or learning).

Like the technologies of communication examined in this book, many uses of bots and machine learning restructure speech, rearranging the positions of speaker, text, and audience—and in doing so, change what it means to be a speaker. What is distinct here is the way this restructuring conflicts with normative theories of speech and legal conceptions of subjectivity. As scholars like John Cheney-Lippold have pointed out, the use of machine learning and big data to surveil and craft predictive models has reconfigured fundamental social relationships involved in communication: where the fundamental scene of speech within legal reasoning is a human reading a message or text, many online communications are characterized by machines or the institutions who employ them, reading traces left by humans.[19] In spaces defined by surveillance, big data, and machine learning, individuals leave traces that become messages that are legible only via the storage capacity and processing power of large computer systems. In this scenario, *we are readable to machines in a way that we are not to each other.* The unwitting messages we send—without mind or will—become the basis for not only the ads we see but also the information and social world that is presented to us, and even state decisions about our mobility and privacy.[20]

A growing body of critical literature on algorithms, big data, and machine learning suggests that the power to interpret and define, long aligned primarily with humans (whether acting as individuals, as part of the state, or as producers of knowledge), is increasingly shared by large commercial entities and, more to the point, by opaque technological processes and systems. This situation reverses the social relations implicit in common uses of the term "expression" (borrowing from the humanist legacy of the term). Individuals, typically the agents creating and interpreting (reading) messages, become more like texts, unwitting sources of information read by machine learning processes, typically in the service either of commerce or security. We transmit signals without thought or intent, and machines read and make decisions based on these signals. The terms of the interaction have been, in other words, switched. Humans act as machines were once thought to, and machines take on work that once defined human mental activity: decisions, judgment, learning, interpretation.

If networks and big data restructure speech so that individual users unwittingly produce traces that are made legible by machinic interpretation (only available to those with large-scale computing capacity, mainly institutions and corporations), many normative principles central to free speech law are subverted. Normative reasons for the existence of free speech include a variety of ends: the autonomy or dignity of the individual and their need for self-expression, the social interest in self-governance and the workings of democracy, the value of discussion and debate as a social safety valve and tool for building tolerance, and the search for truth (or, in lieu of such a lofty goal, the creation of a marketplace of ideas). In the scenario sketched here, where individuals transmit and corporations or institutions interpret these transmissions for institutionally or economically defined ends, neither individuals nor the polity clearly benefit. Such examples of computer communication do not fit within liberal understandings of individual autonomy, nor is it clear that they add to democratic self-government or to discussion and debate. There is little democratic accountability—or discovery—in the opaque processes by which citizens are surveilled and read. There is, as well, little opportunity for discussion or debate. The application of the conception of speech as information to examples of big data analysis could in fact result in decisions that undermine the normative ends traditionally associated with freedom of speech.

As the cases contrasted in chapter 5 suggest, a return to a liberal humanist (or print-liberal) conception of speech is unlikely to solve the problem. Judges and justices are likely to discern speakers and protect their computer-mediated communication when those speakers are seen as legitimate social actors (e.g., Google) than when they are seen as illegitimate or marginal (e.g., hackers like Corley). This will not necessarily serve the ends of individual autonomy, democratic self-determination, safety valves, a competitive marketplace of ideas, or other social and political ends we may wish freedom of speech to serve.

Further, the liberal humanist conception of speech was always a hierarchical mechanism for defining value in human expression and interaction, in which some people's speech mattered more than others. I argued that it was also, crucially, premised on technologies of printing. The definition of speech that judges and justices return to in their deliberations over algorithms and computer programs is one based on authorship and print publicity. Even as jurists declare that the First Amendment is flexible and applies to new technologies as much as old ones, in drawing on this model they are saying that it applies only to expression in newer media that work like expression in print. Applying this model produces a clash between a legal category of speech based in print models of publicity and expression and a communicative environment significantly defined by computational mediation. It is unlikely that applying such a print-based model to algorithms, big data, or natural language processing will produce results that are sociologically, politically, or legally satisfying.

I do not intend the above description as a lament—or at least not as a nostalgic one. While many of these examples have alarming political and social implications, so did many of the arrangements that defined and delimited freedom of speech in the past. Rather, the current moment might be a chance to rethink some of our fundamental assumptions about speech and what it means for it to be free within the contemporary communication landscape. This rethinking will require attention to, or reformulations of, key legal and political assumptions about what it means to speak and the relations of speakers to media and to others. What would our conceptions (and practices) of speech look like if we defined personhood less in terms of mastery over tools, ownership of thoughts, beliefs, and selves? What does expressive agency—and responsibility—look like in complex, distributed sociotechnical systems?

What is needed today and in the future is not a retrenchment to an older ideal, nor obfuscation of the actors and interests involved, but rather a proactive and ethically engaged thinking about the category of speech itself. That is, a broader set of scholars and advocates might proactively do what has been reflexively done by judges and justices in the history analyzed in this book: rethink and define the parameters of "speech." This work could account for the media through which we speak, the constitution of the subjects and collectives that do the speaking, and the technological affordances, social activities, and communicative norms that comprise publicity today (via and off of our communication networks and platforms). The moment might stand as an invitation to engage the ideas and ideals of expression, publicity, dialogue, and advocacy that are so central to the law—and to rethink them in terms of the technical media, cultural techniques, social activities, and relationships that define communication today.

APPENDIX ON METHODS

In additional to traditional methods of discourse analysis and historical research, this book has used computational methods in order to mine the language used in the large corpus of legal decisions involving free speech claims in the twentieth and early twenty-first centuries. Working with the Institute for Advanced Technology in the Humanities at the University of Virginia, I used both probabilistic models of word co-occurrence (topic modeling) and targeted phrase searches to document and analyze historical variations in the specific language used to articulate or concretize the meaning and scope of "speech" in Supreme Court legal decisions since 1900.

To capture all of the cases in which free speech claims were made and discussed (and not only those cases in which these claims were accepted), the team created a large, overinclusive corpus of 897 Supreme Court decisions.[1] We used topic modeling on this corpus to organize and compare topics (or models of likely word co-occurrence, used as indicators of a legal concern or discourse) across decades. This produced many topics that were not of analytical interest. But for those that were (say, a series of words like "radio," "commission," and "license" that seemed to indicate discussion of radio regulation in the 1940s), we searched for later decisions in which the same words co-occurred. This sometimes offered surprising results: for example, suggesting a commonality in language among radio regulation cases of the 1940s and campaign finance decisions of the 1970s and 1990s. These results were the instigation for deeper, qualitative historical research and discourse analysis that became the arguments in chapters 3 and 4.

To create a more concrete archive of the legal language used to define speech, we also used targeted searches to create a large catalog. For this project, we searched the corpus to locate places where the justices stated specific texts, objects, or activities that were coextensive with speech. We searched for phrases like "freedom to … ," "right of … ," and "censorship of…"[2] This produced a large set of results, which my research assistants and I reduced to a smaller set of relevant results, in which the scope of speech or the press was under discussion. We tagged the specific terms that were used to describe or concretize speech (including specifications of what was not speech) and we are currently building a searchable database of these terms. This catalog has provided the basis for some of the specific comparisons in language across eras in the book and for the broader analysis in the shift in terms of legal debate from conceptions of speech as dialogue, persuasion, and expression as externalization of interior mental states to conceptions of speech as both more embodied (picketing, symbols, sitting, sleeping) and then to a more abstract set of terms (information, facts, tabulations, monetary exchanges).

NOTES

Introduction

1. See Mattelart, *Mapping World Communications*; Carey, *Communication as Culture*, 201–230; Gitelman, *Always Already New*; Sterne, *Audible Past*; Peters, "Uncanniness." I borrow the reference to the uncanny aspect of radio from Peters.

2. Print and print circulation are key to many theories of the public from Jürgen Habermas's *Structural Transformation of the Public Sphere* to Michael Warner's *Letters of the Republic*.

3. Before *Hague v. CIO*, municipalities commonly viewed city streets and parks as the property of city government and saw the local police power to regulate activity in the interest of public safety and convenience as a reason to deny access to those who wished to speak on divisive means. In the early twentieth century, city ordinances and permitting practices often denied unions, socialists, anarchists, and feminists from speaking in public places. For more on the specifics of the unionization efforts in Jersey City and Mayor Hague's opposition to the CIO, see Casebeer, "Public."

4. Barbas, "Creating the Public Forum." The term "public forum" was likely borrowed from radio, where forums were staged as a means of granting citizen access and making a space for dialogue in the new broadcast medium.

5. They were, of course, seeking a broader right of advocacy, but the terms of the argument and decision emphasized the reserved activity of passing along public information. In doing so, the legal team for the CIO was building on a recent decision that had ruled that the First Amendment guarded not only against restrictions on publication but also on distribution: *Lovell v. City of Griffin*, 303 U.S. 444 (1938). That these cases made their way to the Court shows that the question of whether distribution was part of the expression covered under freedom of speech was not clear.

6. It is a genealogy in the Foucauldian sense; see Foucault, "Nietzsche, Genealogy, History"; and Foucault, *History of Sexuality*.

7. See Schauer, *Free Speech*.

8. Legal theorists have noted the lack of a clear, coherent definition or theory of speech in the law. See, e.g., Post, "Recuperating"; Greenman, "On Communication"; Bezanson, *Art and Freedom of Speech*; and Tushnet, Chen, and Blochner, *Free Speech beyond Words*.

9. Leslie Kendrick argues that commonsense or popular meanings have shaped this term of art. My analysis here adds specificity and historicity to what constitutes this common sense. Kendrick, "First Amendment Expansionism."

10. Bowker and Star, *Sorting Things Out*; Suchman, "Do Categories Have Politics?";

11 On the role of precedent in legal reasoning, see Dworkin, "Law as Interpretation"; and Lakier, "The Problem isn't the Use of Analogies."

12. Boyle, *Shamans, Software, and Spleens*, 144. He references determinations such as who counts as "men" under the law and what counts as "speech" as two examples of such covert moral determinations, or avoidance.

13. The Supreme Court has not yet decided a case involving the legal status of computer code or programs; to date, district court decisions are the most authoritative.

14. The most common normative theories are (1) individual self-fulfillment or liberty, (2) the search for truth (or, alternately and more skeptically, the idea that the marketplace is a better arbiter of truth than the state), (3) self-governance (democratic decision making), and (4) social stability (that discourse and debate are vehicles for incremental social change, as opposed to more abrupt and violent revolution). See, e.g., Sunstein, *Democracy and the Problem of Free Speech*; Emerson, "Toward a General Theory"; and Schauer, *Free Speech*.

15. Descartes, *Discourse*.

16. The hunger strikes staged by suffragettes in the 1910s to publicize the conditions of imprisonment and to advocate for their classification as political prisoners were a form of publicity, an attempt at public speech from behind prison walls, but were not legally legible as such. The examples of labor protests are discussed further in chapter 1. For more on the way that the speech of people associated too closely with the body is rendered mute, see Anzaldúa, "Speaking in Tongues"; Bordo, *Unbearable Weight*; and Warner, *Publics and Counterpublics*.

17. While they are commonly conflated, speech plus is in fact analytically distinct from the other two (expressive conduct/symbolic speech) with its own genealogy. This is elaborated in chapters 2 and 5.

18. Braidotti, *The Posthuman*; Hayles, *How We Became Posthuman*. Institutions and corporations play a large role as artificial entities in the law, and the decentering of subjects empowers these artificial entities as much as marginal groups.

19. The dynamics of disembodiment shift across the corpus of law examined here. In the early twentieth century, the disembodiment of speech was understood, and policed, along Cartesian lines. By the end of the century, the terms and policing were along the lines of human intent versus computer automation.

20. National security is often cited as the root of the World War I censorship. For more on the way that the repression of speech was based in anti-immigrant sentiment and censorship targeted at immigrants, see Graber, *Transforming Free Speech*. Further, progressive arguments for free speech in the postwar period, like those of Louis Brandeis, were likewise based in notions of ethnic and ideological pluralism. Scholarship like Rabban's "The

Emergence of Modern First Amendment Doctrine" complicates this history by pointing to other less narrowly political understandings of free speech before World War I. The work of Laura Weinrib in *The Taming of Free Speech* pushes more strongly against this origin story.

21. The First Amendment was not understood to apply to state laws until 1925. Before this, most free speech cases were made in terms of state constitutions, most of which guaranteed some form of freedom of speech and publication.

22. Graber, *Transforming Free Speech*. Most actual free speech jurisprudence took place at the state level in the nineteenth century. For more on how the states interpreted free speech during this period, see Blanchard, "Filling in the Void."

23. See, e.g., Bollinger, *Tolerant Society*. The plot points in this narrative are cases that set precedents limiting the ability of state and local governments to restrict speech in the name of public safety or national security. For some evangelists of civil libertarianism, this history reaches its apogee in the infamous Skokie case, in which the Court ruled that the city of Skokie, Illinois, could not prohibit Nazis from wearing swastikas on a march through a community of Holocaust survivors. Recent generations of legal historians have presented a less linear and progressive narrative of civil libertarian free speech law and advocacy. In addition to the work of Graber and Rabban, see Weinrib, *Taming of Free Speech*; Lakier, "Invention of Low-Value Speech"; and Barbas, "Creating the Public Forum."

24. John Durham Peters offers an extended analysis and critique of this liberal narrative in *Courting the Abyss*.

25. Rabban, *Free Speech*; Weinrib, *Taming of Free Speech*.

26. Of course, the intellectual history of free speech goes back much farther, to at least John Milton and John Locke in the seventeenth century. The history of free speech as a legal construct is linked to this longer intellectual and discursive history, but it is distinct from it; the gaps among popular conceptions of free speech, intellectual discourse on free speech as a normative ideal, and the actual legal protections of speech are considerable. On the way that the action and expression of some individuals can silence others, see Matsuda, *Words That Wound*; and Citron, "Cyber Civil Rights."

27. Graber, *Transforming Free Speech*; Sunstein, *Democracy and the Problem of Free Speech*. While references to political speech as "pure speech" or as the primary object of freedom of speech are still common in case law, following the cultural shifts in public and private in the late twentieth century, the line between political and nonpolitical speech has become more difficult to draw in legal arguments.

28. Graber, *Transforming Free Speech*.

29. *Tinker v. Des Moines Independent Community School District*, 393 U.S. 503 (1969); *Garner v. Louisiana*, 368 U.S. 157 (1961); *Brown v. Louisiana*, 383 U.S. 131 (1966).

30. Famously, the Court also raised the bar for suing newspapers for libel, declaring books or other material obscene, and replaced the clear and present danger test with a more stringent standard of incitement of lawless behavior in the 1960s. *New York Times Co. v. Sullivan*, 376 U.S. 254 (1964); *Memoirs v. Massachusetts*, 383 U.S. 313 (1966); *Brandenburg v. Ohio*, 395 U.S. 444 (1969).

31. Barron, "Access to the Press"; Kairys, "Freedom of Speech"; Stein, *Speech Rights*.

32. See, e.g., Graber, *Transforming Free Speech*; Kairys, "Freedom of Speech"; and Sunstein, *Free Speech and the Problem of Democracy*.

33. See, e.g., McChesney, "Free Speech and Democracy!"; Pickard, *America's Battle*; and Weiland, "Expanding the Periphery and Threatening the Core."

34. Kendrick, "First Amendment Expansionism."

35. Starr, *Creation of the Media*.

36. Habermas, *Structural Transformation*; Warner, *Letters of the Republic*; Anderson, *Imagined Communities*. Per Anderson, print was essential to establishing not only norms of publicity but also the affective bonds of nation, or nationalism.

37. The centrality of printing to free speech law and practice remains today. On the print bias of free speech, see Tiersma, *Parchment, Paper, Pixels*; and Marvin, "Theorizing the Flagbody."

38. On the materialization of the word, see Ong, *Orality and Literacy*.

39. Gitelman, *Always Already New*.

40. See Cooley, *Social Organization*; and Small and Vincent, "Psycho-physical Communicating Apparatus."

41. Balkin and Siegel, "Principles, Practices, and Social Movements," 929. The authors are interested in ways that social movements create cases that disrupt these assumptions and open up reinterpretation of constitutional principles. I suggest that new technologies and their uses can do something similar.

42. As is common in histories of free speech, the cases assembled are primarily Supreme Court cases (except in the final chapter, which considers cases that have not yet made their way up to the Supreme Court). The Court is where decisions on constitutional law are made and is also where the authoritative interpretation of the First Amendment takes place.

43. For example, Blanchard, *Revolutionary Sparks*; White, "First Amendment Comes of Age"; Graber, *Transforming Free Speech*; Rabban, *Free Speech*; Weinrib, *Taming of Free Speech*.

44. See Innis, *Empire and Communications*; Kittler, *Discourse Networks*; and many of the essays collected in Gumbrecht, *Materialities of Communication*. On this approach to law, see Vismann, *Files*; and Tiersma, *Parchment, Paper, Pixels*.

45. Gitelman, *Always Already New*. See also Marvin, *When Old Technologies Were New*; and Jackson, "Rethinking Repair."

Chapter 1: Moving Images

1. Lenning, "Myth and Fact."

2. Weinberger, "*Birth of a Nation* and the Making of the NAACP."

3. NAACP member W. E. B. Du Bois, looking back on the campaign against the film, remembered (in 1940) that it was a difficult bind, asking liberals to oppose free expression, but that the high barriers of entry to the mass medium of film had forced them to do so (the NAACP could not afford to mount a filmic "reply"). Du Bois, *Dusk of Dawn*.

4. Weinberger, "*Birth of a Nation* and the Making of the NAACP," 78; Lenning, "Myth and Fact"; Berquist and Greenwood, "Protest against Racism"; Grieveson, *Policing Cinema*.

5. Berquist and Greenwood, "Protest against Racism."

6. Chief Justice White was the guest of honor at this screening. See "Movies at Press Club: Pictures Based on Thomas Dixon's 'Clansman' Shown to Large Gathering," *Washington Post*, February 20, 1915, 5. For more on the screening in the White House, see Lenning, "Myth and Fact."

7. See the recent decision establishing video games as speech, *Brown v. Entertainment Merchants Association*, 564 U.S. 786 (2011), for an example of this reasoning.

8. For excellent examples of this narrative, see Post, "Encryption Source Code"; and Wittern-Keller and Haberski, *Miracle Case*.

9. See, e.g., Jowett, "Significant Medium"; and Wittern-Keller and Haberski, *Miracle Case*.

10. Jowett, "'Capacity for Evil'"; Grieveson, *Policing Cinema*. Concerns about the messages of film are also archived in the early academic work around filmic influence, most famously in the Payne Fund studies and the publication that emerged from these studies, e.g., Herbert Blumer's 1933 book, *The Movies and Conduct*.

11. See the essays collected in Charney and Schwartz, *Cinema*.

12. Other terms for film referenced drama and the theater (e.g., photoplays); less common terms referenced the press (visual newspapers). While the trade press moved toward a more "refined" terminology around 1910, the courts continued to refer to movies as "motion pictures" and "moving images" for some time. Grieveson, *Policing Cinema*, 1–4.

13. Muybridge's scientifically minded films famously captured the mechanics of a horse's gallop and birds in flight; he also did a series of films of human movement (e.g., a nude person descending a staircase). Edison's more popular shorts included depictions of daily life such as children at play, commuters on the street, and a close-up of a kiss.

14. This was only one of the grounds on which the original challenge was made, but it was the center of the arguments before the Supreme Court. Also, the precedent set by the decision was primarily how to apply free speech law to film.

15. It was overturned in *Joseph Burstyn, Inc. v. Wilson*, 343 U.S. 495 (1952).

16. Gunning, "The Cinema of Attractions."

17. The association of film with immigrants and the urban working class may have been more discursive than empirical. For more on the makeup of the audience and the business of movie making and exhibition in the 1910s, see Starr, *Creation of the Media*; and Koszarski, *Evening's Entertainment*. Miriam Hansen, in *Babel and Babylon*, elaborates on the way that studios and exhibitors both capitalized on their association with working-class audiences (to tout their democratic appeal) and at the same time worked to attract a more well-heeled audience.

18. Jowett, "Capacity for Evil"; Czitrom, "Politics of Performance"; Starr, *Creation of the Media*; Grieveson, *Policing Cinema*. Jowett in particular reads the push to regulate films and establish censor boards as the efforts of Protestant religious leaders in a changing twentieth century to maintain a moral and cultural hegemony that they had enjoyed in the nineteenth century.

19. The city of Chicago had been first in censorship, empowering the police to pre-screen movies before they could be exhibited in the city in 1907. In 1911, Pennsylvania established a state censor board, and in 1916 Maryland joined Pennsylvania, Kansas, and Ohio. New York and Florida established censors in 1921, and Virginia followed suit in 1922. Massachusetts used existing blue laws to cobble together a censorship system when attempts to do so legislatively failed. Wittern-Keller, *Freedom of the Screen*.

20. The film industry that had developed by the 1920s depended on national circuits of distribution, in which films made in one place could be distributed across the nation. Local censorship boards were, early on, an obstacle to such distribution. Industry codes and self-censorship were, among other things, a means of working around these obstacles, producing content that would not offend local censors or disrupt national distribution.

21. The free speech arguments began as a secondary claim but were the ones that gained the most traction in the district court. In response to this, Mutual Film and its lawyers emphasized freedom of speech in their appeal of the decision to the US Supreme Court.

22. David Wark Griffith, "The Rise and Fall of Free Speech in America" (1916), https://archive.org/stream/riseandfallfreeoogrifgoog#page/n8/mode/2up. His defense of the film on the grounds of freedom of expression was likely a direct response to the Court's ruling in *Mutual*; see Stokes, *D. W. Griffith's "The Birth of a Nation."*

23. "Freedom of Speech and Boards of Censors for Motion Picture Shows," quoted in Wertheimer, "Mutual Film Reviewed," 170.

24. Rabban, *Free Speech.*

25. *Gitlow v. New York*, 268 U.S. 652 (1925), held that, under the Fourteenth Amendment, the First Amendment applied to state law as well as to federal law.

26. For this reason, I use the general term "free speech laws" to refer inclusively to the different state laws. While these laws were very similar in sentiment, the specific terminology of the laws differed from state to state, and for that reason the cases analyzed here hinge on slightly different terminology.

27. Blanchard, "Filling in the Void."

28. In other words, the justices saw not only a close relationship between images and conduct but also a much closer relationship between words and behavior or conduct than do most today.

29. Noncitizen immigrants today do not enjoy full First Amendment rights and can be deported for participating in political demonstrations. In 2001, the Patriot Act established restrictions reminiscent of those under the early twentieth-century immigration acts, barring entry to the United States for those who support groups designed as terrorist.

30. *Davis v. Massachusetts*, 167 U.S. 43 (1897); see Kairys, "Freedom of Speech." However, the broader track record of state courts in balancing the interest in order (and police power) against individual and group claims of rights to use the streets was more mixed. Anderson, "Formative Period."

31. *Gompers v. Buck's Stove & Range Co.*, 221 U.S. 418 (1911). Political boycotts were formally recognized as protected under the First Amendment in *National Association for the Advancement of Colored People v. Claiborne Hardware Co.*, 458 U.S. 886 (1982).

32. For more on this history, see Rabban, *Free Speech*; and Graber, *Transforming Free Speech.*

33. For more on these free speech claims, see Wertheimer, "Mutual Film Reviewed"; and Rabban, *Free Speech.*

34. Weinrib, *Taming of Free Speech.* On these labor disputes, see also Rabban, *Free Speech.*

35. See the description of freedom of speech and the press in *Mutual*: "the freedom of opinion and its expression, and whether by speech, writing or printing" (242). See also the

distinction between freedom of the press and the news in *Pathé Exchange Incorporated v. George H. Cobb*, 202 App. Div. 450 (1922), discussed later in this chapter.

36. A tension between a view of freedom of speech as an individual right and as a collective social good was nascent during this period. Graber, *Transforming Free Speech*, argues that in nineteenth-century legal theory the right to speak was most often understood as an individual liberty associated with property rights. Progressive legal scholars articulated more collectivist interpretations of freedom of speech in the context of Progressive Era politics and World War I repression. Rabban, *Free Speech*.

37. "Freedom of Speech and Boards of Censors for Motion Picture Shows."

38. Wertheimer, "Mutual Film Reviewed." The lawyers for Mutual Film argued that the Ohio licensing law violated both the First Amendment and the state constitution's guarantee of free speech. The Supreme Court ignored the first claim and focused on the latter.

39. Mnookin, "Image of Truth."

40. Musser, *Emergence of Cinema*, 225.

41. Ohio Constitution, Article 1.11 (1851).

42. To the best of my knowledge, no one at the time had considered recorded speech (phonographs) as a form of speech protected under free speech. It would not be until the 1940s, when records were understood as a form of amplification and public transmission, that they would become part of the speech of free speech.

43. See, for example, the local ordinance upheld by Oliver Wendell Holmes Jr. in *Davis v. Massachusetts* that prohibited the Boston preacher from speaking in Boston Common (see note 32 and accompanying text).

44. "Propaganda" as a term did not yet have a pejorative connotation. Several different typologies were presented. The brief, however, focused on John Collier's typology, which included the following categories: (1) scenic and geographical, (2) scientific and historical, (3) mythological, (4) educational, (5) industrial, (6) classical, (7) manners and customs, and (8) propagandist. In order to argue that film fulfilled a social role similar to the press, the lawyers for Mutual Film emphasized the final category of "propagandist" films, or films designed to educate and to influence public opinion on issues ("campaigns") ranging from women's suffrage to the importance of public playgrounds to Mormonism. *Mutual*, Brief of Appellants, 24–28.

45. *Mutual*, Brief of Appellants, 45. The brief specifically argued that the Ohio constitution would not have been written in broad terms if it was meant to apply only to spoken or written material.

46. Wertheimer, "Mutual Film Reviewed."

47. *Mutual*, 243.

48. Berquist and Greenwood, "Protest against Racism."

49. Indeed, as film historians like Garth Jowett, Lee Grieveson, and Daniel Czitrom argue, it was the very ability of movies to convey ideas and moral lessons that was behind the efforts to regulate, or censor, film. Jowett, "'Capacity for Evil'"; Grieveson, *Policing Cinema*; Czitrom, "Politics of Performance."

50. In this context, the locus of regulatory efforts and other concerns about the moral effects of performance transitioned from the streets (and theaters) to national systems—or industries—of distribution. Czitrom, "Politics of Performance." See also Butsch, *Citizen Audience*.

51. Stokes, *D. W. Griffith's "The Birth of a Nation,"* 132.

52. *Mutual*, 243.

53. This distinction mirrors that in the turn of the twentieth-century discourse on spectatorship, which distinguished between distanced (reasoned) judgment and immersive sensation. Jay, "Diving into the Wreck"; see also Cowie, *Recording Reality*.

54. *Mutual*, 244.

55. *Mutual*, 244. The content of the decisions cited suggests otherwise. In all, the lower courts had upheld the ability of cities to regulate circuses, amusements, and picture shows in the interest of public safety and morals. The challenges to such regulation had included not only property claims but also claims of discrimination (deprivation of liberty), violations of due process, and questions about the extent of the power of local authorities (the latter was among the claims that Mutual Film included in its original suit in the district court). See *Greenberg v. Western Turf Ass'n*, 148 Cal. 126 (1905); *Laurelle v. Bush*, 17 Cal. App. 409 (1911); *Higgins v. Lacroix*, 137 NW 417 (Minn. 1912); and *State v. Loden*, 83 A 564 (Md. 1912). While property and commerce were central to these cases, the claims made and issues discussed in the decisions range beyond property rights.

56. Grieveson, *Policing Cinema*, 149. Grieveson argues that *Mutual* was the culmination of a trend in regulatory discourse and law defining film as commerce.

57. For example, the scathing critique of the press in Upton Sinclair's *The Brass Check* (1919) contrasts starkly with the distinction the justices construct in *Mutual*. The characterization of newspaper owners as press barons dates from the late nineteenth century, as does the denunciation of the sensationalism of the yellow press, which was said to stain the tablecloth with its tawdriness. This idealization of the press is discussed further in chapters 2 and 3.

58. Wertheimer, "Mutual Film Reviewed," 179–181.

59. Starr, *Creation of the Media*.

60. *Mutual*, 244.

61. *Mutual*, 244.

62. How the justices use the term "mechanical reproduction" coincides in some ways with the phenomenon analyzed by Walter Benjamin a few decades later. The justices, too, thought this reproduction meant the loss of a sort of aura, but they did not reach the same conclusion about the democratic implications of this loss. W. Benjamin, "Work of Art."

63. *Mutual*, 243.

64. Habermas, *Structural Transformation*.

65. The categorical separation of original and copy as distinct modes of representation is characteristic of a moment before the dominance of mass communication. W. Benjamin, "Work of Art."

66. Fox Talbot, *Pencil of Nature* (1844–1846), quoted in Sekula, "On the Invention of Photographic Memory"; Snyder, "Res Ipsa Loquitur."

67. A notable exception was *Burrow-Giles Lithographic Co. v. Sarony* 111 U.S. 53 (1884); in the case, the Court recognized the intellectual property of a photographer who had made a photographic portrait of Oscar Wilde. The Court recognized the work of staging and arranging the photograph as a form of authorship; the justices made clear, however, that most photographs did not exhibit such authorship.

68. Decherney, "Copyright Dupes."

69. Gaudreault, "Infringement of Copyright Laws." This was resolved in 1912 when film was included as a copyrightable medium in the law in the Townsend Amendment.

70. Copyright of a photograph was premised on the fact that one person took the photograph and thus the imprint of that person's vision or personality was left in the photo. As Jane Gaines shows in *Contested Culture*, this came about via the remnants of the romantic vision of authorship enshrined in intellectual property law. Film must have posed a problem within this particular way of adjudicating copyright, as there was no one single person who was clearly imprinting his or her personality; it could be the cameraman, the director, the editor, or the scriptwriter.

71. *Kalem Company v. Harper Brothers*, 222 U.S. 55, 62 (1911); Lew, *Ben-Hur*.

72. *Kalem*, 61.

73. *Kalem*, 55–59. Copyright law at the time did not consider a series of photographs illustrating a book to be copyright infringement. It was a translation into the very different, visual idiom of the still photograph. The animation of stills in motion pictures (into a story form) enabled the question of whether film could be considered a similar form of representation as a print story.

74. *Kalem*, 61.

75. Holmes Sr. famously likened the work of the photograph to a mirror with a memory, in which "a sheet of paper reflect[s] images like a mirror and hold[s] them as a picture." Holmes, "Stereoscope and the Stereograph."

76. See Daston and Galison, "Image of Objectivity."

77. The sources of originality in photography had led the Court to decide in the *Burrow-Giles* case that some photographs were the intellectual property of photographers.

78. Indeed, the justices cited *Kalem* in support of the analogy of film to the stage, and thus subject to licensing. *Mutual*, 244.

79. *Mutual*, 244.

80. Amy Adler, "First Amendment and the Second Commandment," has argued that a biblically rooted idea that images are more powerful than words has been (and continues to be) a powerful undercurrent in First Amendment law. I argue, for reasons elaborated below, that the separation of film from opinion and the press was rooted in a more complex set of discourses that might draw on a Protestant suspicion of images but is not reducible to it.

81. *Mutual*, Brief of Appellees, 26.

82. *Mutual*, Brief of Appellees, 29.

83. The outcome of the decision discouraged challenges to *Mutual* until the late 1940s. There were legal challenges to film censorship in the 1920s and 1930s, but these focused on whether particular films should be censored, not on the legality of film censorship itself. See Wittern-Keller and Haberski, *Miracle Case*.

84. Wittern-Keller, *Freedom of the Screen*, 46.

85. *Pathé*, 454.

86. *Pathé*, 457.

87. *Pathé*, 457.

88. *Pathé*, 456 (emphasis added).

89. See, for example, Warner, *Publics and Counterpublics*.

90. Performances themselves are not copyrightable but choreography is; one way

that choreography is copyrighted is through videotaping dancers performing the moves (to give the dance a fixed form). Within this legal setup, the moves of the dancers, when inscribed within a recording technology, become evidence of the mental originality of the choreographer rather than evidence of originality in physical execution or interpretation on the part of the dancers themselves.

91. This distinction maps to the divide in ways of talking about spectatorship in the early twentieth century traced by Martin Jay. On the one hand, people spoke of a mode of spectatorship as distanced judgment (e.g., the work of the critic). On the other, they spoke of a more immersive, "kinaesthetic" spectatorship, in which the audience was thrilled and physically excited or moved. Notably, Jay aligns the former with vision (of the art critic, or we might add the reader) and the latter with the body. Jay, "Diving into the Wreck."

92. *Pathé*, 456.

93. Feffer, *Chicago Pragmatists*; Deegan, *Jane Addams*.

94. The Payne Fund studies were some of the first large-scale studies of media effects. Funded by concerned philanthropists, the studies sought to assess whether and how moviegoing affected young peoples' attitudes, emotions, and behavior. Among the outcomes were sociologist Herbert Blumer's 1933 book, *Movies and Conduct*.

95. William McKeever, "The Moving Picture: A Primary School for Criminals," *Good Housekeeping* (August 1910): 184–186, quoted in Butters, *Banned in Kansas*, 13.

96. Butsch, *Citizen Audience*, 43.

97. Addams, *Spirit of Youth*, 93.

98. George Elliott Howard, "Social Psychology of the Spectator," *American Journal of Sociology* 18, no. 1 (1912): 40, quoted in Grieveson, "Cinema Studies," 12.

99. Münsterberg, *Photoplay*, chapter 11.

100. Münsterberg, *Photoplay*, chapters 11, 4 and 5, respectively. For Münsterberg, the capacities of films did not necessarily mean they were antisocial or disorderly. Like reformers John Collier and Jane Addams, he thought film had the potential to bring the poor and immigrants into better communities than the physical ones in which they resided.

101. Malin, *Feeling Mediated*.

102. Butsch, *Citizen Audience*; social order and stability were tightly linked to democratic society in elite discourse at the time. See Wiebe, *Search for Order*.

103. For more on the history of mass violence in the nineteenth century and its relationship to crowd psychology, see Sandine, *Taming of the American Crowd*.

104. Rabban, *Free Speech*; Weinrib, *Taming of Free Speech*.

105. In fact, many potential members of such crowds were formally excluded from membership. The Immigration Act of 1903, which limited immigration based on race and nationality, was expanded in 1918 to allow for the deportation of anarchists; Emma Goldman was among those expelled.

106. *Mutual*, Brief of Appellees, 25.

107. *Gompers*, 439, cited in *Mutual*, Brief of Appellees, 25.

108. Rabban, *Free Speech*, 171.

109. Many of the fears of crowds were transferred to media audiences as the means and reach of mass communication proliferated in the early decades of the twentieth century. Butsch, *Citizen Audience*.

110. Le Bon, *Crowd*, 36.

111. While Tarde saw imitation in all social life, he argued that in primitive societies such imitation was more gestural and behavioral (more physical), whereas in more advanced societies, imitation was more often an idea or utterance (more linguistic and mental). Tarde, "Extra-Logical Influences." Charles Acland discusses the late nineteenth-century fascination with mesmerism and hypnosis as a context for crowd psychology and early discussions of media effects in *Swift Viewing*.

112. Le Bon, *Crowd*, 13.

113. Le Bon, *Crowd*, 15. His racial hierarchy of suggestibility is explicit: within Europe, Latin crowds are the most agitated and subject to action and Anglo-Saxon the least. Thus, Latin crowds are the most feminine (16). The association between femininity and suggestibility is so extreme that he implies that the testimony of women in court is inherently unreliable (20).

114. The specter of such animation shows up in Victorian fiction like *Dracula* (1897) and *Trilby* (1894) as well as in scientific texts and early twentieth-century ideas of media effects. Acland, *Swift Viewing*.

115. Charles Darwin's *Expressions of the Emotions in Man and Animal* (1872) used photographs of poses and facial expressions (in people and in animals) to demonstrate different emotions. In many of the photographs, electricity had been used to produce the muscular contractions of the facial expression being illustrated, providing a particularly literal link between electrical currents and emotion.

116. Darwin was not particularly interested in the communicative aspects of his study of physical expressions, but he did note that facial expressions and bodily pose constituted a "medium of direct emotional exchange," an "inarticulate language" of a sort. Fleming, "Attitude," 296. This passing note on the communicative aspects of facial expression appears to have influenced the idea of contagion and imitation in later work on crowd psychology (Darwin was a major source of influence on Tarde's work on imitation in particular).

117. A very similar set of ideas about the emotive "surplus value" of the voice circulated in discussions of radio communication in the 1930s (see chapter 2). Similar ideas of the power of embodied speakers were invoked by Justice Jackson in his argument for some limits on the rights of street speakers. *Kunz v. New York*, 340 U.S. 90 (1951), 307.

118. Le Bon, *Crowd*, 27.

119. Schudson, *Discovering the News*; see, e.g., Tarde, "Public and the Crowd."

120. Butsch, *Citizen Audience*; Schudson, *Discovering the News*. That is, public opinion required mental activity, but it was a specific sort of mental activity modeled on that of an educated elite (it was an activity defined therefore by gender, class, and race).

121. For Park, newspapers were a force of modernization and assimilation, through which immigrants would come to form rational, individual opinions rather than rely on group habit, often defined in racial or ethnic terms. Park, *Immigrant Press*. The audience would eventually replace the crowd as the other of publics in US social and political thought; in this substitution, the normative ideal of the public went from being defined in opposition to the unruly activity of crowds to the dangerous passivity and gullibility of the audience. Butsch, *Citizen Audience*. This transformation is discussed in chapter 2.

122. Tarde, "Public and the Crowd"; Lippmann, *Public Opinion*.

123. While it is not how the public was understood at the time, it is worth pointing out

that this conception of the reading public was not only about a way of thinking but also about a set of proper feelings and embodiments. Newspaper reading was likely a key activity aligned with publics not only because it "brought" dispersed people together in a safe fashion but also because it signaled a set of orderly affects that seemed poised to redress the social turmoil of the day.

124. Legal discourse and professionals have a particular bias toward print. For more on the textuality of the law and its bias toward print, see Streeter, "Some Thoughts"; Marvin, "Theorizing the Flagbody"; and Tiersma, *Parchment, Paper, Pixels*.

125. The liberal tradition of thinking about speech rights, or freedoms, is a subject of much legal and humanistic scholarship on the history of free speech, in which a liberal conception of rights is contrasted to republican traditions or libertarian ones. I am focusing instead on liberal conceptions of communication.

Chapter 2: "A Primitive but Effective Means of Conveying Ideas"

1. For examples of histories that focus on the changes in film's social and political status, see Barbas, "How the Movies Became Speech"; and Wittern–Keller and Haberski, *Miracle Case*. By the 1940s, film was discussed as an art form. M. Anderson, "Payne Fund Studies." During World War II, newsreels became important venues for Americans to see and relate to the distant events of the war. The change in film's reputation was tied to shifts in ideas about the type of communication essential to public opinion and democratic self-governance. We miss something important though when we look only at changes in how elites viewed the medium itself; namely, we miss the way in which normative (elite) ideals of not just the medium, but the very nature of communication—and what it means to be a speaker or an audience—were also under revision.

2. Such accounts include Wittern-Keller and Haberski, *Miracle Case*; White, "Analogical Reasoning"; and Jowett, "'Significant Medium.'"

3. *West Virginia State Board of Education v. Barnette*, 319 U.S. 624 (1943), 642 (hereafter cited as *Barnette*).

4. *Barnette*, 632.

5. At the same time, in the late 1930s and early 1940s, the Court was also redefining marching in protest and union picketing as speech—in a legal category that became known as expressive conduct and later "speech plus." Originally, symbolic speech and expressive conduct were differentiated; symbolic speech was expression by nonverbal means (e.g., images, gesture) while expressive conduct was conduct that involved expression (e.g., marching with a sign or placard bearing a slogan or other message). In the latter, the conduct and the expression are heuristically separate; in symbolic speech, they are not. This distinction has been to some extent effaced in recent legal doctrine, in which symbolic speech has been conflated with expressive conduct and "speech plus" (which preserves the heuristic distinction between speech and action in a way that makes it easier to enact content-neutral regulation of such speech). For more on this distinction, see Nimmer, "Meaning of Symbolic Speech."

6. The family name Barnett was misspelled and went on record as "Barnette" after a court clerk erroneously placed an *e* at the end of the girls' names. Once recorded, the mis-

take did not matter—the record took precedence over the actual name of the real people involved. In law, paper and records are paramount.

7. Because of Jehovah's Witnesses' refusal to pledge allegiance, many Americans were suspicious that the Witnesses might be an internal "fifth column" for the Nazis, like those thought to have hastened the downfall of France, Norway, Belgium, Luxembourg, and the Netherlands. This suspicion was deeply ironic, given the persecution of Witnesses in Germany for their failure to salute. Vaughn, *Holding Fast the Inner Lines*; Turner, *Democratic Surround*.

8. *Minersville School District v. Gobitis*, 310 U.S. 586 (1940). The majority had argued that religious freedom could not outweigh the interest in national security and unity and, on the idea of judicial restraint, that this was a matter better decided at the local level through typical political processes. The lone dissenter was Justice Harlan Stone, who was chief justice at the time of the *Barnette* case. The decision was almost immediately controversial, blamed for the subsequent uptick in economic and physical attacks on Jehovah's Witnesses. In a very rare public critique of the decision, two justices went on record to say that they regretted their decision in the case.

9. Frankfurter's dissent in *Barnette* was directed partly at its scope—he argued passionately against the decision in the name of judicial restraint. On the expansion of what constitutes speech in the case, see also Sandman, "West Virginia State Board of Education."

10. It formalized and went further than the 1931 assertion in *Stromberg v. California*, 283 U.S. 359 (1931), that flying a flag was a form of speech protected by the First Amendment.

11. See Gary, *Nervous Liberals*; and Turner, *Democratic Surround*.

12. *Barnette*, 641.

13. See *Lovell v. Griffin* (1938); *DeJong v. Oregon*, 299 US 393 (1937); *Hague v. CIO* (1939); *Thornhill v. Alabama*, 310 U.S. 88 (1939); and *Cantwell v. Connecticut*, 310 U.S. 296 (1939). Many of these cases are discussed further in chapters 3 and 4.

14. The physical conduct, gesture, or bodily pose required by the policy was an explicit theme in the decision; Jackson forcefully and famously declared that any attempt by the state to "force citizens to confess by word or act" a faith or ideology was a violation of the nation's core principles. *Barnette*, 642.

15. *Barnette*, 631.

16. *Barnette*, 628; United Press, "West Virginia Banishes 'Nazi' Salute," *New York Times*, February 2, 1942.

17. Bellamy, "National School Celebration of Columbus Day." The Bellamy salute came into common use in the late nineteenth century in the context of the Spanish-American War and was the common salute to the flag between 1892 and 1942. In the Americanization and patriotic fervor of World War I, many states passed laws requiring the Pledge of Allegiance in school. Twenty states already had such laws when Congress passed a similar federal requirement in 1942. Jacobs, "Conditional Liberty."

18. All three were based on the Roman salute. The similarity led the salute to be replaced in 1942 by the hand-over-the-heart salute still used today. Jacobs, "Conditional Liberty."

19. *Barnette*, 627.

20. United Press, "West Virginia."

21. *Barnette*, 631. Jackson continued throughout the decision to use attitude as a close correlate of opinion, objecting to the flag salute's requirement to adopt an "affirmation of belief and attitude of mind" (633) and objecting to the idea that the state could require individuals to adopt any particular political attitude (636).

22. Tarde, "Public and the Crowd"; Park, *Immigrant Press*. Tarde also discusses the telegraph as a medium that knit the public together, though this applied more to Europe, where the political development of the telegraph tied it more closely to citizen communication. In the United States, the telegraph was used primarily by businesses; its usefulness to public formation was more indirect in the way it formed an infrastructure for the quick exchange of stories among newspapers. See Starr, *Creation of the Media*.

23. Le Bon, *Crowd*, 36.

24. Le Bon, *Crowd*, 36.

25. On the merging of opinion and attitude, as well as on a broader history of the term, from reference to a physical expression (or pose) to a set of mental, psychological preferences, see Fleming, "Attitude."

26. Fleming, "Attitude," 359.

27. Robinson, *Mind in the Making*, 49.

28. For a contemporaneous discussion of the experience of being addressed as a mass subject, see Cantril and Allport, *Psychology of the Radio*.

29. Cantril and Allport, *Psychology of the Radio*, 20. The authors went on to argue that in when attention is held in common by the same stimuli it was "psychologically inevitable" that some conformity would result. In classics like this and Max Horkheimer and Theodor Adorno's critique of the culture industry, the practices and experiences of a new mode of production and dissemination were as important as the content. For more on this, especially in relation to Adorno, see Turner, *Democratic Surround*.

30. For example, see news items like Dorothy Thompson, "Back to Blood and Iron," *Saturday Evening Post*, May 6, 1933; "We Demand!," *Time*, July 10, 1933; Shepard Stone, "Hitler's Showmen Weave Magic Spell: By a Vast Propaganda Aimed at Emotions, Germany's Trance Is Maintained," *New York Times*, December 3, 1933; "Propaganda Show Staged in Berlin: Exhibition for the Olympics Visitors Demonstrates the Success of Nazi Regime," *New York Times*, July 18, 1936; Lois Lochner, "In Germany Today, Individual Is Nothing, Nation Is Everything," *Washington Post*, October 9, 1938; and Junius Wood, "Nazi Coordination Is Accepted by All," *New York Times*, April 3, 1939.

31. For more on the role of media, the corruption of public opinion, and the effects of propaganda, see Turner, *Democratic Surround*; Gary, *Nervous Liberals*; and Sproule, *Propaganda and Democracy*. The idea of "narcotizing dysfunction" was laid out in Lazarsfeld and Merton, "Mass Communication," 238–239.

32. Leach, "'Voices out of the Night'"; Butsch, *Citizen Audience*.

33. *Barnette*, 662.

34. *Barnette*, 632.

35. Robert Jackson Papers, Library of Congress, box 127, *Barnette* folder 1.

36. The symbols in this case differ from those in *Mutual* in one important way. The moving images of film are iconic (mimetic) signs, working via resemblance to an original referent while the symbols here are abstract ones (symbolic signs). Reading a symbolic sign involves more mental work than reading an iconic one (which requires only recognizing

resemblance). However, the type of mental work required is a type of activity aligned more with mesmerism, psychosis, and dreams than with the more valued rational work of giving reasons, deducing principles, or breaking down arguments into component propositions.

37. *Barnette*, 633. An early draft of the decision went into greater detail, noting how the flag might signify differently to "children of disadvantaged parents," Native Americans, and others who "suffer real or fancied discriminations." Robert Jackson Papers, Box 127, *Barnette* folder 1.

38. *Barnette*, 641. Jackson's liberalism about messages and "primitive communication" only went so far. During the red scare of the 1950s, Jackson agreed that advocacy of the overthrow of the government (absent any clear and present danger of action) was not protected under the First Amendment in *Dennis et al., v. United States*, 341 U.S. 494 (1951). And in a case involving a street speaker who disparaged other Catholics and Jews, Jackson argued against an expansive reading of the public forum, to say that the preacher was imposing injury and insults on a captive audience (not organizing a willing one). Embodied speech of this sort, he argued, calling on an idea like the "surplus value" of the human voice, was more likely to incite unrest among the audience, "speech being the primitive and direct communication with the emotions. Few are the riots caused by publication alone, few are the mobs that have not had their immediate origin in harangue." Dissent, *Kunz v. New York*, 340 U.S. 90 (1951).

39. *Barnette*, 662.

40. *Barnette*, 662 (emphasis added).

41. Frankfurter, who was Jewish and thus a member of a minority religion himself, was among the founders of the ACLU. He no doubt had sympathy for the Barnetts. His opposition to these cases was an outcome of his belief in judicial restraint and his understanding of the public/private divide. Frankfurter located religious freedom in the private realm; in the public, he said, we all must be equal under the law. (In other words, liberalism demands that difference be managed in public life.) He further argued that the West Virginia law was not coercive, as the policy, and law in general, dis not govern inner life, only action in the social world. The flag salute had demanded only "submission to conformity of action" and had not robbed the Witnesses of their ability to dissent or express their disagreement in other ways. *Barnette*, 656, 654.

42. The *Gilbert v. Minnesota*, 254 U.S. 325 (1920), decision, which, like *Mutual*, was written by Justice McKenna, argued that protecting the meaning of the flag was part of the state's duty to encourage love of country.

43. *Halter v. Nebraska*, 205 U.S. 34 (1907), 43. A similar idea was at the heart of the West Virginia salute policy: "the flag of our Nation is the symbol of our National Unity transcending all internal differences" and "the Flag is the symbol of the Nation's power; that emblem of freedom in its truest, best sense; that it signifies government resting on the consent of the governed, liberty regulated by law, protection of the weak against the strong, security against the exercise of arbitrary power, and absolute safety for free institutions against foreign aggression." *Barnette*, 626.

44. *Stromberg*. While the Court went back and forth in the years between 1900 and 1943 about whether it was legitimate for states to legislate the meaning and use of the flag, the underlying, telegraphic conception of how the flag communicated remained the same. In this underlying theory of meaning, then, *Barnette* is a departure from *Stromberg*.

45. After *Barnette*, sequences in film, public schools, and eventually the words of the First Amendment itself were discussed as symbols. See *Burstyn v. Wilson* (1952); *McCollum v. Board of Education District 71*, 333 U.S. 203 (1948); and *Dennis v. United States* (1951). In *Dennis*, Frankfurter argued in a concurring opinion that the First Amendment did not protect plots to overthrow the government, and that the words of the First Amendment should not be understood literally, but as symbols of the intent and historical experience of their authors. In this trajectory, institutions that had once seemed firmly rooted in Enlightenment ideals were increasingly discussed in terms of culturally specific codes and psychological processes.

46. *Barnette*, 633.

47. Similarly, the "bad tendency" test was increasingly hard to defend by this point. The idea that some actions and expressions had a tendency to cause moral or physical harm (a "bad tendency") and that the justices could easily identify such provocations and the tendencies they were likely to inspire had been tenable to an earlier generation of justices.

48. Multiple drafts of the decision show these revisions. Robert Jackson Papers, box 127, *Barnette* folder 1.

49. Ferdinand de Saussure, in *Course on General Linguistics*, referred to the system of conventions defining meaning within any given language as a code, a choice of words likely borrowed either from telegraphy or mathematics. In popular parlance, symbols, like signs, pointed to something else, though the term also suggested obfuscation. This borrows something from Freudian dream interpretation, in which dream symbols disguise anxieties and desires (but also, with the proper tools for decoding, represent those same desires and anxieties). See Freud, *Interpretation of Dreams*.

50. Dewey, *Public and Its Problems*; Lippmann, *Public Opinion*. In England, Graham Wallas paralleled Lippmann in many ways in his theory that "the empirical art of politics consists largely in the creation of opinion by the deliberate exploitation of subconscious non-rational inference." Wallas, quoted in Sproule, *Propaganda and Democracy*, 31. I am not suggesting that symbols or symbolic communication was particularly new, or a discovery of this era, but rather that this aspect of communication became an object of social scientific knowledge production used to explain not only mass behavior but also politics and the decision making of elites.

51. In a search of *Time* magazine headlines in EBSCO's Academic Search Complete database, "symbol" appears four times in the 1920s; nine times in the 1930s, with an increased incidence after 1938; and thirteen times in the 1940s. Similarly, a search of the *New York Times* headlines shows that "symbol" and "symbolic" started being used to characterize people and political actions in 1927, becoming more prevalent in the 1930s. A Google Ngram search of the use of "symbol" and related terms within Google's corpus of digitized books also shows a steady upward trend in its usage beginning just before 1920, peaking in 1963.

52. The work of George Herbert Mead provided the basis for symbolic interactionism, as well as the emphasis on symbolic thinking as a uniquely human and social activity, but Blumer pulled the theory together and named it in 1937. Dingwall, "Notes." It is tempting to imagine that Blumer's earlier work on the influence of movies (*Movies and Conduct*), which involved reading moviegoing journals and talking to young people about their re-

sponses to the content of film, might have influenced his approach to the negotiation of meaning.

53. Lerner, "Constitution and Court as Symbols." Others, notably Harold Lasswell in *Psychopathology and Politics,* argued that politics and international relations were essentially driven by unconscious desires and psychologically defined personality types. The concern with symbols and the subconscious were conceptually linked (see, e.g., the quote from Lerner used as an epigraph to this chapter).

54. From the creation of the Office of Radio Research to the Committee on Public Morale, the way that communication scholarship was shaped by public policy concerns and drawn on by government officials in the prewar and wartime years is well documented. See Buxton, "From Radio Research"; Gary, "Communication Research"; and Glander, *Origins of Mass Communication Research.*

55. The unit also coordinated with various academic communication research units, including the Princeton and Stanford radio listening projects, the Library of Congress, the Bureau of Applied Social Research at Columbia University, and the New School for Social Research's Totalitarian Communication Research Project. Gary, *Nervous Liberals.*

56. The unit also coordinated with Lasswell's semi-independent Experimental Division for the Study of Wartime Communication. Lasswell himself was instrumental in the Department of Justice's prosecution of propagandists (under sedition and alien registration laws). Gary, *Nervous Liberals.*

57. Lasswell was deeply influenced by symbolic interactionism and the idea, common to symbolic interactionism and linguistics of the day, that meaning was contextual. The challenge was to devise a method of reading a text that would help to illuminate and measure meaning-making that did not reside solely in the text (or of objectifying the subjective work of connotation). His interest in the project, and perhaps in the method itself, was intriguingly influenced by the work of colleagues at the University of Chicago on cryptographic codes in World War I as well as by Freud. Janowitz, "Harold D. Lasswell's Contribution to Content Analysis."

58. Lasswell, "Provisional Classification of Symbol Data." In the article, Lasswell offers an outline for a behaviorist psychological interview, in which the analyst reads and records the interviewees' words and actions as signs of latent, subconscious meaning.

59. These critiques also focused on the ways in which commercial interests acted to censor and shape news. These discussions are taken up in more detail in chapter 3.

60. For Lasswell, propaganda seemed a potentially valid form of expert management, a liberal tool with which to guide a semirational public (rather than repression or coercion). Perhaps more self-servingly, Edward Bernays offered a similar rationale: "We are governed, our minds are molded, our tastes are formed, our ideas suggested, largely by men we have never heard of. This is a logical result of the way in which our democratic society is organized. Vast numbers of human beings must cooperate in this manner if they are to live together as a smoothly functioning society." Cited in Glander, *Origins of Mass Communication Research,* 26.

61. Sproule, *Propaganda and Democracy;* Gary, *Nervous Liberals;* Glander, *Origins of Mass Communication Research.*

62. Popular perceptions of the scope and effectiveness of World War I propaganda are

most likely overblown. See Jackall and Hirota, "America's First Propaganda Ministry"; and Vaughn, "First Amendment Liberties."

63. V. Edwards, "Group Leader's Guide," 5. The institute aimed at providing Americans critical tools to debunk the messages of figures like Father Coughlin, who effectively used the radio to amplify his sermons, a populist mix of anti-Semitism, critiques of bankers and industrialists, and support for fascist leaders abroad.

64. For example, Paul Lazarsfeld's research center, the Bureau of Applied Social Research (BASR), undertook various studies to assess the difference in print and radio as sources of influence (for propaganda as well as for advertising). In the BASR's reports, researchers regularly noted that one common difference was the authority audiences imputed to print rather than any inherent superiority; they also pointed to the various visual elements of newspaper communication, including layout and pictorial ads. See, e.g., memorandum to Mr. Marion Harper, Sr. Marketing Studies, Inc., "Preliminary Report on Studies Comparing 'Readin' and Listening," October 16, 1946, box 16, BASR Archives, Columbia University; Directors of Radio Research Project, "Foreword," in "Social Stratification of the Radio Audience: A Study Made for the Princeton Radio Research Project," prepared by H. M. Beville, Jr. , research manager, NBC, November 1939, BASR Archives, box 112; Marjorie Fiske, "Memo to Paul Lazarsfeld," June 2, 1943, Retailers' Use of Radio, box 6, folder 4, BASR Archives.

65. Such communication via association and emotion was not strictly representational. It is worth noting that the nonrepresentational aspects of language were an emergent concern in the study of communication in the 1930s. In a 1923 essay, Bronislaw Malinowski coined the term "phatic communication" to label utterances that did not represent anything in the world but rather were about performing sociality (being together, or communion). He first observed phatic utterances in his study of language in "primitive" societies and transferred it to the study of language in industrialized, modern ones—an example of the re-conception of the publics of these countries and the erosion of some of the older lines of distinction between "civilized" and "less civilized" peoples and cultures during this period. Malinowski, "Problem of Meaning."

66. There was a schism between former journalist Creel and Dana Gibson, head of the pictorial division (in charge of most posters). Gibson, who came from the advertising world, preferred sensational images and appeals to fear. Vaughn, *Holding Fast the Inner Lines.*

67. Gary, *Nervous Liberals*; Sproule, *Propaganda and Democracy.*

68. Marjorie Fiske, "Suggested Line of Approach for Script," Retailers' Use of Radio, 1943, box 6, folder 1, BASR Archives. Fiske argued, "The voice has a kind of surplus value, above the printed word. In addition to the actual content which you want to present, the voice of the speaker can express the way he feels about something. Studies have been done showing that even if a man uses nonsense syllables, you can tell whether he means to express anger, or amazement, or any other of a number of emotions" (21). In the context of World War II, the implications were that Hitler might extend his influence not only beyond territorial borders via radio but also beyond linguistic ones. See also Lazarsfeld, *Radio*, 178.

69. Cantril and Allport, *Psychology of the Radio.*

70. Pooley and Socolow, "Myth."

71 See Hayakawa and Hayakawa, *Language*. The general semanticists were influenced by Ogden and Richards's, *Meaning of Meaning*—and, through them, that of Ferdinand de Saussure and Ludwig Wittgenstein. For more on semantics, propaganda, and the intellectual crisis of the 1920s and 1930s, see Sproule, *Propaganda and Democracy*; and Purcell, *Crisis of Democratic Theory*.

72. Actual audiences may not have been so easily swayed or duped. Robert Merton's famous study of persuasion in Kate Smith's war-bond drive argued that audiences were critical of verbal appeals (dismissing the propaganda of words as just talk). Smith's appeals worked, Merton and his collaborators argued, because of the way her appeal was rooted in her body (what they termed a "propaganda of the deed"). One conclusion was that the public needed critical training to inoculate them against such acts of propaganda (propaganda via conduct). Merton, Lowenthal, and Curtis, *Mass Persuasion*.

73. Slesinger, "Film and Public Opinion."

74. I refer here to the rise of cultural, moral, and ethical relativism in the 1920s and 1930s, described by Edward Purcell Jr. In *Crisis of Democratic Theory*, Purcell argues that this relativism was rooted in a loss of faith in the ability to logically deduce answers to moral or ethical problems and the prevalence of examples of divergent ethical systems from the new generation of ethnographic anthropologists (e.g., Margaret Mead's scandalous and popular *Coming of Age in Samoa*). On the gaps inherent to communication and the way these gaps became a topic of scholarly concern and measurement and were in turn institutionalized in the study of communication, see Peters, "Gaps"; and Peters, *Speaking into the Air*.

75. Robert Jackson Papers, box 127, *Barnette* folder 1 (emphasis added). This passage appears in an early draft of the decision that Jackson circulated to his peers in March 1943; this section was considerably condensed in the final decision.

76. The agnosticism about value was not only about the changing legal conception of communication but also shaped by broader cultural and professional trends, many of which also shaped journalism and social science in the midcentury. Smith, *Social Science*; Peters, *Courting the Abyss*; Schudson, *Discovering the News*. On the tensions inherent in the legal formalism described here, see Streeter, "Some Thoughts."

77. *Winters v. New York*, 333 U.S. 507 (1948), 510.

78. *Roth v. United States*, 354 U.S. 476 (1957); *Cohen v. California* 403 U.S. 15 (1971).

79. *Winters* was, in this way, a continuation of the more nuanced take on communication emergent in *Barnette*, attuned to alternate interpretations and the particularity of value judgments—even those of the justices themselves. The justices, just like journalists and social scientists, had to engage in an act of restraint, or self-abstraction, when it came to matters of political value or aesthetic judgment. If Jackson outlined this approach in his discussion of symbols and their similarity to utterances (and the futility of attempting to legislate the use of symbols), the implications of this approach to communication were voiced in *Winters*—and the many decisions built on its precedent. For a critique of this reticence, see Schauer, "Towards an Institutional First Amendment."

80. *Winters*, 510 (emphasis added). The *Winters* decision struck down as overbroad a New York statute that criminalized distribution of publications "principally made up of criminal news, police reports or accounts of criminal deeds or pictures or stories of deeds of bloodshed, lust or crime" thought to incite crime or violence (*Winters*, 507).

81. It would also, in a different set of cases examined later in this book, expand to another set of nonideas on the opposite end of the spectrum: data, dry facts, equations, and information.

82. For example, there is a debate among legal scholars as to whether obscenity is outside the First Amendment because it is not speech (but rather the action or conduct of excitation and arousal, or alternately because it contains no real information) or because it is a particularly harmful form of speech. See, e.g., Sunstein, *Democracy*.

83. By the 1940s, the bad tendency test (which had been used to suppress dissent in World War I) was being replaced by the more rigorous clear and present danger test. Under the latter, regulations of speech were permissible only if they could be linked to a specific danger and that danger was deemed to be likely to take place (this has since been updated to speech that imposes a threat of "immanent lawless action").

84. It was another short step to the community standard for defining obscenity and the idea that what is one man's vulgarity is another's lyric (*Cohen v. California*) or that vulgarity might be protected speech.

85. Lakier, "Invention of Low-Value Speech."

86. See Czitrom, *Media and the American Mind*.

87. Indeed, the similarity of the persuasion research undertaken by the BASR on political decisions and consumer ones is striking.

88. Turner, *Democratic Surround*, 6.

89. *Burstyn*, 501. To support this line of argument, the justices cited two mass-communication texts: a study of film produced by the Hutchins Commission on Freedom of the Press and a work by Paul Lazarsfeld's student Joseph Klapper, who created the "uses and gratifications" school of media research. Inglis, *Freedom of the Movies*, 20–24; Klapper, *Effects of Mass Communication*.

90. *United States v. Paramount Pictures*, 334 U.S. 131 (1948). Between the *Paramount* decision and 1952, the Motion Picture Association of America challenged the censorship of three films for depictions of race (e.g., showing integration, miscegenation). Two of these challenges made their way up to the Supreme Court, but the Court refused to hear them, perhaps fearing the political fallout for challenging the states over rules of racial segregation. Wittern-Keller and Haberski, *Miracle Case*.

91. *Burstyn*, 501–502.

Chapter 3: Transmitters, Relays, and Messages

1. Commission on Freedom of the Press, *Free and Responsible Press*, 108. The Commission on Freedom of the Press, a group of scholars and former government advisors convened to study the state of freedom of the press in 1942, is popularly referred to by the name of its chairman, Robert Hutchins.

2. Many excellent histories focus on the confrontation of negative liberties and positive ones in policy debates in the 1930s and 1940s. See Blanchard, "Associated Press Antitrust Suit"; L. Benjamin, *Freedom of the Air*, 97–106; McChesney, *Problem of the Media*; Stein, *Speech Rights*; and Pickard, *America's Battle*.

3. This impersonality is different from that associated with print. While print is of-

ten associated with the abstraction of utterances from the bodies of authors (e.g., Warner, *Publics and Counterpublics*), the impersonality here is an abstraction from persons to systems.

4. Like many radio stations of the day, Shuler's station, KGEF, shared a frequency with another local radio station.

5. In one instance of the era's equivalent of a phishing scam, he extorted money from multiple listeners with a vague and untargeted threat to the effect that he had dirt on a particular person and would air that dirt if the person did not send him $100. He received several hundred dollars in response. *Trinity Methodist Broadcasting v. FRC*, 62 F. 2d 850 (DC Cir., 1932), 852.

6. L. Benjamin, *Freedom of the Air*, 104.

7. They also made an argument based on Shuler's status as a religious leader, that he had special privileges to proselytize. The Court denied the religious argument but took seriously his free speech claim.

8. In the first claims, most famously that of the "goat gland" doctor, Doc Brinkley, the court did not seriously consider free speech arguments. Rather, the court argued that the station was being operated for private profit (or grievance) rather than the public interest. *KFKB Broadcast Association v. FRC*, 47 F.2d 670 (1931).

9. *Trinity*, Brief for FRC. Caldwell, in "Freedom of Speech," countered that the First Amendment protected against censorship of distribution or circulation as much as against the publication (or production) of speech.

10. Balkin and Siegel, "Principles, Practices and Social Movements," 931. In what followed, both this disjuncture and the maneuvering over how to bridge it shaped the radio industry and speech law.

11. It was for these reasons that universities, funding agencies (e.g., the Rockefeller Institute), and the government spent so much time and money studying the content of radio and its effects, from the Hutchins Commission to the Radio Listening Project at Princeton to the Bureau of Applied Social Research at Columbia.

12. Hobbyists took great pride in tuning in distant signals; skill at such tuning required some level of meteorological knowledge to understand how the weather might affect transmission. Hilmes, *Radio Voices*.

13. The first KDKA broadcast was timed to provide up-to-the-minute results of the 1920 presidential election.

14. US Census Bureau, "20th Century Statistics," *Statistical Abstract of the United States: 1999*, www.census.gov/prod/99pubs/99statab/sec31.pdf. Census data show that households in the South (from Arizona to Virginia) were distinctly less likely to own a radio. Radio adoption was also quicker both in white households than nonwhite ones in urban settings than in rural ones (where radio signals were sparse and spotty). Craig, "How America Adopted Radio."

15. By 1927, there were 733 radio stations on the air, the majority commercially operated. Starr, *Creation of the Media*, 351.

16. To be able to transmit such content, would-be broadcasters had to apply for a Class B license, which required more expensive and up-to-date transmission equipment. License holders would be required to provide live music rather than records. Hilmes, *Radio Voices*.

17. Hilmes, *Radio Voices.*

18. Starr, *Creation of the Media*, 355–356.

19. Lears, *Fables of Abundance*; Cross, *All-Consuming Century.*

20. Smulyan, *Selling Radio*; L. Benjamin, *Freedom of the Air*. Benjamin notes that the general legislative attitude toward radio in these debates was that radio was seen "not so much as a medium of free expression as a medium of commerce, much like motion pictures" (214).

21. See, e.g., Starr, *Creation of the Media*; and Smulyan, *Selling Radio.*

22. Section 18 of the Radio Act of 1927 required that any licensee who granted one candidate for political office access to the air must do the same for all other candidates for that office. This requirement was amended in Section 315 of the Communications Act of 1934 to coverage of only "legally qualified" candidates, with exceptions for news coverage and documentaries.

23. See, e.g., Starr, *Creation of the Media.*

24. *Trinity*, 853. This decision turned on a similar understanding of private and public interests as that in KFKB. The language of this passage also in some ways echoed the critique of commercial radio made by the advocates of educational radio, emphasizing the scientific value of radio and its potential for progress.

25. *Trinity*, 853.

26. Both public speaking and publication were similarly conceptualized as expressions of one's ideas. Today, speeches are often written by one person and performed by another. However, this practice was not so common until the twentieth century. For example, the first president to retain a speech writer was Warren Harding. Earlier presidents may have drawn on the penmanship of others or collaborated on speeches, but it was not an institutionalized and visible practice until the mid-twentieth century. Vilade, *President's Speech.*

27. There were always other views on the role of the editor. For example, Benjamin Franklin's idea of a free press was for the newspaper to act as a conduit for ideas of others, somewhat akin to a common carrier; Starr, *Creation of the Media*, 60. The association of the newspaper and the opinion of an individual, by some accounts, began to change in the late nineteenth century, as editorial opinion moved to the back pages and more factual, "telegraphic" news took over the front pages. Papers distinguished themselves on the speed and breadth of the information they conveyed, rather than on the editorial point of view. Czitrom, *Media and the American Mind*. However, as this chapter will argue, much of the ideological association of editors as speakers remained active in public discourse and law.

28. To make matters more complicated, the license holder was not always the same as the owner of the equipment, leading to some conceptual confusion over whether the radio station was associated with the equipment of transmission or the license to broadcast. Given this, it was difficult to locate ownership and authorship in the new medium. Streeter, *Selling the Air.*

29. In the early 1930s, several states passed laws stating that defamation over the air was not oral defamation (slander) but defamation via publication (libel), due to the broad reach of the medium. L. Benjamin, *Freedom of the Air.*

30. He noted that some other lower courts had agreed with the categorization of radio as a common carrier but that they were wrong. *Sorensen v. Wood*, 123 Neb. 348 (1932).

31. On legislators and the discussion of radio as a common carrier, see L. Benjamin, *Freedom of the Air*.

32. The National Council on Freedom from Censorship drafted a bill in 1932 to try to clarify the situation. It argued that radio stations, like telegraph companies, could not be held responsible for messages they could not exclude. It suggested limits to what could be considered slander and standards for placing responsibility (liability would be restricted to the utterer of the speech, with stations only liable when they were active collaborators with the speaker). The attempt failed and the responsibility of license holders for the speech of political candidates was not clarified until 1959, in *Farmers Educational and Cooperative Union of America v. WDAY*, 360 U.S. 525. L. Benjamin, *Freedom of the Air*.

33. The term "chain" was also applied to newspaper consolidation, in which one publisher (e.g., William Randolph Hearst, Frank Gannett) owned many individual papers.

34. The reach of a station depended on wattage, which was stipulated by the type of license granted by the FRC. The agency issued licenses for local, regional and "clear channel" stations; the latter could reach a large swath of the country (as well as Canada and Mexico), in particular large rural areas that would not be served by local or regional stations.

35. See, e.g., Cantril and Allport, *Psychology of the Radio*; Lazarsfeld and Stanton, *Radio Research*; and other research projects of the Office of Radio Research and the Payne Fund. See also Hilmes, *Radio Voices*, for a cultural history of radio as a force of cultural unification. Hilmes notes that the discussion of radio as a unifying force was particularly strong in the 1920s.

36. Chafee and Meiklejohn used the language of social interests; later Thomas Emerson would use the term "social good." Emerson, "Toward a General Theory."

37. Chafee argued that there were two reasons for, or interests in, freedom of speech: individual autonomy and the broad social interest in democratic discussion and decision making. The latter drew on a long liberal tradition, though Chafee's articulation was framed by the Progressive Era. Legal historians argue that Chafee's grounding of his civil libertarian argument in terms of democracy was a strategy to win over Progressive legal scholars and jurists who were leery of individual rights as property arguments (in part, in the context of the use of individualism in arguments that the right to contract invalidated labor and other Progressive regulation [aka Lochnerism]). Rabban, *Free Speech in Its Forgotten Years*; Graber, *Transforming Free Speech*. See also White, "First Amendment Comes of Age." Graber also argues that Chafee grounded the protection of the minority viewpoint in an argument about the benefits to the majority because he feared courts would not protect the individual rights of immigrants and those holding radical views.

38. Graber, *Transforming Free Speech*. This may have been common in nineteenth-century scholarship on constitutional law, but there were other more radical popular understandings of expressive freedom in circulation. Rabban, *Free Speech in Its Forgotten Years*. There was also a more complicated understanding of freedom of speech in state constitutions and in other areas of law. Blanchard, "Filling the Void."

39. Lebovic, *Free Speech and Unfree News*. The Court had previously employed a nostalgic ideal of the newspaper rather than an empirically grounded description, notably in the *Mutual* case, where the justices had contrasted movies to newspapers based on the commercialism of the former (despite the examples of the Hearst and Pulitzer empires

and the elite criticism of the commercial sensationalism of the "yellow press"). It was not until the late 1940s and early 1950s that the Court acknowledged the commercial aspects of the press, to argue that more crass publications (from lurid picture magazines to movies) existed on a sliding scale with more traditional news, rather than in a distinct category. *Winters v. New York* (1948); *Burstyn v. Wilson* (1952).

40. Morris Ernst, for one, used this rhetoric. Pickard, *America's Battle*. At the same time, there were smaller publishers invested in more nineteenth-century economies of circulation. Sam Lebovic nicely details how opposition to substantive New Deal policies on the part of such publishers (many of whom operated in the South) was linked to opposition to federal publicity and the massification of economies of news circulation. Lebovic, *Free Speech and Unfree News.*

41. Beginning in the late nineteenth century, the mechanical work of printing was thoroughly separated from the editorial work. Printers had unions, while few reporters did. By the 1930s, editorial work was segmented into specialization by topic ("beats") but also by process, so that reporting work was distinct from copy editing. Nerone and Barnhurst, "US Newspaper Types."

42. In the 1930s and 1940s, media reformers and press critics drew on a positive liberties approach to argue that, in order to achieve the social interest in freedom of speech, the government had an affirmative duty to create conditions that allowed a diversity of views.

43. See, e.g., George Seldes's *Lords of the Press* (1938) and *Freedom of the Press* (1935) and Harold Ickes's *America's House of Lords* (1939). Cinematic press criticism ranged from the critique of the effect of commercialism on journalism and journalists in *Five Star Signal* (Mervyn LeRoy, 1931) to the critiques of publishers as cynical political puppeteers in Frank Capra's *Meet John Doe* (1941) and Orson Welles's *Citizen Kane* (1941).

44. Most famously, see Habermas, *Structural Transformation.*

45. Seldes, *Lords of the Press*; Seldes, *Freedom of the Press.*

46. Lebovic, *Free Speech and Unfree News.*

47. FCC commissioner Clifford Durr complained in 1944 that 74 percent of the advertising dollars in radio came from just four industries: food and beverages, drugs, soaps/cleaners, and tobacco. Such a concentrated industry could not be considered "free." Durr, "Freedom of Speech for Whom?"

48. John Rorty, "Order on the Air," *Nation*, May 9, 1934; Caldwell, "Freedom of Speech"; Czitrom, *Media and the American Mind.*

49. The ACLU and advocates for noncommercial radio targeted what they saw as censorship at multiple levels—from the FRC in its allocation of licenses primarily to commercial broadcasters to station managers for their decisions not to air controversial speech or speakers. For more on such efforts, see L. Benjamin, *Freedom of the Air*; and McChesney, "Free Speech and Democracy." Morris Ernst, a leading lawyer for the ACLU, argued that freedom of speech should be understood as an audience's right to listen or receive (see the Mellett epigraph for this section) rather than a right to produce utterances, a position the Court would not be ready to embrace head-on for some years.

50. MacLeish, "Duty of Freedom," 188–189. This criticism echoes and extends the disenchantment with the press expressed by commentators such as Walter Lippmann in the 1920s, in response to official manipulation of information about the war.

51. Blanchard, *Press Criticism*; Starr, *Creation of the Media*; Pickard, *America's Battle*; Lebovic, *Free Speech and Unfree News*.

52. One of the major legal debates going on in this era was over whether press freedoms included freedom from economic regulation. Cases like *Associated Press v. National Labor Relations Board (NLRB)*, 301 U.S. 103 (1937) and *Associated Press v. United States*, 326 U.S. 1 (1945) decided that freedom of the press did not mean that newspapers were immune to labor and antitrust laws. These cases established that freedom of the press did not translate to total freedom in the way a publisher conducted business.

53. The conservatism of this position is illustrated by the fact that it meant the speech of editors superseded that of reporters (as in *AP v. NLRB*). Most reporters favored FDR in the 1936 and 1940s elections, but most newspapers opposed him in each. The job of the reporter was not to express his thoughts and judgments but to ventriloquize the perspectives of editors and owners. Lebovic, *Free Speech and Unfree News*.

54. Lebovic, *Free Speech and Unfree News*. One of the victories of this line of reasoning, and Hanson's legal argumentation, came in *Grosjean v. American Press Co.*, 297 U.S. 233 (1936). The Supreme Court, in striking down a tax levied by Huey Long against the opposition press, treated newspaper corporations as persons, in order to apply the First Amendment to state actions. That the Court was willing to treat corporations as persons (for limited purposes) at roughly the same time as it was defending the line against claims that advertisements were speech (i.e., *Valentine v. Chrestensen*, 316 U.S. 52 [1942]) and specifying that corporations could not claim speech rights in public forum cases (*Hague v. CIO*) is suggestive of how effective the association of newspapers with the views of editors or publishers was. The alignment of the First Amendment with business interests was not only a media phenomenon. In the 1930s, businesses and conservative legal practitioners began to use freedom of expression as an argument in resisting New Deal regulation and refusing to bargain with unions. Weinrib, *Taming of Free Speech*.

55. Broadcasters would develop their own techniques of deflecting regulation. On the way that the "public interest" became the ground for contests between social movements and broadcasters (who attempted to align their interests with the public interests), see Perlman, *Public Interests*.

56. The Court began to consider what would be later called a right to receive information in discussion of the interests or rights of listeners under the First Amendment in the 1940s. The first case to do so involved a street speaker and his record player; *Cantwell v. Connecticut* (1940). The second, discussed here, involved radio; *NBC v. United States* (1943). The Court began to discuss freedom of speech as including a right to hear ideas or information in cases like *United Statues v. Congress of Industrial Organizations*, 335 U.S. 106 (1948). A right to receive literature shows up in *Martin v. City of Struthers*, 319 U.S. 141 (1943).

57. FCC, *Report on Chain Broadcasting* (Persuant to Commission Order no. 37), Docket no. 5060, May 1941. The commission was convened in part in response to a complaint from a would-be competitor, Mutual Broadcasting System, a smaller network run on a less centralized, more cooperative structure than NBC and CBS.

58. FCC, *Report on Chain Broadcasting*, 20.

59. While a concern about the undue influence of a few businessmen accountable only to dispersed stockholders was in the background of the report, its predominant rhet-

oric was of establishing and restoring competition. For a critical analysis of this assumption and framing, see Streeter, *Selling the Air*.

60. *NBC v. United States*, Brief for United States, 118–121.

61. *NBC v. United States*, Brief for United States, 118.

62. Note the passive voice in phrasing such as "the object of the prohibition is to maintain a competitive system under which freedom of speech will not be impaired" (*NBC v. United States*, Brief for United States, 119). The exact nature and identity of those competing and speaking are not clear.

63. The promised competition never materialized. While NBC was forced to divest one of its networks, creating a new national network, ABC, the basic business of the networks was not adversely affected (despite industry predictions that the rules would spell the demise of "quality" radio). There were now four national networks, NBC, CBS, ABC, and Mutual, though the Mutual network was never able to affiliate with high-power stations or attract large sponsors. Three big networks and one weaker network (Mutual) would continue to dominate radio throughout the 1940s; NBC, CBS, and ABC were able to leverage advertising, talent, and equipment to transition to and dominate television until the 1990s.

64. *NBC v. United States*, Appellant's Brief, 39.

65. *Red Lion v. FCC*, 395 U.S. 367 (1969). This meant that a TV station's obligation to provide both sides of an issue trumped the economic or expressive preferences of the station owner.

66. In this discussion, I draw on Streeter's analysis of the ascendency of competition in American policy discourse in the twentieth century, and how the dichotomy of monopoly (restriction) and competition (freedom) impoverishes regulation and free speech discourse. Streeter, *Selling the Air*.

67. Sklar, *Corporate Reconstruction*.

68. Commission on Freedom of the Press, *Free and Responsible Press*, 108.

69. See, e.g., *Stromberg v. California*, 283 U.S. 359 (1931); and *Hague v. CIO*.

70. These concerns have been at the heart of investigations of media effects, from the Payne Fund studies to current investigations of video games. Concerns about the effects of social media veer off from these concerns, in that they are not about mass-produced culture but rather centrally about changes in intimacy, publicity, accountability, and on the flip side, impunity.

71. For examples of arguments that freedom of speech and freedom of the press be distinguished, see Commission on Freedom of the Press, *Free and Responsible Press*; Baker, *Human Liberty*; and Schauer, "Towards an Institutional First Amendment."

72. *Mutual v. Ohio*; *Pathé v. Cobb*.

73. In *Lovell v. Griffin*, the City of Griffin had barred a Jehovah's Witness from distributing literature under a city ordinance restricting such distribution (as a public nuisance). The city argued that it was not a restriction of freedom of speech or press because it did not bar anyone from publishing a pamphlet, just from handing it out in public. The Court disagreed. It appears to be the first time that this distinction was made.

74. In *Schneider v. New Jersey*, 308 U.S. 147 (1938), a series of city ordinances requiring that distribution of literature be preapproved by local authorities was overturned on the same grounds as *Lovell*. The Court noted that the cities could enforce time, place, and manner restrictions on the distribution of literature and could restrict the distribution of

fraudulent (e.g., commercial) literature. On the class politics of the sound-truck cases, see Radovac, "War on Noise." *Saia v. New York*, 334 U.S. 558 (1948), expanded the rights of urban masses to have a voice in the streets, a right that was rolled back in favor of more bourgeois interests in peace and quiet in *Kovacs v. Cooper*, 336 U.S. 77 (1949).

75. Barbas, "Creating the Public Forum." Barbas shows how the concept and terminology of the public forum migrated from efforts to make radio more dialogic and democratic and demonstrates how concerns about the ability of the average citizen to compete with (wealthy and powerful) radio shaped public forum law.

76. This was the decision that was appealed to the Supreme Court in *Hague v. CIO*. *CIO v. Hague*, 101 F.2d 774 (3d Cir. 1939), cited in Barbas, "Creating the Public Forum," 855. A similar logic was applied to picketing in *Milk Wagon Drivers v. Meadowmoor Dairies, Inc.*, 312 U.S. 287 (1941), where the justices said that "picketing is the workingman's communication" (293).

77. Radical speakers like the Industrial Workers of the World had argued for a right to reach a broader audience via the use of the city streets in the 1910s (most famously in the free speech fights). Rabban, *Free Speech in Its Forgotten Years*. Also, arguments that freedom of speech should include a right to proselytize imply a similar address to a broad audience, or dissemination.

78. The ordinance restricting distribution in *Lovell* was not an anomaly. Many cities had turned to restrictions on distribution of literature in order to curb litter and reduce advertising and/or to get around the more stringent First Amendment protections on publishing. This shift is also a testament to the increasing social and political import of distribution and access as axes of power and influence in public communication with the rise of mass media.

79. The other party in the case was a particularly hated (by labor) mayor, Frank Hague, who was roundly critiqued as an American fascist. For a detailed discussion of the case, see Weinrib, *Taming of Free Speech*, 226–269.

80. The ongoing labor disputes were both physical and ideological, and the potential for advocacy to tip into violence was much more present in the jurisprudence of the late 1930s and early 1940s than today. This can be seen in cases decided at roughly the same time, like the *Milk Wagon Drivers* case, where the justices argued when strikes tipped over into violence of intimidation they were no longer speech. The justices had determined that disputes over economic issues were part and parcel of public speech (matters of public and not merely private import), but they worked hard to draw the line between legitimate and illegitimate forms of this dispute. Articulating disputes in disembodied terms—as clashes of ideas rather than bodies—helped to place one's case on the legitimate side of this line.

81. *Hague v. CIO*, Respondent's Brief, 4. This carriage was essential, the brief argued, to the "propagation of an idea"; the language of carriage and propagation both suggest metaphors of radio transmission.

82. *Hague*, 521, 524. This was in part in response to the case presented by Mayor Hague and his lawyers, who argued the CIO was fomenting a communist plot. The court positioned the activity, in contrast, as merely passing along information about the law of the land. The modesty and technicality of the act are of interest to me—the description used in *Hague* foreshadows other forms of expression that do not involve humanist no-

tions of mind, creativity, or conscience, from the "mere tabulations" of the statistician to the mere declarations of a price or commercial transaction (discussed in chapter 4).

83. As in freedom to speak, freedom to publish, and freedom to advocate. The cases in which the freedom to distribute information was extended are *Thornhill v. Alabama* (1940); *Carlson v. California*, 310 U.S. 106 (1940); and *Saia*. *Kovacs* limited the right of citizens to amplification extended in *Saia*.

84. Peters, "Information."

85. See Barbas, "Creating the Public Forum."

86. The justices used "distribution" and "dissemination" interchangeably. While distribution had an industrial set of connotations, the agricultural metaphor of dissemination has close ties with broadcasting, another agricultural metaphor that was by the 1930s closely associated with the working of radio. See Peters, *Speaking into the Air*, for a wide-ranging history of the idea of dissemination and the tensions between dialogue and dissemination in Western thought.

87. This list of terms is derived from a large-scale computational analysis of the language used in twentieth-century Supreme Court decisions involving free speech claims. Using keyword-in-context searches (e.g., "freedom to" + 5 words; "freedom of" + 5 words), I compiled a dated list of the different terms used to define or specify freedom of speech. In the early twentieth century, these terms have an anthropocentric focus on debate and persuasion; by the late 1930s and early 1940s, the terms shift from a dialogic concern with persuasion to a more technological concern with dissemination. For more on the digital methods of text analysis used in this chapter and the next, see the appendix.

88. Printing might be a means of mass dissemination, but prior to the interventions of structuralism and poststructuralism, it was often discussed as a romantic meeting of minds between an individual author and a specific reader.

89. Part of the post–World War I transformation of free speech law taking place in the 1930s and early 1940s was a sense that the most important role of the First Amendment was in protecting dissenting speech (in sharp contrast to the approach of the 1910s, in which dissenting speech was often determined to have a "bad tendency" to harm society and thus could be suppressed). The notion that we must protect the speech we hate dates to this era and these debates.

Radio was not only a one-to-many medium; there were many dialogic aspects of radio in the 1930s and 1940s. See Goodman, *Radio's Civic Ambition*. However, discussions of the power of radio tended to focus on dissemination over dialogue.

90. For more on citizens' rights to amplification and its limits, see *Saia* and *Kovacs*.

91. The report emphasized that this duty and responsibility should remain with the industry. Neither legislators nor the courts could effectively enforce this role. Commission on Freedom of the Press, *Free and Responsible Press*.

92. Meiklejohn, *Free Speech*, 41.

93. The ideal of the town hall as an example of public discourse has been subject to criticism. See, e.g., Post, "Meiklejohn's Mistake"; and Schudson, "Why Conversation Is Not the Soul of Democracy."

94. A view of liberties as "positive" suggests that the government has an active role in securing rights, or even creating opportunities for citizens to exercise those rights, while an understanding of liberties as "negative" holds that rights/freedom is best achieved by

governmental inaction. The clash over positive and negative liberties was a strong current in policy debates of the 1930s and 1940s (attendant to the transformation of the role of the state in the New Deal).

95. *Associated Press v. United States*, 20 (emphasis added).

96 The audience/public's right to receive information would later be recognized in *Red Lion*.

97. Bezanson, *Art and Freedom of Speech*.

98. For more on this case and the normative underpinnings of the audiences' rights in the decision, see Stein, *Speech Rights*.

99. Carey, *Communication as Culture*. Carey locates this economy in the development of the telegraph, in which human messages are encoded as electronic signals in order to be transmitted over the wire.

100. Gleick, *Information*. For an overview of the evolution of computers from number processors to linguistic processors and its consequences, see Streeter, *Net Effect*.

101. The justices first reference the flow of ideas in *Associated Press v. United States*, discussed in this section. Before this, it was primarily goods and commerce that flowed; after, ideas flowed from books differently than from picket lines (*Hughes v. Superior Court of California*, 339 U.S. 460 [1950]); states sought to limit the flow of ideas into the minds of men (*Adler v. Board of Education of the City of New York*, 342 U.S. 485 [1952]); the flow of ideas became the flow within a competitive arena (*CBS v. Democratic National Committee*, 412 U.S. 94 [1973]); and finally, as analyzed in the next chapter, commerce and ideas flowed together in advertisements (*Virginia State Board of Pharmacy v. Virginia Citizens Consumer Council, Inc.*, 425 U.S. 748 [1976]) and in campaigning by corporations (*First National Bank of Boston, et al., v. Bellotti* 435 U.S. 765 [1978]).

Chapter 4: Speech without Speakers

1. Embodied speech was firmly associated with the left, from union picketing to civil rights sit-ins and antiwar actions on campuses across the country. In this light, it is not surprising that conservative justices looked to a more bloodless conceptualization of speech, amenable to institutions and transactions more than rowdy bodies in the streets. In this sense, the posthuman theory of speech is a return to the themes of the early twentieth century, but on very different material and discursive grounds.

2. Sunstein, *Democracy and the Problem of Free Speech*. I suggest this is part of the shift in the broader meanings of speech that Leslie Kendrick argues explains so much of this free speech opportunism. Kendrick, "First Amendment Expansionism."

3. This closely parallels the death of the author, as presented by Roland Barthes and Michel Foucault.

4. Transmission need not be understood this way, but most often in the Anglo-American tradition it is. Carey, *Communication as Culture*. For a more social (and embodied) theory of transmission, see Kramer, *Medium, Messenger, Transmission*.

5. Embodied acts like flag burning and naked dancing have, of course, been recognized as expressive since this point. It is not absolute. But even in these decisions (flag burning and naked dancing), there have been powerful tensions between embodiment

and artifactualism. See Marvin, "Theorizing the Flagbody"; and Bezanson, *Art and Freedom of Speech*.

6. In "Artifactual Speech," Ronald Bezanson tracks this shift and terms it an "artifactual" strand of free speech theory.

7. In chapter 1, we saw a similar focus on the ontology of film as a medium. Here, the legal rationales rest on an ontology of communication itself rather than a particular medium or form of communication.

8. See Blanchard, *Press Criticism*; and Kairys, "Freedom of Speech." A decade sometimes overlooked in histories of free speech, the 1950s were marked by Cold War hysteria and the restriction of free speech when it came to communists. Particularly illustrative of this hysteria is the contrast between Justice Jackson's rhetoric in *Barnette* (that no official may define orthodoxy in opinion) and his willingness to throw the head of the Communist Party in jail for his views, which Jackson defined as a "well organized, nationwide conspiracy" and existential threat in *Dennis et al., v. United States*, 341 US 494 (1951).

9. While it was decided in 1972, *Cohen v. California* (1971) seems a part of the general legal spirit of the 1960s. The case is notable for the fact that it explicitly included the emotional force of a particular phrase (here, "Fuck the draft!" emblazoned on a jacket worn in court), and not only the ideas conveyed by words, as a component of the speech in free speech.

10. This expansion was curbed by the creation of the *O'Brien* test in 1968, discussed in chapter 5.

11. *Red Lion v. FCC* (1969). The primacy of the public interest would be walked back a few years later in favor of the rights of owners in *CBS v. Democratic National Committee*, 412 US 94 (1973). For more on this, see Stein, *Speech Rights*.

12. Rights of access to mass media were a major theme of progressive legal scholars in the 1960s (most famously associated with Jerome Barron). For more on the failures of the right to access in the 1960s, see Sunstein, "New Deal for Speech"; and Stein, *Speech Rights*.

13. This is, of course, a simplification. Many liberal justices remained on the Supreme Court, and the early 1970s in particular saw some famous liberal decisions. In terms of free speech, these included the decision that the Nixon administration could not prevent publication of the Pentagon Papers in the name of national security, and also the extension of free speech to include the emotional force of a message. But it also was the era in which the Court reversed itself on the relation of the public and media owners, saying that the editorial discretion of broadcasters (and newspapers) trumped the interests of the public, in *CBS v. DNC* (1973) and *Miami Herald Publishing v. Tornillo*, 418 US 241 (1974).

14. Sunstein, *Democracy and the Problem of Free Speech*. For more on the political, economic, and regulatory reasons that corporations turned to the First Amendment (and other parts of the Bill of Rights) to combat regulation, see Mayer, "Personalizing the Impersonal."

15. See *Sorrell v. IMS Health, Inc.*, 564 US 552 (2011); and *Cicilline v. Jewel Food Stores, Inc.*, 542 F. Supp. 2d. 842 (2008).

16. The case was a challenge to the 1974 amendments to the Federal Election Campaign Act of 1971, which were enacted in response to the allegations of abuses in the Nixon campaign.

17. *Buckley v. Valeo*, 424 US 1 (1976). The decision distinguished between campaign expenditures, which were necessary aspects of the expression of particular political ideas by candidates, and campaign contributions by others. Contributions, the justices reasoned, were more general expressions of support; restricting the amount of these contributions did not censor this communication of support.

18. *First National Bank v. Bellotti* (1978). It is worth noting that Schauer's empirical definition of the legal term of art speech involving a sender, message, and receiver was published just before these cases, in which we begin to see speech without speakers. Schauer, *Free Speech*.

19. This conceptualization of social relations in terms of psychology and personality did not go away in the 1960s and 1970s, but rather was transferred to other, less institutional sites of discourse, in particular that of the counterculture and feminism. Cohen-Cole, *Open Mind*; Illouz, *Cold Intimacies*.

20. In *The Net Effect*, Thomas Streeter notes that by the 1970s the substratum of computation was commonly understood as symbols—and computers as communication machines—a process that began with the move to programming languages (in which programming a computer became a practice of symbol manipulation).

21. Geoghegan, "Information"; Peters, "Information." Per Peters, in the seventeenth and eighteenth centuries, information referred to sense data, the impressions of the outside world on the mind of an individual. By the late nineteenth and early twentieth centuries, information had become abstracted from human bodies and senses—the data desired by the state in order to make that which one could formerly only imagine into something "factual and manageable" ("Information," 14).

22. Peters, "Information," 15. Similarly, in *How We Became Posthuman*, N. Katherine Hayles describes the changes in cultural and scientific conceptions of intelligence, life, and agency that she terms "posthumanism" as a process via which "information lost its body."

23. The brief-lived Office of Emergency Management (1940–42) also contained a Division of Information; the OWI took over the work that had formerly been housed there.

24. Searches for uses of the term "information" in legal decisions involving free speech claims show that prior to the late 1930s, it appeared only as a technical legal term: "an information" was a formal charge or complaint. This use was replaced by information as communication in the late 1930s and 1940s. For more on the methodology employed here, see the appendix.

25. A year later, in *Milk Wagon Drivers v. Meadowmoor Dairies, Inc.* (1941), the Court placed limits on the right to picket, deciding that when picketing turned violent, free speech rights ended. The case argued conduct that was accompanied by speech could be regulated, even if it interfered with speech (as long as the regulation targeted only the conduct and did so in service of a significant government interest). This is distinct from symbolic speech (or expressive conduct) in which the action itself conveys ideas. On the distinction, see Nimmer, "Meaning of Symbolic Speech."

26. *Cantwell v. Connecticut* (1940); *Chaplinsky v. New Hampshire*, 315 US 568 (1942). The latter described "fighting words, which were" likely to produce violence rather than thought or debate. In 1952, the Court upheld an Illinois law prohibiting the publication or

exhibition of any depiction arguing the "depravity, criminality, unchastity, or lack of virtue of a class of citizens of any race, color, creed or religion" because it conveyed no (useful) information and because it was highly likely to cause immediate harm or disorder (*Beauharnais v. Illinois*, 343 US 250 [1952]). The *Beauharnais* decision has since been superseded but not overturned. The reasoning in *Chaplinsky* and *Beauharnais* about speech as the conveyance of ideas was in tension with the contemporaneous reasoning in *Winters v. New York* (1949), where the justices argued that freedom of speech was not restricted to the exposition of ideas.

27. See Lippmann, *Liberty and the News*, on information as the raw material for the production of public opinion. Only a few years later, Lippmann would more famously and pessimistically abandon the hope that better information might produce better opinion. The amount and complexity of information about the world, the trickery of symbols, and the political economy of the mass media confounded the ability of average individuals to be truly informed. Lippmann, *Public Opinion*; see also Lippmann, *Phantom Public*.

28. In tracing this history back to the 1920s and communications engineering, I wish to—along with other scholars like Jonathan Sterne in *MP3*—complicate histories of cybernetics and information theory that begin with World War II and defense research.

29. Hayles, *How We Became Posthuman*.

30. It was easy to quantify the number of letters carried by the post office, or the number of newspapers published. The invisibility of the data of electronic communication made it hard to quantify for bureaucrats as well as engineers. The census measured the number of radio stations and telephone receivers and lines, but it could not measure what was transmitted. Geoghegan, "Information." See also Sterne, *MP3*; and Mills, "Deaf Jam."

31. Compare the approach to information as a resource that could be maximized for profit in the Bell Labs research and the concept of the information economy or society (e.g., Porat, "Information Economy"). For a transnational history of this report, see Kline, *Cybernetics Moment*, 202–228.

32. Hartley, "Transmission of Information." The psychological factors here include those like linguistic systems, shared cultural knowledge, and other codes that introduced confounding and unpredictable variables into the assessment of channel capacity. Bracketing questions of interpretation (or mutual intelligibility) and focusing on signals alone (irrespective of intelligibility) allowed for an assessment of the physical capacity of the line for signal transmission—a key step in maximizing efficiency of the lines.

33. Hartley, "Transmission of Information," 536 (emphasis added). The paper was based on a presentation by Hartley and coworker Harry Nyquist at a conference in Italy in 1927.

34. It is notable that this turn toward a quantification of symbols took place at the same time as the rise in discussions of polysemy and interpretation. This coincidence raises questions as to whether this turn was about not only efficiency but was also a response to and defense against psychological indeterminacy.

35. Mills, "Media and Prosthesis"; Mills, "Deafening"; Sterne, *MP3*.

36. The mathematical modeling of continuous wave transmission, such as human speech or music, in terms of discrete signals (sampling) was a key contribution of Claude Shannon's influential article, "Mathematical Theory." Sterne, *MP3*.

37. Shannon, "Mathematical Theory," 379 (emphasis in original). This point, however,

was already central to Hartley's 1928 publication. See Sterne, *MP3*, for more on Hartley's and Nyquist's works and the political economy of Bell Labs foundations of information theory.

38. Mills, "Deafening."

39. Sterne, *MP3*; Liu, *Freudian Robot.*

40. Communication, as successful transmission, is understood in this engineering discourse as replication or repetition, terms that were, in earlier decades of sociology (e.g., Le Bon) and legal reasoning, associated with degraded or primitive communication, not the speech of "civilized" liberal subjects.

41. This point is illustrated in Shannon's experiments to determine the statistical structure of English. As Lydia Liu points out in *Freudian Robot,* these experiments mimicked and reversed the surrealist game of exquisite corpse by revealing the working of statistics and probability in the place of a subconscious. These games are preserved in Shannon's papers, where one can see various experiments in predicting the next letter in any given message. See, in particular, Shannon Papers, Library of Congress, Washington, DC, box 7.

42. Liu, *Freudian Robot*; Geoghegan, "From Information Theory to French Theory." Roman Jakobson in particular drew on Shannon's model and was an early participant in the discussions of cybernetics at the Macy conferences. Lacan described the unconscious on the model of the circuit in "Circuit" (89). And Derrida draws on computation and cybernetics—as well as on examples of machinic and embodied "writing" to argue that there was no "soul" or consciousness that guaranteed the meaning of an utterance—in *Of Grammatology* (9).

43. The justices described speech in terms of utterances three times in the 1920s, once in the 1930s, sixteen times in the 1940s, eleven times in the 1950s, three times in the 1960s, and not at all after that. The "utterance" (and other terms used to describe and define speech, such as "argument" or "dissent") was the vehicle for the beliefs, thoughts, convictions, ideas, and conscience—all understood as individual creations and/or property—that the justices sought to safeguard through freedom of expression. Publication was similarly figured as a vehicle for an individual's or group's ideas or convictions. This assessment is based on a large-scale, digital catalog of the definitions of and cognates for speech in twentieth-century Supreme Court cases. See the appendix.

44. Geoghegan, "Information," 178 (emphasis added). He could have added "for the extraction of monetary value."

45. I do not mean to suggest that the legal discourse analyzed here is responding to or drawing explicitly on the academic discussion of posthumanism, but rather that the analytic term applies to the legal discourse. Further, I argue that the legal discourse was not the product of poststructural or posthuman theory but that both theory and legal discourse are seen as products of social, cultural, and technological changes surrounding computation.

46. Geoghegan, "Information"; Liu, *Freudian Robot.* See also Hayles, *How We Became Posthuman.*

47. Roughly a decade later, Wiener gave a similar take on human-machine interactions in a description of his World War II research predicting the flight paths of enemy pilots. Wiener noted that in predictions that encompassed mechanical capabilities and

human behavior, it was necessary to reduce the whole "system" to a single basis, and because we had a better (more rigorous) understanding of mechanics, the behavior of the human element should be placed within the framework of math and engineering. On the centrality of this move to cybernetics and post–World War II social science in the United States, see Galison, "Ontology of the Enemy."

48. Galison, "Ontology of the Enemy"; Shannon and Weaver, *Mathematical Theory*. In this translation from technical journal to more and more popular audiences, the shift in title from "A Theory . . . " to *The Mathematical Theory* telegraphs a broadening of the scope of the theory, pushed by Wiener but not altogether rejected by Shannon. Kline, *Cybernetics Moment*.

49. Weaver, "Mathematics," 11.

50. See Wiener, *Human Use of Human Beings*.

51. Models of behavior based on information theory can be seen in game theory and its adoption in social theory like Erving Goffman's *The Presentation of Self in Everyday Life*, which drew on game theory as a model (and which is fundamentally as concerned with the cybernetic theme of control via information as it with dramaturgy). The role of the Cold War in the adoption and popularization of information theory is arguably neglected here. For more thorough treatments of this key conjuncture, see Erickson et al., *How Reason Almost Lost Its Mind*; Kline, *Cybernetics Moment*; and P. Edwards, *Closed World*.

52. And in a different vein, as early as the late 1930s, commercial transactions were becoming legible as expression (though legal claims of expressiveness for commercials failed in this era). It was in the 1960s that advertisements took on a more creative and expressive social meaning—which no doubt was a key cultural precedent for *Virginia*. For more on this moment in the history of advertising, see Frank, *Conquest of Cool*; and Ewan, *Captains of Consciousness*.

53. Ruesch and Kees, *Nonverbal Communication*. The work is clearly indebted to cybernetics and information theory, with sections on feedback, control, and coding as well as on the information value of movement and gestures. The book begins with a quote from Weaver's 1949 *Scientific American* article. In addition, Gregory Bateson, an early cybernetics enthusiast and organizer of the Macy conferences, was a consultant for the book.

54. Ruesch and Kees, *Nonverbal Communication*, 36–37. While Darwin's study of emotion in humans and animals is an obvious precursor, the uptake of nonverbal communication as a subfield did not take place till the 1950s and 1960s, and the popularization of the idea of "body language" can be dated to the best-selling book *Body Language* in 1970. (The cover of the book, tellingly, promises to read the body of an attractive woman, providing ways to assess questions such as whether her body says she is loose, or a manipulator; other guides about how to read the bodies of potential job applicants and other ways of rendering the bodies of others as consumable or productive soon followed.)

55. The idea that symbols are effectively signals, which convey information about the sender, is in fact the rationale that Eric Posner offers for the importance of symbols and their legal protection in a 1989 article, "Symbols, Signals and Social Norms." The article was a continuation of Posner's work, begun in the early 1970s, on using economic and other rational behavioral models as a basis for jurisprudence.

56. The Macy conferences were one of the sites of this transfer. The Macy group be-

gan to shift its focus of research and discussion from "feedback" to "information" in 1949, after the publication of Shannon and Weaver's book. By the 1951 meeting, "information" had replaced "feedback" as a key metaphor linking social, biological, and mathematical systems. Kline, *Cybernetics Moment*, 56.

57. For the influence of information theory and its sibling, cybernetics, on these fields, see Kline, *Cybernetics Moment*; Gleick, *Information*; P. Edwards, *Closed World*; and Hobart and Schiffman, *Information Ages*.

58. James Carey's 1985 essay advocating for a "ritual" view of communication in which poetics, social roles, and association are as important as the transfer of information was a pushback against the dominance of this model. See Carey, *Communication as Culture*.

59. The essay was structured on the S > M > R flow (a complication of it). While the model reinserts audience activity (acknowledged in the work of the 1930s and 1940s but downplayed in much postwar research on media effects), in theorizations of communication, it does so within the structured confines of an ideological system rather than the wilds of individual psychology. Hall, "Encoding/Decoding."

60. The way that postwar mass communication studies occluded the industrial aspects of mass communication was heavily critiqued by the more critical scholarship emerging in the late 1970s and 1980s. See, e.g., Gitlin, "Media Sociology"; and McQuail, *Mass Communication Theory*.

61. McLuhan was influenced by the work of Norbert Wiener; his famous slogan "the medium is the message" most likely drew on Wiener's theorization of society in terms of message transmission. McLuhan's *Understanding Media* is particularly full of discussions of cybernetics and the shift from a mechanical to informational social and economic order.

62. Turner, *From Counterculture to Cyberculture*. But see the concerns held by many on the left about the power of automation to take away jobs, detailed in Kline, *Cybernetics Moment*.

63. Kline, *Cybernetics Moment*.

64. Bell, *Coming of the Post-Industrial Society*; Drucker, *Age of Discontinuity*. See also Beniger, *Control Revolution*. Alvin and Heidi Toffler promoted a set of similar ideas in popular magazines and books starting in the mid-1960s (where they introduced and popularized the idea of "information overload").

65. The labels "information society" and "postindustrial society" were closely tied, if not interchangeable, underscoring the idea that what came after industry in the phrase "postindustrial society" was information work. For more on this, see Kline, *Cybernetics Moment*.

66. The report was spurred in part by the academic studies noted above and in part by the fact that a major economic rival, Japan, had in the late 1960s begun to measure information as a portion of its national economy. Kline, *Cybernetics Moment*.

67. Porat, "Information Economy," 2 (emphasis added).

68. Mayer, "Personalizing the Impersonal."

69. Redish may in fact have been the one to insert the term "commercial speech" into legal discourse. His article is the first reference I found to the term in scholarly databases, and the first use of the term I found in a legal decision dates to 1973, two years after the publication of his article. It was adopted by the Court in 1976, in *Virginia State Board*

of Pharmacy v. Virginia Citizens Consumer Council, 425 US 748 (1976). The term has since been used to characterize legal decisions about advertising in the 1940s and 1950s.

70. Redish, "First Amendment in the Marketplace." Redish devoted most of his argumentation to the informational value of commercials, though he somewhat hastily acknowledged that many ads were irrational, as was consumer behavior. He argued, somewhat contradictorily, that this was not a problem for granting ads First Amendment protection because (1) many political expressions and decisions were irrational, yet fully protected; and at the same time (2) the irrationality of consumer behavior might be the result of poor information, which could be remedied by increasing advertising (which would seem to be contradicted by the example he sketched of fully protected commercial speech and the irrationality of voter behavior). Redish also briefly argued that advertisements (especially those that had a low informational value) were forms of artistic creation and should be protected as part of the free speech of their creators. However, most of his focus was on the informational content of ads and their benefit to their audience, both as an individual matter and as a social good.

71. My argument is not that these more difficult discussions went away, but rather that the engineering discourse provided an excellent alternative for those who wanted to resolve uncertainties.

72. This is the source of one argument for stronger protection of commercial speech. For example, when activists attack Nike's practices, their speech is granted greater protection than Nike's PR rebuttals. In "Commercial Speech," Martin Redish used this example to argue that providing less protection to commercials and PR messages is a form of viewpoint discrimination.

73. Such arguments have been repeated in social media policies on electoral ads. Facebook's decision to allow political ads without vetting them for lies or misinformation was draped in free speech rhetoric (as was the contrasting policy of Twitter, which was not to allow political ads).

74. *Virginia*, oral arguments, https://www.oyez.org/cases/1975/74-895. Lawyers for the state also argued that the law was intended to keep consumers from seeing drugs as mere commodities and from shopping around for pharmacists, on the logic that a stable (nonmarket) relationship among patient, physician, and pharmacist was in the interest of the public's health.

75. *Bigelow v. Virginia*, 421 US 809 (1975). The law at issue in this case was also a Virginia state law, which had been used to censure (fine) the publisher of a newspaper in Charlottesville, Virginia, for running advertisements for abortion services in New York, where they were legal.

76. *Virginia*, 762.

77. *Virginia*, 761.

78. See, in particular, *Valentine v. Chrestensen* (1942).

79. The justices in these cases cite *Thornhill v. Alabama* (1940) as the precedent for including factual information (and not only opinion or ideas) within speech and not *Hague v. CIO* (1939), which made a similar argument. *Hague* expanded speech rights of dissenters, and *Thornhill* stepped back the decision, crafting limits. Thus, it is the more restrictive logic that is reiterated and referred to within the legal system of citation. As is often the case, the more radical logic and rhetoric is forgotten. The other case they might

have drawn on as precedent is *Winters v. New York*; to have done so would have drawn on a different line of reasoning, in which movies and other commercial entertainments are protected because the justices cannot find solid grounds on which to draw the line between idea and amusement, propaganda and entertainment. This would have been a fitting, though perhaps less lofty, lineage to invoke.

80. *Virginia*, 757.

81. *New York Times v. Sullivan*, 376 US 254 (1964).

82. In *Fables of Abundance*, Jackson Lears describes the more informational ads of the nineteenth century and the turn toward psychologically driven advertising in the early twentieth century.

83. *Cohen v. California*. The case is credited with including elements of a message that are not strictly cognitive—emotional valence and aesthetics—as part of what is conveyed in any utterance, or example of speech.

84. *Virginia*, 765.

85. In the rhetoric of information as a great equalizer, or leveler, are the seeds of what would by the 1990s be a full-blown rhetoric of digital utopianism, in which digital networks and the information economy would erase hierarchies of race, gender, nation, and inheritance. On this discourse, see Turner, *From Counterculture to Cyberculture*; and Streeter, *Net Effect*.

86. *Bellotti*, 776.

87. The amicus briefs submitted for the appellants (First National Bank et al.) argued that the Massachusetts law had infringed businesses' political speech and that this both limited their ability to conduct business and hurt the American public by depriving them of information. In particular, the briefs submitted by Associated Industries of Massachusetts, the Greater Boston Chamber of Commerce, and the Massachusetts Taxpayer's Association and by the Northeastern Legal Foundation and Mid-America Legal Foundation contained lengthy defenses of corporate speech rights, in the name of the interests of both the corporations and the public.

88. It is worth noting that when looked at in conjunction with *Virginia*, this is a very fractured if not contradictory take on speech. In the former case, the justices avoid the connotations of meaning aligned with messages and "ideas" to include ads. Here, they look for meaning in order to avoid scrutinizing the rights of the speakers (corporations).

89. I refer here to the work of scholars who have argued that the First Amendment is becoming a popular tool to ward off economic regulation. See, e.g., Schauer and Sunstein, "Lochner's Legacy"; Balkin, "Some Realism about Pluralism"; and Wu, "Is the First Amendment Obsolete?"

90. New England Merchants National Bank, Gillette, Digital Equipment Corporation, and Wyman-Gordon Corporation were the other appellants in the case. There was organized support (amicus briefs detailing a variety of legal arguments and lists of suggested precedents) for the corporations. In contrast, only the state of Montana and the Federal Elections Commission submitted amicus briefs on behalf of the state of Massachusetts.

91. Lewis F. Powell Jr., "Attack on American Free Enterprise System" (1971), Snail Darter Documents, Paper 79, http://lawdigitalcommons.bc.edu/darter_materials/79.

92. *Bellotti*, 778.

93. In *Virginia*, the Court had made a similar argument: that "speech does not lose its

First Amendment protection because money is spent to project it" (61, summarizing the outcome of *Buckley*).

94. *Citizens United v. Federal Election Commission*, 558 US 310 (2010).

95. *Citizens United*, 341.

96. *Citizens United*, 391.

97. The use of the marketplace of ideas metaphor, while it has a long pedigree, did not become a common rationale and way of describing freedom of speech in legal decisions until the 1940s; its use skyrocketed in the 1960s. I would argue that, as well, the vision of the markets referred to in the metaphor changed during this time from the farmer's market to the stock exchange.

98. *Bellotti*, 783. Powell argued that restrictions on corporate messages depleted the general "stock of information" available to the public. His use of the term echoed its use in economics, where stock is a synchronic variable and flow is a diachronic variable. See, e.g., Boulding, *Image*.

99. While this equivalence among messages aligns well with the judicial agnosticism about value described in chapter 2, it is distinct. The withholding of judgment described in chapter 2 was more about the role of judges and judicial interpretation, while the equivalences described here are more descriptive (they contain more evaluation of messages and the public sphere).

100. I should note that categories of unprotected speech like "fighting words" and "obscenity" rely heavily on social context—as does the clear and present danger test; no justice would place speech at the center of First Amendment law across the board. Rather, it is one of the argumentative moves that legal practitioners can make in their own efforts to persuade.

101. These notions of flow, and regulation as a blockage of information, continue to animate net neutrality and other telecom policy debates. Weiland, "Expanding the Periphery."

102. *Citizens United*, 340.

103. This argument about anti-corporate discrimination was repeated in another recent case, *Sorrell v. IMS*, in which the Court struck down a Vermont patient privacy law that barred pharmacies from sharing patient information with pharmaceuticals.

104. While the "marketplace of ideas" can be traced back to John Stuart Mill (and was famously referenced by Justice Holmes in 1919), it was not a common metaphor in Supreme Court decisions until the 1960s.

105. In the 1990s, the Court found that the exclusion of gays and lesbians from parades and from the Boy Scouts were both protected speech (of those who wished to exclude the speakers) in *Hurley v. Irish-American Gay, Lesbian and Bisexual Group of Boston*, 515 US 557 (1995) and *Dale v. Boy Scouts of America*, 530 US 640 (2000). In the latter, the justices argued that the presence of James Dale, a gay man, in the Boy Scouts amounted to a message about the values of the Boy Scouts—and that an antidiscrimination suit to force the Scouts to keep Dale would violate the organization's freedom of speech. This was, as Ronald Bezanson argues in *Art and Freedom of Speech*, a decision in which there was a (somewhat inchoate) message but no speaker in the traditional sense.

106. Indeed, speech becomes coterminous with communication in some Supreme Court decisions in the late 1950s and 1960s, when the justices begin to refer to the First Amendment in terms of a freedom of communication.

107. One answer is nonsense and noise. Perhaps this is why some scholars are attempting to theorize the place of nonsense in free speech law. See Bezanson, *Art and Freedom of Speech*; and Tushnet et al., *Free Speech beyond Words*, 134–148.

Chapter 5: Speaking Machines

1. Massaro, Norton, and Kaminski, "Siri-ously 2.0"; Massaro and Norton, "Siri-ously?"

2. The Court endorsed the internet as one big site for the dissemination of personal opinion (and viewed personal computers both as individualized printing presses that enabled anyone to become a pamphleteer and as soapboxes that enabled anyone to be the town crier) in *Reno v. ACLU*, 521 US 824 (1994), 870.

3. In various lower court decisions, judges have examined whether computer programs or code can be considered speech, defining code as speech only when it speaks to other people (e.g., programs as a means of communication among programmers). See *Junger v. Daley*, F.3d 481 (2000); and *Commodity Futures Trading Commission v. Vartuli* 228 F.3d 94 (2000).

4. This has not put a halt to analyzing actions that speak in and of themselves. In the flag burning case *Texas v. Johnson*, 491 US 397 (1989), the majority did not attempt to disarticulate the message of the burning from the act. The justices referred to the burning as inherently expressive. They said the *O'Brien* test would apply if the Texas law was not aimed at curtailing expression (which it clearly was). Yet the law upheld in *O'Brien* had also been aimed at curtailing expression.

5. This is telegraphed by headlines such as "Does Computer Code Count as Free Speech?," CNBC, March 1, 2016; "Apple's Code = Speech Mistake," MIT *Technology Review*, March 1, 2016; and "Code Is Free Speech," *Time*, March 17, 2016. The claim was discussed and dissected in a variety of mainstream media outlets and tech blogs.

6. For more on the development of the code is speech argument, see Coleman, *Coding Freedom*. See also Streeter, *Net Effect*.

7. Several prominent legal scholars wrote amicus briefs in support of Corley's legal arguments against the DMCA, among them Peter Jaszi, Julie Cohen, Yochai Benkler, and Lawrence Lessig. (Rodney Smolla submitted an amicus brief in support of the studios.) *Universal City Studios v. Corley*, 273 F.3d 429 (2001), 433.

8. Gillespie, *Wired Shut*.

9. There being no DMCA in Norway, the Norwegian authorities charged the teen with illegally accessing information. He argued that because he owned the DVDs he hacked, accessing them via DeCSS was not illegal. He was acquitted.

10. Postigo, *Digital Rights Movement*.

11. The amicus briefs of prominent intellectual property scholars testified to this effect. Further, the politics of Corley and his defenders were formed in the free software movement and its critique of the extension of corporate power via copyright. See Coleman, *Coding Freedom*.

12. If the regulation in question targets only the action, it will receive intermediate scrutiny rather than strict scrutiny—a level of review in which it is easier to justify regula-

tion. On the difference between expressive conduct as symbolic speech and speech plus, see Nimmer, "Meaning of Symbolic Speech."

13. Gitelman, *Always Already New*. The legal code is similarly both text and instrument. In *Files*, Cornelia Vismann in particular argues that the law (as a set of documents, or written rules) is more instrumental than textual.

14. On the way that definitions of speech work to limit the scope of the First Amendment, see Wu, "Machine Speech."

15. *Universal City Studios, Inc. v. Reimerdes*, 111 F. Supp. 2d 294 S.D.N.Y. (2000), brief of amici curiae. https://cryptome.org/mpaa-v-2600-bac.htm.

16. See Petersen, "How Speech Lost Its Voice."

17. Amy Harmon, "Free Speech Rights for Computer Code; Suit Tests Power of Media Concerns to Control Access to Digital Content," *New York Times*, July 31, 2000. In the text of his decision in the appeal, Judge Newman referenced a different type of key—a skeleton key. Either way, looking at the program, the judges saw a key that might be used to access the property of others.

18. With the advent of the internet as a site of publication, and the ability to download and use programs immediately, the restriction on exports was interpreted as a restriction on online publishing. Two earlier legal cases had alleged that these restrictions violated freedom of speech (*Bernstein v. United States Department of Justice* [1999] and *Junger v. Daley* [2000]).

19. *Reimerdes*, 326. This followed in a tradition of analogizing computer code to print or writing by earlier programmers like Phil Salin and Donald Knuth. See Salin's influential 1991 essay "Freedom of Speech in Software," PhilSalin.com, July 14, 1991, http://philsalin.com/patents.html.

20. *Corley*, 445–446.

21. Schauer, "Boundaries." See also Post, "Encryption Source Code." Post argues that discussion of whether code is covered by the First Amendment (questions of coverage preceding questions of protection) should focus less on the ontology of code and more on the way that it is circulated or situated for use.

22. Music is a bit of a hard case for First Amendment scholars; judges and justices have declared classical and instrumental music (that is, music without words) to be speech, but they have a hard time explaining why it is so. Legal scholars have pointed out that existing justifications for free speech do not clearly explain why such music should be considered speech. See Tushnet, Chen, and Blochner, *Free Speech beyond Words*; and Munkittrick, "Music as Speech." In "On Communication," John Greenman argues that musical scores might be seen as ideational, but that the sound of music (represented by those very scores) cannot be.

23. Galloway, "Language Wants to Be Overlooked"; Hayles, "Speech, Writing, Code"; Gitelman, *Always Already New*. But compare with Chun, *Programmed Visions*.

24. In writing and print, intelligibility is also limited by factors such as the implement of inscription and quality of the page. Yet, in code the locus of intelligibility arguably resides more in the machine (which does the interpreting) than in human interlocutors.

25. Hayles, "Speech, Writing, Code." See also Chun, *Programmed Visions*. While their diagnoses of code (in particular, its performativity) differ, both Hayles and Chun emphasize the material, machinic substrate of intelligibility in computer code. Chun emphasizes

the gaps between code and its execution, problematizing the idea that code does what it says; rather, she argues, the requirements of operating systems, the libraries, and hardware (e.g., in compilation) affect—or mediate—the functionality of code. The idea that code does what it says is a fantasy of both dematerialization and of mastery: we act as if software were pure logos.

26. *Corley*, 447. The precedents on building explosive devices are mixed and seem to vary at least in part based on who the potential bomb builders are. The case that the judge cited to show that instructions could be suppressed was *United States v. Featherston*, 461 F.2d 1119 (1972), in which several Black militants were prosecuted for instructing others in making incendiary devices. On the other hand, the *Anarchist Cookbook*, a similar set of instructions created by a white antiwar protestor (and largely circulated among white dissidents, teenagers, and extremists), has been granted protection.

27. *Corley*, 451. Judge Kaplan (in a passage quoted at length in *Corley*) also, on the example of viruses (computer and biological), argued that copyright infringement could no longer penalize only those who made illegal copies but must include the circulation of tools that could be used to make copies. As with a virus where transmission risks an epidemic, he argued, dissemination itself carried substantial risk. *Reimerdes*, 331–332.

28. *Bland v. Roberts*, No. 12-1671 (4th Cir., Sept. 18, 2013); CFTC v. *Vartuli* (2000).

29. In the lower court decision, Judge Kaplan made this argument through a viral metaphor that Judge Newman quoted at length on appeal. Essentially, they argued that the responsibility for the execution of the code lay in the person who made it available, as it was inevitable that someone would run the program. In this case, the decision of the audience to act was inconsequential, not a real example of agency or a site of accountability—a stark contrast to the reasoning about words and deeds used in incitement cases.

30. *Reimerdes*, 304.

31. *Corley*, 447. Newman clarified that he was not implying that all speech was at heart informational, and that speech might also convey ideas, emotions, or thoughts.

32. For an example of this rhetoric, see "Pigdog Journal DeCSS Distribution Center," *Pigdog Journal*, February 16, 2000, https://www.pigdog.org/decss/. In Corley's deposition, the lawyers for the movie studios refer to a post on Corley's website calling the linking an act of civil disobedience. Deposition of Emmanuel Goldstein, United States District Court, Southern District of New York, June 27, 2000, archived at *2600 News*, accessed August 9, 2021, https://www.2600.com/dvd/docs/2000/0627-goldstein.txt. See also Postigo, *Digital Rights Movement*, 118–119.

33. *Virginia*, 761. Posting a program arguably does more than this, making it available for viewing and critique, as well as for decrypting DVDs. By providing information about how to program a computer, programs contribute to the production of knowledge in a general way.

34. They did, however, see the troll or prankster (esp. Judge Kaplan). The decision was in many ways crafted around the idea that bad actors might use code to create viruses or engage in other disruptive behavior (e.g., stealing domain names, hacking into the computer systems of businesses). *Reimerdes*, 308–309.

35. In "Recuperating," Post argues that discussions of whether objects or actions are speech should focus on such social actions and contexts.

36. Though the justices began to attempt to dis-articulate action and expression in

the 1940s and 1950s, debating whether the First Amendment protected only carrying placards or also "patrolling" in cases involving picketing.

37. Lawyers for O'Brien provided a particularly compelling argument that Congress had passed the amendment to quash this type of dissent, with quotes from multiple lawmakers saying as much. *United States v. O'Brien*, 391 U.S. 367 (1968), Respondent's Brief, 16–22. Despite an equally cogent argument about the legitimacy and precedents for using such evidence of legislative motive, the Supreme Court argued in a 7–1 majority that they were not convinced of a censorious motive and that legislative motive was not a valid line of argumentation. First Amendment scholars today agree that one fact that should be taken into account when determining whether or not the First Amendment applies is whether or not the law is aimed at suppressing a particular type of message, speaker, or medium. Post, "Recuperating."

38. In the 1940s and 1950s, sound trucks were understood as platforms of the workers or the poor, an alternative means of amplification to privately controlled media outlets (see chapter 3).

39. Lisa Gitelman notes the similarities between the draft card and the computer punch-card program, as simultaneously information carriers and instruments. She also points out the way that the status of the card itself became an important line of reasoning in the *O'Brien* decision: O'Brien's lawyers argued that the value of the card was in the information it carried, which was available elsewhere (in Gitelman's terms, they argued that the card was pure text). If this was true, then burning the draft card did no real harm (O'Brien could just as easily be drafted with or without the card) and was purely symbolic. Justice Warren disagreed, arguing that the card had value as a physical object and instrument. Like a receipt, it carried information and was a talisman with evidentiary power. Gitelman, *Always Already New*, 89–121. The nature of the receipt in Warren's analogy testifies to the predigital, or pre-internet, context of the decision: information requires a place (or a body) as a token, the draft card is the container of that information, and its physicality is key to its ability to travel with and track the body and identity of the potential conscript. *O'Brien*.

40. In *From Counterculture to Cyberculture*, Fred Turner describes how the punch-card ID operated as a symbol of the inhuman "machine" of warfare and corporate and institutional rationality, and the bodies of the students operated as symbols of organic human experience in the free speech movement.

41. *O'Brien*, Respondent's Brief. O'Brien's lawyers cited *Barnette, Thornhill*, and two cases involving sit-ins staged to protest segregation: Justice Harlan's concurrence in *Garner v. Louisiana*, 338 U.S. 157 (1961) (a sit-in at a lunch counter was protected speech) and the majority decision in *Brown v. Louisiana*, 383 U.S. 151 (1966) (silent sit-in and stand-up demonstrations to desegregate a library were protected speech and protestors could not be fined or arrested for breach of peace). The lawyers, further, argued that the First Amendment should protect the right to use the most "dramatic and compelling" means available to make a statement or speech. While the Court seems to have rejected this argument in *O'Brien*, several years later they accepted a similar argument, when applied to words, in arguing that banning obscenities (wearing a jacket emblazoned with "Fuck the draft!" in a courthouse) was unconstitutional as it restricted the emotional force and meaning of the utterance, in *Cohen v. California*.

42. The Warren Court was generally quite liberal on free speech issues. The *O'Brien* decision departs from this, seeming to bend over backward to accommodate the arguments of the state against compelling arguments and the evidence that the criminalization of burning draft cards was an effort by Congress to quash a particular form of dissent (in other words, pretty bald censorship).

43. Gitelman, *Always Already New*.

44. He most famously said this during a 1968 speech called "The Other America," though he had used the line before in interviews with white journalists, suggesting white America listen to the violence of the disenfranchised not as outbursts of private passions (or, worse, "primitivity") but as a political message that the conditions they were forced to live under were untenable. On King's earlier uses of the line, see Lily Rothman, "What Martin Luther King Really Thought about Riots," *Time*, April 28, 2015, http://time.com/3838515/baltimore-riots-language-unheard-quote/.

45. Turner, *From Counterculture to Cyberculture*; Gitlin, *The Whole World Is Watching*. Gitlin famously discussed how the need to attract the attention of mainstream media created incentives to spectacle and symbolic protest in the antiwar movements of the 1960s.

46. I refer here to the formal study of nonverbal behavior as a form of visual signaling, game theory, and the application of information theory to the study of DNA. Ruesch and Kees, *Nonverbal Communication*; Bateson and Kees, "Interaction"; Hayles, *How We Became Posthuman*.

47. *O'Brien*, 376.

48. This problem was at the heart of Warren's dismissal of draft-card burning as speech.

49. For example, saluting the flag or mutely occupying a segregated space. See *West Virginia State Board of Education v. Barnette* (1943); *Brown v. Louisiana*. Arguably, picketing and strikes might be included as well; in the 1940s, the justices wrestled with whether picketing was an inherently expressive activity, or whether the expressive elements might be distinguished from "patrolling" (as mere conduct). See, e.g., *Labor Board v. Fruit Packers*, 377 U.S. 58 (1964); *Cox v. Louisiana*, 379 U.S. 536 (1965); and *Walker v. Birmingham*, 388 U.S. 307 (1967).

50. It also, importantly, rendered gestural communication equivalent to linguistic communication. In doing so, it overlooked all the aspects of body language that cannot be rendered by words alone. See, e.g., Bateson, "Why Do Frenchmen?"

51. Rehnquist was dissenting in the case that declared flag burning to be speech. He argued, "Far from being a case of 'one picture being worth a thousand words,' flag burning is the equivalent of an inarticulate grunt or roar that, it seems fair to say, is most likely to be indulged in not to express any particular idea, but to antagonize others." *Texas v. Johnson*, 432.

52. There is another standard, or test—the *Spence* test—that the judges might have applied to determine whether or not the DeCSS program as a whole was expressive. Developed to determine when flag desecration was expressive and when it was merely conduct, the *Spence* test asks whether there is a speaker with the intent to send a "particularized message" (not an inchoate one) and the likelihood that this message will be understood by an audience. *Spence v. Washington*, 418 U.S. 405 (1974).

53. *Reimerdes*, Transcript of Oral Arguments.

54. There were other ways to decide the case. For example, the *Spence* test could be used to distinguish expressive uses of code from nonexpressive uses. For many examples, the First Amendment simply would not be implicated. For those in which it is, *O'Brien* could be used to determine the legitimacy of regulation. There are still other solutions. Tim Wu suggests that there is a "functionality doctrine" implicit in First Amendment law that can be used to limit opportunistic uses of the law. The functionality doctrine, he argues, holds that instruments or tools (conduits or platforms) are not speech but are relevant to First Amendment law only to the extent that they provide means for the speech of others (Tweets are speech, but Twitter as a platform is not). Wu, "Machine Speech."

55. To borrow a phrase from Morgan Weiland's analysis of a different set of cases, the legal rationales in *Corley* expanded the periphery of speech (which is most open to opportunistic claims) while threatening the core values and types of speech protected by the First Amendment. Weiland, "Expanding the Periphery."

56. Hayles, *How We Became Posthuman*; Chun, *Programmed Visions*; Inoue, "Word for Word"; and, on the work of scriveners and clerks in legal history, Halliday, "Authority in the Archives."

57. The quote comes from Douglas's dissent in *United States v. Auto Workers*, 52 U.S. 567 (1957), 595–596. To protect such speech, he argued, would be "to give constitutional dignity to an irrelevance" and to elevate meaningless communication above more important speech, such as "the impassioned plea of the orator."

58. The ability of the term search engine to refer to either a company like Google or the technological system performing the search (a product of the company) is rhetorically and politically useful. Here, I use the term "search engine" only to talk about the companies.

59. Introna and Nissenbaum, "Shaping the Web"; Vaidhyanathan, *Googlization of Everything*; Gillespie, "Relevance of Algorithms."

60. And, somewhat ironically in the context presented here, this index is made up of unauthorized copies of websites, a violation of copyright law that no one in particular seems to mind. Vaidhyanathan, *Googlization of Everything*.

61. That the arguments for treating search results as speech are not made in the name of users is, I would argue, a testament to the extent to which messages or information have come to substitute the public in arguments about the free flow of information (and market-based arguments about speech in general), documented in chapter 4. For an analysis of the relation of search results to the speech of website creators and to the expressive interests of users, see Bracha, "Folklore of Informationalism"; and Grimmelman, "The Structure of Search Engine Law."

62. Langdon was the only plaintiff in these cases to argue that his speech rights had been violated by the search engines. The court disagreed, on grounds that the First Amendment does not offer citizens any rights claims in privately owned property, or channels; the upshot was that the court ruled that in a search, search engines are the only speakers (the creators of websites cannot claim speech rights). Langdon and his lawyers also argued in vain that, like company towns, search engines had a governmental-enough function to be a public forum. *Langdon v. Google*, 474 F. Supp. 2d 622 (2007), 631.

63. Zhang had argued expressly that Baidu was not engaging in speech, but in discriminatory conduct, physically blocking his site.

64. *Zhang v. Baidu*, 10 F. Supp. 3d 433 (2014), 441, citing a key ruling about speech rights in cable TV, *Turner Broadcasting System v. FCC*, 512 U.S. 622 (1994), 641. It is hard to overlook the fact that the "person" doing the deciding in this case was (1) a corporation and (2) most likely not actually making this determination but rather carrying out a state determination about allowable speech (usually understood as censorship).

65. The agitation and press criticism of the 1930s and 1940s discussed in chapter 3 had introduced to First Amendment law the vexing problem that there were many potential constituencies, or groups of people (owners, content creators who were employees, and the public), who might claim speech rights in commercial media and whose interests might be in conflict. *Miami v. Tornillo* addressed this problem by determining that, in newspapers, the only legal speaker—or rightsholder—was the owner. In contrast, in earlier decisions, the Court had determined that content creators and the public had some legal claims in broadcast and cable. Stein, *Speech Rights*.

66. While the fairness doctrine was retired by the FCC, it would be perfectly legal for the agency to reinstate those or similar rules about content.

67. Bracha and Pasquale, "Federal Search Commission?"; Whitney, "Search Engines." Whitney grounds her comparison of search results to a grocery store in a comparison made by a former Google employee, describing the way the designs of social media, apps, and devices seek to manipulate users. See Tristan Harris, "How Technology Is Hijacking Your Mind: From a Magician and Google Design Ethicist," *Thrive Global*, May 18, 2016, http://journal.thriveglobal.com/how-technology-hijacks-peoples-minds-from-a-magician-and-google-s-design-ethicist-56d62ef5edf3. Whitney also suggests another analogy, which comes with a precedent: the curatorial activity of search engines is like that of law schools determining which groups can speak on their premises, an activity that the Supreme Court has decided is not expressive (law schools may not bar some groups or agencies from recruiting on their premises due to political or conscientious objections).

68. Volokh and Falk, "First Amendment Protection." The authors have since used many of these arguments in an article in the *Journal of Law Economics and Policy*.

69. That search engines have different outputs has been important in convincing some judges that algorithms reflect the judgments of engineers (rather than being neutral tools). See, e.g., *Zhang*. The assumption is that the primary source of differentiation among search engines is the algorithm and not the other components of completing a search (e.g., indexing, differences in how search query language is parsed, or the judgments of dispersed others, discussed below).

70. For more on the problematic use of the editorial analogy in cases dealing with search engines, see Whitney, "Search Engines." But compare with Lakier, "Problem Isn't the Use of Analogies."

71. Tarleton Gillespie specifically contrasts editorial logics to algorithmic logics in these terms in "Relevance of Algorithms," 192. On the linkages between algorithmic and journalistic objectivity and the difference between algorithmic and journalistic judgment, see Carlson, "Automating Judgement"; and Bilić, "Search Algorithms, Hidden Labor, and Information Control."

72. For a discussion of this overlap, see Gillespie, "Algorithmically Recognizable."

73. In the legal discussions, these distributed judgments are subsumed under the work of programmers.

74. This relevance is calculated based on a set of cultural assumptions and a statistical model of what the users' preferences are likely to be based on, according to the data each user has produced about themselves and data culled from other users. As the trade press notes, Google's definition of quality has little direct connection to content. A quality website (result) is one that satisfies the user's intentions and goals. Roger Montti, "5 Strategies Unlocked from Google's Quality Rating Guidelines," *Search Engine Journal*, March 21, 2016.

75. The harvester also favored large-scale industrial farms over smaller ones (leading to concentration of ownership), and mechanical labor over that of the tomato pickers and sorters. Winner, "Do Artifacts Have Politics?" This type of indirect agency is less likely to be legally binding or recognized (see Burke, "Patenting Speech" for a discussion of this in relation to the First Amendment) than others—including the sort of agency behind the more famous example from Winner's essay, Robert Moses's purportedly segregationist design of the bridges on the Long Island Expressway. Recognizing the more dilute agency and responsibility of the tomato harvester is, however, ethically and politically powerful.

76. On the influence of mathematical models of power, including those structuring impact-factor ratings, see Rieder, "What Is in PageRank?" See also the critique of using links as a proxy for approval (or even as a simple citation) in Vaidhyanathan, *Googlization of Everything*.

77. Noble, *Algorithms of Oppression*; Benjamin, *Race after Technology*.

78. There are exceptions. Recently, Google prioritized Wikipedia entries as a top result in all searches due to trust in Wikipedia as a reliable source. Still, this is distinct from the vision of editorial judgment called on in legal discourse, as it does not rely on decisions about which stories to run or which issues to cover, but rather which institutions or sources to trust (more akin to the politics of source selection in journalism).

79. As noted in chapter 3, the normative rationales for protecting editorial choices are generally either the individual freedom and expressive liberties of editors or publishers or the broad public interest served by editors and journalists in selecting and providing useful information (sometimes articulated in terms of the rights or interest of the audience).

80. Whether or not editorial judgments work this way in practice, the normative rationale for protecting them presumes that they are judgments on what constitutes an issue of public import and which perspectives on this issue matter most.

81. Most famously, Google for a long time offered to autocomplete searches beginning "Are Jews ... " with "evil." Similarly, Google suggested people looking for information on the Islamic faith might want to know whether Islam permits terrorism. Google's autocomplete suggestions involving queries about Black people suggested "loud," "athletic," and "lazy," among others; for searches about Black women, Google's top suggestions were "angry," "loud," and "mean." (The top suggestion for searches about feminists was "feminists are sexist.") The top results of these searches include neo-Nazi and other hate-group sites. Issie Lapowsky, "Google Autocomplete Still Makes Vile Suggestions," *Wired*, February 2, 2018, https://www.wired.com/story/google-autocomplete-vile-suggestions/; Noble, *Algorithms of Oppression*. As of spring 2018, Google had disabled autocompletes involving groups of people and verbs like "are." Also, changes were implemented for other searches ("is Islam ..." suggested "polytheistic or monotheistic" and "universalizing or ethnic"; "is feminism ..." suggested "capitalized," "a word," "a movement," or "Marxist"; and "is Black Lives Matter ..." suggested a single term: "trademarked").

82. In general, services that act like neutral conduits are not liable for the messages they convey. Online platforms act as more than mere conduits, but were granted immunity from liability (for all offenses except copyright infringement) for the messages they carry under section 230 of the Communications Decency Act.

83. Vaidhyanathan, *Googlization of Everything*; Gillespie, "Relevance of Algorithms."

84. See, e.g., Davies, "How Machine Learning in Search Works."

85. These judgments may not be good—and this more distributed evaluation is certainly not free of bias or bad politics.

86. Although some are better than others. Baidu's exclusion of pro-democracy sites is more like a cable operator deciding not to carry Fox News—or to carry only Fox News—than a newspaper's decision not to publish a letter to the editor (*Miami v. Tornillo*). And Google's alleged manual de-listing of e-solutions clients and de-ranking of Search King client sites also seems to me closer to anti-trust questions than like editorial ones (e.g. whether to run a letter to the editor). More promising than finding the perfect analogy for what search engines are, we might pay more attention to the different things search engines are *doing*—and how the law applies to this type of activity, along the lines that Kate Klonick suggests for social media platforms in "New Governors." See also Balkin, "Free Speech."

87. For example, in *Algorithms of Oppression*, Safiya Noble nicely breaks down and critiques the idea that sexualized search results for "Black girls" were a reflection of popular "taste" or demand, showing these results rather to have been the product of an organized effort by the pornography industry. Other examples of gaming search engine parameters include organized efforts of white nationalist groups to promote racist and anti-Semitic messages and the work of reputation management services to cultivate search results for clients.

88. For an example of a more promising framework for assessing the social and political work—expressive and otherwise—of algorithms, see Ananny, "Toward an Ethics of Algorithms."

89. *Zhang* was different in that the public interest was invoked.

90. Users, or the public, rarely show up in this debate. They are implied, the passive background in whose name information is produced and circulates. Their interests and actions as users of programs or search engines are overlooked, to the point that user search queries are not usually factored into discussions of algorithms and free speech.

Conclusion

1. Such AIs, which convincingly mimic human speech patterns, are the subject of a California law, known as the "bot bill," that bans such programs from pretending to be real people in order to "incentivize a purchase or sale of goods or services in a commercial transaction or to influence a vote in an election." The law requires these agents to disclose that they are machines.

2. It is not unreasonable to imagine a political effort to craft some version of a Fairness Doctrine applied to social media platforms. (The fairness doctrine applied to broadcast media for much of the twentieth century, requiring broadcasters to air more than one

side of a controversial issue, in an attempt to prevent them from becoming too-powerful editorial voices.)

3. My genealogy explains the economic uses of free speech more than the conservative political uses, which rely more on ideas of liberty often associated with classic liberalism; yet the scope of speech has also been essential to many efforts to use the First Amendment to undo antidiscrimination law. In *Hurley v. Irish American Gay, Lesbian and Bisexual Group of Boston* (1995) and *Dale v. Boy Scouts of America* (2000), the Court arguably stretched the definition of speech to find that the inclusion of gays and lesbians in parades and organizations was a form of compelled speech, and thus their exclusion was part of the freedom of speech of those who wished to discriminate. As well, in *Masterpiece Cakeshop v. Colorado Civil Rights Commission*, 138 S. Ct. 1719 (2018), the baker who refused to serve a gay couple hinged his defense on the claim that cake decoration was a form of expression ("speech") and that the Colorado antidiscrimination law infringed this expression. *Masterpiece* in particular echoed the circumstances of attempts to fight civil rights laws in the 1960s (where some restaurant owners argued they had a right to refuse to serve Black customers or to segregate customers by race); it is unlikely that the free speech argument would have worked to block civil rights laws in that era. Much of the change may indeed be a political shift in the discourse of freedom and individual rights, but the definition of speech (the ability to argue that cake decoration is speech) is part of this story. Frederick Schauer warns that this expansion of what freedom of speech means threatens to reduce the level of protection afforded to political speech, democratic dialog, and other forms of "core" expression. Schauer, "Towards an Institutional First Amendment."

4. On liberalism and the stoic subject of free speech law and discourse, see Peters, *Courting the Abyss*. On the way that autonomy has been limited to adult white males and its history, see Williams, "On Being the Object of Property"; Cornell, "Autonomy Reimagined"; Hirshmann, *Rethinking Obligation*; Bordo, *Unbearable Weight*; and Anzaldúa, *Borderlands / La Frontera*.

5. Balkin and Siegel, "Principles, Practices, and Social Movements," 948.

6. Like the commercial nature of the press, the historical reliance of the press on content that originated elsewhere seems to have been overlooked or repressed by the judges and justices in *Mutual* and *Pathé*, in favor of a romanticized view of the press as a vehicle for the expression of the ideas of authors.

7. For justices in the early twentieth century, it was clear that freedom of speech was a means for protecting ideas, or the freedom of thought. Today, speech is broader and vaguer.

8. *Dale v. Boy Scouts; Hurley v. Irish American Gay, Lesbian and Bisexual Group of Boston. Hurley* has been an important precedent in cases dealing with algorithms, in which the owner-creators of algorithms are likened to the discriminatory parade organizers, free to decide which messages—or bodies—to include and which to exclude.

9. Kittler, *Gramophone, Film, Typewriter*. See also Winthrop-Young, *Kittler and the Media*.

10. See, e.g., Haraway, "Cyborg Manifesto"; Braidotti, *Posthuman*.

11. The animating, immaterial spirit posited by Descartes's mind/body dualism was derided as a "ghost in the machine" by the more materialist twentieth-century philoso-

pher Gilbert Ryle. The ghost has migrated to our digital devices. Today, the term is used as well to refer to computer technologies that seem to have minds of their own.

12. Massaro and Norton, "Siri-ously?"; Massaro, Norton, and Kaminski, "Siri-ously 2.0"; Wu, "Is the First Amendment Obsolete?"; and Wu, "Machine Speech." In theory, this is because the public has a right to this information. Courts have been skeptical of judges' ability to determine when information is a boon to the public and when it is disadvantageous or even harmful to the public.

13. The term "bot" has been used to describe a number of simple agents (e.g., web crawlers) and uses of computers (e.g., a computer that has been taken over by a hacker, used to carry out some task). My interest—and much recent attention—has been on how automated agents use natural language processing to produce automated machinic speech. For a typology of bots, see Gorwa and Guilbeault, "Unpacking the Social Media Bot."

14. Woolley, Shorey, and Howard, "Bot Proxy"; Woolley, "Automating Power"; Amnesty Global Insights, "Mexico's Misinformation Wars: How Organized Troll Networks Attack and Harass Journalists and Activists in Mexico," *Medium*, January 24, 2017, https://medium.com/amnesty-insights/mexico-s-misinformation-wars-cb748ecb32e9.

15. Tay was presented as entertainment, but the results of the experiment also would have helped Microsoft engineer artificial assistants like Cortana and other projects that involve processing oral communication.

16. Such ambiguities over responsibility (fears of liability) continue to keep social bots (e.g., Open AI's GPT-3) from being used in many commercial applications.

17. Woolley et al., "Bot Proxy." To date, in First Amendment law, discussion of speech via proxy has focused on financial transactions; in these discussions the assumption is a match between the rightsholding individual's intent or message and the message of the proxy (the money is used to purchase or promote a message via an intermediary). Here, the relationship of proxy to individual is different.

18. Woolley et al., "Bot Proxy." The authors argue for a definition of bots not as extensions of programmers' agency (or prostheses) or as mere inert tools, but rather as proxies that have an agency of their own that is harnessed in the interests of the programmer but is not identical or fully reducible to these interests. As such, they do not fit into the typology of speech products or communication tools proposed by Tim Wu. See also Gillespie, "Platforms Intervene"; and Shah, "When Machines Speak."

19. Cheney-Lippold, *We Are Data*.

20. As Cheney-Lippold shows, models or data doppelgangers built on the profiles we create with our online activity are used to determine individuals' roles and relations to the national security apparatus. In a particularly chilling and fascinating example, he shows how predictive modeling of who is likely to be a "citizen" (rather than actual citizenship status) is used to determine whether legal protections granted to citizens and their communications apply in digital surveillance. Cheney-Lippold, *We Are Data*. If such examples are speech situations, they are ones in which social relations are fundamentally altered from those presumed in existing legal precedent (not to mention philosophy and social science). Individuals are no longer speakers or audiences but are the source of materials intelligible only to machines (and only at scale).

Appendix

1. The corpus was curated to be overinclusive, in order to capture all Supreme Court decisions in which the justices considered free speech claims. It included all decisions in which the terms "freedom of speech," "free speech," "freedom of expression," "free expression," "free press," "freedom of the press," "press freedom," or "First Amendment" occurred in the headnotes (in both Westlaw and LexisNexis databases). This list included decisions in which the discussion of free speech was minimal, or claims were not made. As is common in First Amendment scholarship, we selected only Supreme Court cases as these decisions are the most authoritative source of law.

2. We searched for the specific phrases "freedom of," "freedom to," "right of," "right to," "abridged by," and "censorship." In addition, we searched for the following sets of terms when in close proximity: "protected" and "First Amendment"; "protected" and "speech"; "covered" and "First Amendment"; and "covered" and "freedom."

BIBLIOGRAPHY

Acland, Charles. *Swift Viewing: The Popular Life of Subliminal Influence*. Durham, NC: Duke University Press, 2012.

Addams, Jane. *The Spirit of Youth and the City Streets*. New York: Macmillan, 1909.

Adler, Amy. "The First Amendment and the Second Commandment." *New York Law School Law Review* 57, no. 41 (2012–2013): 41–58.

Ananny, Mike. "Toward an Ethics of Algorithms: Convening, Observation, Probability, and Timeliness." *Science, Technology, and Human Values* 41, no. 1 (2016): 93–117.

Anderson, Alexis. "The Formative Period of First Amendment Theory, 1870–1915." *American Journal of Legal History* 24, no. 1 (1980): 56–75.

Anderson, Benedict. *Imagined Communities: Reflections on the Origin and Spread of Nationalism*. London: Verso, 1983.

Anderson, Mark Lynn. "The Payne Fund Studies and the Creation of the Media Expert." In *Inventing Film Studies*, edited by Lee Grieveson and Haidee Wasson, 38–65. Durham, NC: Duke University Press, 2008.

Anzaldúa, Gloria. *Borderlands / La Frontera: The New Mestiza*. San Francisco: Aunt Lute Books, 1987.

Anzaldúa, Gloria. "Speaking in Tongues." In *This Bridge Called My Back: Writings by Radical Women of Color*, edited by Cherríe Moraga and Gloria Anzaldúa, 165–173. Latham, NY: Kitchen Table / Women of Color Press, 1983.

Baker, C. Edwin. *Human Liberty and Freedom of Speech*. New York: Oxford University Press, 1989.

Baker, C. Edwin. "Scope of the First Amendment Freedom of Speech." *UCLA Law Review* 25, no. 5 (1978): 964–1041.

Balkin, Jack. "Free Speech in the Algorithmic Society: Big Data, Private Governance, and New School Speech Regulation." *UC Davis Law Review* 51, no. 3 (2018): 1149–1210.

Balkin, Jack. "The Path of Robotics Law." *California Law Review Circuit* 6 (2015): 45–60.

Balkin, Jack. "Some Realism about Pluralism: Legal Realist Approaches to the First Amendment." *Duke Law Journal* 1990, no. 3 (1990): 375–430.

Balkin, Jack, and Reva B. Siegel. "Principles, Practices, and Social Movements." *University of Pennsylvania Law Review* 154, no. 4 (2006): 927–950.

Barbas, Samantha. "Creating the Public Forum." *Akron Law Review* 44, no. 3 (2011): 809–866.

Barbas, Samantha. "How the Movies Became Speech." *Rutgers Law Review* 64, no. 3 (2012): 665–745.

Barron, Jerome A. "Access to the Press: A New First Amendment Right." *Harvard Law Review* 80, no. 8 (1967): 1641–1678.

Barthes, Roland. "The Death of the Author." In *Image-Music-Text*, translated by Steven Heath, 142–148. New York: Hill and Wang, 1977.

Bateson, Gregory. "Why Do Frenchmen?" In *Steps to an Ecology of Mind*, 9–13. Chicago: University of Chicago Press, 2000.

Bateson, Gregory, and Weldon Kees. *Interaction and Communication in Three Families* (film). Bateson Papers, University of California, Santa Cruz.

Bell, Daniel. *The Coming of the Post-Industrial Society: A Venture in Social Forecasting.* New York: Basic Books, 1976.

Bellamy, Francis. "National School Celebration of Columbus Day: The Official Programme." *Youth's Companion* 65 (1892): 446–447. Available at http://historymatters .gmu.edu/d/5762/.

Beniger, James R. *The Control Revolution: Technological and Economic Origins of the Information Society.* Cambridge, MA: Harvard University Press, 1989.

Benjamin, Louise. *Freedom of the Air and the Public Interest: First Amendment Rights in Broadcasting to 1935.* Carbondale: Southern Illinois University Press, 2001.

Benjamin, Ruha. *Race after Technology: Abolitionist Tools for the New Jim Code.* Cambridge: Polity, 2019.

Benjamin, Walter. "The Work of Art in the Age of Mechanical Reproduction." In *Illuminations*, translated by Harry Zohn, 217–252. 1968. Reprint, New York: Schocken, 1986.

Berquis, Goodwin, and James Greenwood. "Protest against Racism: *Birth of a Nation* in Ohio." *Journal of the University Film Association* 26, no. 3 (1974): 39–44.

Bezanson, Randall P. *Art and Freedom of Speech.* Urbana: University of Illinois Press, 2009.

Bezanson, Randall P. "Artifactual Speech." *Journal of Constitutional Law* 3, no. 3 (2001): 819–849.

Bilić, Paško. "Search Algorithms, Hidden Labour and Information Control." *Big Data and Society* 3, no. 1 (2016): 1–9.

Blanchard, Margaret. "The Associated Press Antitrust Suit: A Philosophical Clash over Ownership of First Amendment Rights." *Business History Review* 61, no. 1 (1987): 43–85.

Blanchard, Margaret. "Filling in the Void: Speech and Press in State Courts Prior to *Gitlow*." In *The First Amendment Reconsidered: New Perspectives on the Meaning of Freedom of Speech and Press*, edited by Bill Chamberlin and Charlene Brown, 14–59. New York: Longman, 1982.

Blanchard, Margaret. "Press Criticism and National Reform Movements: The Progressive Era and the New Deal." *Journalism History* 5, no. 2 (1978): 33–55.

Blanchard, Margaret. *Revolutionary Sparks: Freedom of Expression in Modern America.* Oxford: Oxford University Press, 1992.

Bollinger, Lee C. *The Tolerant Society.* New York: Oxford University Press, 1986.

Bordo, Susan. *Unbearable Weight: Feminism, Western Culture, and the Body.* Berkeley: University of California Press, 2004.

Boulding, Kenneth E. *The Image: Knowledge in Life and Society.* Ann Arbor: University of Michigan Press, 1961.

Bowker, Geoffrey, and Susan Leigh Star. *Sorting Things Out: Classification and Its Consequences.* Cambridge, MA: MIT Press, 1999.

Boyle, James. *Shamans, Software, and Spleens: Law and the Construction of the Information Society.* Cambridge, MA: Harvard University Press, 1996.

Bracha, Oren. "The Folklore of Informationalism: The Case of Search Engine Speech." *Fordham Law Review* 82, no. 4 (2014): 1629–1687.

Bracha, Oren, and Frank Pasquale. "Federal Search Commission? Access, Fairness, and Accountability in the Law of Search." *Cornell Law Review* 93, no. 6 (2008): 1149–1209.

Braidotti, Rosi. *The Posthuman.* Cambridge: Polity, 2013.

Burk, Dan. "Patenting Speech." *Texas Law Review* 79, no. 1 (2000): 99–162.

Butsch, Richard. *The Citizen Audience: Crowds, Publics, and Individuals.* New York: Routledge, 2007.

Butters, Gerald, Jr. *Banned in Kansas: Motion Picture Censorship, 1915–1966.* Columbia: University of Missouri Press, 2007.

Buxton, William. "From Radio Research to Communications Intelligence: Rockefeller Philanthropy, Communications Specialists, and the American Policy Community." In *The Political Influence of Ideas: Policy Communities and the Social Sciences,* edited by Stephen Brooks and Alain G. Gagnon, 187–230. Westport, CT: Praeger, 1994.

Caldwell, Louis G. "Freedom of Speech and Radio Broadcasting." *Annals of the American Academy of Political and Social Science* 177, no. 1 (1935): 179–207.

Cantril, Hadley, and Gordon Allport. *The Psychology of the Radio.* New York: Peter Smith, 1941.

Carey, James. *Communication as Culture: Essays on Media and Society.* New York: Routledge, 1992.

Carlson, Matt. "Automating Judgement? Algorithmic Judgement, News Knowledge, and Journalistic Professionalism." *New Media and Society* 20, no. 5 (2018): 1755–1772.

Casebeer, Kenneth M. "Public—Since Time Immemorial: The Labor History of *Hague v. CIO.*" *Rutgers Law Review* 66, no. 1 (2013): 147–178.

Charney, Leo, and Vanessa R. Schwartz, eds. *Cinema and the Invention of Modern Life.* Berkeley: University of California Press, 1995.

Cheney-Lippold, John. *We Are Data: Algorithms and the Making of Our Digital Selves.* New York: New York University Press, 2017.

Chun, Wendy Hui Kyong. *Programmed Visions: Software and Memory.* Cambridge, MA: MIT Press, 2013.

Citron, Danielle Keats. "Cyber Civil Rights." *Boston University Law Review* 89, no. 1 (2009): 61–125.

Cohen-Cole, Jamie. *The Open Mind: Cold War Politics and the Sciences of Human Nature.* Chicago: University of Chicago Press, 2014.

Coleman, Gabriella. *Coding Freedom: The Ethics and Aesthetics of Hacking.* Princeton, NJ: Princeton University Press, 2013.

Commission on Freedom of the Press. *A Free and Responsible Press: A General Report on Mass Communication; Newspapers, Radio, Motion Pictures, Magazines, and Books*, edited by Robert D. Leigh. Chicago: University of Chicago Press, 1947.

Cooley, Charles Horton. *Social Organization: A Study of the Larger Mind*. New York: Charles Scribner's Sons, 1929.

Cornell, Drucilla. "Autonomy Re-imagined." *Journal for the Psychoanalysis of Culture and Society* 8, no. 1 (2003): 144–149.

Cowie, Elizabeth. *Recording Reality, Desiring the Real*. Minneapolis: University of Minnesota Press, 2011.

Craig, Steve. "How America Adopted Radio: Demographic Differences in Set Ownership Reported in the 1930–1950 U.S. Census." *Journal of Broadcasting and Electronic Media* 48, no. 2 (2004): 179–195.

Cross, Gary. *An All-Consuming Century: Why Commercialism Won in Modern America*. New York: Columbia University Press, 2000.

Czitrom, Daniel. *Media and the American Mind: From Morse to McLuhan*. Chapel Hill: University of North Carolina Press, 1982.

Czitrom, Daniel. "The Politics of Performance: Theater Licensing and the Origins of Movie Censorship in New York." In *Movie Censorship and American Culture*, edited by F. G. Couvares, 16–42. Washington, DC: Smithsonian Institute, 1996.

Darwin, Charles. *Expressions of the Emotions in Man and Animal*. New York: D. Appleton and Company, 1898.

Daston, Lorraine, and Peter Galison. "The Image of Objectivity." *Representations*, no. 40 (1992): 81–128.

Davies, Dave. "How Machine Learning in Search Works: Everything You Need to Know." *Search Engine Journal*, June 21, 2018. https://www.searchenginejournal.com/how -machine-learning-in-search-works/257837/#close

Decherney, Peter. "Copyright Dupes: Piracy and New Media in Edison v. Lubin (1903)." *Film History* 19, no. 2 (2007): 109–124.

Deegan, Mary Jo. *Jane Addams and the Men of the Chicago School, 1892–1918*. New Brunswick, NJ: Transaction, 1990.

Delgado, Richard, and Jean Stefancic. *Critical Race Theory: An Introduction*. 1995. Reprint, New York: New York University Press, 2012.

Derrida, Jacques. *Of Grammatology*. Translated by Gayatri Chakravorty Spivak. 1974. Reprint, Baltimore, MD: Johns Hopkins University Press, 1997.

Descartes, René. *Discourse on Method*. Translated by John Veitch. 1637. Reprint, London: J. M. Dent and Sons, 1916.

Dewey, John. *The Public and Its Problems*. New York: Henry Holt and Company, 1927.

Dingwall, Robert. "Notes toward an Intellectual History of Symbolic Interactionism." *Symbolic Interaction* 24, no. 2 (2001): 237–242.

Drucker, Peter. *The Age of Discontinuity: Guidelines to Our Changing Society*. London: Heinemann, 1969.

Du Bois, W. E. B. *Dusk of Dawn: An Essay toward an Autobiography of a Race Concept*. 1940. Reprint, New York: Schocken, 1968.

Durr, Clifford. "Freedom of Speech for Whom?" *Public Opinion Quarterly* 8, no. 3 (1944): 391–401.

Dworkin, Ronald. "Law as Interpretation." *Critical Inquiry* 9, no. 1 (1982): 179–200.

Edelman, Bernard. *Ownership of the Image: Elements for a Marxist Theory of Law*. Translated by Elizabeth Kingdom. London: Routledge and Kegan Paul, 1979.

Edwards, Paul. *The Closed World: Computers and the Politics of Discourse in Cold War America*. Cambridge, MA: MIT Press, 1996.

Edwards, Violet. *Group Leader's Guide to Propaganda Analysis*. New York: Institute for Propaganda Analysis, 1938.

Emerson, Thomas. "Toward a General Theory of the First Amendment." *Yale Law Journal* 72, no. 5 (1963): 877–956.

Erickson, Paul, Judy Klein, Lorraine Daston, and Rebecca Lemov. *How Reason Almost Lost Its Mind: The Strange Career of Cold War Rationality*. Chicago: University of Chicago Press, 2013.

Ernst, Morris. "Radio Censorship and the 'Listening Millions.'" *Nation*, April 28, 1926.

Ewan, Stewart. *Captains of Consciousness: Advertising and the Social Roots of the Consumer Culture*. New York: McGraw-Hill, 1977.

Feffer, Andrew. *The Chicago Pragmatists and American Progressivism*. Ithaca, NY: Cornell University Press, 1993.

Fleming, Donald. "Attitude: The History of a Concept." In *Perspectives in American History*, vol. 1, edited by Donald Fleming and Bernard Bailyn, 287–365. Cambridge, MA: Harvard University Press, 1967.

Foucault, Michel. *The History of Sexuality*. Vol. 1, *An Introduction*. Translated by Robert Hurley. 1978. Reprint, New York: Knopf, 1990.

Foucault, Michel. "Nietzsche, Genealogy, History." In *The Foucault Reader*, edited by Paul Rabinow, 76–100. New York: Random House, 1984.

Foucault, Michel. "What Is an Author?" In *The Foucault Reader*, edited by Paul Rabinow, 101–20. New York: Random House, 1984.

Frank, Thomas. *The Conquest of Cool: Business Culture, Counterculture and the Rise of Hip Consumerism*. Chicago: University of Chicago Press, 1997.

Freud, Sigmund. *The Interpretation of Dreams*. Translated by A. A. Brill. New York: Macmillan, 1913.

Gaines, Jane. *Contested Culture: The Image, the Voice, and the Law*. Chapel Hill: University of North Carolina Press, 1991.

Galison, Peter. "The Ontology of the Enemy: Norbert Wiener and the Cybernetic Vision." *Critical Inquiry* 21, no. 1 (1994): 228–266.

Galloway, Alexander. "Language Wants to Be Overlooked: On Software and Ideology." *Journal of Visual Culture* 5, no. 3 (2006): 315–331.

Gary, Brett. "Communication Research, the Rockefeller Foundation, and Mobilization for the War on Worlds, 1938–1944." *Journal of Communication* 46, no. 3 (1996): 124–148.

Gary, Brett. *The Nervous Liberals: Propaganda Anxieties from World War I to the Cold War*. New York: Columbia University Press, 1999.

Gaudreault, André. "The Infringement of Copyright Laws and Its Effects (1900–1906)." In *Early Cinema: Space, Frame, Narrative*, edited by Thomas Elsaesser, 114–122. London: British Film Institute, 1990.

Geoghegan, Bernard Dionysius. "From Information Theory to French Theory: Jakobson, Lévi-Strauss, and the Cybernetic Apparatus." *Critical Inquiry* 38, no. 1 (2011): 96–126.

Geoghegan, Bernard Dionysius. "Information." In *Digital Keywords: A Vocabulary of Information and Society*, edited by Benjamin Peters, 173–183. Princeton, NJ: Princeton University Press, 2016.

Gillespie, Tarleton. "Algorithmically Recognizable: Santorum's Google Problem, and Google's Santorum Problem." *Information Communication and Society* 20, no. 1 (2016): 1–18.

Gillespie, Tarleton. "The Relevance of Algorithms." In *Media Technologies: Essays on Communication, Materiality, and Society*, edited by Tarleton Gillespie, Pablo Boczkowski, and Kirsten Foot, 167–194. Cambridge, MA: MIT Press, 2014.

Gillespie, Tarleton. *Wired Shut: Copyright and the Shape of Digital Culture.* Cambridge, MA: MIT Press, 2007.

Gitelman, Lisa. *Always Already New: Media, History, and the Data of Culture.* Cambridge, MA: MIT Press, 2006.

Gitlin, Todd. "Media Sociology: The Dominant Paradigm." *Theory and Society* 6, no. 2 (1978): 205–254.

Gitlin, Todd. *The Whole World Is Watching: Mass Media in the Making and Unmaking of the New Left.* Berkeley: University of California Press, 1989.

Glander, Timothy. *Origins of Mass Communications Research during the American Cold War: Educational Effects and Contemporary Implications.* New York: Routledge, 1999.

Gleick, James. *The Information: A History, a Theory, a Flood.* New York: Vintage, 2011.

Goffman, Erving. *The Presentation of Self in Everyday Life.* New York: Doubleday, 1959.

Goodman, David. *Radio's Civic Ambition: American Broadcasting and Democracy in the 1930s.* New York: Oxford University Press, 2011.

Gorwa, Robert, and Douglas Guilbeault. "Unpacking the Social Media Bot: A Typology to Guide Research and Policy." *Policy and Internet* 10, no. 2 (2018): 1–29. doi: 10.1002/poi3.184.

Graber, Mark. *Transforming Free Speech: The Ambiguous Legacy of Civil Libertarianism.* Berkeley: University of California Press, 1991.

Greenman, John. "On Communication." *Michigan Law Review* 106, no. 7 (2007): 1338–1378.

Grieveson, Lee. "Cinema Studies and the Conduct of Conduct." In *Inventing Film Studies*, edited by Lee Grieveson and Haidee Wasson, 3–37. Durham, NC: Duke University Press, 2008.

Grieveson, Lee. *Policing Cinema: Movies and Censorship in Early Twentieth-Century America.* Berkeley: University of California Press, 2004.

Grimmelmann, James. "The Structure of Search Engine Law." *Iowa Law Review* 93, no. 1 (2007): 1–64.

Gumbrecht, Hans Ulrich, ed. *Materialities of Communication.* Translated by William Whobrey. Stanford, CA: Stanford University Press, 1994.

Gunning, Tom. "The Cinema of Attractions: The Early Film, Its Spectator, and the Avant Garde." In *Early Cinema: Space, Frame, Narrative*, edited by Thomas Elsaesser, 56–62. London: British Film Institute, 1990.

Habermas, Jürgen. *The Structural Transformation of the Public Sphere.* Translated by Thomas Burger. Cambridge, MA: MIT Press, 1991.

Hall, Stuart. "Encoding/Decoding." In *Culture, Media, Language*, edited by Stuart Hall, Dorothy Hobson, Andrew Love, and Paul Willis, 128–139. London: Hutchison, 1980.

Halliday, Paul. "Authority in the Archives." *Critical Analysis of Law* 1, no. 1 (2014): 110–142.

Hansen, Miriam. *Babel and Babylon: Spectatorship in American Silent Film*. Cambridge, MA: Harvard University Press, 1991.

Haraway, Donna J. "Cyborg Manifesto." In *Simians, Cyborgs, and Women: The Reinvention of Nature*, 149–182. New York: Routledge, 1991.

Hartley, R. V. L. "Transmission of Information." *Bell System Technical Journal* 7, no. 3 (1928): 535–563.

Hayakawa, S. I., and Alan R. Hayakawa. *Language in Thought and Action*. 1939. Reprint, San Diego, CA: Harcourt Brace Jovanovich Publishers, 1990.

Hayles, N. Katherine. *How We Became Posthuman: Virtual Bodies in Cybernetics, Literature, and Informatics*. Chicago: University of Chicago Press, 1999.

Hayles, N. Katherine. "Speech, Writing, Code: Three Worldviews." In *My Mother Was a Computer: Digital Subjects and Literary Texts*, 39–61. Chicago: University of Chicago Press, 2005.

Hilmes, Michelle. *Radio Voices: American Broadcasting, 1922–1952*. Minneapolis: University of Minnesota Press, 1997.

Hirshmann, Nancy. *Rethinking Obligation: A Feminist Method for Political Theory*. Ithaca, NY: Cornell University Press, 1992.

Hobart, Michael, and Zachary Schiffman. *Information Ages: Literacy, Numeracy, and the Computer Revolution*. Baltimore, MD: Johns Hopkins University Press, 1998.

Holmes, Oliver Wendell. "The Stereoscope and the Stereograph." *Atlantic Monthly* 3, no. 20 (June 1859): 738–749.

Illouz, Eva. *Cold Intimacies: The Making of Emotional Capitalism*. Cambridge: Polity, 2007.

Inglis, Ruth. *Freedom of the Movies*. Chicago: University of Chicago Press, 1947.

Innis, Harold. *Empire and Communications*. Toronto, ON: Dundurn Press, 2007.

Inoue, Miyako. "Word for Word: Verbatim as Political Technologies." *Annual Review of Anthropology* 47 (2018): 217–232.

Introna, Lucas, and Helen Nissenbaum. "Shaping the Web: Why the Politics of Search Engines Matters." *Information Society* 16, no. 3 (2000): 169–185.

Jackall, Robert, and Janice Hirota. "America's First Propaganda Ministry: The Committee on Public Information during the Great War." In *Propaganda*, edited by Robert Jackall, 137–173. New York: New York University Press, 1995.

Jackson, Steven. "Rethinking Repair." In *Media Technologies: Essays on Communication, Materiality, and Society*, edited by Tarleton Gillespie, Pablo Broczkowski, and Krtisten Foot, 221–239. Cambridge, MA: MIT Press, 2014.

Jacobs, Jennifer. "Conditional Liberty: The Flag Salute before *Gobitis* and *Barnette*." *Journal of Church and State* 47, no. 4 (2005): 747–768.

Janowitz, Morris. "Harold D. Lasswell's Contribution to Content Analysis." *Public Opinion Quarterly* 32, no. 4 (1968): 646–658.

Jay, Martin. "Diving into the Wreck: Aesthetic Spectatorship at the Turn of the Millennium." In *Refractions of Violence*, 103–117. London: Routledge, 2003.

Jowett, Garth. "'A Capacity for Evil': The 1915 Supreme Court *Mutual* Decision." *Historical Journal of Film, Radio, and Television* 9, no. 1 (1989): 59–78.

Jowett, Garth. "'A Significant Medium for the Communication of Ideas': The *Miracle* Decision and the Decline of Motion Picture Censorship." In *Movie Censorship and*

American Culture, edited by F. G. Couvares, 258–276. Washington, DC: Smithsonian Institute, 1996.

Kairys, David. "Freedom of Speech." In *The Politics of Law: A Progressive Critique*, edited by David Kairys, 190–215. New York: Basic, 1998.

Kendrick, Leslie. "First Amendment Expansionism." *William and Mary Law Review* 56, no. 4 (2015): 1199–1219.

Kittler, Friedrich. *Discourse Networks 1800/1900*. Translated by Michael Meteer, with Chris Cullens. Stanford, CA: Stanford University Press, 1990.

Kittler, Friedrich. *Gramophone, Film, Typewriter*. Translated by Geoffrey Winthrop-Young and Michael Wutz. Stanford, CA: Stanford University Press, 1999.

Klapper, Joseph. *The Effects of Mass Communication*. New York: Free Press, 1950.

Kline, Ronald. *The Cybernetics Moment: Or, Why We Call Our Age the Information Age*. Baltimore, MD: Johns Hopkins University Press, 2015.

Klonick, Kate. "The New Governors: The People, Rules, and Processes Governing Online Speech." *Harvard Law Review* 131, no. 6 (2018): 1598–1667.

Koszarski, Richard. *An Evening's Entertainment: The Age of the Silent Feature Picture, 1915–1928*. Vol. 3 of *History of the American Cinema*, edited by Charles Harpole. New York: Scribner, 1990.

Krämer, Sybille. *Medium, Messenger, Transmission: An Approach to Media Philosophy*. Amsterdam: Amsterdam University Press, 2015.

Lacan, Jacques. "The Circuit." In *The Seminar of Jacques Lacan: Book 2, The Ego in Freud's Theory and in Psychoanalysis, 1954–1955*, translated by Sylvana Thomaselli, 77–92. Cambridge: Cambridge University Press, 1988.

Lakier, Genevieve. "The Invention of Low-Value Speech." *Harvard Law Review* 128, no. 8 (2015): 2166–2233.

Lakier, Genevieve. "The Problem Isn't the Use of Analogies, but the Analogies Courts Use." Knight First Amendment Institute at Columbia University, February 26, 2018. https://knightcolumbia.org/content/problem-isnt-use-analogies-analogies-courts-use.

Lasswell, Harold. "A Provisional Classification of Symbol Data." *Psychiatry* 1, no. 2 (1939): 197–204.

Lasswell, Harold. *Psychopathology and Politics*. Chicago: University of Chicago Press, 1930.

Lazarsfeld, Paul. *Radio and the Printed Page*. New York: Duell, Sloan and Pearce, 1940.

Lazarsfeld, Paul, Bernard Berelson, and Hazel Gaudet. *The People's Choice: How the Voter Makes Up His Mind in a Presidential Campaign*. New York: Columbia University Press, 1944.

Lazarsfeld, Paul, and Robert Merton. "Mass Communication, Popular Taste and Organized Social Action." In *The Communication of Ideas*, edited by L. Bryson, 95–118. New York: Harper, 1948.

Lazarsfeld, Paul, and Frank Stanton, *Radio Research, 1942–1943*. New York: Essential Books, 1944.

Leach, Eugene E. " 'Voices Out of the Night': Radio Research and Ideas about Mass Behavior in the United States, 1920–1950." *Canadian Review of American Studies* 20, no. 2 (1989): 191–209.

Lears, Jackson. *Fables of Abundance: A Cultural History of Advertising in America*. New York: Basic, 1994.

Le Bon, Gustav. *The Crowd: A Study of the Popular Mind*. 1986. Reprint, Kitchener, ON: Batoche Books, 2000.

Lebovic, Sam. *Free Speech and Unfree News: The Paradox of Press Freedom in America*. Cambridge, MA: Harvard University Press, 2016.

Lenning, Arthur. "Myth and Fact: The Reception of *Birth of a Nation*." *Film History* 16, no. 2 (2004): 117–141.

Lerner, Max. "Constitution and Court as Symbols." *Yale Law Journal* 46, no. 8 (1937): 1290–1319.

Levinas, Emmanuel. "Freedom of Speech." In *Difficult Freedom: Essays on Judaism*, translated by Sean Hand, 205–207. 1963. Reprint, Baltimore, MD: Athlone, 1990.

Lew, Wallace. *Ben-Hur: A Tale of the Christ*. New York: Harper Brothers, 1880.

Lippmann, Walter. *Liberty and the News*. New York: Harcourt, Brace, and Company, 1920.

Lippmann, Walter. *The Phantom Public*. New York: Macmillan, 1927.

Lippmann, Walter. *Public Opinion*. New York: Harcourt, Brace, and Company, 1922.

Liu, Lydia. *The Freudian Robot: Digital Media and the Future of the Unconscious*. Chicago: University of Chicago Press, 2010.

MacLeish, Archibald. "The Duty of Freedom." In *Freedom of the Press Today*, edited by Harold Ickes, 187–191. New York: Van Guard Press, 1941.

Malin, Brenton. *Feeling Mediated: A History of Media Technology and Emotion in America*. New York: New York University Press, 2014.

Malinowski, Bronislaw. "The Problem of Meaning in Primitive Languages." In *The Meaning of Meaning*, edited by C. K. Ogden and I. A. Richards, 296–336. New York: Harcourt, 1927.

Marvin, Carolyn. "Theorizing the Flagbody: Symbolic Dimensions of the Flag Desecration Debate, or, Why the Bill of Rights Does Not Fly in the Ballpark." *Critical Studies in Mass Communication* 8, no. 2 (1991): 119–138.

Marvin, Carolyn. *When Old Technologies Were New: Thinking about Electric Communication in the Late Nineteenth Century*. New York: Oxford University Press, 1988.

Massaro, Toni, and Helen Norton. "Siri-ously? Free Speech and Artificial Intelligence." *Northwestern University Law Review* 110, no. 5 (2016): 1169–1194.

Massaro, Toni, Helen Norton, and Margot E. Kaminski. "Siri-ously 2.0: What Artificial Intelligence Reveals about the First Amendment." *Minnesota Law Review* 101, no. 6 (2017): 2481–2525.

Matsuda, Mari. *Words That Wound: Critical Race Theory, Assaultive Speech, and the First Amendment*. Boulder, CO: Westview, 1993.

Mattelart, Armand. *Mapping World Communication: War, Progress, Culture*. Translated by Susan Emanuel and James A. Cohen. Minneapolis: University of Minnesota Press, 1994.

Mayer, Carl. "Personalizing the Impersonal: Corporations and the Bill of Rights." *Hastings Law Journal* 41, no. 3 (1989–1990): 577–667.

McChesney, Robert. "Free Speech and Democracy! Louis G. Caldwell, the American Bar Association, and the Debate over the Free Speech Implication of Broadcasting Regulation, 1928–1938." *American Journal of Legal History* 35, no. 4 (1991): 351–392.

McChesney, Robert. *The Problem of the Media: U.S. Communication Politics in the 21st Century*. New York: Monthly Review Press, 2004.

McLuhan, Marshall. *Understanding Media: The Extensions of Man*. Cambridge, MA: MIT Press, 1994.

McQuail, Denis. *Mass Communication Theory: An Introduction*. London: Sage, 1983.

Meiklejohn, Alexander. *Free Speech and Its Relation to Self-Government*. New York: Harper, 1948.

Merton, Robert K., Marjorie Fiske Lowenthal, and Alberta Curtis. *Mass Persuasion: The Social Psychology of a War Bond Drive*. New York: Harper and Bros., 1946.

Mills, Mara. "Deafening: Noise and the Engineering of Communication in the Telephone System." *Grey Room* no. 43 (2011): 118–143.

Mills, Mara. "Deaf Jam: From Inscription to Reproduction to Information." *Social Text* 28, no. 1 (2010): 35–58.

Mills, Mara. "Media and Prosthesis: The Vocoder, the Artificial Larynx, and the History of Signal Processing." *Qui Parle* 21, no. 1 (2012): 107–149.

Mnookin, Jennifer. "The Image of Truth: Photographic Evidence and the Power of Analogy." *Yale Journal of Law and the Humanities* 10, no. 1 (1998): 1–74.

Munkittrick, David. "Music as Speech: A First Amendment Category unto Itself." *Federal Communications Law Journal* 62, no. 3 (2010): 665–690.

Münsterberg, Hugo. *The Photoplay: A Psychological Study*. New York: D. Appleton, 1916. http://www.gutenberg.org/ebooks/15383.

Musser, Charles. *The Emergence of Cinema: The American Screen to 1907*. Vol. 1 of *History of American Cinema*, edited by Charles Harpole. New York: Scribner, 1990.

Nerone, John, and Kevin Barnhurst. "US Newspaper Types, Newsrooms, and the Division of Labor, 1750–2000." *Journalism Studies* 4, no. 4 (2003): 435–449.

Nimmer, Melvin. "The Meaning of Symbolic Speech under the First Amendment." *UCLA Law Review* 21, no. 29 (1973–1974): 29–61.

Noble, Safiya Umoja. *Algorithms of Oppression: How Search Engines Reinforce Racism*. New York: New York University Press, 2018.

Ogden, C. K., and I. A. Richards. *The Meaning of Meaning*. 1923. Reprint, Orlando, FL: Harcourt Brace, 1989.

Ong, Walter. *Orality and Literacy: The Technologizing of the Word*. London: Methuen, 1982.

Park, Robert E. *The Immigrant Press and Its Control*. New York: Harper and Brothers, 1922.

Perlman, Allison. *Public Interests: Media Advocacy and Struggles over US Television*. New Brunswick, NJ: Rutgers University Press, 2016.

Peters, John Durham. *Courting the Abyss: Free Speech and the Liberal Tradition*. Chicago: University of Chicago Press, 2005.

Peters, John Durham. "The Gaps of Which Communication Is Made." *Critical Studies in Mass Communication* 11, no. 2 (1994): 117–140.

Peters, John Durham. "Information: Notes toward a Critical History." *Journal of Communication Inquiry* 12, no. 2 (1988): 9–23.

Peters, John Durham. *Speaking into the Air: A History of the Idea of Communication*. Chicago: University of Chicago Press, 2001.

Peters, John Durham. "The Uncanniness of Mass Communication in Interwar Social Thought." *Journal of Communications* 46, no. 3 (1996): 108–123.

Petersen, Jennifer. "How Speech Lost Its Voice: The Informational Turn in US Free Speech Law." *History of Humanities* 6, no. 1 (2021): 179–197.

Pickard, Victor. *America's Battle for Media Democracy: The Triumph of Corporate Libertarianism and the Future of Media Reform.* Cambridge, MA: Cambridge University Press, 2015.

Pooley, Jefferson, and Michael Socolow. "The Myth of the *War of the Worlds* Panic." *Slate,* October 12, 2013. http://www.slate.com/articles/arts/history/2013/10/orson_welles_war_of_the_worlds_panic_myth_the_infamous_radio_broadcast_did.html.

Porat, Marc. "The Information Economy: Definition and Measurement." Washington, DC: Office of Telecommunications, Department of Commerce, 1977.

Posner, Eric. "Symbols, Signals, and Social Norms in Politics and Law." *Journal of Legal Studies* 27, no. 2 (1989): 765–798.

Post, Robert. "Encryption Source Code and the First Amendment." *Berkeley Technology Law Journal* 15, no. 2 (2000): 713–723.

Post, Robert. "Meiklejohn's Mistake: Individual Autonomy and the Reform of Public Discourse." Yale Law School, Faculty Scholarship Series (1993), paper 203. http://digitalcommons.law.yale
.edu/cgi/_viewcontent.cgi?article=1202&context=fss_papers.

Post, Robert. "Recuperating First Amendment Doctrine." *Stanford Law Review* 47, no. 6 (1995): 1249–1281.

Postigo, Hector. *The Digital Rights Movement: The Role of Digital Technology in Subverting Digital Copyright.* Cambridge, MA: MIT Press, 2012.

Purcell, Edward, Jr. *The Crisis of Democratic Theory: Scientific Naturalism and the Problem of Value.* Lexington: University Press of Kentucky, 1973.

Rabban, David. "The Emergence of Modern First Amendment Doctrine." *University of Chicago Law Review* 50, no. 4 (1983): 1207–1355.

Rabban, David. *Free Speech in Its Forgotten Years, 1870–1920.* Cambridge: Cambridge University Press, 1997.

Radovac, Lilian. "The War on Noise: Sound and Space in LaGuardia's New York." *American Quarterly* 63, no. 3 (2011): 733–760.

Redish, Martin. "Commercial Speech and the Values of the First Amendment." Washington, DC: Cato Institute, June 19, 2017. https://object.cato.org/sites/cato.org/files/pubs/pdf/pa_813.pdf.

Redish, Martin. "The First Amendment in the Marketplace: Commercial Speech and the Values of Free Expression." *George Washington Law Review* 39, no. 3 (1971): 429–473.

Rieder, Bernhard. "What Is in PageRank? A Historical and Conceptual Investigation of a Recursive Status Index." *Computational Culture* 2 (2012). http://computationalculture.net/what_is_in_pagerank/.

Robinson, James Harvey. *The Mind in the Making: The Relation of Intelligence to Social Reform.* New York: Harper and Bros., 1921.

Ruesch, Jurgen, and Weldon Kees. *Nonverbal Communication: Notes on the Visual Perception of Human Relations.* Berkeley: University of California Press, 1956.

Sandine, Al. *The Taming of the American Crowd: From Stamp Riots to Shopping Malls.* New York: Monthly Review Press, 2009.

Sandman, Warren. "West Virginia State Board of Education v. Barnette." In *Free Speech on Trial: Communication Perspectives on Landmark Supreme Court Cases,* edited by Richard Parker, 100–115. Tuscaloosa: University of Alabama Press, 2003.

Saussure, Ferdinand de. *Course on General Linguistics*. Translated by Roy Harris. Peru, IL: Open Court, 1986.

Schauer, Frederick. "The Boundaries of the First Amendment: A Preliminary Exploration of Constitutional Salience." *Harvard Law Review* 117, no. 6 (2004): 1765–1809.

Schauer, Frederick. "First Amendment Opportunism." Harvard Kennedy School of Government, Faculty Working Paper Series (2000). https://papers.ssrn.com/s013/papers.cfm?abstract_id=253832.

Schauer, Frederick. *Free Speech: A Philosophical Enquiry*. Cambridge: Cambridge University Press, 1982.

Schauer, Frederick. "Towards an Institutional First Amendment." *Minnesota Law Review* 89, no. 5 (2005): 1256–1279.

Schudson, Michael. *Discovering the News: A Social History of American Newspapers*. New York: Basic, 1978.

Schudson, Michael. "Why Conversation Is Not the Soul of Democracy." *Critical Studies in Mass Communication* 14, no. 4 (1997): 297–309.

Sekula, Allan. "On the Invention of Photographic Memory." In *Thinking Photography*, edited by Victor Burgin, 84–109. London: Macmillan, 1982.

Seldes, George. *Freedom of the Press*. New York: Bobbs Merrill Company, 1935.

Seldes, George. *Lords of the Press*. New York: J. Messner, 1938.

Shah, Nishant. "When Machines Speak to Each Other: Unpacking the 'Social' in 'Social Media.'" *Social Media + Society* 1, no. 3 (2015). doi: 10.1177/2056305115580338.

Shannon, Claude E. "A Mathematical Theory of Communication." *Bell System Technical Journal* 27 (1948): 379–423.

Shannon, Claude E., and Warren Weaver. *The Mathematical Theory of Communication*. Urbana: University of Illinois Press, 1949.

Siegert, Bernard. "Cultural Techniques: Or the End of the Intellectual Postwar Era in German Media Theory." *Theory, Culture, and Society* 30, no. 6 (2013): 48–65.

Sklar, Martin. *The Corporate Reconstruction of American Capitalism, 1890–1916: The Market, the Law, and Politics*. Cambridge: Cambridge University Press, 1988.

Slesinger, Donald. "The Film and Public Opinion." In *Print, Radio, and Film in a Democracy: Ten Papers on the Administration of Mass Communications in the Public Interest*, edited by Douglas Waples, 79–98. Chicago: University of Chicago Press, 1942.

Small, Albion W., and George E. Vincent. "The Psycho-physical Communicating Apparatus." In *An Introduction to the Study of Society*, 215–36. New York: American Book Company, 1894.

Smith, Mark C. *Social Science in the Crucible: The American Debate over Objectivity and Purpose, 1918–1941*. Durham, NC: Duke University Press, 1994.

Smulyan, Susan. *Selling Radio: The Commercialization of Broadcasting, 1920–1934*. Washington, DC: Smithsonian Institution Press, 1994.

Snyder, Joel. "Res Ipsa Loquitur." In *Things That Talk: Object Lessons from Art and Science*, edited by Lorraine Daston, 195–221. Brooklyn, NY: Zone, 2004.

Sproule, Michael. *Propaganda and Democracy: The American Experience of Media and Mass Persuasion*. Cambridge: Cambridge University Press, 2005.

Starr, Paul. *The Creation of the Media: Political Origins of Modern Communication*. New York: Basic, 2004.

Stein, Laura. *Speech Rights in America: The First Amendment, Democracy, and the Media.* Urbana: University of Illinois Press, 2006.

Sterne, Jonathan. *The Audible Past.* Durham, NC: Duke University Press, 2003.

Sterne, Jonathan. *MP3: The Meaning of a Format.* Durham, NC: Duke University Press, 2012.

Stokes, Melvin. *D. W. Griffith's "The Birth of a Nation": A History of "The Most Controversial Motion Picture of All Time."* New York: Oxford University Press, 1997.

Streeter, Thomas. *The Net Effect: Romanticism, Capitalism, and the Internet.* New York: New York University Press, 2010.

Streeter, Thomas. *Selling the Air: A Critique of the Policy of Commercial Broadcasting in the United States.* Chicago: University of Chicago Press, 1996.

Streeter, Thomas. "Some Thoughts on Free Speech, Language, and the Rule of Law." In *Freeing the First Amendment: Critical Perspectives on Freedom of Expression*, edited by Robert Jensen and David S. Allen, 31–53. New York: New York University Press, 1995.

Suchman, Lucy. "Do Categories Have Politics? The Language/Action Perspective Reconsidered." *Computer Supported Cooperative Work* 2, no. 3 (1994): 170–190.

Sunstein, Cass. *Democracy and the Problem of Free Speech.* New York: Free Press, 1993.

Sunstein, Cass. "Lochner's Legacy." *Columbia Law Review* 873, no. 5 (1987): 873–919.

Sunstein, Cass. "A New Deal for Speech." *Hastings Communication and Entertainment Law Journal* 17, no. 1 (1994): 137–160.

Tarde, Gabriel. "Extra-Logical Influences." In *The Laws of Imitation*, translated by Elsie Clews Parsons, 189–243. New York: Henry Holt and Company, 1903.

Tarde, Gabriel. "The Public and the Crowd" (1901). In *Gabriel Tarde on Communication and Social Influence: Selected Papers*, edited by Terry Clark, 277–294. Chicago: University of Chicago Press, 2010.

Tiersma, Peter. *Parchment, Paper, Pixels: Law and the Technologies of Communication.* Chicago: University of Chicago Press, 2010.

Turner, Fred. *The Democratic Surround: Multimedia and American Liberalism from World War II to the Psychedelic Sixties.* Chicago: University of Chicago Press, 2013.

Turner, Fred. *From Counterculture to Cyberculture: Stewart Brand, the Whole Earth Network, and the Rise of Digital Utopianism.* Chicago: University of Chicago Press, 2006.

Tushnet, Mark V., Alan K. Chen, and Joseph Blocher. *Free Speech beyond Words: The Surprising Reach of the First Amendment.* New York: New York University Press, 2017.

Vaidhyanathan, Siva. *Copyrights and Copywrongs: The Rise of Intellectual Property and How It Threatens Creativity.* 1994. Reprint, New York: New York University Press, 2003.

Vaidhyanathan, Siva. *The Googlization of Everything: (And Why We Should Worry).* Berkeley: University of California Press, 2011.

Vaughn, Steven. "First Amendment Liberties and the Committee on Public Information." *American Journal of Legal History* 23, no. 2 (1979): 95–119.

Vaughn, Steven. *Holding Fast the Inner Lines: Democracy, Nationalism, and the Committee on Public Information.* Chapel Hill: University of North Carolina Press, 1980.

Vilade, Edwin. *The President's Speech: The Stories behind the Most Memorable Presidential Addresses.* Guilford, CT: Lyons, 2012.

Vismann, Cornelia. *Files: Law and Media Technology.* Translated by Geoffrey Winthrop-Young. Stanford, CA: Stanford University Press, 2008.

Volokh, Eugene, and Donald Falk. "First Amendment Protection for Search Engine
     Results." White paper commissioned by Google. https://www.volokh.com/uploads
     /2012/05/SearchEngineFirstAmendment.

Warner, Michael. *Letters of the Republic: Publication and the Public Sphere in Eighteenth-
     Century America*. Cambridge, MA: Harvard University Press, 1992.

Warner, Michael. *Publics and Counterpublics*. London: Zone, 2002.

Weaver, Warren. "The Mathematics of Communication." *Scientific American* 181, no. 1 (July
     1949): 12–13.

Weiland, Morgan. "Expanding the Periphery and Threatening the Core: The Ascendant
     Libertarian Speech Tradition." *Stanford Law Review* 69, no. 5 (May 2017): 1389–1472.

Weinberger, Stephen. "*The Birth of a Nation* and the Making of the NAACP." *Journal of
     American Studies* 45, no. 1 (2011): 77–93.

Weinrib, Laura. *The Taming of Free Speech: America's Civil Liberties Compromise*. Cam-
     bridge, MA: Harvard University Press, 2016.

Wertheimer, John. "Mutual Film Reviewed: The Movies, Censorship, and Free Speech in
     Progressive America." *American Journal of Legal History* 37, no. 2 (1993): 158–189.

White, G. Edward. "Analogical Reasoning and Historical Change in Law: The Regulation of
     Film and Radio Speech." In *History, Memory, and the Law*, edited by Austin Sarat and
     Thomas Kearns, 283–318. Ann Arbor: University of Michigan Press, 1999.

White, G. Edward. "The First Amendment Comes of Age: The Emergence of Free Speech
     in Twentieth Century America." *Michigan Law Review* 95, no. 2 (1996): 299–392.

Whitney, Heather. "Search Engines, Social Media, and the Editorial Analogy." In *The Per-
     ilous Public Sphere: Structural Threats to Free Expression Today*, edited by David E.
     Pozen, 115–145. New York: Columbia University Press, 2020.

Wiebe, Robert H. *The Search for Order, 1877–1920*. New York: Hill and Wang, 1967.

Wiener, Norbert. *Cybernetics, or Control and Communication in the Animal and the Ma-
     chine*. 1948. Reprint, Cambridge, MA: MIT Press, 2013.

Wiener, Norbert. *The Human Use of Human Beings: Cybernetics and Society*. New York:
     Houghton Mifflin, 1954.

Williams, Patricia J. "On Being the Object of Property." *Signs* 14, no. 1 (1988): 5–24.

Winner, Langdon. "Do Artifacts Have Politics?" *Daedalus* 109, no. 1 (1980): 121–136.

Winthrop-Young, Geoffrey. *Kittler and the Media*. Cambridge: Polity, 2011.

Wittern-Keller, Laura. *Freedom of the Screen: Legal Challenges to State Film Censorship,
     1915–1981*. Lexington: University Press of Kentucky, 2008.

Wittern-Keller, Laura, and Raymond Haberski Jr. *The Miracle Case: Film Censorship and the
     Supreme Court*. Lawrence: University Press of Kansas, 2008.

Woolley, Samuel. "Automating Power: Social Bot Interference in Global Politics." *First
     Monday* 21, no. 4 (2016). https://firstmonday.org/article/view/6161/5300.

Woolley, Samuel, Samantha Shorey, and Phil Howard. "The Bot Proxy: Designing Auto-
     mated Self-Expression." In *A Networked Self and Platforms, Stories, Connections*, ed-
     ited by Zizi Papacharissi, 59–76. New York: Routledge, 2018.

Wu, Tim. "Is the First Amendment Obsolete?" In *The Free Speech Century*, edited by Lee
     Bollinger and Geoffrey Stone, 272–291. New York: Oxford University Press, 2019.

Wu, Tim. "Machine Speech." *University of Pennsylvania Law Review* 161, no 6 (2013):
     1495–1534.

INDEX

American Civil Liberties Union (ACLU), 13, 32, 60, 101, 150, 221n41

American Journal of Sociology, 47

American Newspaper Publishers' Association (ANPA), 102

amplification, 76, 109–111, 114–115, 128, 194, 198, 213n42

analogies, 33–38, 41, 181–183, 186–187

antidiscrimination laws, 155, 190, 195, 244n105, 254n3

antiregulatory politics, 14, 100, 102–103, 116–117, 122, 150, 190, 243n89

antitrust regulation, 85, 102, 116–117, 181, 231n52, 253n86

Apple, 159–160

Arnold, Thurman, 72

artifacts, 111, 113; agency decentered in favor of, 120–122; messages as, 10–11, 15, 20, 89, 120–123, 139, 151; technocultural, 11, 15, 184; tomato harvester example, 184, 252n75

artificial entities, 121–123, 189, 195–196, 208n18

Associated Press v. United States (1945), 116–117

AT&T, 97

"Attack on the American Free Enterprise System" (Powell), 150

attitude, 65–66, 84, 87, 109; and interwar communication research, 73–80

audiences, 3–5, 103, 193, 196, 217n121, 225n72, 241n59, 247n29; distanced from speaker, 17, 28, 121–123; for film, 28–30, 211n17; rights of, 108, 112–115, 117, 123, 125, 145, 148, 179, 181, 231n56. *See also* public

bad tendency test, 13, 31, 35, 82–83, 222n47, 226n83, 234n89

Baidu (Chinese search engine), 179–181

Balkin, Jack, 18, 192

Barbas, Samantha, 4, 112

Barnette. See West Virginia State Board of Education v. Barnette (1943)

Barnett family, 59–60

Bateson, Gregory, 137

Bell, Daniel, 140

Bellamy flag salute, 59, 61–62, *62, 63*, 219n17

Bell Labs, 129–132, 135

Ben-Hur: A Tale of the Christ (film adaptation), 39–41

Benjamin, Ruha, 184

Berelson, Bernard, 81

Bernays, Edward, 74

big data, 200–202, 255n20

Bigelow v. Virginia (1975), 146–147, 242n75

Birth of a Nation, The, 24–27, 30, 35, 210n3, 211n6

Blackmun, Harry, 144

Blumer, Martin, 72, 222–223n52

bodies: computer code as proxy for, 158; and crowd, 28, 32; embodiment of speech, 9, 12, 18–19; film, role in, 27–28, 45; as metaphor for society, 16; and mimicry, 47, 192; mind-body distinction, 8–9, 43, 45, 254–255n11; and protest, 172–173; re-animation of in film, 27–28, 45. *See also* crowds; expressive conduct; gestures

bots, 22, 169–170, 190, 198–200, 253n1, 255n13, 255n15, 255n18; Tay (chatbot), 199, 255n15

boycotts, 32, 49–50, 212n31

Boyle, James, 6, 208n12

Brandeis, Louis, 12, 32, 99, 208n20

Buckley v. Valeo (1976), 124, 142, 143, 144–145, 154, 237n17

Bureau of Applied Social Research (BASR), 224n64

Burrow-Giles Lithographic Co. v. Sarony (1884), 214n67

Burstyn v. Wilson (1952). *See Joseph Burstyn, Inc. v. Wilson* (1952)

cable operators, 181

campaign finance, 123–124, 143, 205, 235n101. *See also Buckley v. Valeo* (1976)

Cantril, Hadley, 76, 220n29

Carey, James, 118, 241n58

Carlson v. California (1940), 128, 145

computer code/programs, 157–177, 208n13; action/speech distinction, 163, 166–170; agency, concerns about, 158–159, 164, 167–168, 176–180, 182, 185–188; anxieties about, 158, 178, 181, 188–189; coding as creative act, 160, 168–169, 176; duality of, 165–166; as equivalent to other languages, 164–165; executability, 158, 163, 166–167, 176, 247n29; as form of speech, 161–162; functional aspects, 162, 165–167, 169; as information, 168–169; instructions, 7, 158–159, 166–168, 247n26; instructions as "speech," 159–177; intelligibility of, 246–247n25; interaction with social world, 169–170; as language, 133, 164–170; and personhood, 168–169, 178, 196, 202; programmers, roles of, 158–163, 166–169, 175–179, 185, 187–189, 198–200, 245n3, 246n19, 251n73, 255n18; as proxy for body, 158; regulation of, 160–161, 163, 167; as text, 164–168; as text and instrument, 163, 165, 246n13

computer punch card IDs, 171, 248n40

computers, 118, 156; automated utterances, 157; business use of, 140–141; female operators, 176; hardware, 159, 166, 176–177, 188, 191, 199, 247n26; human intent looked for, 156, 157–158; lower court hesitance to extend speech to, 157–158; machine learning, 184, 187, 200–201; operating systems, 166, 247n26; personal assistants, 22, 190. *See also* algorithms

conduct. *See* action; expressive conduct; gestures

conformity/homogeneity, concerns about, 67, 97–98, 100–101, 220n29, 221n41

conservative legal movement, 150–155, 190

constitutions, state, 31, 34, 213n45

consumer privacy, 124

consumer rights movement, 142–143, 143–144

consumer society, 93

content creation: and algorithms, 177, 186, 188; radio, 92–93, 97–98

content industry, 160–164

content neutrality, 14, 155, 162, 218n5

content scrambling systems (CSS), 160–164

"control revolution," 118

conversation, as model for speech, 114, 116

copies, 38–41, 47, 192; crowds and imitation, 50–51; vs. original publications, 18, 27, 34, 111; radio speaker's role, 89, 93–98

copyright (intellectual property), 41, 141, 214n67, 215–216n90, 215n70, 215n69, 215n73, 245n11, 247n27, 250n60, 253n82; and computer code, 160–164, 174; and film, 39–41, 45; and romantic vision of authorship, 215n70

Corley, Eric (alias Emmanuel Goldstein), 161–170, 178, 188. *See also Universal City Studios v. Corley* (2001)

corporate speech, 10–11, 20; 1970s, 120, 124–125, 187, 235n101, 243n87; alleged discrimination against, 151, 153–154, 195–196, 244n103; speakers legally replaced by information, 142–154. *See also Citizens United v. Federal Election Commission;* corporations

corporations, 17; anti-big business atmosphere, 1930s, 98; as artificial entities, 121, 195–196, 208n18; as beneficiaries of Court rulings, 14, 89, 120, 124, 143–146, 151, 178–179, 190, 194–195, 198; capture of free speech law, 14, 150; civil rights discourse used by, 151, 153–155, 180–181, 254n3; film and free speech, 33; personhood, 158, 185, 251n64. *See also* advertising; commerce; commercial speech; corporate speech

coverage, 6, 160, 173, 188, 191, 246n21

Creel, George, 74, 127, 224n66

criminal law, 173–174

crowds, 217n116; and bodies, 28, 32; fear of, and film, 28, 32, 37, 46–48, 216n109; and imitation, 50–51; as irrational, 18–19, 50, 67; motor system and influence on, 51, 66; public as civilized version of, 52-54; as raced, gendered, and classed, 53, 216n105; social psychology of, 48-52

culture, ownership of, 160-164

culture industries critique, 68

cyberlibertarian rhetoric, 153, 157

cybernetics, 136-138, 140, 239-240n47, 240n51, 240n53

Darwin, Charles, 217nn115-116, 240n54

Davis, William F., 31

Decherney, Peter, 39

decryption code, 159-170; DeCSS decoding program, 160-170, 174, 247n32, 249n52; as "munitions," 164; as political speech, 162-163, 174, 177; as protest, 159-161, 168, 169. *See also* computer code/programs; *Universal City Studios v. Corley* (2001)

democracy, 12, 16, 151-152, 201, 208n14; and distribution, 115; and individual choice, 83-84, 107-108; and publicity, 39; and radio regulation, 98-99; regulation in the name of, 100, 102

Derrida, Jacques, 133, 239n42

Descartes, René, 8, 24, 208n19, 254-255n11

Dewey, John, 72

Digital Millennium Copyright Act (DMCA), 161-163, 174, 245n7

discrimination: against gays and lesbians, 155, 195, 244n105, 254n3; rhetoric of used by corporations, 151, 153-154, 195-196, 244n103

disembodiment of speech, 9, 129-130, 208n19; and computer code, 158-160, 163-164, 170, 174-176; and expressive conduct, 20, 120, 158-159, 170-177; and information, 130-139, 142, 151, 154, 158-160, 194-195; and personal assistants, 190

dissenting/minority speech, 1, 5, 8, 12, 99, 112-116, 193, 234n89; and *Barnette*, 59-62, 249n50; corporations cast in light of, 151, 154-155; efforts to rebal-

ance public sphere, 116; and film, 46; of Jehovah's Witnesses, 59-64, 219n8; and literature distribution, 19; suppression of, 31-32; in technological terms, 114-115. *See also* labor movement/union organizing; literature/pamphlet distribution

distribution, 207n5; and amplification, 76, 109-111, 114-115, 128; as free speech, 89, 115, 121; and film, 30, 33-34, 42, 212n20; of ideas, 88-89; as industrial metaphor, 104, 109-115; internet as site for, 3, 189, 245n2, 246n18; national systems of, 212n20, 213n50; and newspapers, 100; prioritized, 103-104; radio as medium of, 89, 94-98; speech as, 4, 19-20, 89, 104-108, 111-117, 193-194. *See also* film distribution; literature/pamphlet distribution

Douglas, William O., 176, 250n57

draft-card burning, 159, 163, 170-177, *171*, 249n45; draft card as symbol and instrument, 172; law criminalizing (1965), 170-171

Drucker, Peter, 140

Du Bois, W. E. B., 210n3

Durr, Clifford, 101

DVD decryption, 160-164

economics, 138-139; of speech, 13-14, 20, 87-88, 108, 125

economy of the signal, 118, 132

Edison, Thomas, 27, 211n13

editorial judgments: algorithmic outputs as, 177-187; biases in, 184-185; subjects of algorithmic decision-making, 183-187, 252nn78-81, 254n8; types of judgment, 182-185

editor-publisher, 94-95, 99, 100, 103, 106, 109, 192, 214n57, 228n27, 231n54

elections: ballot measures, 149-154; campaign finance, 123-124, 143, 205, 235n101; Nixon campaign (1972), 124; use of bots in, 198, 253n1

electricity, 27-28, 47, 118, *135*, 217n115

libertarian tradition and, 12; drafted in 1789, 15; extended to distribution, 112–113; federal laws as focus of, 31;opportunism and, 14–15, 32, 102–103, 150, 235n2; press, freedom of, 12, 98–104, 106, 110, 115; progressive narrative of, 3, 5, 12; scope of, 16; separation of speech and conduct under, 8; shaped by technology, 15–16, 19, 23, 192, 195, 197; and state laws, 209n21; as technocultural artifact, 11, 15. *See also* free speech; press, freedom of

First National Bank of Boston, 149–151

First National Bank of Boston v. Bellotti (1968), 120, 124–125, 149–154, 237n18, 243nn87–88, 243n90, 244n98

Fiske, Marjorie, 76, 224n68

flag: burning, 59, 235n5, 245n4, 249n51; restriction on uses of, 71; as symbol, 82, 221nn43–44

flag salutes, 19, 163; Bellamy version, 59, 61–62, *62, 63,* 219n17; hand on heart, 62; Roman salute, 219n18; as speech, 58–66; as symbolic, 69–72, 79–80. *See also* gestures

Fleming, Donald, 66

Fly, James, 101

"four freedoms," 60

four-minute men, 75, 76

Fourteenth Amendment, 154, 212n25

Frank, Donald, 182

Frankfurter, Felix, 68, 70–71, 83, 173, 219n9, 221n41, 222n45

Frankfurt school, 109–110

Free and Responsible Press, A (Commission on Freedom of the Press), 87

"Freedom of Speech" (Levinas), 119

"freedom of the air," 98–104

free software movement, 160, 162, 174–175, 245n11

free speech: in 1910s, 30–33; in 1970s, 123–126; and classification politics, 5–11; coverage, determination of, 6, 173, 188, 191, 246n21; distribution as, 20, 89–90, 113–116, 121–122, 128, 142,

194–195; "free" as focus of, 14, 18; future of, 198–203; hierarchy of, 107; histories of, 1–7, 11–17, 210n42; individualization of, 4, 8, 32–33, 94; listening within, 18–19, 67, 117; nineteenth century understandings of, 12–13; opportunism, 15, 76, 186, 235n2, 250nn54–55; radical theories of, 12, 32, 48–49, *49,* 111–112, 172, 233n77, 242n79; social good theory of, 19, 98–103, 107, 113, 116, 213n36, 229n36; two-tier system, 13; used as antiregulatory tool, 14, 100, 102–103, 116–117, 122, 190; wartime expansion of, 60–61. *See also* speech

"free speech fights," 48

free speech law, 31, 212n26, 212n30; speech as subject of, 5–6, 151

Free Speech League, 32

free speech movement, 119, 171, 172, 248n40

Freudian theory, 51, 66–67, 72–74, 222n49

functionality doctrine, 250n54

Gary, Brett, 73

Gaudet, Hazel, 81

gays and lesbians, discrimination against, 155, 195, 244n105, 254n3

gender, 13, 53, 139, 149, 155, 176

general semantics, 78–79

general theory of communication, 131–134, *135,* 136, 166; popularization of, 134–139. *See also* information theory

Geoghegan, Bernard, 133–134

gestures, 58; empty, 61; and general theory of communication, 136–137; inchoate, 173–174, 249n51; as nonverbal communication, 40, 50, 58, 137–138, 173, 192, 218n5, 240n54, 249n46; as speech, 19, 58–59, 64, 79–80, 137. *See also* action; bodies; expressive conduct; flag salutes; symbols

Gitelman, Lisa, 21, 163, 172, 246n13, 248n39

Gitlin, Todd, 249n45

Goldman, Emma, 48, *49,* 216n105

Gompers v. Buck's Stove & Range Co. (1911), 49

Google, 178, 180; bad faith use of free speech claims, 186; citation ranking, use of, 184; *Langdon v. Google* (2007), 179, 180, 184, 250n62; PageRank system, 183; *Search King v. Google* (2003), 179, 180, 184; white paper, 182

Graber, Mark, 213n36, 229n37

Great Depression, 76, 88, 98

Grieveson, Lee, 37

Griffith, D. W., 24, 30, 35, 212n22

Gunning, Tom, 28–29

hacking. See *Universal City Studios v. Corley* (2001)

Hague, Frank "Boss," 3–4, 113

Hague v. Congress of Industrial Organizations (1939), 3–5, 18, 111–114, 127–128, 144–145, 207n3, 242n79

Hand, Learned, 107, 117

Haraway, Donna, 157

Harlan, John Marshall, 248n41

Hartley, Ralph, 129–131, 135

hate speech, 25, 199, 252n81

Hayles, N. Katherine, 129–130, 246n25

Hays Code (1930s), 78

Hinman, Harold J., 44–46

histories of free speech, 1–7, 11–17, 210n42; media history, 5, 14–17, 22, 29, 58

Hitler, Adolf, 63, 67–68, 75, 224n68

Holmes, Oliver Wendell, Jr., 12, 31, 32, 40–41, 99, 213n43

How We Advertised America (Creel), 74

Hutchins Commission. *See* Commission on Freedom of the Press

icons, 26, 75–76, 79, 220–221n36

ideas: advertising as, 144; distribution of, 88–89; and gestures, 61; as opinion, 57–58; symbolism as "primitive" way of communicating, 58, 69, 135–136

images, 2, 215n80; and algorithms, 177, 191; influence of, 50–52, 212n28; moving, 16–17, 28, 33–34, 43–44, 47, 192–193; still, 34, 40, 215n73; as symbols, 58, 73–74, 78–79

immaterial good, information as, 121, 134–135, 137–140, 153, 160

immigrants, 11–12, 31–32, 208n20, 217n121; 229n37; anti-immigrant sentiment, 11–12, 29, 48, 208n20; deportation of, 31, 212n29, 216n105; and film, 29, 37, 46, 211n17; Jewish filmmakers, 29, 37

Immigration Act of 1903, 216n105

impersonal speech, 89, 121–122, 128, 226–227n3

"incitement" standard, 7, 13, 209n30, 247n29

indeterminacy, of information, 130

individual, 10–11, 208n14; rights-bearing, 11, 104; speech as act of, 8, 32–33, 94

individual rights, 60, 83, 213n36, 254n3; as suspect, 19, 98–100, 229n37

Industrial Commission of Ohio, 42, 49

industrialization of media, 19–20, 88–89, 95, 100, 108–115, 193, 228n20

Industrial Workers of the World, 48

influence, 136, 211n10, 212n28, 224n64; as coercive, 8, 44, 46; film as, 38, 42–55, 65, 213n49; and human will, 45–46, 50, 54–55; of images, 50–52, 212n28; and motor system, 47, 51, 65–66

information: advertising as, 141, 143–148; algorithms as, 179, 181; as artifact, 10, 20; blurred lines between types of, 82–83; computer code as, 168–170, 175–176; as content, 129–130; and disembodiment of speech, 130–139, 142, 151, 154, 158–160, 194–195; as engineering problem, 128–134, 141–142; fungibility of, 135, 143, 153; as immaterial good, 121, 134–135, 137–140, 153, 160; late 1960s and 1970s discussions, 119–120; legibility prioritized, 137–138; as official, public communication, 127–128; as organized data, 140; pamphlet distribution as, 127–128, 148; procedure, metrics, and efficiency prioritized, 159, 168–169; as property, 141; as proxy for social interests, 125, 138–139, 145–146, 148, 151–152, 179, 184;

right to receive, 14, 91–92, 108, 117, 123, 144, 148, 181, 193, 231n56, 235n96; rise and influence of in twentieth-century thought, 126–142; as site of agency and freedom, 122–123; "stock" of, 153. *See also* messages

information economy, 139–142

information society, 128, 129, 140, 241n65

information theory, 20, 118, 125–126, 130–134, 140–142, 238n28, 240n51, 240n51, 240n53, 249n46; and disembodiment of speech, 130, 139, 142; popularization of, 134–139, 141. *See also* general theory of communication

infrastructures, 14, 21–22, 119, 176, 181, 184, 189, 190, 192, 220n22

inscription, 16–17, 41, 176, 183–184, 216n90, 246n24

Institute for General Semantics, 78

Institute for Propaganda Analysis, 75, 78, 224n63

instructions, 7, 158–159, 166–168, 247n26

intellectual property. *See* copyright (intellectual property)

"intelligence," 121, 127, 129, 133

interiority of speech, 1, 8, 110–115, 134, 137–138, 144, 163–164, 206

interpretation, 54, 56, 64, 134–135, 137, 195, 225n79; and computer code/programs, 168, 174–176, 201; of gestures, 45–46, 216n90; of symbols, 70–72, 78–80, 83

Jackson, Robert, 60, 61, 65, 69–73, 79, 79–80, 83, 219n14, 220n21, 221nn37–38, 225n75, 225n79

Jakobson, Roman, 133, 239n42

Jay, Martin, 216n91

Jehovah's Witnesses, 59–64, 219n8

Jersey City, New Jersey, 3–4, 113, 114

Joseph Burstyn, Inc. v. Wilson (1952), 26, 52, 57, 64, 81, 84, 148

journalism, 66, 127, 183, 225n76. *See also* objectivity

journalists, 3, 48, 60, 72, 74, 76, 81, 100, 162, 193, 230n43

judicial activism, 60

Jump, Herbert, 46

justice, and equality of messages, 12, 152–155

Justice Department, 73, 160

Kalem Company v. Harper Brothers (1911), 39–41

Kaplan, Lewis A., 164, 167, 247n27

Kazan, Roman, 161–162

Kees, Weldon, 137–138, 240n53

Kennedy, Anthony, 151–152, 153–154

King, Martin Luther , Jr., 146, 172, 249n44

Kittler, Friedrich, 196

Kline, Ronald, 140

Ku Klux Klan, 24–25

labor movement/union organizing, 28, 32, 48; boycotts as verbal acts, 49–50; *Hague v. Congress of Industrial Organizations* (1939), 3–5, 18, 111–114, 127–128, 144–145, 207n3, 242n79; picketing and sign-bearing, 111, 113–114, 128, 148, 218n5, 247–248n36, 249n49

Lacan, Jacques, 133, 239n42

Lakier, Genevieve, 83

Langdon v. Google (2007), 179, 180, 184, 250n62

language: computer code as, 164–170; structure, 132–133

Lasswell, Harold, 73, 75–76, 79, 223n53, 223nn56–58, 223n60

latent meaning, 22, 51, 70, 73–76, 78–79, 130, 222n50, 223n53, 223n58

law and economics movement, 142

Lazarsfeld, Paul, 76, 81, 224n64

Le Bon, Gustave, 50–51, 52, 53, 67, 217n113

Lebovic, Sam, 99

leftists, 67–68, 98, 100–101, 152

legal category of speech, 2, 5–11, 18, 21, 23, 202, 218n5; and computer code/programs, 158, 170, 175–176, 191; coverage, 6, 160, 173, 188, 191, 246n21; expressive conduct as, 170, 212n28;

legal category of speech (*continued*)
and film, 26, 54–59; less-protected
speech, 124–125, 128, 242n72; pure
speech, 13, 144, 169, 170, 209n27;
speech plus, 9, 163, 173, 208n17, 218n5,
237n25; as substitution for deliberation, 175–176; unprotected speech, 8–9,
244n100; verbal acts, 49–50, 65, 78,
84, 133, 225n72. *See also* classification;
commercial speech; speech
legal discourse, 9, 40, 246n13; 1930s and
1940s, 90–91, 99; 1960s and 1970s,
120–121; 1970s, 119–120; conceptualization of speech as information, 133, 139;
contradictions in, 2, 10, 15, 116, 243n88;
and general theory of communication,
136; and popularized information theory, 141. *See also* civil libertarian theory
of free speech; political/ideological
contexts of legal discourse
Lerner, Max, 57, 72
less-protected speech, 124–125, 128, 242n72
Levinas, Emmanuel, 119
liability, 95–96, 186, 190, 229n32, 253n82,
255n16
libel, 42–43, 146–147, 209n30, 228n29,
229n32; responsible speaker, 95–97;
Sorensen v. Wood, 95–96, 228n30
liberal humanist conceptions of speech,
10–11, 110–111, 120, 192, 198; and
computer code, 163–164, 167–168; and
film, 55–56; inversion of, 201–202; and
search engines as speech, 180
Liberty and the News (Lippmann), 66
licensing, 213n38; radio license holders,
76, 92–97, 103, 227n16, 228n22, 228n28,
229n32, 229n34; theater regulation, 33,
34–35, 37
linguistics, 78, 223n57; structural, 132–133
Lippmann, Walter, 53, 57, 72; *Liberty and
the News,* 66; *Public Opinion,* 66–67,
74
literature/pamphlet distribution, 1, 3, 13,
18–20, 31–32, 49, 94, 112–113, 232n73; as
information, 127–128, 148; local ordi-

nances, 61; and workers' rights, 3–4, 19.
See also film distribution
Liu, Lydia, 133, 239n41
Locke, John, 209n26
Lovell v. City of Griffin (1938), 112–113, 114,
207n5
lower courts, 30, 124, 149, 210n42, 214n55,
228n30; computation and algorithm
cases, 20, 157–158, 164, 245n3, 247n29;
search engine cases, 177–181, 184; *Decisions: Langdon v. Google* (2007), 179,
180, 184, 250n62; *NBC v. United States*
(1943), 106–108, 110, 111, 117; *Search King
v. Google* (2003), 179, 180, 184; *Zhang v.
Baidu* (2014), 179, 180–181, 184. See also
Universal City Studios v. Corley (2001);
US Supreme Court
Luce, Henry, 88

MacLeish, Archibald, 102
Macy conferences, 134, 138, 239n42,
240–241n56, 240n53
Malinowski, Bronislaw, 224n65
marketplace of ideas, 33, 84, 89, 108,
117–118, 142, 150, 153–154, 201, 244n97,
244n103
Marshall, James, 72
Massaro, Toni, 157, 198
mass communication, 16, 75, 83, 109, 116,
134, 138, 193–194, 216n109, 241n61
mass media, 13, 19, 22, 34, 74; and power
dynamics, 89, 97–98, 100–101, 104–106,
115–116, 121–122. *See also* film; newspapers; radio
mass society thesis, 67
mathematical formulae, as protected
speech, 164–165
mathematical theory of communication,
22, 128, 133, 135–140, 142, 238n36
Mayflower doctrine, 107
McKeever, William, 46
McKenna, Joseph, 35–36, 39
McLuhan, Marshall, 138, 241n61
Mead, George Herbert, 222n52
meaning: in engineering terms, 131; latent,

picketing and sign-bearing, 111, 113–114, 128, 148, 218n5, 247–248n36, 249n49

Pledge of Allegiance. *See* flag salutes

political economy of media, 75, 99, 115–116, 132, 192, 195, 238n27; radio, 89–90, 103, 108

political/ideological contexts of legal discourse, 121–122, 125, 177–180; conservative legal movement, 150–155, 190

political speech, 12–13, 61, 81, 83, 124, 159, 209n27, 243n87, 254n3; and *Bellotti*, 150–151; decryption code as, 162–163, 174, 177; and film, 31–32; as "pure speech," 13, 144, 169, 209n27

positive and negative liberties, 89, 102, 226n2

Posner, Eric, 240n55

posthuman conception of speech, 10–11, 20, 120–123, 128, 134, 152, 154–155, 196, 235n1, 237n22, 239n45

Powell, Lewis F., 149–150, 153, 244n98; memorandum, 150

Powell memorandum, 150

power dynamics, 13–14; and computer code decisions, 177; of film, 28–30, 37–38, 42–47; and mass media, 89, 97–98, 100–101, 104–106, 115–116, 121–122; and propaganda, 71, 74; and state, 35; and symbols, 57, 67–68, 71, 74–75

presence, metaphysics of, 133

press: film compared to, 33–34, 36–37, 41; meanings of word, 17; newsreels as, 43–44

press, freedom of, 12, 42–44, 87–88, 98–104, 106, 110, 115

"primitive" thought, 9, 19, 80, 137, 193–194, 217n111; and crowds, 50–51, 221n38; film associated with, 27, 48–52; included in speech, 55–59; as open to interpretation, 70; symbolism as, 58, 69, 135–136

printing, 8, 15, 33, 45, 56, 210nn36–37, 230n41; merged with speaking, 164; model of applied to algorithms and computers, 189, 202; political economy of, 103, 192; and publicity, 15–16, 180, 192, 196, 202, 210n36; romantic views of, 189, 192, 234n88

printing press, 3, 15–17, 106, 191–192, 202, 245n2

prior restraint, 11–12, 30, 31, 34, 94

privacy, 122, 124, 190, 198, 200, 244n103

probability, and language analysis, 132

profanity, 14, 59, 81

progressivism/Progressivism, 29, 46, 99, 213n36, 229n37

progress narratives, 3, 5, 12, 228n24

propaganda, 22, 34, 72–79, 81, 107, 223n60; 1930s and 1940s concerns, 64; meanings of term, 74, 213n44; "of the deed," 225n72; social science research on, 19, 72–74, 222n50, 224n64; through fiction, 82; World War I experience of, 74–77, 77

property: information as, 141; ownership, 99; private ownership and decryption code, 160

property rights, 12, 163, 175, 213n36, 241n55

protest, 110, 218n5, 249n44; 1960s, 119; 1970s against corporations, 143; and bodies, 172–173; and computer code/programs, 159–161, 168, 169; draft-card burning, 159, 163, 170–177, 171, 249n45; in image of "machine-using institution" of the press, 110. See also *United States v. O'Brien* (1968); *Universal City Studios v. Corley* (2001)

proxies: and algorithms, 179, 183; computer code for body, 158; information as proxy for social interests, 125, 138–139, 145–146, 148, 151–152, 179, 184

public, 217–218n123, 253n90; choice equated with freedom, 107–108; as civilized version of crowd, 52–54; demographic shifts in, 66; elites as part of, 68, 74–75; rationality of, 18–19, 43, 49–55, 66–67, 163–164; right to receive information, 90, 102–103, 107–108, 110. *See also* audiences

148, 181, 193, 231n56, 235n96; as technocultural artifacts, 11, 15

Robinson, James Harvey, 66

Roosevelt, Franklin Delano, 60, 75, 76, 95,
96

Rorty, James, 101

Ruesch, Jurgen, 137–138, 240n54

Saussure, Ferdinand de, 133, 222n49

Scalia, Antonin, 152, 194

Scientific American, 135, 135–137

search engines, 177–187, 250n58, 250n62,
251n69, 253n86; Baidu, 179–181; biases
in, 184–185; indexing, 178–179; newspaper analogy with, 180–183; output as
protected language, 177–178; priorities
vs. intentionality, 184–185; process of
search, 178–179, 183; ranked results as
indication of agency, 182; results as
speech, 179; search results, 177–180,
182–188, 250n61, 251n67, 253n87. *See
also* algorithms; Google; social media

Search King v. Google (2003), 179, 180, 184

Seldes, George, 74, 98

self-governance, 141, 201, 208n14

semantics, 78–79

semiotics, 72, 147

sender-message-receiver schema, 126, 132,
135, 138, 140, 241n59

Shannon, Claude, 128, 131–134, *135,* 140,
142, 166, 239nn41–42; "A Mathematical
Model of Communication," 135

Shuler, Bob, 90–91, 94–95, 227nn4–5,
227n7

Siegel, Reva, 18, 192

signal: and content creation, 186; economy
of, 118, 132; electronic, 16–17, 118, 132;
and social relations, 134, 138, 173

Sinclair, Upton, 214n57

Small, Albion, 53

Smith, Kate, 225n72

social good theory, 19, 98–103, 107–108,
116, 229n36; and marketplace of ideas,
108, 113

social interests, information as proxy for,

125, 138–139, 145–146, 148, 151–152, 179,
184

social media, 232n70, 251n67, 253–254n2,
253n86; Facebook, 167, 242n73; Twitter,
198–199. *See also* search engines

social movements, 1, 7, 21, 210n41, 231n55

social psychology, 18, 46–47, 53, 126, 130,
138, 222n50; of crowds, 48–52; opinion
psychologized, 64–69; of symbols,
72–74. *See also* information theory

social relations: ignored by focus on
technology, 175–177; reversed by
algorithms and machine learning,
200–201; and signal, 134, 138, 173

social sciences, 27, 43, 81, 121, 126–127, 130,
134, 137; crowd, view of, 53, 56; interwar
communication research, 72–80; public opinion, views of, 64, 67

sociotechnical systems, 91, 136, 189,
199–200, 202, 250n58

Sorenson, C. A., 95–96

Sorensen v. Wood (1932), 95–96, 228n30

Sorrell v. IMS Health (2011), 124, 244n103

sound trucks, 13, 110, 111–115, 171, 248n38

speaker: audience distance from, 17, 28,
121–123; decentering of in radio, 88–89,
93–98, 106; legal replacement of by information, 142–154; responsible, 95–97;
role of in radio, 89, 93–98; speech
disarticulated from, 9–11, 120–121,
141–142, 149–154, 196–197, 237n18. *See
also* speech

Special Defense Unit (SDU; Department of
Justice), 73

spectatorship, 47, 52, 214n53, 216n91

speech: "artisanal," 111; basic unit of, 125,
133; Cartesian connotations, 8–9, 24,
208n19; changing conceptions of, 14–17,
57–59, 103–104, 125, 127–128, 187–188;
choice as, 83–84, 107–108; and classification politics, 5–11; commonsense
understandings of, 5; communication
distinguished from, 8, 24, 121, 155,
244n106; compelled, 60, 69, 160, 254n3;
computer code as language, 160–170;

symbol analysis (content analysis), 73–80, 222nn49–50, 223n53; general semantics, 78–79

symbolic interactionism, 72, 222–223n52, 223n57

symbolic speech, 9, 22, 57, 59, 163, 173, 208n17, 218n5, 237n25

symbols, 126, 130, 222n51, 240n55; flag and flag salute as, 69–72, 82, 221nn43–44; icons vs., 220–221n36; images as, 58, 73–74, 78–79; interpretation of, 70–72, 78–80; interwar communication research, 64, 73–80; "latent" meaning, 22, 70, 73–76, 78–79, 223n53, 223n58; in the law, 69–80; mental engagement required for, 69–70, 80, 94; news as deployment of, 67; as open to interpretation, 70–72, 78–80, 81; as "primitive but effective way of communicating ideas," 58, 137; selection of, as communication, 130–135; as stable referents, 70–71, 82; word and print media as, 68–69, 75–76, 79. *See also* gestures; images

Symbols of Governance, The (Arnold), 72

systems, 10–11; of communication, 10, 125, 129, 131–132; general theory of communication, *135*; sociotechnical, 91, 136, 189, 199–200, 202, 250n58; speech as phenomenon of, 20, 89

Tarde, Gabriel, 50–51, 53, 217n111, 217n116, 220n22

technocultural artifacts, 11, 15, 184

technology, 2–3; and changes in public sphere, 2, 56, 79, 88–89; comparisons between forms of, 33; film, 27–29, 46–47, 54–56, 192; First Amendment shaped by, 15–16, 19, 23, 192, 195, 197; radio as, 87, 89, 90–92, 94, 106, 114–116, 118; social relations ignored by focus on, 175–177; studies, 5–6

telegraph, 16, 125, 129, 132, 133–134, 220n22

telephony, 21, 125, 129, 132, *135*, 176

television, 125, 136, 181, 232n63

Texas v. Johnson (1989), 245n4

theatrical performances, 33–36, 214n55; adaptations and copyright, 40–41

Thornhill v. Alabama (1940), 111, 127, 144–145, 242n79

Time magazine, 88

Toffler, Alvin, 140, 241n64

Toffler, Heidi, 140, 241n64

totalitarianism, 60–61, 67, 80, 103, 109–110

Touretzky, David, 164–165

town hall, 116, 234n93

transmission, 17, 193; communication as, 125–126, 141; information as engineering problem, 128–134; linearity concept, 65, 70, 122, 138–139; radio, 4–5, 19, 76, 89, 91–92, 95–97, 103, 107, 233n81

Trinity Methodist Church, South v. Federal Radio Commission (1932), 90–91, 94

Triumph of the Will (film), 75

Trump, Donald, 198

truth, search for, 7, 201, 208n14

Turner, Fred, 84, 139

2600: The Hacker Quarterly, 161

unfair trade practices, 108

United States Information Service, 127

United States v. Featherston (1972), 247n26

United States v. O'Brien (1968), 163, 170–175, 236n10, 245n4, 248n37, 248n39, 248n41, 250n54

United States v. Paramount Pictures, Inc. (1948), 85, 226n90

Universal City Studios v. Corley (2001), 160–164, 174, 178, 188, 246nn26–27, 246n29, 246nn31–32, 246n34, 250n55; amicus briefs, 245n7, 245n11; code and language in, 164–170

Universal City Studios v. Reimerdes (2000), 161–162, 246n19

University of Chicago, 79, 142

unprotected speech, 8–9, 244n100

US Constitution, 15–17

US Court of Appeals, Second Circuit, 161

US Court of Appeals, Third Circuit, 112

US Department of Commerce, 92, 140

US Department of State, 164